Essays on Relativism

2001–2021

CRISPIN WRIGHT

OXFORD
UNIVERSITY PRESS

Great Clarendon Street, Oxford, OX2 6DP,
United Kingdom

Oxford University Press is a department of the University of Oxford.
It furthers the University's objective of excellence in research, scholarship,
and education by publishing worldwide. Oxford is a registered trade mark of
Oxford University Press in the UK and in certain other countries

Published in the United States of America by Oxford University Press
198 Madison Avenue, New York, NY 10016, United States of America

British Library Cataloguing in Publication Data
Data available

Library of Congress Control Number: 2023934399

ISBN 978-0-19-284599-3

DOI: 10.1093/oso/9780192845993.001.0001

Printed and bound by
CPI Group (UK) Ltd, Croydon, CR0 4YY

Links to third party websites are provided by Oxford in good faith and
for information only. Oxford disclaims any responsibility for the materials
contained in any third party website referenced in this work.

For Paul Boghossian

Contents

Preface and Acknowledgements

A recent discussion published in the blog of the American Philosophical Association on July 30, 2021, concludes with these words:

> Relativism is not just some bad idea, but the mother lode of bad ideas. It's about time we stamp it out.[1]

This is a vivid expression of the widespread notion that identifies relativism with the denial that there is anything that it is determinately objectively correct to think about any subject matter whatever, that truth is invariably a function of non-compulsory attitudes of the believer. Maybe that idea indeed deserves no better fate than a "stamping out." (Though good luck with that project!) In any case, I need to emphasize straight away such an immoderate anti-objectivism is not the focus of the chapters in this book, which centres on the much more nuanced, selective, and technically sophisticated versions of relativism about truth—*alethic relativism*—that, variously developed in contemporary treatments by authors such as Max Kölbel, John MacFarlane, and Mark Richard, have generated an astonishing amount of to-ing and fro-ing in the journals over the last quarter of a century. The seas of this modern debate having now subsided a little, it seemed good to put together this collection of some of my own attempts to contribute to the discussion.

It is doubtful whether the majority of the ten chapters included here would have been written had I not had the opportunity to lead two successive collaborative research projects on the issues during the first fifteen years of the millennium. The first, 'Contextualism and Relativism', ran at the St. Andrews research centre, Arché, from around 2005 onwards, and was awarded major funding from the UK Arts and Humanities Research Council from 2008 to 2012. The second, 'Relativism and Rational Tolerance', was sponsored by the Leverhulme Trust at the Northern Institute of Philosophy at Aberdeen between 2012 and 2015. I am extremely grateful to the AHRC and to the Leverhulme Trust for their generous support.

The team at Arché included Herman Cappelen as co-investigator and Sebastiano Morruzzi, Richard Dietz, Derek Ball, and Dilip Ninan as project postdocs, with additional support from the regularly visiting Arché professorial fellows of the day, Francois Reçanati, Jonathan Schaffer, Jason Stanley, and Brian

---

[1] The author is Maarten Boudry, current holder of the Etienne Vermeersch Chair of Critical Thinking at Ghent University,

Weatherson. In Aberdeen at the Northern Institute, Patrick Greenough and Paula Sweeney served as co-investigators and the postdocs were Carl Baker, Filippo Ferrari, Giacomo Melis, and Alex Plakias. My debts to both groups of colleagues, for the intensively productive research culture they helped to create in each place and for invaluable critical feedback on my early thoughts about the issues herein discussed, are unfathomable.

Many others have, naturally, helped me with this work, not least in the course of the various presentations of drafts of the chapters at conferences and departmental colloquia over the years. Appropriate acknowledgements are usually made at the end of the respective chapters. But two special additional debts stand out, one to a staunch foe of relativism and one to perhaps its most formidable friend in its modern guise. The latter is John MacFarlane, who more than anyone else has reinvigorated the discussion of alethic relativism by his masterly development of a new paradigm for it to assume, and by his skilful applications thereof to a whole plethora of subject areas. The foe is my former departmental colleague, Paul Boghossian, to whom I am indebted both for his powerful writings on the issues and for our many conversations about them over the years. My collection is dedicated to him in gratitude and affection.

Finally I must thank Sebastiano Morruzzi and Filippo Ferrari for allowing me to reprint here the papers I respectively co-authored with them. I am especially grateful to Susanna Melkonian-Altshuler for her tireless work in preparing the final manuscript and collating the Bibliogaphy; and Peter Momtchiloff and Imogene Haslam at OUP for their very efficient and courteous editorial support.

Crispin Wright

Kemback, Fife
July 2022

Origins of the Essays

Chapter 1, "On Being in a Quandary: Relativism, Vagueness, Logical Revisionism" was first published in *Mind* 110:437 (2001), 45–98. It was reprinted in the *Philosopher's Annual* for the same year.

Chapter 2, "Intuitionism, Realism, Relativism, and Rhubarb" was first published in Patrick Greenough and Michael Lynch (eds.), *Truth and Realism*, Clarendon Press, 2006, 38–60.

Chapter 3, "New Age Relativism and Epistemic Possibility: The Question of Evidence" was first published in *Philosophical Issues* 17 (2007), 262–83.

Chapter 4, "Relativism about Truth Itself: Haphazard Thoughts about the Very Idea" was first published in Manuel García-Carpintero and Max Kölbel (eds.), *Relative Truth*, Oxford: Oxford University Press, 2008, 157–85.

Chapter 5, "Fear of Relativism?," was first published as a contribution to a book symposium on Paul Boghossian's *Fear of Knowledge*, in *Philosophical Studies* 141:3 (2008), 379–90.

Chapter 6. "Trumping Assessments and the Aristotelian Future," co-authored with Sebastiano Moruzzi, was first published in *Synthese* 166:2 (2009), 309–31.

Chapter 7. "Assessment-Sensitivity: The Manifestation Challenge," was first published as a contribution to a book symposium on John MacFarlane's *Assessment-Sensitivity*, in *Philosophy and Phenomenological Research*, 92 (2016), 189–96. doi:10.1111/phpr.12262

Chapter 8. "Talking with Vultures," co-authored with Filippo Ferrari, was first published as a critical study of Herman Cappelen and John Hawthorne's *Relativism and Monadic Truth*, in *Mind* (2017). doi: 10.1093/mind/fzw06610

Chapter 9. "The Variability of 'Knows': An Opinionated Overview" was first published in Jonathan Jenkins Ichikawa (ed.), *The Routledge Handbook of Epistemic Contextualism*, Taylor and Francis, 2017, 13–31.

Chapter 10. "Alethic Pluralism, Deflationism, and Faultless Disagreement" is an extended, previously unpublished version of the abridged paper of the same title that was first published in *Metaphilosophy* 52:3–4 (2021), 432–48.

Introduction

Overview of the Chapters

The chapters gathered here anthologize my researches over the last two decades on three interconnected sets of issues:

- the intense renaissance of interest in the metaphysics of relativism about truth and its application in semantic theory;
- the significance of the "variability" phenomena that seem to afflict ascriptions of knowledge and claims featuring epistemic 'mights' and 'coulds'; and
- the challenge to find the best formulation of anti-realism about certain areas of our thought and discourse in such a way as to make sense of the intuitive idea that disagreement about matters within these areas can be and often is "faultless."

Concerning the last of these, one of the most natural and, at first blush, most important 'folk' anti-realist thoughts about basic taste, for instance, or comedy, or perhaps (some aspects of) etiquette, is that their lack of objectivity crystallizes in the possibility of situations where one party accepts a certain assessment and another something overtly apparently inconsistent with it and neither need be guilty of any kind of mistake of substance or shortcoming of cognitive process, broadly understood. However on close inspection it has proved, familiarly, very challenging to make coherent sense of this idea and it is fair to say that the majority of theorists who have thought about it, even those antecedently drawn to some form of anti-realism about some of the relevant range of discourses, have come to reject it as incoherent and to fall back on one of three views: viz. that in cases of the kind concerned there is *either* no real disagreement *or* that what disagreement there may be is not a matter of the antagonists' endorsement of mutually contradictory propositions, *or* that there is after all some form of fault involved.

To this trilemma there are two important exceptions in the contemporary literature: relativists, of various stripes, often hold it up as something of a *coup* for their stance that it can, supposedly, make straightforward sense of faultless disagreement; and there is also the quite different strategy for doing so, prefigured in *Truth and Objectivity* (Wright 1992) and developed in Chapters 1 and 2 of this

Essays on Relativism: 2001–2021. Crispin Wright, Oxford University Press. © Crispin Wright 2023.
DOI: 10.1093/oso/9780192845993.003.0001

volume, that argues that making judicious revisions to classical logic akin to those of the *mathematical intuitionists* can provide the resources to stabilize the notion of faultless disagreement as pre-theoretically understood against the aporia that otherwise seems to overtake it. These proposals are scrutinized in Chapters 2 and 10. The upshot is that neither relativism nor intuitionism does after all meet all the desiderata that a satisfactory account of the folk notion should satisfy; relativism because, in all foreseeable forms, it rehabilitates only an emasculated notion of disagreement; intuitionism because, without additional moves, it offers nothing to explain how, when you and I have a disagreement of the kind concerned, we can both rationally regard the other's opinion as "as good as mine." An account to overcome these drawbacks, involving a significant investment in the framework, especially the alethic pluralism, of *Truth and Objectivity*, is proposed in Chapter 10.

The specific focus assumed by much of the recent debate about relativism is very striking in one respect. In the heyday of the debates about realism in the last century, it fell to three rather different forms of anti-realism—expressivism, error-theory, and the Dummettian 'verificationist' rejection of evidence-transcendence truth—to provide the principal challengers. In hindsight, the lack of almost any explicit discussion of relativism about truth—surely one of the oldest and most natural anti-objectivist tendencies in all philosophy—may seem to have been a surprising omission. The broadly Protagorean idea that, whether globally or locally, the idea of *absolute* truth is an illusion—that there is only 'your truth' and 'my truth', or perhaps 'our truth' and 'their truth'—continues to provide a standing temptation for the anti-realist instincts of freshmen and the folk. Why didn't it get more of a look-in in the C20 debates? Why wasn't it centre stage, in particular, in *Truth and Objectivity*?

The answer is that, with the exception, perhaps, of the debates about ethical theory, where the term 'relativism', loosely understood to encompass any repudiation of the idea of absolute moral standards, remained in currency largely as a result of its employment, sympathetic or critical, by writers such as Gilbert Harman and Bernard Williams, the twentieth-century debates about realism and objectivity had largely relegated the idea of relative truth to the scrapheap. Non-factualist, non-cognitivist, and error-theoretic proposals attracted development precisely as more competitive—more resilient, and intuitively more felicitous—ways of trying to do justice to the anti-realist impulse than anything that might be provided by the dubious idea that the truth of a proposition would be best conceived as involving an extra argument place, to be filled by a culture, or society, or, worst of all, a single thinker. Had not serious doubts about the very coherence of this notion emerged as early as Socrates' dissection of it in the *Theaetetus*? And even in the case of morals, where it continued to be debated, did not even the more defensible versions of it have obviously unacceptable consequences?[1]

---

[1] Perhaps most salient is the emasculation of any potent notion of moral normativity. That an argument is valid is a reason to accept its conclusion if you accept its premises. That it is valid by such

So what a sea-change may seem to have taken place! But the appearance is somewhat deceptive. The dramatic resurgence of interest in alethic relativism in recent philosophy, as is in keeping with the contemporary analytic philosophical *milieu*, has been driven not so much by a renewed confidence in the ability of relativistic proposals to contribute to the traditional metaphysical debates about objectivity—to provide a stable, theoretically coherent home for certain kinds of anti-realist sympathies—as by the thought that relativism may have a crucial part to play in *descriptive philosophical semantics*. More specifically, the suggestion, elaborated by John MacFarlane and others,[2] has been that an empirically adequate semantics for certain areas of discourse, including knowledge-ascriptions and talk of epistemic 'mights', will best incorporate the idea of the truth of an utterance of one of the relevant sorts as relative to a *context of assessment*. Only thereby, so it is suggested, can it accommodate certain *prima facie* striking 'data' concerning the linguistic practices in question. These data, principally involving patterns of retraction and reassessment—but also embracing the kinds of things that can properly be said by eavesdroppers![3]—have impressed as crucial precisely because they apparently exclude any kind of indexical or contextualist account of constructions for which an ordinary invariantist semantic story already impresses as inappropriate for other reasons.[4]

Issues raised by this 'New Age' empirico-linguistic relativistic tendency are explored in several of the later chapters of this collection. While Chapters 4 and 5 are primarily concerned with relativism in its traditional garb as a metaphysical thesis, Chapters 3, 6, and 9 centre squarely on the idea that for certain discourses, the truth-value of an utterance may indeed vary with the context in which it is assessed: Chapter 3 focuses on the case of epistemic possibility; Chapter 6 (co-authored with Sebastiano Morruzzi) critiques MacFarlane's attempt to bring this brand of relativism to the aid of an Aristotelian conception of the open future;

---

and such standards is no such reason unless you think the standards are correct. That the current (as I write this) refusal of the US to intervene in the Assad regime's oppression of the Syrian people is morally unacceptable is a reason to work to see the policy changed. That it is unacceptable by such and such standards is no such reason unless you think the standards are correct. But moral relativism, in its purest form, holds not merely that all moral truth is relative to standards but that *there is no further issue* about the correctness of moral standards.

[2] John Macfarlane's magisterial (2014), encompassing chapters covering the ground of many of his earlier papers, bestrides all the debates and specific areas of application recently proposed. But relativism about epistemic modals has been defended, in addition, by Egan (2007 and 2011); and Gillies (2010). Among the advocates of relativism about knowledge are Kompa (2002); Richard (2004); Stephenson (2007); and Brogaard (2008a). Advocates of relativism about taste include Kölbel (2004); Lasersohn (2005); Richard (2008); and Egan (2010). Relativism about indicative conditionals is sympathetically discussed by Weatherson (2009) and Kolodny and MacFarlane (2010). Relativism about probability statements has been proposed by Douven (2011) and discussed by Yu (2016); a relativistic treatment of future contingents has been discussed by Belnap, Perloff, and Xu (2001).

[3] The importance of eavesdropping data may have eluded many theorists in the field! It looms large in Egan, Hawthorne, and Weatherson (2004).

[4] It is my impression that this part of the argument—the basis for the disjunction: either contextualism or relativism, for the kinds of discourse concerned—never quite received the clarity or attention in the early stages of these debates needed to justify the disjunctive syllogism.

Chapter 9 argues that relativism, so conceived, is actually inadequate to the very linguistic data, concerning retraction, that have been argued to scupper rival contextualist accounts of 'knows'. However Chapter 9 also argues that the contextualist offerings have in any case essential and decisive shortcomings of their own. Chapter 7 argues more generally that the specific linguistic practices that its sympathizers have generally referenced in support of New Age relativist semantics actually fall short of evidence for any such thing. In Chapter 8, co-authored with Filippo Ferrari, the attention switches to a critique, and rejection, of Herman Cappelen and John Hawthorne's book-length attempt to undercut any motivation for assessment-sensitive semantics, most especially in the treatment of discourse concerning personal taste, and their efforts to restore the prospect of a contextualist account.

Returning to the issue of faultless disagreement, if neither relativism nor contextualism offers resources sufficient to stabilize and vindicate the idea in areas where it may seem attractive—and if a realist invariantism about the funny, the tasty, and the exciting is reckoned to be beyond the pale in any case—a quite different style of approach is needed. Chapters 8 and 10 propose for the regions of discourse concerned a broadly use-theoretic account whose hallmarks are the integration of a locally deflationary notion of truth within an alethic pluralist framework and the distinction of a range of norms of use, embracing not just conditions of assertibility but supplementary independent norms of denial, retraction, and silence. Readers familiar with Chapter 1 of *Truth and Objectivity* will anticipate that this strategy requires rebuttal of the 'Inflationary' argument developed there, which contended that there is actually no fully deflated notion of truth available anywhere consistently with acceptance of the validity of the Disquotational Scheme for the truth-predicate. Chapter 10 explains what is correct about that argument and why, all the same, it does not quite perform as, in 1992, I advertised.

1

On Being in a Quandary

Relativism, Vagueness, Logical Revisionism

This chapter addresses three problems: the problem of formulating a coherent relativism, the Sorites paradox, and a seldom noticed difficulty in the best intuitionistic case for the revision of classical logic. A response to the latter is proposed which, generalized, contributes towards the solution of the other two. The key to this response is a generalized conception of indeterminacy as a specific kind of intellectual bafflement—Quandary. Intuitionistic revisions of classical logic are merited wherever a subject matter is conceived both as liable to generate Quandary and as subject to a broad form of evidential constraint. So motivated, the distinctions enshrined in intuitionistic logic provide for both a satisfying resolution of the Sorites paradox and a coherent outlet for relativistic views about, e.g., matters of taste and morals. An important corollary of the discussion is that an epistemic conception of vagueness can be prised apart from the strong metaphysical realism with which its principal supporters have associated it, and acknowledged to harbour an independent insight.

In this chapter, I shall propose a unified treatment of three *prima facie* unrelated problems. Two are very well known. One is the challenge of providing an account of vagueness which avoids the Sorites paradox. This has been discussed almost to tedium, but with the achievement, it is fair to say, of increasing variety rather than convergence in the proffered solutions.[1] Another is the problem of formulating a coherent relativism (in the sense germane to matters of taste, value, etc.) This is also well known. However it has had rather less intense recent attention; part of my project in what follows (Section 1) will be to recommend a view about what the real difficulty is. But the third problem—an awkward-looking wrinkle in the standard kind of case for revision of classical logic first propounded by the Intuitionists and generalized in the work of Michael Dummett—has, I think,

---

[1] I am afraid that the direction of the present treatment will be to add to the variety. My hope is that it will draw additional credibility from its association with resources to treat the other problems.

Essays on Relativism: 2001–2021. Crispin Wright, Oxford University Press. © Crispin Wright 2023.
DOI: 10.1093/oso/9780192845993.003.0002

not been widely perceived at all, either by revisionists[2] or their conservative opponents.[3]

The link connecting the problems, according to the diagnosis here entertained, runs via the notion of *indeterminacy*. Specifically: I will propose and commend a—broadly epistemic—conception of what (at least in a very wide class of cases) indeterminacy *is* which not merely explains how vagueness does *not* ground the truth of the major premises in Sorites paradoxes but also assists with the question of what form an interesting relativism (whether global or restricted to a local subject matter) may best assume, and helps to bring out what the basic intuitionistic—'anti-realist'—misgiving about classical logic really is. Though differing in at least one—very significant—respect from the conception of indeterminacy defended in the writings of Timothy Williamson, Roy Sorensen, and other supporters of the so-called Epistemic Conception of vagueness,[4] I doubt if it would have occurred to me to explore the ensuing proposal without their precedent. Indeed, a second important sub-project of the discussion to follow is indirectly to make a case that the Epistemicists have hold of an insight which may be detached from the extreme and, for many, bizarre-seeming metaphysical realism which—with their own encouragement—is usually regarded as of the essence of their view.

Our work will be in eight sections. Sections 1–3 will lay out the problems in the order indicated in the sub-title; Sections 4–6 will then take them in the reverse order and develop the advertised uniform treatment. Section 7 will comment on the relation of the proposal to the Epistemic Conception of vagueness. Section 8 is a concluding summary.

1. Relativism

1.1 Let me begin with a reminder of the crude but intuitive distinction from which the relativistic impulse springs. Any of the following claims would be likely to find both supporters and dissenters:

That snails are delicious
That cockroaches are disgusting
That marital infidelity is alright provided nobody gets hurt
That a Pacific sunset trumps any Impressionist canvas

---

[2] Henceforward, I restrict 'revisionism' and its cognates to the specific form of logical revisionism canvassed by the Intuitionists and their 'anti-realist' descendants.

[3] An insightful exception to this general myopia is Salerno (2000).

[4] See Sorensen (1988, pp. 199–253); Williamson (1992 and 1994). The Epistemic view receives earlier sympathetic treatment in Cargile (1969 and 1979, §36) and Campbell (1974) and is briefly endorsed in Horwich (1998 at p. 81). For further references, see Williamson (1994, p. 300, n. 1).

and perhaps

That Philosophy is pointless if it is not widely intelligible
That the belief that there is life elsewhere in the universe is justified
That death is nothing to fear.

Disputes about such claims may or may not involve quite strongly held convictions and attitudes. Sometimes they may be tractable disputes: there may be some
other matter about which one of the disputing parties is mistaken or ignorant,
where such a mistake or ignorance can perhaps be easily remedied, with the result
of a change of heart about the original claim; or there may be a type of experience
of which one of the disputing parties is innocent, and such that the effect of
initiation into that experience is, once again, a change of view. But there seems no
reason why that should have to be the way of it. Such a dispute might persist even
though there seemed to be nothing else relevant to it about which either party was
ignorant or mistaken, nor any range of relevant experience which either was
missing. The details of how that might happen—how the dispute might be
intransigent—vary with the examples. But in a wide class of cases, it would likely
be a matter of one disputant placing a value on something with which the other
could not be brought to sympathize; or with their being prone to an emotional or
other affect which the other did not share; or with basic differences of propensity
to belief, perhaps associated with the kinds of personal probability thresholds
which show up in such phenomena as variations in agents' degrees of risk
aversion.

Intuitively, claims of the above kinds—potentially giving rise to what we may
call *disputes of inclination*—contrast with claims like these:

That the kind of snails eaten in France are not found in Scotland
That cockroaches feed only on decomposing organic matter
That extra-marital affairs sometimes support a marriage
That sunset tonight will be at 7.31 pm
That there are fewer professional analytical philosophers than there were
That there are living organisms elsewhere in the solar system
That infant mortality was significantly higher in Victorian times than in Roman.

Any of these might in easily imaginable circumstances come into dispute, and in
some cases at least we can imagine such disputes being hard to resolve. Relevant
data might be hard to come by in some cases, and there are also material
vaguenesses involved in most of the examples, on which a difference of opinion
might turn. Then there is the possibility of prejudice, ignorance, mistake, delusion,
and so on, which in certain circumstances—perhaps far-fetched—it might be
difficult to correct. However what doesn't seem readily foreseeable is that we

might reach a point when we would feel the disputants should just 'agree to differ', as it were, without imputation of fault on either side. Opinions about such matters are not to be exculpated, to use a currently modish term, by factors of personal inclination, but have to answer to—it is almost irresistible to say—*the facts*.

This crude but intuitive distinction—disputes of inclination versus disputes of fact—immediately gives rise to a problem. Both types of dispute are focused on straightforward-seeming, indicative contents. But all such contents are naturally treated as truth-evaluable, and truth, one naturally thinks, is a matter of fit with the facts. So the very form of disputes of inclination seems tailor-made to encourage the idea that they are disputes of fact after all: disputes in which, *ceteris paribus*, someone is out of touch with how matters really stand. The problem is therefore: how to characterize disputes of inclination in such a way as to conserve the species, to disclose some point to the lay-philosophical intuition that there are such things at all, genuinely contrasting with—what one's characterization had better correlatively explain—disputes about the facts.

1.2 So far as I can see, there are exactly four broadly distinguishable types of possible response:

(i) *Rampant Realism* denies that the illustrated distinction has anything to do with non-factuality. For rampant realism, the surface form of disputes of inclination has precisely the significance just adumbrated: such disputes *do* centre on truth-evaluable contents, and truth *is* indeed a matter of fit with the facts. So, even in a radically intransigent dispute of inclination, there will, *ceteris paribus*, be a fact of the matter which one of the parties will be getting wrong. It may be that we have not the slightest idea how a particular such dispute might in principle be settled, and that if charged to explain it, we would hesitate to assign any role to ignorance, or prejudice, or mistake, or vagueness. These facts, however, so far from encouraging relativism, are best attributed to the imperfection of our grasp of the type of subject matter which the dispute really concerns.

I mean this option to be parallel in important respects to the Epistemic Conception of vagueness. The Epistemicist[5] holds that vague expressions like 'red', 'bald', and 'thin' actually denote properties of perfectly definite extension. But we do not (or, in some versions, cannot) know which properties these are— our concepts of them, fixed by our manifest understanding of the relevant expressions, fail fully to disclose their nature. There is thus a quite straightforward sense in which when I say that something is, for instance, red,

---

[5] I shall capitalize—'Epistemicist', 'Epistemicism', etc.—whenever referring to views which, like those of Sorensen and Williamson, combine a conception of vagueness as, broadly, a matter of ignorance with the retention of classical logic and its associated Bivalent metaphysics.

I (necessarily) imperfectly understand what I have said.[6] Clearly there is space for a similar view about the subject matter of a dispute of inclination. It can happen that we express a concept by 'delicious' which presents a property whose nature it fails (fully) to disclose. This property may or may not apply to culinary snails. There is no way of knowing who is right in the dispute, but somebody will be. At any rate, the issue is no less factual than that of whether culinary snails are indigenous to Scotland.

I do not propose to discuss the rampant realist proposal in any detail here. No doubt a fuller discussion of it would recapitulate many of the moves and counter-moves made in the recent debates about the Epistemic Conception of vagueness. Still, there are some interesting, foreseeably additional issues. Here are three:

First, is there any principled ground whereby a theorist might propose an Epistemicist treatment of vagueness but refuse to go rampant realist over what we are loosely characterizing as matters of inclination?

Second, can a rampant realist treatment of matters of inclination match the conservatism of the Epistemic Conception of vagueness? The Epistemicist does

---

[6] Experience shows that Epistemicists incline to protest at this. Suppose 'tall', say, as a predicate of human beings, applies to an individual just if they are precisely 5′ 11″ tall or more—that *5′ 11″ tall or more* is the property actually denoted by the vague, 'tall', so used. Then why, in saying that an individual is tall, should I be regarded as understanding what I have said to any lesser extent than when, in circumstances where I do not know the identity of the culprit, I say that whoever broke the clock had better own up? Why should ignorance of what, in fact, I am talking *about* be described as an imperfection of *understanding*?

Although it is not my purpose here to develop criticisms of the Epistemic Conception, I'll take a moment to try to justify the charge. The foregoing protest assumes that the epistemicist is entitled to regard us as knowing what *type* of sharply bounded property an understood vague expression denotes, and as ignorant only of *which* property of that type its use ascribes. I know of no justification for that assumption. What type of sharply bounded property does 'red' denote? Something physical? Or a manifest but sharply bounded segment of the 'colour wheel'? Or something else again? On what basis might one decide? And if the understanding of some common-or-garden vague expressions gives rise to no favoured intuitive *type* of candidate for their putative definitely bounded denotations, why should we favour the obvious candidates in cases—like 'tall'—where there are such?

Intuitively, to understand a simple, subject-predicate sentence, say, is to know what object is being talked about and what property is being ascribed to it. To be sure, the purport of that slogan should not be taken to require that one invariably has an *identifying* knowledge of the former: I can fully understand an utterance of 'Smith's murderer is insane' without knowing who the murderer is. But it is different with predication. Here what is demanded of one who understands is, at least in the overwhelming majority of cases, that they know—*in a sense parallel to the possession of identifying knowledge of the referent of a singular term*—what property the use of a particular predicate ascribes. Since the overwhelming majority of natural language predicates are vague, that is what the Epistemicist denies us. It would be no good for her to reply: 'But you *do* know what property "red" denotes—it is the property of being red!' On the Epistemic account, I know neither which property that is, nor what type of property it is, nor even—in contrast to, say, my understanding of 'has Alex's favourite property' where while ignorant in both those ways, I at least know what a property has to do in order to fit the bill—what would make it true that a particular property was indeed ascribed by the normal predicative use of 'red'. It is the last point that justifies the remark in the text; if you were comparably ignorant in all three respects about the content of a definite description—thus ignorant, in particular, of what condition its bearer, if any, would have to meet—it would be absolutely proper to describe you as failing fully to understand it.

not, properly understood, *deny* there is any such thing as vagueness; rather, she attempts a distinctive account, in epistemic terms, of what vagueness consists in. A similar account would be desirable, if the approach is to be extended to matters of inclination, of what it is that really distinguishes them from those matters which the opposing, mistaken view takes to be the only genuinely factual ones. A satisfying account must somehow *save* the crude and intuitive distinction, rather than merely obliterate it.

Third, the question arises whether rampant realism can be reconciled with the good-standing of our ordinary practice of the discourses in question. If irremediable ignorance—for instance, a gulf between our concept of the property denoted by 'delicious' and the nature of that property—is at work in disputes of inclination, one might wonder with what right we take it that there is no serious doubt in cases where there is *consensus* that the property applies. Of course, the same issue arises for Epistemicist treatments of vagueness: if we do not know enough about the sharply bounded property we denote by 'red' to be sure where its boundaries lie, what reason have we to think we have not *already* crossed those boundaries in cases where we are agreed that something is red? However, the problem may be a little more awkward for an epistemic treatment of matters of inclination. For the Epistemicist can presumably rejoin that however the reference of 'red' is fixed, a good account will constrain the word to refer to a property which does at least apply to the paradigms, on which we concur. The possible awkwardness for the extended, rampant realist view is that there are not, in the same way, *paradigms* for many of the examples of matters of inclination. That is: there are shades of colour that must be classified as red on pain of perceptual or conceptual incompetence, but there are no tastes that *must* similarly be classified as delicious. If matters of inclination—for instance, of gastronomic taste—even where not contested in fact, are as a class *essentially contestable*, at least in principle, without incompetence, then in contrast with the situation of 'red' and vague expressions generally, there would seem to be no clear candidates for the *partial* extensions that a competitive account of the reference of the distinctive vocabulary—'delicious', 'over-salted', etc.—might plausibly be required to conserve.

(ii) The second possible response to the problem of characterizing disputes of inclination is that of *Indexical Relativism*. On this view, truth-conditional contents are indeed involved in 'disputes' of inclination, but actually there are no *real disputes* involved. Rather, the seemingly conflicting views involve implicit reference to differing standards of assessment, or other contextual parameters, in a way that allows both disputants to be speaking the literal truth. Snails are delicious *for you*—for someone with your gastronomic susceptibilities and propensities—but they are not delicious for me—for one whose culinary taste is as mine is. Hurt-free infidelities can be acceptable to you—perhaps, to anyone inclined to judge the moral worth of an action by its pleasurable or painful effects alone—but they are not acceptable to me—to one inclined to value openness and integrity in close personal relationships for its own sake, irrespective of any independently beneficial or harmful consequences.

This, very familiar, kind of relativistic move is still supported in recent philosophy—for instance by Gilbert Harman on morals.[7] Its obvious drawback is that it seems destined to misrepresent the manner in which, at least as ordinarily understood, the contents in question embed under operations like the conditional and negation. If it were right, there would be an analogy between disputes of inclination and the 'dispute' between one who says 'I am tired' and her companion who replies, 'Well, I am not' (when what is at issue is one more museum visit). There are the materials here, perhaps, for a (further) disagreement but no disagreement has yet been expressed. But ordinary understanding already hears a disagreement between one who asserts that hurt-free infidelity is acceptable and one who asserts that it is not. And it finds a distinction between the denial that hurt-free infidelity is acceptable and the denial that it is generally acceptable by the standards employed by someone who has just asserted that it is acceptable. Yet for the indexical relativist, the latter should be the proper form of explicit denial of the former. In the same way, the ordinary understanding finds a distinction between the usual understanding of the conditional, that if hurt-free infidelity is acceptable, so are hurt-free broken promises, and the same sentence taken on the understanding that both antecedent and consequent are to be assessed relative to some one particular framework of standards (that of an actual assertor of the sentence, a framework which might or might not treat infidelity and promise-breaking in different ways).

Of course there is room for skirmishing here, some of it no doubt quite intricate. But it is not clear that we should expect that indexical relativism can save enough of the standard practice of discourses within which disputes of inclination may arise to avoid the charge that it has simply missed their subject matter.

(iii) The third possible response to the problem of characterizing disputes of inclination is that of *Expressivism*: the denial that the discourses in question genuinely deal in truth-conditional contents at all. Of course, on this view there are, again, no real *disputes* of inclination at all—merely differences of attitude, feeling, and reaction. There has been a significant amount of recent discussion of this kind of approach, stimulated by the sophisticated versions of it proposed by writers such as Simon Blackburn

---

[7] Harman has been, of course, a long-standing champion of the idea. The most recent extended defence of his views is in Harman and Thomson (1996, part one). For a many-handed discussion, see Railton, Harman, and Thomson (1998).

and Alan Gibbard.[8] But it confronts a very general dilemma. What is to be the expressivist account of the propositional—seemingly truth-conditional—surface of the relevant discourses? The clean response is to argue that it is misleading—that what is conveyed by discourse about the delicious, the morally acceptable, or whatever this kind of view is being proposed about, can and may be better expressed by a regimented discourse in which the impression that truth-conditional contents are being considered, and denied, or hypothesized, or believed, etc., is analysed away. However it seems fair to say that no-one knows how to accomplish this relatively technical project, with grave difficulties in particular attending any attempt to reconstruct the normal apparatus of moral argument in such a way as to dispel all appearance that it moves among truth-evaluable moral contents.[9] The alternative is to allow that the propositional surface of moral discourse, to stay with that case, can actually comfortably consist in there being no genuinely truth-conditional contents at issue, no genuine moral beliefs, no genuine moral arguments construed as movements from possible beliefs to possible beliefs, and so on. But now the danger is that the position merely becomes a terminological variant for the fourth response, about to be described, with terms like 'true' and 'belief' subjected to a (pointless) high redefinition by expressivism, but with no substantial difference otherwise.

(iv) Of the options so far reviewed, the first allows that a dispute of inclination is a real dispute, but at the cost of conceding that one of the disputants will be undetectably wrong about a subject matter of which both have an essentially imperfect conception, while the other two options deny, in their respective ways, that there is any genuine dispute at all. The remaining option—I'll call it *True Relativism*—must, it would seem, be the attempt to maintain that, while such disputes may indeed concern a common truth-evaluable claim, and thus may be genuine—may involve incompatible views about it—there need be nothing about which either disputant is mistaken, nor any imperfection in their grasp of what it is that is in dispute. Opinions held in disputes of inclination may, in particular cases, be flawed in various ways. But in the best case, the true relativist thought will be, such a dispute may oppose two opinions with which there is no fault to be found, even in principle, save by invocation of the idea that there is an ulterior, undecidable fact of the matter about which

---

[8] Blackburn (1984, ch. 6): "Evaluations, Projections and Quasi-realism," still remains the best introduction to his view, but the most recent official incarnation is Blackburn (1998); Alan Gibbard's ideas are developed systematically in his magisterial work (Gibbard 1990).

[9] For exposition and development of some of the basic difficulties, see Hale (1986, 1992, and 2002).

someone is mistaken. That hypothesis, distinctive of the first option, is exactly what true relativism rejects: for true relativism, genuinely conflicting opinions about a truth-evaluable claim may each be unimprovable and may involve no misrepresentation of any further fact.

1.3 In the light of the shortcomings, briefly noted, of the three available alternatives— and because it has, I think, some claim to be closest to the commonsense view of the status of disputes of inclination—it is of central importance to determine whether the materials can be made out for a stable and coherent true relativism. In *Truth and Objectivity* (Wright 1992), I proposed—without, I think, ever using the word 'relativism'—a framework one intended effect of which was to be just that. The key was the contrast between areas of discourse which, as it is there expressed, would be merely *minimally truth-apt*, and areas of discourse where, in addition, differences of opinion would be subject to the constraint of *cognitive command.*

The idea that there are merely minimally truth-apt discourses comprises two contentions, about truth and aptitude for truth respectively. The relevant— minimalist—view about truth, in briefest summary, is that all it takes in order for a predicate to qualify as a truth predicate is its satisfaction of each of a basic set of platitudes about truth: for instance, that to assert is to present as true, that statements which are apt for truth have negations which are likewise, that truth is one thing, justification another, and so on.[10] The view about truth-aptitude, likewise in briefest summary, itself comprises two contentions:

---

[10] A fuller list might include:

the transparency of truth—that to assert is to present as true and, more generally, that any attitude to a proposition is an attitude to its truth—that to believe, doubt or fear, for example, that *P* is to believe, doubt or fear that *P* is true. (*Transparency*)

the opacity of truth—incorporating a variety of weaker and stronger principles: that a thinker may be so situated that a particular truth is beyond her ken, that some truths may never be known, that some truths may be unknowable in principle, etc. (*Opacity*)

the conservation of truth-aptitude under embedding: aptitude for truth is preserved under a variety of operations—in particular, truth-apt propositions have negations, conjunctions, disjunctions, etc., which are likewise truth-apt. (*Embedding*)

the Correspondence Platitude—for a proposition to be true is for it to correspond to reality, accurately reflect how matters stand, 'tell it like it is', etc. (*Correspondence*)

the contrast of truth with justification—a proposition may be true without being justified, and vice versa. (*Contrast*)

the timelessness of truth—if a proposition is ever true, then it always is, so that whatever may, at any particular time, be truly asserted may—perhaps by appropriate transformations of mood, or tense—be truly asserted at any time. (*Timelessness*)

that truth is absolute—there is, strictly, no such thing as a proposition's being more or less true; propositions are completely true if true at all. (*Absoluteness*)

The list might be enlarged, and some of these principles may anyway seem controversial. Moreover it can be argued that the Equivalence Schema underlies not merely the first of the platitudes listed— Transparency—but the Correspondence and Contrast Platitudes as well. For elaboration of this claim, see Wright (1992, pp. 24–7). For further discussion of the minimalist conception, and adjacent issues, see Wright (1998 and 2001).

that any discourse dealing in assertoric contents will permit the definition upon its sentences of a predicate which qualifies as a truth predicate in the light of the minimalist proposal about truth;

and

that a discourse should be reckoned to deal with suitable such contents just in case its ingredient sentences are subject to certain minimal constraints of *syntax*—embeddability within negation, the conditional, contexts of propositional attitude, etc.—and *discipline*: their use must be governed by commonly acknowledged standards of warrant.

A properly detailed working out of these ideas[11] would foreseeably have the effect that almost all the areas of discourse which someone intuitively sympathetic to the 'crude but intuitive' distinction might want to view as hostage to potential disputes of inclination will turn out to deal in contents which, when the disciplinary standards proper to the discourse are satisfied, a supporter is going to be entitled to claim to be true. That however—the proposal is—ought to be consistent with the discourse in question failing to meet certain further conditions necessary to justify the idea that, in the case of such a dispute, there will be a further fact in virtue of which one of the disputants is in error.

What kind of condition? The leading idea of someone—the *factualist*—who believes that a given discourse deals in matters of fact—unless she thinks that its truths lie beyond our ken—is that soberly and responsibly to practise that discourse is to enter into a kind of *representational* mode of cognitive function, comparable in relevant respects to taking a photograph or making a wax impression of a key. The factualist conceives that certain matters stand thus and so independently of us and our practice—matters comparable to the photographed scene and the contours of the key. We then engage in the appropriate investigative activity—putting ourselves at the mercy of the standards of belief-formation and appraisal appropriate to the discourse in question (compare taking the photograph or impressing the key on the wax)—and the result is to leave an imprint on our minds which, in the best case, appropriately matches the independently standing fact.

This kind of thinking, while doubtless pretty vague and metaphorical, does have certain quite definite obligations. If we take photographs of one and the same

---

[11] A partial development of them is offered in Wright (1992, chs. 1–2).

scene which somehow turn out to represent it in incompatible ways, there has to have been some kind of shortcoming in the function of one (or both) of the cameras, or in the way it was used. If the wax impressions we take of a single key turn out to be of such a shape that no one key can fit them both, then again there has to have been some fault in the way one of us went about it, or in the materials used. The tariff for taking the idea of representation in the serious way the factualist wants to is that when subjects' 'representations' prove to conflict, then there has to have been something amiss with the way they were arrived at or with their vehicle—the wax, the camera, or the thinker.

That's the key thought behind the idea of cognitive command. The final formulation offered in *Truth and Objectivity* was that a discourse exerts cognitive command just in case it meets this condition:

> It is a priori that differences of opinion formulated within (that) discourse, unless excusable as a result of vagueness in a disputed statement, or in the standards of acceptability, or variation in personal evidence thresholds, so to speak, will involve something which may properly be regarded as a cognitive shortcoming.
> (Wright 1992, p. 144)

To stress: the constraint is motivated, in the fashion just sketched, by the thought that it, or something like it, is a commitment of anyone who thinks that the responsible formation of opinions expressible within the discourse is an exercise in the *representation* of self-standing facts. Conversely: any suggestion that conflicts in such opinions can be *cognitively blameless*, yet no vagueness be involved of any of the three kinds provided for in the formulation, is a suggestion that the factualist—seriously representational—view of the discourse in question is in error. Broadly, then, the implicit suggestion of *Truth and Objectivity* was that true relativism about a particular discourse may be formulated as the view that, while qualifying as minimally truth-apt, it fails to exhibit cognitive command.

1.4 However there is an awkwardness to be confronted by any proposal of this general kind. The key to true relativism, as we have it so far, is somehow to make out that a discourse deals in contents which are simultaneously truth-apt yet such that, when they fall into dispute, there need in principle be nothing wrong with— nothing to choose between—the disputed opinions. But in granting that the contents in question are minimally truth-apt, the relativist allows, presumably, that they are subject to ordinary propositional-logical reasoning. So, where P is any matter of inclination which comes into dispute between a thinker A, who accepts it, and a thinker B, who does not, what is wrong with the following *Simple Deduction*?

1	(1) *A* accepts *P*	—	Assumption
2	(2) *B* accepts Not-*P*	—	Assumption
3	(3) *A*'s and *B*'s disagreement involves no cognitive shortcoming	—	Assumption
4	(4) *P*	—	Assumption
2,4	(5) *B* is guilty of a mistake, hence of cognitive shortcoming	—	2, 4
2, 3	(6) Not-*P*	—	4, 5, 3 RAA
1, 2, 3	(7) *A* is guilty of a mistake, hence of cognitive shortcoming	—	4
1,2,	(8) Not-[3]	—	3, 3, 7 RAA

The Simple Deduction seems to show that whenever there is a difference of opinion on *any*—even a merely minimally—truth-apt claim, there *is*—quite trivially—a cognitive shortcoming, something to choose between the views. And since this has been proved *a priori*, cognitive command holds for all truth-apt discourses. So the alleged gap between minimal truth-aptitude and cognitive command, fundamental to the programme of *Truth and Objectivity*, disappears.

Obviously there has to be *something* off-colour about this argument. So much is immediately clear from the reflection that the disagreement it concerns could have been about some borderline case of a *vague* predicate: nothing that happens in the Simple Deduction is sensitive to the attempt made in the formulation of cognitive command to exempt disagreements which are owing to vagueness (one way or another). Yet the Deduction would have it that even these must involve cognitive shortcoming. And the notion of shortcoming involved is merely that of bare *error*—mismatch between belief and truth-value. So if the argument shows anything, it would appear to show *a priori* that any difference of opinion about a borderline case of a vague predicate will also involve a mismatch between belief (or unbelief) and actual truth-value. It would therefore seem that there has to *be* a truth-value in all such cases, even if we have not the slightest idea how it might be determined. We appear to have been saddled with the Epistemic Conception! I believe that means, with all due deference to the proponents of that view, that the Simple Deduction proves too much.[12]

---

[12] It may be rejoined (and was, by Mark Sainsbury, in correspondence) that we could accept the Simple Deduction without commitment to the stark bivalence espoused by the Epistemic Conception if we are prepared to allow that *A*'s and *B*'s respective opinions may indeed both reflect cognitive shortcoming where *P*'s truth-status is borderline—on the ground that, in such circumstances, both ought to be *agnostic* about *P*. The point is fair, as far as it goes, against the gist of the preceding paragraph in the text. However I believe—and this will be a central plank of the discussion to follow— that it is a profound mistake to regard positive or negative verdicts about borderline cases as *eo ipso* defective. If that were right, a borderline case of *P* should simply rank as a special kind of case in which—because things are *other than P says*—its negation ought to hold. In any case the Simple Deduction will run no less effectively if what *B* accepts is not 'Not-*P*' when understood narrowly, as holding only in *some* types of case where *P* fails to hold, but rather as holding in *all* kinds of case where things are not as described by *P*—*all* kinds of ways in which *P* can fail of truth, including being borderline (if, *contra* my remark above, that is how being borderline is conceived.) So even if Bivalence is rejected, the Simple Deduction still seems to commit us to the more general principle Dummett once called *Determinacy*: that *P* always has a determinate *truth-status*—of which Truth and Falsity may be only two among more than two possibilities—and that at least one of any pair of conflicting opinions

So where does it go wrong? It may be felt that the trouble lies with an overly limited conception of 'cognitive shortcoming'. The considerations used to motivate the cognitive command constraint—the comparison with the idea of representation at work in the examples of the photograph or the wax impression—license something richer: a notion of cognitive shortcoming that corresponds to failure or limitation of process, mechanism, or materials, and not merely a mismatch between the product and its object. The two cameras that produce divergent—conflicting—representations of the same scene must, one or both, have functioned less than perfectly, not merely in the sense that one (or both) gives out an inaccurate snapshot but in the sense that there must be some independent defect, or limitation, in the process whereby the snapshot was produced. So too, it may be suggested, with cognitive command: the motivated requirement is that differences of opinion in regions of genuinely representational discourse should involve imperfections of *pedigree*: shortcomings in the manner in which one or more of the opinions involved were arrived at, of a kind that might be appreciated as such independently of any imperfection in the result. Once shortcoming in that richer sense is required, it can no longer be sufficient for its occurrence merely that a pair of parties disagree—it needs to be ensured in addition that their disagreement betrays something amiss in the way their respective views were arrived at, some independently appreciable failure in the representational mechanisms. That, it may be felt, is what the cognitive command constraint should be understood as really driving at.

Such an emended understanding of cognitive shortcoming is indeed in keeping with the general motivation of the constraint. But it does not get to the root of our present difficulties. For one thing, the Simple Deduction would still run if we dropped all reference to cognitive shortcoming—thereby finessing the issue of how that notion should be understood—and replaced line (3) with:

(3*) *A*'s and *B*'s disagreement involves no *mistake.*

The resulting reasoning shows—if anything—that any pair of conflicting claims involve a mistake. If it is sound, there just isn't any fourth, i.e., true-relativistic response to the original problem. To suppose that *P* is merely minimally truth-apt in the sense of allowing of hypothesis, significant negation, and embedding within propositional attitudes is already, apparently, a commitment to rampant realism. Surely that cannot be right. But the modified Deduction, with (3*) replacing (3), shows that refining the idea of cognitive shortcoming in the manner just indicated has nothing to contribute to the task of explaining why not.

Perhaps more important, however, is the fact that we can run an argument to much the same effect as the (unamended) Simple Deduction even when 'cognitive shortcoming' *is* explicitly understood in the more demanding sense latterly

---

about *P* must involve a mistake about this status, whatever it is. That is still absolutely in keeping with the realist spirit of the Epistemic Conception, to which it still appears—at least in spirit—the Simple Deduction commits us if unchallenged.

proposed.[13] One reason why rampant realism is unattractive is because by insisting on a fact of the matter to determine the rights and wrongs of any dispute of inclination, no matter how intransigent, it is forced to introduce the idea of a truth-making state of affairs of which we have a necessarily imperfect concept,[14] and whose obtaining, or not, thus necessarily transcends our powers of competent assessment. This is unattractive in direct proportion to the attraction of the idea that, in discourses of the relevant kind, we are dealing with matters which essentially *cannot* outrun our appreciation: that there is no way in which something can be delicious, or disgusting, or funny, or obscene, etc., without being appreciable as such by an appropriately situated human subject because these matters are, in some very general way, constitutively dependent upon *us*. What we—most of us—find natural to think is that disputes of inclination typically arise in cases where *were* there a 'fact of the matter', it would have to be possible—because of this constitutive dependence—for the protagonists to know of it. Indeed, the ordinary idea that such disputes need concern no fact of the matter is just a *modus tollens* on that conditional: were there a fact of the matter, the disputants should be able to achieve consensus about it; but it seems manifest in the character of their disagreement that they cannot; so there isn't any fact of the matter. So for all—or at least for a wide class of cases—of claims, *P*, apt to figure in a dispute of inclination, it will seem acceptable—and the recoil from rampant realism will provide additional pressure—to hold to the following principle of *evidential constraint* (EC):

$P \rightarrow$ it is feasible to know that P[15]

and to hold, moreover, that the acceptability of this principle is, *a priori*, dictated by our concept of the subject matter involved.[16,17]

---

[13] This point was first made in Shapiro and Taschek (1996).

[14] See footnote 6 above.

[15] One substitution instance, of course, is:

Not-$P \rightarrow$ it is feasible to know that not-P.

[16] To forestall confusion, let me quickly address the quite natural thought that, where EC applies, cognitive command should be assured—since any difference of opinion will concern a knowable matter—and hence that any reason to doubt cognitive command for a given discourse should raise a doubt about EC too. This, if correct, would certainly augur badly for any attempt to locate disputes of inclination within discourses where cognitive command failed but EC held! But it is not correct. What the holding of EC for a discourse ensures is, just as stated, that each of the conditionals

$P \rightarrow$ it is feasible to know that P

Not-$P \rightarrow$ it is feasible to know that not-P,

is good for each proposition P expressible in that discourse. That would ensure that any difference of opinion about P would concern a knowable matter, and hence involve cognitive shortcoming, only if in any such dispute it would have to be determinate that one of P or not-P would hold. But of course it is of the essence of (true) relativism to reject precisely that—(and to do so for reasons unconnected with any vagueness in the proposition that P.)

[17] The modality involved in *feasible knowledge* is to be understood, of course, as constrained by the distribution of truth-values in the actual world. The proposition that, as I write this, I am in Australia is one which it is merely (logically or conceptually) possible to know—the possible world in question is

Consider, then, the following *EC-Deduction*:

1	(1)	A believes P, B believes not-P, and neither has any cognitive shortcoming.	—	Assumption
2	(2)	P	—	Assumption
2	(3)	It is feasible to know that P	—	2, EC
1,2	(4)	B believes the negation of something feasibly knowable.	—	1,3
1,2	(5)	B has a cognitive shortcoming	—	4
1	(6)	Not-P	—	2,1,5 RAA
1	(7)	It is feasible to know that not-P	—	6,EC
1	(8)	A believes the negation of something feasibly knowable.	—	1,7
1	(9)	A has a cognitive shortcoming	—	8
	(10)	Not-[1]	—	1,1,9 RAA

This time 'cognitive shortcoming', it is perhaps superfluous to remark, must involve less than ideal procedure, and not just error in the end product, since it involves mistakes about feasibly knowable matters.

So: it seems that (1) and EC are inconsistent, i.e. evidential constraint is incompatible with the possibility of cognitively blameless disagreement. If the EC-Deduction is sound, then it seems that wherever EC is *a priori*, cognitive command is met. And it is plausible that EC *will* be *a priori* at least for large classes of the types of claim—*par excellence* simple predications of concepts like *delicious*—where relativism is intuitively at its most attractive, and where a gap between minimal truth-aptitude and cognitive command is accordingly called for if we are to sustain the *Truth and Objectivity* proposal about how relativism should best be understood.[18]

1.5 What other objection might be made to either Deduction? Notice that there is no assumption of Bivalence in either argument; both can be run in an intuitionistic logic. But one might wonder about the role of *reductio* in the two proofs. For instance, at line (6) in the Simple Deduction, the assumption of P having run into trouble, RAA allows us to infer that its negation holds. Yet surely, in any context where we are trying seriously to make sense of the idea that there may be 'no fact of the matter', we must look askance at any rule of inference which lets us advance to the negation of a proposition just on the ground that its assumption has run into trouble. More specifically: in any circumstances where it is a possibility that a

---

one in which the proposition in question is true, and someone is appropriately placed to recognize its being so. By contrast, the range of what is feasible for us to know goes no further than what is actually the case: we are talking about those propositions whose actual truth could be recognized by the implementation of some humanly feasible process. (Of course there are further parameters: recognizable when? where?, under what if any sort of idealization of our actual powers?, etc. But these are not relevant to present concerns.)

[18] To stress: it is not merely *Truth and Objectivity*'s implicit proposal about *relativism* that is put in jeopardy by the EC-Deduction. According to the project of that book, cognitive command is a significant watershed but is assured for all discourses where epistemic constraint fails and realism, in Dummett's sense, is the appropriate view. Thus if the EC-Deduction were to succeed, cognitive command would hold universally and thus fail to mark a realism-relevant crux at all.

proposition's failing to hold may be a reflection merely of there being no 'fact of the matter', its so failing has surely to be distinguished from its negation's holding.

Natural though the thought is, it is not clear that there is much mileage in it. Let's make it a bit more specific.[19] The idea is best treated, we may take it, as involving restriction of the right-to-left direction of the *Negation Equivalence*,

$$T\neg P \leftrightarrow \neg TP,$$

expressing the commutativity of the operators, 'it is true that' and 'it is not the case that'. In circumstances where there is no fact of the matter whether or not P, it will be the case both that $\neg TP$ and $\neg T\neg P$. The proper conclusion, on the assumptions in question, of the *reductio* at line (6) of the Simple Deduction is thus not that the negation of P holds, but merely that it is not the case that P is true. And from this, since it is consistent with there being 'no fact of the matter' whether or not P, we may not infer (at line (7)) that A is guilty of any mistake in accepting P. Or so, anyway, the idea has to be.

Rejecting the Negation Equivalence has repercussions, of course, for the Equivalence Schema itself:

$$TP \leftrightarrow P$$

since one would have to reject the ingredient conditional:

$$P \to TP^{20}$$

That flies in the face of what would seem to be an absolutely basic and constitutive property of the notion of truth, that P and TP are, as it were, *attitudinally equivalent*: that any attitude to the proposition that P—belief, hope, doubt, desire, fear, etc.—is equivalent to the same attitude to its truth. For if that's accepted, and if it is granted that any reservation about a conditional has to involve the taking of some kind of differential attitudes to its antecedent and consequent, then there simply can be no coherent reservation about $P \to TP$.

A more direct way of making essentially the same point is this. At line (6) of each Deduction, even with RAA modified as proposed, we are entitled to infer that it is not the case that P is true. By hypothesis, however, A accepts P. Therefore unless that somehow does fall short of an acceptance that P is true, A is guilty of a mistake in any case. But how could someone accept P without commitment to its truth?

Indeed, there is actually a residual difficulty with this whole tendency, independent of issues to do with the attitudinal transparency of truth. Simply

---

[19] I draw here on a suggestion of Patrick Greenough.
[20] There will be no cause to question the converse conditional, which is needed for the derivation of the uncontroversial $T \neg P \to \neg TP$.

conceived, the mooted response to the two Deductions is trying to make out/exploit the idea that A and B may each be neither right nor wrong because there is 'no fact of the matter', where this conceived as a *third possibility*, contrasting with either A or B being right. That idea may well demand some restriction on the form of *reductio* utilized in the two Deductions. But the problem they are bringing to light will persist even after the restriction. For the simple fact now seems to be that A is taking matters to be one way, and B is taking them to be another, when in truth they are *neither*—when, precisely, a third possibility obtains. In that case there is indeed nothing to choose between A's and B's respective views, but only because they are both equally *off-beam*. We achieve the parity between their views essential to any satisfactory working out of a true relativism only by placing them in *parity of disesteem*. This general point—broadly, the intuitive inadequacy of 'third possibility' approaches to the construal of indeterminacy—will recur in the sequel.

So, that is the first of the three problems to which I want to work towards a unified approach: it is the problem of stabilizing the contrast between minimal truth-aptitude and cognitive command or, more generally, the problem of showing how there can indeed be a coherent true relativism—a coherent response of the fourth kind to the challenge of providing a proper account of the character of disputes of inclination.

2. The Sorites

2.1 Even after all the attention meted out to it, the simplicity of the Sorites paradox can still seem quite breathtaking. Take any example of the standard sort of series. Let F be the predicate in question. Let x' be the immediate successor in the series of any of its elements, x. The first element in the series—call it 'o'— will be F and the last—'k'—will be non-F. And of course F will be vague. If it were precise, there would be a determinate cut-off point—a last F-element in the series, immediately succeeded by a first non-F one. It would be true that $\exists x\,(Fx \land \neg Fx')$. So since F is vague, that claim is false. And its being false would seem to entail that every F-element is succeeded by *another* F-element: that $\forall x\,(Fx \rightarrow Fx')$. But that is trivially inconsistent with the data that Fo and that not-Fk.

What is startling is that it is, seemingly, child's play to replicate this structure with respect to almost every predicate that we understand; and that the motivation for the troublesome major premiss—

$$\forall x\,(Fx \rightarrow Fx')$$

—seems to flow directly just from the very datum that F is vague, that is, from the denial that it is precise. Again: if $\exists x\,(Fx \land \neg Fx')$ just *says*—falsely—that F is precise in the relevant series, then surely it's (classical) contradictory, $\forall x\,(Fx \rightarrow Fx')$, just says—*truly*—that F is vague. But it was given that Fo and that not-Fk. Seemingly incontrovertible premisses emerge—extremely simply, if a little long-windedly—as incompatible. Vague predicates, in their very nature, seemingly have all-inclusive extensions.

2.2. Hilary Putnam once suggested that an intuitionistic approach might assist (see Putnam 1983, pp. 271–86). How exactly? Not, anyway, by so restricting the underlying logic that the paradox cannot be derived.[21] It is true that it takes classical logic to motivate the major premiss, $\forall x\,(Fx \to Fx')$, on the basis of denial of the *unpalatable existential*, $\exists x\,(Fx \land \neg Fx')$. But the paradox could as well proceed directly from that denial:

$$\neg \exists x (Fx \land \neg Fx')$$

in intuitionistic logic. To be sure, we cannot then reason intuitionistically from Fo to Fk. (To do so would require double negation elimination steps.) But we can still run the Sorites reasoning backwards, from not-Fk to not-$F(o)$, using just n applications of an appropriate sub-routine of conjunction introduction, existential introduction and RAA. So what profit in Intuitionism here?

Putnam's thought is best taken to have been that there is no option but to regard the major premisses,

$$\neg \exists x (Fx \land \neg Fx')$$

or

$$\forall x\,(Fx \to Fx'),$$

as reduced to absurdity by the paradox, and that we are therefore constrained to accept their respective negations,

$$\neg\neg\exists x (Fx \land \neg Fx')$$

and

$$\neg \forall x\,(Fx \to Fx'),$$

as demonstrated. The advantage secured by an intuitionistic framework is then that, lacking double negation elimination—and also the classical rule, $\neg \forall x (\ldots x \ldots) \Rightarrow \exists x \neg (\ldots x \ldots)$, in consequence—we are not thereby constrained to accept the *unpalatable existential*:

---

[21] I do not suggest that Putnam was under any illusion about this.

$$\exists x \, (Fx \wedge \neg Fx').$$

So we can treat the Sorites reasoning as a straightforward *reductio* of its major premiss without thereby seemingly being forced into denying the very datum of the problem, viz. that F is vague.

The trouble is that this suggestion, so far, deals with only half the problem. Avoiding the unpalatable existential is a good thing, no doubt. Yet equally we have to explain what is wrong with its denial. And does not recognition of the vagueness of F in the relevant series precisely *enforce* that denial? Does not the vagueness of F just *consist in* the fact that no particular claim of the form, $(Fa \wedge \neg Fa')$, is true? And is not the problem compounded by the fact that the usual style of anti-realist/ intuitionist semantics will require us to regard recognition that nothing could justify such a claim as itself a conclusive reason for denying each particular instance of it for the series in question? It is true that intuitionistic resources would avoid the need to treat the Sorites reasoning as a proof of the unpalatable existential claim. But that thought goes no way to explaining how to resist its *negation*, which seems to be both an apt characteristic expression of F's vagueness and mandated by intuitionist style semantics in any case. And to stress: the negation leads straight to the paradox, whether our logic is classical or intuitionist (cf. Read and Wright 1985).

This brings out sharply what I regard as the most natural perspective on what a solution to the Sorites has to accomplish. Since the reasoning *is a reductio* of the major premiss, we have to recognize that $\neg\neg\exists x (Fx \wedge \neg Fx')$ is true. So we need to understand

(i) how the falsity of $\neg\exists x \, (Fx \wedge \neg Fx')$ can be consistent with the vagueness of F; and

(ii) how and why it can be a principled response to refuse to let $\neg\neg\exists x (Fx \wedge \neg Fx')$ constitute a commitment to the unpalatable existential, and hence—apparently—to the precision of F.[22]

3. Revisionism

3.1 It is generally though not universally assumed among interested philosophers that anti-realism in something close to Dummett's sense—the adoption of an evidentially constrained notion of truth as central in the theory of meaning— should lead to revisions in classical logic. But why? Truth plays a role in the

---

[22] This perspective is not mandatory, of course. In particular, it will not appeal to any dyed-in-the-wool classicists. Supervaluationist and Epistemicist approaches try, in their different ways, to allow us the unpalatable existential while mitigating its unpalatability. But those are not the approaches we follow here.

standard semantical justification for classical logic. Persuasion that truth is essentially—or locally—evidentially constrained might thus lead to (local) dissatisfaction with classical *semantics*—and hence with the standard justification for classical logic. But why should that enjoin dissatisfaction with the logic itself? There would seem to be an assumption at work that classical logic needs its classical justification. But maybe it might be justified in some other way. Or maybe it needs no semantical justification at all.[23] Is there a revisionary argument that finesses this apparent lacuna?

Here is one such proposal—I will call it the Basic Revisionary Argument—advanced by myself (see Wright 1992, ch. 2, pp. 37–44). Assume the discourse in question is one for which we have no guarantee of decidability: we do not know that it is feasible, for each of its statements P, to come to know P or to come to know not-P. Thus this principle holds

$$\text{(NKD)} \quad \neg K(\forall P)\,(\text{FeasK}(P) \vee \text{FeasK}(\neg P))$$

Then given that we also accept

$$\text{(EC)} \quad P \rightarrow \text{FeasK}(P)$$

—any truth of the discourse in question may feasibly be known—we get into difficulty if we also allow as valid

$$\text{(LEM)} \quad P \vee \neg P$$

For LEM and EC sustain simple reasoning to the conclusion that any P is such that either it or its negation may feasibly be known.[24] If we *know* that both LEM and

---

[23] I pursued these doubts about Dummett's revisionary line of thought in Wright (1993, ch. 15, pp. 433–57).

[24] For a reason to emerge in the next footnote, we should formulate the reasoning like this:

LEM	(i)	$P \vee \neg P$	
EC	(ii)	$P \rightarrow \text{FeasK}(P)$	
	(iii)	$\text{FeasK}(P) \rightarrow (\text{FeasK}(P) \vee \text{FeasK}(\neg P))$	
EC	(iv)	$P \rightarrow (\text{FeasK}(P) \vee \text{Feas K}(\neg P))$	(ii). (iii)
EC	(v)	$\neg P \rightarrow \text{FeasK}(\neg P)$	
	(vi)	$\text{FeasK}(\neg P) \rightarrow (\text{FeasK}(P) \vee \text{FeasK}(\neg P))$	
EC	(vii)	$\neg P \rightarrow (\text{FeasK}(P) \vee \text{FeasK}(\neg P))$	(vi), (vii)
LEM, EC	(viii)	$\text{FeasK}(P) \vee \text{FeasK}(\neg P)$	(i), (iv), (vii) disjunction elimination

EC are good, this reasoning presumably allows us to know that, for each P, (FeasK$(P) \vee$ FeasK$(\neg P)$). But that knowledge is inconsistent with NKD. Thus it cannot stably be supposed that each of EC, LEM, and NKD is known. Anti-realism supposes that EC is known *a priori*, and NKD seems incontrovertible—(for does it not merely acknowledge that, relative to extant means of decision, not all statements are decidable?) So the anti-realist must suppose that LEM is not known—agnosticism about it is mandated so long as we know that we don't know that it is feasible to decide any significant statement. Since logic has no business containing first principles that are uncertain, classical logic is unacceptable in our present state of information.

Of course, there are *three* possible responses to the situation: to deny, with the anti-realist, that LEM is known; to deny, with the realist, that EC is known; or to accept the reasoning as a proof that NKD is after all wrong. The last might be reasonable if one had provided consistent and simultaneous motivation for LEM and EC. But it is not a reasonable reaction when the grounds—if any—offered for LEM pre-suppose an evidentially unconstrained notion of truth (or at least have not been seen to be compatible with evidential constraint).

Note that provided disjunction sustains reasoning by cases, it is LEM—the *logical law*—that is the proper target of the argument, not just the semantic principle of Bivalence. (And reasoning by cases would be sustained in the relevant case if, e.g., the semantics was standard-supervaluational, rather than Bivalence-based.)[25]

---

[25] Actually, as Tim Williamson has reminded me, this point depends on how reasoning by cases (disjunction elimination) is formulated. If '$P \vee Q$' is supertrue and so is each of the conditionals, '$P \to R$' and '$Q \to R$', then so is R. That is ungainsayable, and enough to sustain the proof in footnote 30 and the letter of the argument of the text that one who believes that EC and NKD are each known should be agnostic about LEM. However reasoning by cases fails from the supervaluational perspective if the required auxiliary lemmas take the form

$$P \vdash R, \quad Q \vdash R,$$

rather than the form

$$\vdash P \to R, \quad \vdash Q \to R$$

A counterexample would be the invalidity of the inference from

$$P \vee \neg P \text{ to Definitely } P \vee \text{Definitely } \neg P,$$

notwithstanding the validity of each of

$$P \vdash \text{Definitely } P,$$

and

$$\neg P \vdash \text{Definitely} \neg P$$

(From the supervaluational perspective, we lose the inference from

$$P \vdash \text{Definitely } P$$

to

$$\vdash P \to \text{Definitely } P$$

so that the premises for the form of disjunction elimination that is supervaluationally sound are unavailable in the particular instance. Cf. Williamson 1994, p. 152 and Fine 1975, p. 290.

So this really is an argument for suspension of classical *logic*, not just classical semantics.

Note too that the argument is for not endorsing LEM in our present state of information. It is not an argument that the Law allows counterexamples—that it is *false*. That view is indeed inconsistent with the most elementary properties of negation and disjunction, which entail the *double negation* of any instance of LEM.[26]

3.2 But there is a problem—the advertised 'awkward wrinkle'—with the Basic Revisionary Argument. It is: what justifies NKD? It may seem just obvious that we do not know that it is feasible to decide any significant question (what about vagueness, backwards light cones, Quantum Mechanics, Goldbach, the Continuum Hypothesis, etc.?) But for the anti-realist, though not for the realist, this modesty needs to be able to stand alongside our putative knowledge of EC. And there is a doubt about the stability of that combination.

To see the worry, ask: what does it take *in general* to justify the claim that a certain statement is not known? The following seems a natural *principle of agnosticism*:

(AG)   *P* should be regarded as unknown just in case there is some possibility *Q* such that if it obtained, it would ensure not-*P*, and such that we are (warranted in thinking that we are) in no position to exclude *Q*.[27]

If AG is good, then justification of NKD will call for a *Q* such that, were *Q* to obtain, it would ensure that

$$\neg \forall P (\text{FeasK}(P) \vee \text{FeasK}(\neg P)).$$

And now the problem is simply that it would then follow that there is some statement such that neither it nor its negation is feasibly knowable—which in turn, in the presence of EC, entails a contradiction. So given EC, there can be no such appropriate *Q*.[28] So given EC and AG, there can be no justifying NKD. Thus the intuitive justification for NKD is, seemingly, not available to the anti-realist.

---

[26] Here is the simplest proof. Suppose $\neg[P \vee \neg P]$. And now additionally suppose *P*. Then $P \vee \neg P$ by disjunction introduction—contradiction. So $\neg P$, by *reductio*. But then $P \vee \neg P$ again by disjunction introduction. So $\neg\neg(P \vee \neg P)$. This proof is, of course, intuitionistically valid.

[27] If 'are in no position to exclude' means: do not know that not, then of course this principle uses the notion it constrains—but that is not to say that it is not a correct constraint.
Admirers of 'relevant alternatives' approaches to knowledge may demur at the generality of (AG) as formulated; but it will make no difference to the point to follow if 'there is some possibility *Q*' is replaced by 'there is some *epistemically relevant* possibility *Q*', or indeed any other restriction.

[28] Epistemically relevant or otherwise.

3.3 There is a response to the problem which I believe we should reject. What NKD says is that it is not known that *all* statements are such that either they or their negations may feasibly be known. So an AG-informed justification of NKD, will indeed call for a Q such that, if Q holds, *not all* statements, P, are such that FeasK(P) ∨ FeasK($\neg P$). But the advertised contradiction is in effect derived from the supposition that *some particular P* is such that ¬(FeasK(P) ∨ FeasK($\neg P$)). So to refer that contradiction back to the above, we need the step from $\neg \forall P(\ldots P \ldots)$ to $\exists P \neg(\ldots P \ldots)$—a step which is, of course, not generally intuitionistically valid. In other words: provided the background logic is intuitionistic, no difficulty has yet been disclosed for the idea that there are grounds for NKD which are consistent with AG.

The trouble with this, of course, is that we precisely may not take it that the background logic *is* (already) intuitionistic; rather the context is one in which we are seeking to capture an argument to the effect that it *ought* to be (at least to the extent that LEM is not unrestrictedly acceptable.) Obviously we cannot just help ourselves to distinctively intuitionistic restrictions in the attempt to stabilize the argument if the argument is exactly intended to motivate such restrictions.

A better response will have to improve on the principle AG. Specifically it will need to argue that it is not in general necessary, in order for a claim of ignorance whether P to be justified, that we (recognize that we) are in no position to exclude circumstances Q under which not-P would be true—that, at least in certain cases, it is possible to be in position to exclude any such Q while *still* not knowing or being warranted in accepting P.

And of course it is actually obvious that the intuitionist/anti-realist needs such an improved account in any case. For while the right-hand side of AG is presumably uncontentious as a *sufficient* condition for ignorance, it cannot possibly give an acceptable *necessary* condition in any context in which it is contemplated that the *double negation of* P *may not suffice for* P. In any such case, we may indeed be in a position to rule out any Q sufficing for not-P, yet still not in a position to affirm P. What the anti-realist needs, then, is a conception of *another* sufficient condition for ignorance which a thinker can meet even when in position to exclude the negation of a target proposition. And that there is this type of sufficient condition needs to be appreciable independently and—since we are seeking this in order to refurbish an argument for revising classical logic—in advance of an endorsement of any broadly intuitionistic understanding of the logical constants.

Is there any such alternative principle of ignorance? Our third problem[29] is the challenge to make out that there is and thereby to stabilize the Basic Revisionary Argument.

---

[29] Of course friends of classical logic are not likely to perceive this as a *problem*.

4. Revisionism Saved

4.1 We shall work on the problems in reverse order. To begin with, then, how might AG fail—how might someone reasonably be regarded as ignorant of the truth of a proposition who rightly considered that they were in a position to exclude (any proposition entailing) its negation?

A suggestive thought is that a relevant shortcoming of AG is immediate if we reflect upon examples of indeterminacy.[30] Suppose we take the simplest possible view of indeterminacy—what I will call the *third possibility view*: that indeterminacy consists/results in some kind of status other than truth and falsity—a *lack* of truth-value, perhaps, or the possession of some other truth-value. Then it is obvious—at least on one construal of negation, when not-*P* is true just when *P* is false—how being in position to exclude the negation of a statement need not suffice for knowledge of that statement. For excluding the negation would leave open *two* possibilities: that *P* is true and that it is indeterminate—that it lacks, or has a third, truth-value. Hence if that were the way to conceive of indeterminacy, we should want to replace AG with, as a first stab, something like:

(AG*)   *P* should be regarded as unknown just in case *either* there is some possibility *Q* such that if it obtained, it would ensure not-*P*, and such that we are (warranted in thinking that we are) in no position to exclude *Q or P* is recognized, in context, to be indeterminate.

This (in one form or another very widespread[31]) conception of indeterminacy is however, in my view, *un premier pas fatal*. It is quite unsatisfactory in general to represent *in*determinacy as any kind of determinate truth-status—any kind of middle situation, contrasting with both the poles (truth and falsity)—since one cannot thereby do justice to the absolutely basic datum that in general borderline cases come across as *hard* cases: as cases where we are baffled to choose between conflicting verdicts about which polar verdict applies, rather than as cases which

---

[30] Under this heading, I mean at this point to include both linguistic vagueness—the phenomenon, whether semantic or epistemic, or however it should be understood, which is associated with the Sorites paradox—and also indeterminacy *in re*, as might be exhibited by quantum phenomena, for instance, or the future behaviour of any genuinely indeterministic physical system.

[31] It is a common assumption, for instance, both of any supervaluational theorist of vagueness who accepts it as part of the necessary background for a supervaluational treatment that vague statements give rise to a class of cases in which we may stipulate that they are true, or that they are false, without (implicit) reclassification of any case in which they would actually be true, or false; and of defenders of degree-theoretic approaches (in accepting that there are statements which are neither wholly true nor wholly false.)

we recognize as enjoying a status inconsistent with both. Sure, sometimes people may non-interactively agree—that is, agree without any sociological evidence about other verdicts—that a shade of colour, say, is indeterminate (though I do not think it is clear what is the *content* of such an agreement); but more often—and more basically—the indeterminacy will be initially manifest not in (relatively confident) verdicts of indeterminacy but in (hesitant) differences of opinion (either between subjects at a given time or within a single subject's opinions at different times) about a polar verdict, which we have no idea how to settle—and which, therefore, we do not recognize as wrong.

In any case, even if indeterminacy is taken to be third possibility indeterminacy, AG* is indistinguishable from AG in the present dialectical setting. The standard anti-realist/intuitionist semantics for negation will have it that *P*'s negation is warranted/known just when the claim is warranted/known that no warrant for / knowledge of *P* can be achieved.[32] It follows that for the intuitionist/anti-realist, *recognizable* third possibility indeterminacy would be a situation where the negation of the relevant statement should be regarded as holding and is hence no ground for agnosticism about anything. (*Unrecognizable* third possibility indeterminacy, for its part, would be a solecism in any case, in the presence of EC for the discourse in question.)

4.2 A better conception of indeterminacy will allow that it is not in general a determinate situation and that indeterminacy about which statement, *P* or its negation, is true, is not to be conceived as a situation in which neither is. The latter consideration actually enjoins the former. For to comply with the latter, indeterminacy has to be compatible both with *P* and with its negation being true and clearly no determinate truth-status can be so compatible: if it is a truth-conferrer for either, it is inconsistent with the other; if it is a truth-conferrer for neither, then neither is true, and contradictions result (at least in the presence of the Disquotational Scheme). To reject the third possibility view is thus to reject the idea that in viewing the question, whether *P*, as indeterminate, one takes a view with any direct bearing on the question of the truth-value of *P*. I know no way of making that idea intelligible except by construing indeterminacy as some kind of *epistemic* status.

To accept this view—I shall call it the *Quandary view*—is, emphatically, less than to subscribe to the Epistemic Conception of vagueness, according to which vague expressions do actually possess sharp, albeit unknowable limits of extension. But it is to agree with it this far: that the root characterization of indeterminacy will be by reference to *ignorance*—to the idea, as a starting

---

[32] This account of negation is actually enforced by EC and the Disquotational Scheme—see Wright (1992, ch. 2).

characterization, of cases where we do not know, do not know how we might come to know, and can produce no reason for thinking that there is any way of coming to know what to say or think, or who has the better of a difference of opinion.[33] The crucial question how a Quandary view of indeterminacy can avoid becoming a version of the Epistemic Conception will exercise us in due course.

How does AG look in the context of the Quandary view? Consider for P a borderline case predication of 'red'. The materials about it which the Quandary view, as so far characterized, gives us are that we do not know, do not know how we might come to know, and can produce no reason for thinking that there is any way of coming to know whether the item in question is correctly described as 'red'. Now if what we are seeking to understand—in our attempt to improve on AG—is how someone could remain ignorant of the correctness of this predication who already knew that no Q inconsistent with it was true, then clearly the Quandary view helps not at all. For if I knew that no Q entailing not-P was true, that would surely be to *resolve* the indeterminacy, since it would rule out the case of not-P and—on the Quandary view, though not the Third Possibility view—no other case than P is then provided for. If all I am given is, not some additional possibility *besides P* and not-P but merely that I do not know, and do not know how to know, and can produce no reason for thinking that there is any way of coming to know which of them obtains, then there seems to be no obstacle to the thought that to learn that one does *not* obtain would be to learn that the other does.

4.3 The situation interestingly changes, however, when we consider not simple indeterminate predications like 'x is red' but *compounds* of such indeterminate components, as conceived under the Quandary view. In particular the Basic Revisionary Argument, that LEM is not known to hold in general, arguably becomes quite compelling when applied to instances of that principle whose disjuncts are simple ascriptions of colour to surfaces in plain view. It is a feature of the ordinary concept of colour that colours are *transparent* under suitable conditions of observation: that if a surface is red, it—or a physical duplicate[34]— will appear as such when observed under suitable conditions; *mutatis mutandis* if

---

[33] All three clauses are active in the characterization. If a subject does not know the answer to a question nor have any conception of how it might be decided, she is not thereby automatically bereft of any ground for thinking it decidable. One such ground might be to advert to experts presumed to be in position to resolve such a question. Another might be some general reason to think that such questions were decidable, even while lacking any specific idea of how. Neither will be available in the range of cases on which we shall shortly focus—simple predications of colour of surfaces open to view in good conditions. A difference of descriptive inclination in such a case among otherwise competent and properly functioning subjects is not open to adjudication by experts, nor do we have any general reason to think that the issue must be adjudicable in principle, in a way beyond our present ken. To be sure, we are forced to say so if we cling to the Law of Excluded Middle while retaining the belief that these predications are subject to EC. But then—again—we owe a ground for LEM consistent with that belief. I shall add a fourth clause in due course.

[34] The complication is to accommodate 'altering'—the phenomenon whereby implementing the very conditions which would normally best serve the observation of something's colour might, in special cases, actually change it. Rapid-action chameleons would be an example.

it is not red. Colour properties have essentially to do with how things visually appear and their instantiations, when they are instantiated, may always in principle be detected by our finding that they do indeed present appropriate visual appearances. So, according to our ordinary thinking about colour—though not of course that of defenders of the Epistemic Conception—EC is inescapable in this setting: when x is any coloured surface in plain view under what are known to be good conditions, each of the conditionals:

if x is red, that may be known,

and

if it is not the case that x is red, that may be known,

is known.

Now EC for redness, so formulated, would of course be inconsistent with recognizable third possibility indeterminacy: with our recognition, of a particular such x, that it could not be known to be red and could not be known not to be red. But it is perfectly consistent with our recognition merely that among some such possible predications, there will be a range where we do not know, and do not know how we might come to know, and can produce no reason for thinking that there is any way of coming to know whether the objects in question are red or not—it is only knowledge that we *cannot* know that is foreclosed. (If we could know that we couldn't know, then we would know that someone who took a view, however tentative—say that x was red—was wrong to do so. But we do *not* know that they are wrong to do so—the indeterminacy precisely leaves it open.) The key question is therefore the status of NKD as applied to these predications: the thesis that the disjunction, that it is feasible to know P or feasible to know not-P, is not known to hold for all P in the range in question. Sure, in the presence of EC, it cannot be that—so we cannot know that—*neither* disjunct is good in a particular case; that's the point just re-emphasized. But we surely do know of suitable particular instances—particular sample surfaces, in good view—that we do not know, and do not know how we might know, and can produce no reason for thinking that there is any way of coming to know what it is correct to say of their colour or who has the better of a dispute. And it may therefore seem plain that, the contradictoriness of its negation notwithstanding, we are thus in no position to affirm of such an instance, x, that the disjunction, that either it is feasible to know that x is red or it is feasible to know that it is not the case that x is red, may be known. Since LEM—in the presence of EC—entails that disjunction, it follows—granted that there is a compelling case for EC over the relevant subject matter—that we should not regard LEM as known.

4.4. But there is a lacuna in this reasoning. An awkward customer may choose to query the passage from the compound ignorance described by the three conditions on Quandary to the conclusion that we do not know the target disjunction, that either it is feasible to know that x is red or it is feasible to know that it is not the case that x is red. Suppose I do not know, and do not know how I might know, and can produce no reason for thinking that there is any way of coming to know that P; likewise for not-P. Then I might—loosely— describe myself as not knowing, and not knowing how I might know, and able to produce no reason for thinking that there is any way of coming to know what it is correct to think about P or who has the better of a dispute about it. Still, might I not have all those three levels of ignorance and still know that it is the case *either that* P *is knowable or that its negation is*? For not knowing what it is correct to think about P might naturally be taken as consisting in the conjunction: not knowing that it is correct to think P *and* not knowing that it is correct to think not-P; likewise not knowing who has the better of a difference of opinion about P might be taken as the conjunction: not knowing that the proponent of P has the better of it and not knowing that the proponent of not-P has the better of it. And all that, of course, would still be consistent with knowing that there *is* a correct verdict—that *someone* has the better of the dispute.

The objection, then, is that it does not strictly follow from the too-informal characterization offered of Quandary that if 'x is red' presents a quandary, then we have no warrant for the disjunction,

FeasK(x is red) $\vee$ FeasK(it is not the case that x is red)

All that follows, the awkward customer is pointing out, is that we are, as it were, thrice unwarranted in holding either disjunct. To say that someone does not know whether A or B is ambiguous. Weakly interpreted, it implies, in a context in which it is assumed that A or B is true, that the subject does not know which. Strongly interpreted, it implies that the subject does not know that the disjunction holds. The objection is that we have illicitly mixed this distinction: that to suggest that to treat borderline cases of colour predicates as quandaries enjoins a reservation about the displayed disjunction is to confuse it. It is uncontentious that such examples may be quandaries if that is taken merely to involve ignorance construed as an analogue of the weak interpretation of ignorance whether A or B. But to run the Basic Revisionary Argument, a case needs to be made that borderline cases of colour predicates present quandaries in a sense involving ignorance under the strong interpretation. What is that case?

A first rejoinder would be to challenge the objector to say, in the examples that concern us, what if any ground we possess for the claim that our ignorance *goes no further* than the weak interpretation—what residual ground, that is, when x is a borderline case of 'red', do we have for thinking that the disjunction,

FeasK(x is red) $\vee$ FeasK(it is not the case that x is red)

is warranted? It will not do, to stress, to cite its derivation from EC and classical logic—not before a motivation for classical logic is disclosed consistent with EC. Yet no other answer comes to mind.

However a second, decisive consideration is to hand if I am right in thinking that the kind of quandary presented in borderline cases has so far been under-described. As stressed, it is crucial to the conception of indeterminacy being proposed that someone who takes a (presumably tentative) view for or against the characterizability of such a case as 'red' is *not known to be wrong*. But that is consistent with allowing that it is also not known whether knowledge, one way or the other, about the redness of the particular case is even *metaphysically possible*— whether there is metaphysical space, so to speak, for such an opinion to constitute knowledge. I suggest that we should acknowledge that borderline cases do present such a fourth level of ignorance: that, when a difference of opinion about a borderline case occurs, one who feels that she has no basis to take sides should not stop short of acknowledging that she has no basis to think that anything amounting to knowledge about the case is metaphysically provided for. And if that is right, then there cannot be any residual ground for regarding the above disjunction as warranted. The strong interpretation of our ignorance whether it is feasible to know that x is red or feasible to know that it is not the case that x is red is enforced.

4.5 Let's take stock. Our project was to try to understand how it might be justifiable to refuse to endorse a claim in a context in which we could nevertheless exclude the truth of its negation. For the case of simple predications of colour on surfaces open to view in good conditions, the situation is seemingly this:

(i) that what I termed the transparency of colour enjoins acceptance of EC, in the form of the two ingredient conditionals given above;

(ii) that we know that there is a range of such predications where we do not know or have any idea how we might come to know whether or not they are correct, and moreover where we can produce no independent reason for thinking that there must be a way of knowing, or even reason to think that knowledge is metaphysically possible.

Nevertheless

(iii) we have a perfectly general disproof of the negation of LEM. (see footnote 26).

If we now essay to view the latter as a proof of LEM, something will have to give: either we must reject the idea that even simple colour predications obey

EC—specifically its two ingredient conditionals—and so reject the transparency of colour or we must repudiate (ii), treating the putative proof of LEM precisely as a ground for the claim that there must be a way of adjudicating all borderline colour predications. But, again, it just seems plain that the proof does not show *that*; what it shows is merely that denial of the law cannot consistently be accommodated alongside the ordinary rules for disjunction and *reductio ad absurdum*. The move to 'So one of the disjuncts must be knowably true' should seem like a complete *non sequitur*.

If that is right, then one who accepts both the transparency of colour and that borderline cases present quandaries as most recently characterized must consider that there is no warrant for LEM as applied to colour predications generally—even though the negation of any instance of it may be disproved—and hence that double negation elimination is likewise without warrant. Thus there *has* to be a solution to the problem the Intuitionist has with the Basic Revisionary Argument if it is ever right to accept EC for a given class of vague judgements and simultaneously allow that some of them present quandaries. And the solution must consist in the disclosure of a better principle of ignorance than AG.

4.6 Does the example of colour guide us towards a formulation of such a principle? According to AG it is a necessary and sufficient for a thinker's ignorance of *P* that there be some circumstances *Q* such that if *Q* obtained, not-*P* would be true and such that the thinker has no warrant to exclude *Q*. The improved principle the anti-realist needs will allow this to be a sufficient condition, but will disallow it as necessary. Here is a first approximation. Consider any compound statement, *A*, whose truth requires that (some of) its constituents have a specific distribution of truth-values or one of a range of such specific distributions. And let the constituents in question be subject to EC. Then

(AG$^+$) *A* is known only if there is an assurance that a suitably matching distribution of evidence for (or against) its (relevant) constituents may feasibly be acquired.[35, 36]

A purported warrant for a compound statement meeting the two stated conditions thus has to ground the belief that some appropriate pattern of evidence may be

---

[35] As it stands, this—more specifically, its contrapositive—provides a second sufficient condition for ignorance, restricted to the kind of compound statement it mentions. That is all that is necessary to explain how someone can be properly regarded as ignorant of a statement who, by being in position to discount any *Q* inconsistent with that statement, fails to meet the other sufficient condition of ignorance offered by AG.

[36] This is, to stress, only a first approximation to a full account of the principle required. Quantified statements, for instance, do not literally have constituents in the sense appealed to by the formulation—though it should be straightforward enough to extend the formulation to cover them. More needs to be said, too, about how the principle should apply to compounds in which negation is the principal operator. But the provisional formulation will serve the immediate purpose.

disclosed for its constituents. In particular, nothing is a basis for knowledge of a disjunction which does not ensure that at least one of the disjuncts passes the evidential constraint in its own right. More generally, when the truth of any class of statements is evidentially constrained, knowledge of statements compounded out of them has to be conservative with respect to the feasibility of appropriate patterns of knowledge of their constituents. One may thus quite properly profess ignorance of such a compound statement in any case where one has no reason to offer why an appropriate pattern of knowledge for its constituents should be thought achievable.

The great insight of the Mathematical Intuitionists—and the core of their revisionism—was that a thinker may simultaneously both lack any such reason and yet be in a position to refute the *negation* of such a compound using only the most minimal and uncontroversial principles governing truth and validity. The proof of the double negation of LEM sketched in footnote 26, for instance, turns only on the standard rules for disjunction, *reductio ad absurdum* in the form that no statements collectively entailing contradictory statements can all be true, and the principle (enjoined, remember, by the Equivalence Schema) that the negation of a statement is true just in case that statement is not. These principles are themselves quite neutral on the question of evidential constraint but are arguably constitutive of the content of the connectives—disjunction and negation— featuring in LEM. The assurance they provide of the validity of its double negation is thus ungainsayable. But when the truth of the ingredient statements is taken to involve evidential constraint, then that assurance does not in general amount to a reason to think that the appropriate kind of evidence for one disjunct or the other must in principle be available in any particular case. The assurance falls short in quandary cases—like borderline cases of simple colour predications—where we do not know what to say, do not know how we might find out, and can produce no reason for thinking that there is a way of finding out or even that finding out is metaphysically possible.

Quandaries are not, of course, restricted to cases of vagueness as usually understood. They are also presented, for instance, by certain unresolved but—so one would think—perfectly precise mathematical statements for which we possess no effective means of decision. So add the thought—whatever its motivation—that mathematical truth demands proof and there is then exactly the same kind of case for the suspension of classical logic in such areas of mathematics.[37] That is what the Intuitionists are famous for. But if the account I have outlined is sound, then— whether or not there are compelling reasons derived within the philosophy of

---

[37] Note that this way of making a case for basic intuitionistic revisions needs neither any suspect reliance on AG nor appeal to specific non-truth-based proposals—in terms of assertibility conditions, or conditions of proof—about the semantics of the logical constants. The key is the combination of epistemic constraint and the occurrence of quandary cases. Any *semantical* proposals offered can sound exactly the same as those of the classicist.

meaning for regarding EC as globally true—there will always be a case for suspension of classical logic wherever locally forceful grounds for EC combine with the possibility of quandary.[38]

5. An Intuitionistic Solution to the Sorites

5.1 Our problem was to make out how the Sorites reasoning could justly be treated as a *reductio* of its major premiss without our incurring an obligation to accept the unpalatable existential, and further—when the existential is unpalatable precisely because it seems to express the precision of the relevant predicate in the Sorites series—to explain how the major premiss might properly be viewed as a misdescription of what it is for that predicate to be vague. The essence of the solution that now suggests itself is that the vagueness of F should be held to consist not in the falsity of the unpalatable existential claim but precisely in its association with quandary in the sense latterly introduced.

To expand. Assume that F is like 'red' in that, though vague, predications of it are subject to EC. Then any truth of the form, $Fa \land \neg Fa'$, would have, presumably, to be recognizably true. The unpalatable existential, $\exists x (Fx \land \neg Fx')$, has only finitely many instances in the relevant type of (Sorites) context. So its truth too would have to be recognizable. And to recognize its truth would be to find an appropriate Fa and $\neg Fa'$ each of which was recognizably true. We know that there is no coherently denying that there is any such instance, since that denial is inconsistent, by elementary reasoning, with the data, $F(o)$ and $\neg F(n)$. But we

---

[38] An interesting supplementary question is now whether a revisionary argument might go through without actual *endorsement* of EC, just on the basis of agnosticism about it in the sense of reserving the possibility that it might be right. The line of thought would be this. Suppose we are satisfied that the outlined revisionary argument would work if we knew EC, but are so far open-minded—unpersuaded, for instance, that the usual anti-realist arguments for EC are compelling, but sufficiently moved to doubt that we know that truth is in general subject to *no* epistemic constraint. Suppose we are also satisfied that NKD, as a purely general thesis, is true: we have at present no grounds for thinking that we can in principle decide any issue. The key question is then this: can we envisage—is it rational to leave epistemic space for—a type of argument (which a global proponent of the revisionary argument thinks we already have) for EC which would ground its acceptance but would not improve matters as far as NKD is concerned? If the possibility of such an argument is open, then it must be that our (presumably *a priori*) grounds for LEM are *already* inconclusive—for what is open is precisely that we advance to a state of information in which EC is justified and yet in which NKD remains true. But in that case we should recognize that LEM already lacks the kind of support that a fundamental logical principle should have—for that should be support which would be robust in any envisageable future state of information.

That seems intriguing. It would mean that revisionary anti-realism might be based not on a positive endorsement of EC but merely on suspicion of the realist's non-epistemic conception of truth.

Would this provide a way of finessing Fitch's paradox?—the well-known argument (Fitch 1963) that, in the presence of EC, it is contradictory to suppose that some truths are never known? No: if nothing else was said, the paradox would stand as a reason for doubting that it *is* rational to reserve epistemic space for a convincing global argument for EC.

also know that we cannot find a confirming instance so long as we just consider cases where we are confident respectively that Fa, or that $\neg Fa'$. Thus, if there is a confirming pair, Fa and $\neg Fa'$, it must accordingly be found among the borderline cases. If these are rightly characterized as presenting quandary—that is, if we do not know whether to endorse them, do not know how we might find out, and can produce no reason for thinking that there is, or even could be, a way of finding out—then the status of $\exists x\,(Fx \wedge \neg Fx')$ is *likewise* a quandary, notwithstanding the proof of its double negation. And the plausibility of its (single) negation, notwithstanding the paradox it generates, is owing to our misrepresentation of this quandary: we are prone to deny the *truth* of the unpalatable existential when we should content ourselves with the observation that all its instances in the series in question are either false or quandary-presenting—an observation that merits denial of no more than its (current or foreseeable) assertibility.

5.2 Again, it is crucial to this way with the problem that the quandary posed by borderline cases be exactly as characterized and in particular that it falls short of the certitude that there can be no deciding them. There can be no intuitionistic treatment of the Sorites unless we hold back from that concession. The indeterminacy associated with vague predicates has to fall short of anything that fits us with knowledge that one who takes a determinate—positive or negative—view of such an example, however tentative, makes a mistake. For once we allow ourselves to cross that boundary—to rule out all possibility of finding a confirming instance of the unpalatable existential—EC, where we have it,[39] will enforce its denial and the paradox will ensue.

This limitation—that we lack the certitude that there can be no finding a validating instance of the unpalatable existential—may seem very difficult to swallow. Let it be that atomic predications of vague expressions present quandaries in just the sense characterized; in particular, that we do not know that there is no knowing that such a predication is true, or that it is false. Still, that both P and Q present quandaries is not in general a reason for regarding their conjunction as beyond all knowledge: if Q is not-P, for instance, we can know—one would think— that the conjunction is false even though each conjunct is a quandary. It may seem evident that instances of the unpalatable existential are in like case: that even if Fx and $\neg Fx'$ are quandaries, we *do* still know that there is no knowing that both are true. In general, quandary components are sure to generate quandary compounds only if verdicts on those components are mutually unconstrained; but the whole point about Sorites series is that adjacent terms lie close enough together to ensure that differential verdicts cannot be justified—*ergo* cannot be known.

Plausible as this train of thought may seem, it must be resisted—at least by a defender of EC for the range of predications in question. For suppose we knew

---

[39] Is EC always plausible for basic Sorites-prone predicates? It does seem to be a feature of all the usual examples. See concluding remarks below.

that any adjacent terms in a Sorites series lie close enough together to ensure that differential verdicts about them cannot both be known. Then we would know that

$$\text{FeasK}\,(Fx) \rightarrow \neg\text{FeasK}\,(\neg Fx')$$

By EC, we have both

$$Fx \rightarrow \text{FeasK}\,(Fx)$$

and

$$\neg Fx' \rightarrow \text{FeasK}\,(\neg Fx')$$

So, putting the three conditionals together,

$$Fx \rightarrow \neg\neg Fx'$$

Hence, contraposing and collapsing the triple negation,[40]

$$\neg Fx' \rightarrow \neg Fx$$

So if we think we know that any adjacent terms in a Sorites series lie close enough together to ensure that differential verdicts about them cannot both be known, we have to acknowledge that each non-F item in the series is preceded by another. Thus we saddle ourselves with a Sorites paradox again.[41]

---

[40] The equivalence of triple to single negation is of course uncontroversial.

[41] The general thrust of our discussion involves—as one would naturally expect of an advertised intuitionistic treatment—a heavy investment in EC. As I have said, I believe the principle is plausible for the kinds of statement that feature in the classic examples of the Sorites paradox—though the relationship between vagueness and evidential constraint is a crucial and relatively unexplored issue (see remarks at the end of the chapter). But I should stress that I regard the conception of borderline cases which I am proposing, of which it is an essential feature that we do not know that there is no knowledgeable verdict to be returned about a borderline case, as plausible independently of the incoherence of its denial when EC is accepted. Let me quickly rehearse a further corroborative consideration.

According to the opposing view—*the verdict exclusion view*—a borderline case is something about which we know that a knowledgeable positive or negative verdict is ruled out. The verdict exclusion view would be imposed by the third possibility view, but whatever its provenance, it faces great difficulty in accommodating the intuitions that ground the idea of higher-order vagueness. For consider: if a (first-order) borderline case of P is something about which one can know that one ought to take an agnostic stance—a situation where one ought not to believe P and ought not to believe not-P—then (one kind of) a higher-order borderline case is presumably a situation where one can know that one ought not to believe P and ought not to believe that P is (first-order) borderline. Since on the view proposed P's being first-order borderline is a situation where one ought not to believe P and

Let me again stress the two morals:

(i) EC plus knowledge of the *irresolubility* of borderline cases is a cocktail for disaster. Any compelling local motivation for EC with respect to a vague discourse enforces an acknowledgement that our ignorance with respect to the proper classification of borderline cases can extend no further than Quandary, as characterized, allows. We—innocent witnesses, as it were, to a difference of opinion—don't know what to say about such a case, don't know how to know, cannot produce any reason for thinking that there is any way of knowing nor even that there could be. But we do *not* know that there is none.

(ii) EC plus knowledge of the *undifferentiability* of adjacents in a Sorites series—the unknowability of the truth of contrasting verdicts about them—is similarly explosive. So we must take it that, where the statements in question are quandaries, we do not know that verdicts of the respective forms, *Fa* and not-*Fa'*, can never knowingly be returned. That allows each conjunction of such quandaries, *Fa* $\land$ ¬*Fa'*, to be itself a quandary;

ought not to believe not-*P*, it follows that, confronted with a higher-order borderline case, one can know that:

    (i) one ought not to believe *P*;

and

    (ii) one ought not to believe that one ought not to believe *P* and ought not to believe not-*P*. However in moving in the direction of (putative) borderline cases of *P* and the first-order *P*/not-*P* borderline, we have moved *towards P*, as it were, and away from not-*P*. Since—according to the verdict exclusion view—the first-order borderline cases were already cases where it could be known that

    (iii) one ought not to believe not-*P*,

it should follow that the relevant kind of higher-order borderline cases are likewise cases where (iii) may be known. So one gets into a position where one may knowledgeably endorse both (i) and (iii) yet simultaneously know—by dint of knowing (ii)—that one ought not to endorse their conjunction—a Moorean paradox (at best).

In sum: the idea that agnosticism is always mandated in borderline cases cannot make coherent sense of higher-order vagueness. The distinction between cases where a positive or negative view is mandated and cases where agnosticism is mandated cannot itself allow of borderline cases, on the verdict exclusion view. That is very implausible, and provides a powerful reason to be suspicious of the verdict exclusion view.

This conclusion would be blocked, of course, if the verdict exclusion view were qualified: if it were conceded that agnosticism is only mandated for *some* borderline cases and that for others, perhaps less 'centrally' borderline, something like the permissibility-conception which I have been recommending—that in such cases those who incline to return positive or negative verdicts are not known to be incorrect but are, as it were, 'entitled to their view'—is the stronger account. Arguably, though, such a compromise would give the game away. For if the permissibility-conception is correct at least for cases towards the borderline between definite cases of *P* and—the alleged—definite cases on the borderline between *P* its negation, the question must immediately arise what good objection there could be to allowing the negation of *P* to cover the latter, agnosticism-mandating cases. None if they are conceived as by the third possibility view—for then they are exactly cases where *P* is other than—so not—true. But after that adjustment, the only remaining borderline cases would be just those where conflicting opinions were permissible, and the permissibility-conception would therefore seem to have the better case to capture the basic phenomenon.

whence we may infer that the unpalatable existential is also a quandary, by the reasoning outlined in Section 5.1.[42]

5.3 What are we now in position to say about the following conditional:

$$\exists x(Fx \wedge \neg Fx') \to \text{'}F\text{'} \text{ is not vague,}$$

rightly focused on by Timothy Chambers in recent criticism of Putnam (Chambers 1998)? If it is allowed to stand as correct, then—contraposing—any vague expression will be characterized by the negation of the antecedent and the all too familiar aporia will ensue. What fault does the broadly intuitionistic approach I have been canvassing have to find with it?

Well, there *is* no fault to be found with it as a *conditional of assertibility*: to be in position to assert the antecedent with respect to the elements of a Sorites series must be to be in position to regard 'F' as sharply defined over the series. So an intuitionist who insists on the familiar kind of assertibility- conditional semantics for the conditional, whereby 'P → Q' is assertible just if it is assertible that any warrant for asserting P would be (effectively transformable into) a warrant for asserting Q, will be put in difficulty by Chambers' simple point. However that style of semantics is arguably objectionable in any case, obliterating as it does the distinction in content between the conditionals,

If P, then Q

and

If P is assertible, then Q.[43]

What is wrong with the Chambers conditional from our present perspective is rather that, if its antecedent—the unpalatable existential—is rightly regarded as presenting a quandary in cases where F is vague in the series in question, then it is not something whose truth we are in a position to exclude. So for all we know, the antecedent of the Chambers conditional may be true while its consequent is false;

---

[42] Timothy Williamson's (1996a) otherwise cogent recent criticisms of Putnam—specifically, his *reductio* of the combination of Putnam's proposal about vagueness and the ideal-justification conception of truth which Putnam favoured at the time—precisely assume that our knowledge of the status of borderline cases extends far enough to let us know that there can be no justified differentiation of adjacents, even under epistemically ideal circumstances. But we have seen, in effect, that Putnam should refuse to grant that assumption. A would-be intuitionistic treatment of vagueness must respect the two morals just summarized.

[43] This assumes that 'P' and 'P is assertible' are always co-warranted.

for F is vague by hypothesis. So there is—as there needs to be—principled cause to regard the conditional as unacceptable.[44]

This is not inconsistent with allowing that the unpalatable existential does indeed characterize what it is for F to be *precise* relative to the series of objects in question. But if that is insisted upon, then we learn that it was a mistake to view vagueness as entailing a *lack of precision*. Rather, the vagueness of a predicate involves the combined circumstances that atomic predications of it are prone to present quandary and that we are unwarranted in regarding Bivalence/Excluded Middle as valid for such predications. Vagueness so conceived is an epistemic notion; precision, if enjoined by the truth of the unpalatable existential, is a matter of ontology—of actual sharpness of extension. I'll return to the issue of the characterization of vagueness below.

5.4 Earlier we set two constraints on a treatment of the Sorites: it was to be explained

(i) how the falsity of $\neg\exists x\,(Fx \land \neg Fx')$ can be consistent with the vagueness of F; and

(ii) how and why it can be a principled response to refuse to let $\neg\neg\exists x\,(Fx \land \neg Fx')$

---

[44] A skirmish about this is possible. If the unpalatable existential is justly regarded as a presenting a quandary, then we shouldn't rule out the possibility of coming to know that $\exists x(Fx \land \neg Fx')$ is true. But if we did know it, we should presumably not then know that the relevant predicate, F, is vague—for we would know that it was sharply bounded in the series in question. So it seems we can rule out

$$(*)\quad \exists x(Fx \land \neg Fx') \ \& \ `F` \text{ is vague}$$

as a feasible item of knowledge. And now, if (*) is subject to EC, it follows that it is false and hence—again, an intuitionistically valid step—that the Chambers conditional holds after all. (I am grateful to Timothy Williamson for this observation.)

On the other hand, if (*) is *not* subject to EC; then the question is why not—what principled reason can be given for the exception when so much of our discussion has moved under the assumption that many contexts involving vague expressions are so?

The answer is that (*) cannot be subject to EC—at least in the simple conditional form in which we have been considering that principle—for just the reason that Fitch's well-known counterexamples cannot be. These counterexamples are all contingent conjunctions where knowledge of one conjunct is inconsistent with knowledge of the other. The simplest case is: P and it is not known that P. Knowledge of the second conjunct would require—by the factivity of knowledge—that the first conjunct was not known; but if the conjunction could be known, so could each conjunct simultaneously. Hence EC must fail if the Fitch schema has true instances. It now suffices to reflect that, on the conception of vague expressions as giving rise to quandary, (*) is merely a more complex Fitch case. For to know that `$F$` is vague is to know that predications of it give rise to quandaries in a series of the appropriate kind and hence—by the reasoning sketched in the second paragraph of Section 5.1—that the unpalatable existential is itself a quandary and hence is not known. Of course this comparison would not be soothing for someone sympathetic to the sketched intuitionistic response to the Sorites who was also a proponent of EC *globally*. But there is no evident reason why the viability of the intuitionistic response to the Sorites should depend upon the global proposition. For one for whom the case for EC always depends on the nature of the local subject matter, there should be no discomfort in recognizing that 'blind-spot' truths—truths about truths of which we are, *de facto* or essentially, ignorant—will provide a region of counterexamples to EC.

constitute a commitment to the unpalatable existential, and hence—apparently—to the precision of *F*.

The answers of the present approach, in summary, are these. The major premiss for the Sorites may unproblematically be denied, without betrayal of the vagueness of *F*, if *F*'s vagueness is, in the way adumbrated, an epistemic property—if it consists in the provision of quandary by some of the atomic predications of *F* on objects in the series in question. And such a denial need be no commitment to the unpalatable existential—or other classical equivalents of that denial which seem tantamount to the affirmation of precision—if the latter are also quandaries and are thus properly regarded as objects of agnosticism. Rather, the classical-logical moves which would impose such commitments are to be rejected precisely because they allow transitions from known premisses to quandary conclusions.[45]

6. Relativism Stabilized

6.1 Our problem was to block both the apparent lesson of the Simple Deduction, that any dispute about a truth-apt content involves a mistake, and that of the EC-Deduction, that any dispute about an evidentially constrained truth-apt content involves a substantive cognitive shortcoming—so that, at least with subject matters constrained by EC, the intended gap between minimal truth-aptitude and cognitive command collapses. It should now be foreseeable how a principled response to these awkward arguments may run.

The truth is that each Deduction is actually fine, as far as it goes—(to the stated line (8) in the case of the Simple Deduction, and line (10) in the case of the EC-Deduction.) The problem, rather, consists in a *non sequitur* in the way their conclusions were *interpreted*. Take the EC-Deduction. (The response to the Simple Deduction is exactly parallel.) What is actually put up for *reductio* is the claim that a certain dispute involves no cognitive shortcoming. That is a negative existential claim, so the *reductio* is in the first instance a proof of *its* negation, i.e. a doubly negated claim: that it is not true that *A*'s and *B*'s conflicting opinions involve no cognitive shortcoming. This is indeed established *a priori* (if EC is locally *a priori*). However to achieve the alleged demonstration of cognitive command—that it is *a priori* that cognitive shortcoming is involved—we have first to eliminate the double negation. And the needed DNE step, like that

---

[45] The reader should note that no ground has been given for reservations about Double Negation Elimination as applied to atomic predications, even in quandary-presenting cases. For—in contrast to the situation of the double negation of the unpalatable existential—no purely logical case will be available to enforce acceptance of $\neg\neg Fa$ in a case where Fa presents a quandary. However an acceptance of DNE for vague atomic predications will not, of course, enforce an acceptance of the Law of Excluded Middle for them. (Recall that the proof of the equivalence of DNE and LEM requires that the former hold for *compound* statements, in particular for LEM itself.)

involved in the classical 'proof' of LEM and the Sorites-based proof of the unpalatable existential, involves a violation of AG$^+$. As the reader may verify, the reasoning deployed in the EC-Deduction up to its conclusion at line (10) draws on no resources additional to those involved in the proof of the double negation of LEM save *modus ponens* and the suggestion that one who holds a mistaken view of a knowable matter is *per se* guilty of cognitive shortcoming. Neither of those additions seems contestable, so the EC-Deduction should be acknowledged as absolutely solid. However the transition from its actually doubly negated conclusion to the advertised, double negation eliminated result—that cognitive command holds wherever conflict of opinion is possible—demands, in the presence of EC, that there be an *identifiable* shortcoming in A's and B's conflicting opinions—for the shortcoming precisely consists in holding the wrong view about a knowable matter. If the example is one of quandary, the DNE step is thus a commitment to the view that an error may be identified in a case where we do not know the right opinion, do not know how we might know, and have no general reason to suppose that there is, or could be, a way of knowing nonetheless. Once again, the logical and other resources involved in the simple proof (up to line (10)) seem manifestly inadequate to sustain a conclusion with that significance. So although indeed in position to rule out the suggestion that any disagreement is cognitively blameless, just as the two Deductions show, we remain—in the light of the enhanced principle of ignorance AG$^+$—unentitled to the claim that there will be cognitive shortcoming in any difference of opinion within a minimally truth-apt discourse. We remain so unentitled precisely because that would be a commitment to a *locatability* claim for which the proof of the double negation provides no sufficient ground and for which we have, indeed, no sufficient ground.

The immediate lesson is that it is an error (albeit a natural one) to characterize failures of cognitive command—or indeed what is involved in True Relativism generally—in terms of the possibility of blameless differences of opinion.[46] Indeed, it is the same root error as the characterization of failures of Bivalence in terms of third possibilities, truth-value gaps, and so on. Failures of cognitive command, like failures of Bivalence, must be viewed as situations where we *have no warrant for* a certain claim, not ones where—for all we know—its negation may be true. We *do* know—the two Deductions precisely teach—that the negation will not be true. But that's not sufficient for cognitive command. The distinction once again turns on the intuitionistic insight that one may, in contexts of evidential constraint and potential quandary, fall short of knowledge of a claim whose negation one is nevertheless in position to exclude.

---

[46] Regrettably, the error is encouraged by the wording of some passages in *Truth and Objectivity*. See, for instance, pp. 94 and 145.

The point does not depend on the sources of any potential quandary. But my implicit proposal in *Truth and Objectivity*—the reason why the cognitive command constraint was formulated so as to exempt disagreements owing to vagueness—was that it is a feature of discourse concerning the comic, the attractive, and the merely minimally truth-apt generally, that differences of opinion in such regions may present quandaries for reasons *other than* vagueness. It is not (just) because 'funny' and 'delicious' are vague in the way 'red' is that the kind of differences of opinion about humour and gastronomy are possible which we do not know how to resolve, do not know how we might get to know, and do not know that there is, or could be, any getting to know. Merely minimally truth-apt discourses, in contrast with discourse exerting cognitive command, provide examples of indeterminacy *in re*. But we need to correct the usual understanding of this, epitomized by the rhetoric of phrases like 'no fact of the matter'. That rhetoric, it should now be superfluous to say, is simply inconsistent with the most basic constitutive principles concerning truth and negation. The indeterminacy consists rather in the fact that provision exists for quandaries which, because they arise in contexts governed by evidential constraint, enforce agnosticism about principles—like Bivalence—which if they could be assumed to hold, would ensure that there was a 'fact of the matter', about which we would merely be ignorant. It is a matter, if you like, of lack of warrant to believe in a fact of the matter, rather than a reason to deny one—a subtle but crucial distinction whose intelligibility depends on a perception of the inadequacy of AG and the basic intuitionistic insight.

7. Epistemic Indeterminacy

7.1 Let me return to the issue of the relation between the epistemic conception of indeterminacy I have been proposing and the rampantly realist Epistemic Conception. Writing in criticism of Williamson's and Sorensen's respective defences of the latter, I once observed that

> Perhaps the most basic problem for the indeterminist—the orthodox opponent of the Epistemic Conception—is to characterize what vagueness consists in—to say what a borderline case is. It is also one of the least investigated. The epistemic conception should not be allowed to draw strength from this neglect. There is no cause to despair that the situation can be remedied.   (Wright 1995, p. 146)

Well, how close do the foregoing considerations come to remedying the situation? My proposal in that earlier essay was that borderline cases of F should be characterized in the natural way, using an operator of definiteness, as cases which are neither definitely F nor definitely not-F but—prefiguring what I have been suggesting here—that the definiteness operator should be construed epistemically, with genuine borderline cases marked off from determinate matters lying beyond our ken—including borderline cases as conceived by the Epistemicist—by examples of the latter sort being characterized by the principle of Bivalence, there characterized as the hypothesis of 'universal determinacy in truth-value' (Wright 1995, p. 145).

Williamson later responded:

> So far the parties do not disagree; the epistemicist has merely said more than the indeterminist. But that is not the only difference between them. The indetermin- ist regards the epistemicist's account of borderline cases as *positively incorrect* [my emphasis]. The epistemicist is supposed to regard borderline claims as determinate in truth-value, while the indeterminist regards them as not deter- minate in truth-value.   (Williamson 1996b, p. 44)

This gloss on the differences between the protagonists enabled Williamson to advance the following line of criticism. Part of the indeterminist characterization of borderline claims is that they are not determinate in truth-value. What does 'determinate' mean? If not being determinate in truth-value involves *lacking* a truth-value then we are back with third possibility indeterminacy. But 'not determinate in truth-value' cannot just mean 'not definitely true and not definitely false' since that claim—with 'definitely' understood epistemically, as now by both sides in the dispute—is one the Epistemicist is prepared to make; whereas the denial of determinacy was supposed to crystallize a point of disagreement between the indeterminist and the Epistemicist. So, Williamson concluded, the indeter- minist bugbear—of giving some non-epistemic account of borderline cases— recurs.

This was a curious criticism, given that the notion of determinacy in truth-value was involved in the first place only as a paraphrase of the principle of Bivalence. For in that case, Williamson's supposition that my indeterminist was someone who regarded borderline claims as not determinate in truth-value would be equivalent to attributing to her the thesis that Bivalence *failed* for such claims. And then, given that I explicitly did not want any traffic with third possibilities, Williamson would have had a much more forceful criticism to make than merely that the implicated notion of determinacy had still not been properly explained.

In fact, however—the important point for our present concerns—Williamson mischaracterized the opposition in the first place. It was a misunderstanding to suppose that the 'indeterminist'—my theorist in the earlier chapter—regarded borderline claims as 'not determinate in truth-value'. Rather, the difference between that theorist and the Epistemicist was precisely that the former draws back from, rather than denies, a view which the Epistemicist takes: the negation belongs with the attitude, not the content. The 'indeterminist' regarded the

Epistemicist's bivalent view of borderline cases (the view of them as determinate in truth-value) not as positively wrong—where that is taken to mean: something she is prepared to *deny*—but as positively unjustified: something which she knows of no sufficient grounds to accept.

In fact, the involvement of an (unexplicated) notion of determinacy was inessential to the view that was being proposed. The claim of determinacy in truth-value just is the claim that Bivalence holds in the cases in question. So the heart of the 'indeterminist' thesis was just that borderline cases are these: cases where—in an appropriate epistemic sense of the definiteness operator—a target predication is not definitely true and not definitely false and where there is no extant warrant for the assertion of Bivalence. Williamson's short response contained nothing to threaten the stability of this view.

That said, it merits acknowledgement that 'indeterminist' was not the happiest label for the type of position I was trying to outline, and that it may have misled Williamson. For it is hard to hear it without gathering a suggestion of a *semantic* or an *ontological* thesis: of vagueness conceived as involving matters left unresolved not (merely) in an epistemic sense, but in fact, by the very rules of language, or by the World itself. For someone who wants one of those directions made good—and who read my remark quoted above as calling for just that—the direction taken in my earlier discussion, and in this one, will puzzle and disappoint. In any case—save in one crucial detail—it is still no part of the view I have been developing in *this* chapter to regard the Epistemicist's account of borderline cases as 'positively incorrect'. There is agreement that the root manifestations of vagueness are captured by epistemic categories: bafflement, ignorance, difference of opinion, and uncertainty—and that to conceive of the phenomenon in semantic or ontological terms is to take a *proto-theoretical* step which, absent any coherent further development, there is cause to suspect may be a mistake. The 'crucial detail' of disagreement—prescinding, of course, from the major conflict over warrant for the principle of Bivalence—is merely over the thesis that borderline cases are known to defy all possibility of knowledgeable opinion. While the coherence of the Quandary view depends on its rejection, Williamson perceives it as a theoretical obligation of his own view to defend it.[47] But setting that apart, it deserves emphasis that the view of vagueness here defended is consistent with the

---

[47] I am not myself certain that the Epistemicist does have any obligation to defend anything so strong. Someone who believes that vague expressions have sharp extensions ought to explain, sure, why we don't actually know what they are nor have any clear conception of how we might find out. But there would seem to be no clear obligation to conceive of them as unknowable—(though that might be a consequence of the theorist's best shot at meeting the less extreme explanatory demand). I suspect that matters proceed differently in Williamson's thinking: that he regards the impossibility of knowledgeable (positive or negative) opinion about borderline cases as a datum, which would straightforwardly be explained by semantic and ontological conceptions of indeterminacy (could we but explain *them*) and of which he therefore conceives that his own, Bivalence-accepting conception must provide an alternative explanation. I do not think it is a datum.

correctness of the Epistemic Conception (and on the other hand, *pari passu*, with agnosticism about whether it even could be correct). The Quandary view is consistent with the correctness of the Epistemic Conception in just the sense in which the Intuitionist philosophy of mathematics is consistent with the actual correctness of the principle of Bivalence and classical mathematical practice. The basic complaint is not of *mistake*—though the Epistemic Conception may well prove to be committed to collateral mistakes (for instance about the conditions on possible semantic reference: on what it takes for a predicate to stand for a property)—but of *lack of evidence*.

7.2 One—albeit perhaps insufficient—reason to retain the term 'indeterminist' for the conception of vagueness defended in my earlier chapter was the retention of a definiteness operator and the characterization of borderline cases as 'not definitely . . . and not definitely not . . .'. But I now think *that* was a mistake—and the operator itself at best an idle wheel. My earlier proposal was that P is definitely true just if any (what I called) *primary* opinion—any opinion based on neither testimony nor inference, nor held groundlessly—that not-P would be 'cognitively misbegotten', i.e. some factor would contribute to its formation of a kind which, once known about, would call its reliability into question in any case and could aptly be used to explain the formation of a mistaken opinion. No doubt this proposal could be pressured in detail, but—with the notion of cognitive command recently before us—the guiding idea is plain: the definite truths were to be those disagreements which would have to involve cognitive shortcoming *tout court*, with no provision for excuses to do with vagueness.

So a claim which is not definitely true and not definitely false ought to be one—I seem to have wanted to suggest—about which 'neither of a pair of conflicting opinions need be cognitively misbegotten' (Wright 1995, p. 145). This proposal was intended to capture the idea

that the phenomenon of permissible disagreement at the margins is of the very essence of vagueness . . . the basic phenomenon of vagueness is one of the possibility of faultlessly generated—cognitively un-misbegotten—conflict. (p. 145)

However we have in effect seen that this will not do. What we learned from the EC-Deduction was that, wherever we have evidential constraint, hence each of the conditionals

$P \rightarrow$ it is feasible to know that P, and
$\neg P \rightarrow$ it is feasible to know that $\neg P$,

the idea of a 'faultlessly generated' disagreement rapidly destabilizes. For if the disagreement were faultless, it could not be that it was feasible to know either of the protagonists' opinions to be correct, or there would have to be fault in the generation of the other. And in that case, contraposing on both conditionals, contradiction ensues.

But we know the remedy now: retreat to the double negation and invoke the enhanced principle of ignorance, AG^+. My proposal should have been not that faultlessly generated disagreements are possible where vague claims are concerned, but that we are in no position to claim that any disagreement about such a claim involves fault. Thus the root phenomenon of vagueness cannot after all, when cautiously characterized, be that of permissible disagreement at the margins; rather it is the possibility of disagreements of which we are in no position to say that they are *impermissible*, in the sense of involving specific shortcomings of epistemic pedigree. We are in no position to say that because, notwithstanding the incoherence of the idea that such a disagreement is actually fault-free, the claim that there are specific shortcomings involved must, in the presence of EC, involve a commitment to their identifiability, at least to the extent of pointing the finger at one disputant or the other. And that is exactly what we have no reason to think we can generally do.

The upshot is that even when 'definitely' is interpreted along the epistemic lines I proposed, we should not acquiesce in the characterization of borderline claims as ones which are *neither* definitely true *nor* definitely false.[48] Rather, they will be claims for which *there is no justification for the thesis that they are* definitely true or definitely false—again, with 'definitely' epistemic—nor any justification for the application of Bivalence to them. But now the former point is swallowed by the latter. For in the presence of EC, justification for Bivalence just is justification for the thesis that any statement in the relevant range is knowably—so definitely— true or false. So the definiteness operator is (harmless but) *de trop*.

One more very important qualification. None of this is to suggest that we may give a complete characterization of vagueness along these Spartan lines: that vague statements are just those which give rise to quandary and for which Bivalence is unjustified. That's too Spartan, of course. The view proposed has indeed, after all, no need for the expressive resource of an operator of indeterminacy. But some quandaries—Goldbach's conjecture, for instance—feature nothing recognizable as vagueness; and others—that infidelity is alright provided nobody gets hurt, perhaps—may present quandaries for reasons other than any ingredient vagueness. So the task of a more refined taxonomy remains—the notion of quandary is just a first step.[49] But if the general tendency of this discussion is right, it is a crucial step.

---

[48] I leave it as an exercise for the reader to adapt the EC-Deduction to a proof of this claim.

[49] Relevant initial thoughts, already bruited, are these: it is known—in our present state of information, in the absence of proof—that nobody's opinion about Goldbach is knowledgeable; whereas, on

8. Summary Reflections

8.1 To recapitulate the gist of all this. A proposition *P* presents a quandary for a thinker *T* just when the following conditions are met:

   (i) *T* does not know whether or not *P*
  (ii) *T* does not know any way of knowing whether or not *P*
 (iii) *T* does not know that there is any way of knowing whether or not *P*
 (iv) *T* does not know that it is (metaphysically) possible to know whether or not *P*.

The satisfaction of each of these conditions would be entailed by

  (v) *T* knows that it is impossible to know whether or not *P*,

but that condition is excluded by Quandary as we intend it—a quandary is uncertain through and through.

Note that, so characterized, quandaries are relative to thinkers—one person's quandary may be part of another's (presumed) information—and to states of information—a proposition may present a quandary at one time and not at another. There are important classes of example which are acknowledged to present quandaries for all thinkers who take an interest in the matter. Goldbach's conjecture is currently one such case. But for the protagonists in an (intransigent) dispute of inclination, it will naturally not seem that the target claim presents a quandary; likewise when conflicting verdicts are returned about a borderline case of some vague expression. Yet to a third party, the contested claim in such cases—and hence the question who is right about it—may always reasonably be taken to present a quandary nonetheless.

It should seem relatively uncontroversial to propose that unresolved mathematical conjectures, borderline cases of vague expressions, and the foci of disputes of inclination meet the four defining conditions of quandary. To say that much is simply to report on our epistemic situation in relation to the claims in question. It is to say nothing about their metaphysical or semantical status. What is not uncontroversial, of course, is the contention that clause (v) fails—the contention that we do not know that there is no knowing the truth of either of two conflicting verdicts about a borderline case, or either of the two conflicting views in a dispute of inclination. As I have acknowledged, this modesty may go against the grain. But it is imposed

---

the view proposed, we precisely do not know that a positive or negative verdict about a borderline case of '*x* is red' is unknowledgeable. And unlike 'red', predications of 'funny' have no definite cases—they are always contestable.

if we accept that the disputed statement is subject to EC.[50] And it is imposed in any case if we are inclined to think that we should be permissive about such disputes—for otherwise we ought to convict both disputants of over-reaching, of unwarranted conviction about an undecidable matter, and they should therefore withdraw. The thought that they are, rather, *entitled* to their respective views has to be the thought that we do not know that they are wrong to take them—do not know that neither of their views is knowledgeable.

I do not expect many immediate converts—at least not from among those who start out convinced that clause (v) should be part of the account of vagueness. But maybe I have done a little to erode that conviction—or at least to bring out other intuitions and theses that it holds hostage. In any case, Epistemicists will abjure the role played by Evidential Constraint in the foregoing discussion. And inde-terminists proper will equally abjure the suggestion that the proponents of the Epistemic Conception of vagueness have the matter half right: that indeterminacy *is* an epistemic matter, that borderline cases should be characterized as cases of (a complicated kind of) ignorance. According to the present view, the Epistemic Conception takes us in the right general direction. It goes overboard in its additional (gratuitous and unmotivated) assumption that the principle of Bivalence holds for all statements, including quandary-presenting ones, so that we are constrained to think of, e.g., predicate expressions which are prone to give rise to such statements as denoting—by mechanisms of which no-one has the slightest inkling how to give an account—sharply bounded properties of which we may lack any clear conception.[51] But the general conception of vagueness it involves is otherwise—at least in the round—quite consistent with the present proposal.

I have suggested that the Intuitionists' revisionism is best reconstructed as driven by a mixture of quandary and evidential constraint: the belief that truth in mathematics cannot outrun proof, together with a recognition that unresolved mathematical conjectures can present quandaries in the sense characterized. If this is right, then, my point has been, the revisionary argument will generalize, and classical logic—especially the Law of Excluded Middle and, correlatively, the principle of double negation elimination—should not be accepted (since it has not been recognized to be valid) for any area of discourse exhibiting these two features. The result, I have argued, is that we have the resources for a principled, broadly intuitionistic response to the Sorites paradox. And we can stabilize the contrast between minimal truth-aptitude and cognitive command against the Deductions that threatened to subvert it, and which do indeed show that it is unstable in the setting of classical logic. To be sure, we do not thereby quite recover the materials for a coherent *true relativism* as earlier characterized—which

---

[50] See also footnote 41 above.   [51] See footnote 6 above.

involved essential play with the possibility of fault-free disagreement. But an *anti-relativistic* rubric in terms of cognitive command: that it hold *a priori* of the discourse in question that disagreements within it (save when vagueness is implicated) involve cognitive shortcoming, may once again represent a condition which there is no guarantee that any minimally truth-apt discourse will satisfy. The relativistic thesis, for its part, should accordingly be the denial that there is— for a targeted discourse—any such *a priori* guarantee (or merely the claim that it is unwarranted to suppose that there is.) Thus the ancient doctrine of relativism, too, now goes epistemic. I do not know if Protagoras would have approved.

8.2 It merits emphasis, finally, that—for all I have argued here—these proposals can be extended no further than to discourses which exhibit the requisite combination of characteristics: quandary-propensity and evidential constraint. Without that combination, no motive has been disclosed for suspension of classical logic[52]—but classical logic would serve to reinstate the intended conclusions of the two Deductions and to obliterate the distinction between the proper conclusion of the Sorites paradox—the denial of its major premiss—and the unpalatable existential. One question I defer for further work is whether the two characteristics co-occur sufficiently extensively to allow the mooted solutions to have the requisite generality.

Two initially encouraging thoughts are these. First, as noted earlier, people's ordinary willingness to think in terms of 'no fact of the matter' in cases of intransigent disputes of inclination is in effect the manifestation of an acceptance of evidential constraint for the relevant discourse. (For if they were comfortable with the idea that such a dispute could in principle concern an undecidable fact, why would they take its intransigence as an indicator that there wasn't one?) I therefore conjecture that whatever exactly it is that we are responding to when we engage in the kind of taxonomy I illustrated right at the beginning with the two 'crude but intuitive' lists, the contents which we are inclined to put in the first list will indeed be cases where we will not want to claim any conception of how the facts could elude appreciation by the most fortunately generated human assessment.

Second, if classical logic is inappropriate, for broadly intuitionistic reasons, for a range of atomic statements, it could hardly be reliable for compounds of them, even if the operations involved in their compounding—quantifiers, tenses, and so on—were such as to enable the construction of statements which are not subject to EC. Thus what the intuitionistic response to the Sorites requires is not that *all* vague sentences be both potentially quandary-presenting and evidentially constrained but only that all *atomic* vague sentences be so. The standard examples of the Sorites in the literature—'red', 'bald', 'heap', 'tall', 'child'—do all work with

---

[52] But see, however, footnote 38 above.

atomic predicates, and all are, plausibly, evidentially constrained. But that is merely suggestive. If a finally satisfactory intuitionistic philosophy of vagueness is to be possible, we need an insight to connect basic vague expressions and evidential constraint. The notions of observationality, and of response dependence, would provide two obvious foci for the search. For now, however—in a contemporary context in which a few theorists of vagueness have argued against its prospects but most have simply paid no serious heed to the idea at all—it will be enough to have conveyed (if I have) something of the general shape which a stable intuitionistic philosophy of vagueness might assume.[53]

References

Blackburn, Simon (1984), *Spreading the Word*, Oxford: Clarendon Press.

Blackburn, Simon (1998), *Ruling Passions*, Oxford: Clarendon Press.

Campbell, R. (1974), "The Sorites Paradox," *Philosophical Studies* 26, 175–91.

Cargile, J. (1969), "The Sorites Paradox," *British Journal for the Philosophy of Science* 20, 193–202.

Cargile, J. (1979), *Paradoxes*, Cambridge: Cambridge University Press.

Chambers, Timothy (1998), "On Vagueness, *Sorites*, and Putnam's 'Intuitionistic Strategy'," *The Monist* 81, 343–8.

Fine, Kit (1975), "Vagueness, Truth and Logic," *Synthese* 30, 265–300.

Fitch, Frederic B. (1963), "A Logical Analysis of Some Value Concepts," *The Journal of Symbolic Logic* 28, 135–42.

Gibbard, Alan (1990), *Wise Choices, Apt Feelings*, Cambridge, MA: Harvard University Press.

Hale, Bob (1986), "The Compleat Projectivist," *The Philosophical Quarterly* 36, 65–84.

Hale, Bob (1992), "Can There Be a Logic of Attitudes?" in John Haldane and Crispin Wright (eds.), *Reality, Representation and Projection*. Oxford: Oxford University Press, 337–63.

---

[53] Versions of the material on revisionism were presented at colloquia at the University of Bologna, the City University of New York Graduate Center, and at Rutgers University in autumn 1998. I was fortunate enough to have the opportunity to present a discussion of all three problems at two seminars at Ohio State University in December of that year, and to have a precursor of the present draft discussed at the Language and Mind seminar at NYU in April 1999, where Stephen Schiffer's commentary resulted in a number of improvements. The NYU draft also provided the basis for three helpful informal seminars at Glasgow University in May 1999. More recently, I took the opportunity to present the material on the Sorites at an Arché Workshop on Vagueness which, with the sponsorship of the British Academy, was held at St Andrews in June 2000. I am extremely grateful to the discussants on all these occasions, and in addition to John Broome, Patrick Greenough, Richard Kimberley Heck, Fraser MacBride, Sven Rosenkranz, Mark Sainsbury, Joe Salerno, Tim Williamson, and a referee for Mind for valuable comments and discussion. Almost all the research for the chapter has been conducted during my tenure of a Leverhulme Research Professorship; I gratefully acknowledge the support of the Leverhulme Trust.

Hale, Bob (2002), "Can Arboreal Knotwork Help Blackburn Out of Frege's Abyss?" A Book Symposium on Blackburn's (1998), in *Philosophy and Phenomenological Research* Vol. 65, No. 1 (Jul., 2002), pp. 144–9.

Harman, Gilbert and Judith Jarvis Thomson (1996), *Moral Relativism and Moral Objectivity*, Oxford: Basil Blackwell.

Harman, Gilbert, Judith Jarvis Thomson et al. (1998), "Book Symposium on Gilbert Harman and Judith J. Thomson (1996)," *Moral Relativism and Moral Objectivity*, *Philosophy and Phenomenological Research* 58, 161–222.

Horwich, Paul (1998), *Truth*, Oxford: Clarendon Press (second edition).

Putnam, Hilary (1983), "Vagueness and Alternative Logic," *Realism and Reason*. Cambridge: Cambridge University Press, 271–86.

Railton, Peter, Gilbert Harman, and Judith Jarvis Thomson (1998), "Moral Explanation and Moral Objectivity Moral Relativism and Moral Objectivity," *Philosophy and Phenomenological Research* 58 (1), 175.

Read, Stephen and Crispin Wright (1985), "Hairier than Putnam Thought," *Analysis* 45, 56–8.

Salerno, Joseph (2000), "Revising the Logic of Logical Revision," *Philosophical Studies* 99, 211–27.

Shapiro, Stewart and William Taschek (1996), "Intuitionism, Pluralism and Cognitive Command," *Journal of Philosophy* 93, 74–88.

Sorensen, Roy (1998), *Blindspots*, Oxford: Oxford University Press.

Williamson, Timothy (1992), "Vagueness and Ignorance," *Proceedings of the Aristotelian Society*, Supplementary Volume 66, 145–62.

Williamson, Timothy (1994), *Vagueness*, London and New York: Routledge.

Williamson, Timothy (1996a), 'Putnam on the Sorites Paradox'. *Philosophical Papers* 25, 47–56.

Williamson, Timothy (1996b), "Wright on the Epistemic Conception of Vagueness," *Analysis* 56, 39–45.

Wright, Crispin (1992), *Truth and Objectivity*, Cambridge, MA: Harvard University Press.

Wright, Crispin (1993), "Anti-Realism and Revisionism," *Realism, Meaning and Truth*, Oxford: Basil Blackwell (second edition), 433–57.

Wright, Crispin (1995), "The Epistemic Conception of Vagueness," *The Southern Journal of Philosophy* Supplementary Volume XXXIII, 133–59 (on "Vagueness," edited by Terence Horgan).

Wright, Crispin (1998), "Truth: A Traditional Debate Reviewed," *Canadian Journal of Philosophy* Supplementary Volume 24, 31–74 (on "Pragmatism," edited by Cheryl Misak). Reprinted in Simon Blackburn and Keith Simmons (eds.) (1999), *Truth*, Oxford: Clarendon Press, 203–38.

Wright, Crispin (2001), "Minimalism, Deflationism, Pragmatism, Pluralism," in Michael P. Lynch (ed.), *The Nature of Truth: From the Classic to the Contemporary*, Cambridge, MA: MIT Press.

2

Intuitionism, Realism, Relativism, and Rhubarb

1. The Ordinary View of Disputes of Inclination

Imagine that Tim Williamson thinks that stewed rhubarb is delicious and that I beg to differ, finding its dry acidity highly disagreeable. There is, on the face of it, no reason to deny that this is a genuine disagreement—each holding to a view that the other rejects. But it is a disagreement about which, at least at first pass, the Latin proverb—*de gustibus non est disputandum*—seems apt. It is, we feel—or is likely to be—a disagreement which there is no point in trying to settle, because it concerns no real matter of fact but is merely an expression of different, permissibly idiosyncratic tastes. Nobody's wrong. Tim and I should just agree to disagree.

Call such a disagreement a *dispute of inclination*. The view of such disputes just gestured at—I'll call it the *Ordinary View*—combines three elements:

1. that they involve genuinely incompatible attitudes (*Contradiction*);
2. that nobody need be mistaken or otherwise at fault (*Faultlessness*); and
3. that the antagonists may, perfectly rationally, stick to their respective views even after the disagreement comes to light and impresses as intractable (*Sustainability*).

Assuming that there are indeed disputes as so characterized, it is of course an important and controversial issue how far they extend—whether, for example, certain differences of opinion about ethics, or aesthetics, or justification, or even theoretical science come within range. But my question here is more basic: it is whether the three noted elements can be combined coherently—whether there *are* any disputes of inclination, as characterized by the Ordinary View, at all.

The question is given urgency by the fact that the four most salient alternatives to the Ordinary View all seem rebarbative or misconceived. There is, first, the *rampant realist* proposal—an analogue of the epistemic conception of vagueness. Rampant realism holds that there have to be facts of the matter which either Tim or I are missing. Rhubarb just has to be either delicious or not, so one of us has to be mistaken, even if there is no way of knowing who. Such a view is vulnerable to a

Essays on Relativism: 2001–2021. Crispin Wright, Oxford University Press. © Crispin Wright 2023.
DOI: 10.1093/oso/9780192845993.003.0003

charge of semantical and metaphysical superstition. It also arguably precludes Sustainability—the possibility of persisting in the dispute with rational integrity—since neither Tim nor I have the slightest reason to think that our own tastes reflect the putative real facts about deliciousness, rampant-realistically conceived.

Realism need not be rampant. A more moderate realism might try to domesticate the relevant facts by attempting to construe them as, in one way or another, *response dependent*—proposing, for instance, that what is delicious is what (a majority of) well-qualified judges find to be so. But this seems a misdirection too: for one thing, I don't think we really believe in 'well qualifiedness' in *basic* matters of taste—that's the point of the Latin proverb. For another, the proposal promises no better than its rampant counterpart in accommodating Faultlessness and Sustainability.

Recoiling from these views, one may be tempted by the thought that perhaps no genuine dispute is involved after all. Perhaps the impression to the contrary is somehow an artefact of language. One—*expressivist*—version of that idea has it that we are misled by the indicative surface of the dispute: maybe Tim's avowal that rhubarb is delicious serves merely to give expression to the pleasure he takes in the stuff and is thus something with no properly negatable content; maybe my avowal to the contrary serves merely to give expression to my corresponding distaste for it. Such a proposal will face all the familiar difficulties in the philosophy of language—difficulties for example in accounting for routine conditional, disjunctive, tensed, and attitudinal constructions embedding such apparent indicative contents—which are faced by strict expressivist proposals in general, and to which many believe they have no satisfactory response.

An alternative strategy for denying that there is any genuine disagreement is to take the indicative appearances at face value, but hold that the contents in question are not really in conflict—for instance, that they are elliptical and that when the ellipsis is unpacked, the impression of incompatibility vanishes. It may be suggested, for instance, that Tim's view is properly characterized as being that rhubarb is delicious *by his standards*, and that I am saying that rhubarb is not delicious *by mine*. So we are talking past each other and may both well be right.

This suggestion is open to the charge that it distorts the meaning of what we intend to say when we give voice to judgements of taste. There is, for example, a challenge involved in the question: 'If, as you say, rhubarb is delicious, how come nobody but you here likes it?', which goes missing if the proper construal of it mentions an explicit standard-relativity in the antecedent. So it looks as though a larger package will be called for, involving not just hidden constituents but an error-theory concerning our ordinary understanding of the relevant kinds of claim. A related consideration points out that, on our ordinary understanding, the explicitly standard-relativized kind of formulation represents a fall-back claim if the original, unqualified claim gets into difficulty—a puzzling phenomenon if they coincide in content.

There are other forms of semantic contextualism, of course, besides those which postulate ellipsis or hidden constituents. But the awkwardnesses just noted will remain on any such view. If Tim's and my differing tastes are sufficient, one way or another, to ensure that we express different concepts of the delicious in our respective assessments of rhubarb, and hence that there is no obstacle to our both being right, then why will we each be inclined to withdraw if suitably many others don't concur? Why doesn't the contextualist explanation of why my judgement is not in conflict with Tim's survive as a means to explain why I can be right *no matter how idiosyncratic my view*? And why fall back on an explicitly standard-relativized claim if the content of my original claim was already implicitly relativized?

Each of the four views canvassed—that there is a real but undetectable fact of the matter about whether rhubarb is delicious, that there is a real but response-dependent fact of the matter, that there is no real matter in dispute because no truth-evaluable content is involved, and that there is no real dispute because the contents involved are elliptical, or otherwise contextually distinct—each of these four views not merely involves compromise of one or more of the three components of the Ordinary View but seems open to additional objection. If we want to avoid metaphysical hypostasis, snobbery in matters of taste, unplayable philosophy of language, or misrepresentation of linguistic practice, then we should want the Ordinary View. So it comes as an unpleasant surprise that it seems, under quite modest pressure, to collapse.

2. The Simple Deduction

The collapsing argument is what in earlier work I dubbed the Simple Deduction.[1] It is disarmingly straightforward. The idea that there is genuine disagreement involved in the dispute goes with the idea that there is a genuinely indicative content, capable of featuring in attitudes and standing in relations of incompatibility to other such contents. Any such genuine content can also be *supposed*. So: suppose that rhubarb is delicious. Then I'm mistaken. But the Ordinary View has it that no one is mistaken (Faultlessness). So rhubarb isn't delicious. But then Tim is mistaken. So someone has to be mistaken after all. Contradiction precludes Faultlessness.

More explicitly, see Table 2.1. The occurrence of genuine disagreement seems to demand, by elementary and uncontroversial logical moves, the existence of mistakes.[2] Further, once that's recognized, it becomes impossible to see how Tim and I can persist in our disagreement with rational integrity. Apparently one of us

---

[1] Wright (2001, 2002).
[2] Note in particular that there is no appeal to the Law of Excluded Middle.

Table 2.1

1	(1) *A* accepts *P*	_____	Assumption
2	(2) *B* accepts Not-*P*	_____	Assumption
3	(3) *As* and *Bs* disagreement involves no mistake	_____	Assumption
4	(4) *P*	_____	Assumption
2, 4	(5) *B* is making a mistake	_____	2, 4
2, 3	(6) Not-*P*	_____	4, 5, 3 *Reductio*
1, 2, 3	(7) *A* is making a mistake	_____	1, 6
1,2	(8) Not-(3)	_____	3, 3, 7 *Reductio*

has to be mistaken. But if one of us is mistaken, how can we tell who? Isn't it just a conceit to think it has to be the other? So Sustainability is compromised too. Thus the three components in the Ordinary View fall apart.

Faced with this difficulty, the natural temptation for a proponent of the Ordinary View is to try to refine the second component—to qualify Faultlessness. Maybe it's too much to demand that there need be no mistake involved in the dispute. Maybe the most that can be asked is that there be no *epistemically blameworthy* mistake. Perhaps Faultlessness should be replaced by something like the idea that neither Tim nor I need have done anything which would have opened our opinions to proper suspicion when considered in isolation, by someone with no view on the matter in hand but otherwise as knowledgeable as you like. Or something like that.

But this suggestion doesn't really help. For one thing, part of the attraction of Faultlessness is that, while we want to acknowledge that there may be no settling a dispute of inclination, we precisely don't want that acknowledgement to commit us to the idea of potentially unknowable facts of the matter—that's why the rampant realist proposal strikes us as so bizarre. The rhetoric of 'no fact of the matter' expresses the natural, folk-philosophical view: such disputes are potentially irresolvable, we think, not because the facts in question can transcend our impressions but because the impressions themselves are in some way basic and constitutive; so when they conflict, there need be no further court of appeal. If that thought can be reconciled with the idea of truth at all, then truth—at least in matters of taste—had better be *per se* knowable. But then the Simple Deduction is easily emended to argue not just that Tim's and my disagreement must involve a mistake but that it must involve a cognitive shortcoming in the stronger sense proposed, since one of us fails to know something that can be known.[3]

And indeed, even if the Ordinary View can somehow avoid commitment to evidential constraint, the situation is still not stable. For the conclusion of the Simple Deduction, that there is a mistake—false belief—involved in any such dispute, still stands unchallenged, even if no cognitive blame need attach to either

[3] For elaboration, see the 'EC-Deduction' at p. 60 of Wright (2001). This volume at page 19.

disputant. And now, since for all I can tell it may as well be me who has a false belief as Tim, and since Tim is in an analogous position, it still seems impossible to understand how it can be rationally acceptable for us to agree to differ and persist in our respective views. The threat to Sustainability is already posed by the concession that Faultlessness *in the weak sense* is precluded by Contradiction.

So far I've not said anything about relativism. It may be thought that the Ordinary View—the suggestion of the possibility of genuine but fault-free disagreements in which the protagonists are fully rationally entitled to persist in their conflicting opinions—is tantamount to relativism: specifically, to the idea that truth in the region of discourse in which the dispute is articulated should be viewed as relative to the differences in standard, or context, or whatever, which generate the disagreement in the first place. But this is not correct. Relativism, I want to suggest, is best viewed as a *theoretical attempt* to underwrite and reconcile the elements in the Ordinary View. It is a response to the problem, rather than merely a label for the amalgam of ideas which gives rise to it. Whether it is an adequate, or theoretically attractive, response remains to be seen.

3. An Intuitionistic Response

First I want to table a different response. The Simple Deduction—exploiting, be it noted, only the most elementary logic and placing no reliance on any distinctively classical moves—elicits a contradiction from the three assumptions, that Williamson believes that rhubarb is delicious, that Wright believes that rhubarb is not delicious, and that nobody is mistaken. The conclusion seems to be forced, accordingly, that somebody has to be mistaken in any genuine such dispute. But it's not forced. There is a distinctively classical move involved in the interpretation of the *reductio* as indicative that mistake always has to be involved. Specifically, take the third assumption as that:

It is not the case that Williamson is mistaken and it is not the case the Wright is mistaken.

Then to interpret the *reductio* as showing that someone must have made a mistake is to take it that the negation of that conjunction licenses us in concluding:

Either Williamson is mistaken or Wright is mistaken.

That's to make an inferential transition of the form:

$$\frac{\text{Not-}(\text{Not-}A\ \&\ \text{Not-}B)}{A \lor B}$$

—a pattern whose classical validation demands elimination of double negations, and which is not in general intuitionistically valid.

Very well. But so what? How might sticking at the intuitionistically valid conclusion—the negated conjunction—put us in a position to accommodate the components in the Ordinary View, and to reconcile them with each other? And even if resisting the transition to the disjunction would help, how might intuitionistic restrictions sufficient to block the relevant de Morgan Law be motivated in the type of context at hand?

Let's consider the second question first. The key issue, as always, concerns the status of the principle of Bivalence for statements of the relevant kind. For since:

Not-(Not-A & Not-B)

is, by uncontroversial steps, equivalent to:

Not-Not-($A \lor B$),[4]

the move at which it is being suggested we may balk is tantamount to double negation elimination for disjunctions. If this class of cases of double negation elimination is accepted, Excluded Middle will hold quite generally, since its own double negation may likewise be established by wholly uncontroversial steps. Thus assuming—as we may in this dialectical context[5]—that Excluded Middle rests upon Bivalence, the defensibility of the transition from the thesis that Tim and I cannot both be right to the uncomfortable claim that *someone in particular*—either Tim or me—is mistaken about rhubarb rests on the defensibility of Bivalence for claims like: 'rhubarb is delicious'.

In intuitionistic mathematics, the challenge to Bivalence is best seen as flowing from a combination of two claims: first an insistence on a form of evidential constraint—that truth in mathematics may not defensively be supposed to outrun decidability in principle by a certain loosely characterized class of constructively acceptable methods; second, that, for any theory at least as rich as number theory, we possess no guarantee that any given statement is indeed decidable by such methods. Simply put: if Bivalence holds for Goldbach's conjecture—if either the

---

[4] Assume *Not-(Not-A & Not-B)* and *Not-(A ∨ B)*. Use the latter, *vel-intro* and *Reductio* to derive each of *Not-A* and *Not-B*. Conjoin them to derive a contradiction with *Not-(Not-A & Not-B)*, and discharge *Not-(A ∨ B)* by a further *Reductio.*

Assume *Not-Not-(A ∨ B)* and *Not-A & Not-B*. Assume A ∨ B and reason by *vel-elim* and *Reductio* to *Not-[Not-A & Not-B]*. A further step of *Reductio* yields *Not-[A ∨ B]* on *Not-A & Not-B* as assumption. One more step of *Reductio* then gives *Not-[Not-A & Not-B]* on *Not-Not-(A ∨ B)* as assumption.

[5] To explain: the present dialectical context is one in which we are assuming that disjunction is distributive—that the truth of a disjunction requires the truth of at least one of its disjuncts in particular. Otherwise, the conclusion that either Tim is mistaken about rhubarb or I am carries no implication of the actual existence of a mistake. But where disjunction is distributive, the validity of Excluded Middle rests on Bivalence.

conjecture or its negation is true—then, by evidential constraint, one or the other will be verifiable by intuitionistically acceptable methods. So since we do not, in our present state of information, know that either can be so verified, we do not, in our present state of information, have any right to claim that Bivalence holds for Goldbach's conjecture, nor therefore throughout number-theoretic statements as a class.

The intuitionistic reservation about Bivalence is thus one of agnosticism. But it is not an agnosticism based on the spectre of third possibilities—additional truth-values, or truth-value gaps. Rather it is based on our inability to guarantee the possibility of knowledge, along with the thesis—held for independent reasons—that the truth requires that possibility for the type of statement for which the validity of Bivalence is under review.

Either of these claims may of course be contested for a given class of statements. But both may seem attractive for each of two non-mathematical kinds of example, for which, accordingly, the validity of Bivalence may consequently come into question. One comprises those vague statements typified by predications of adjectives like 'red' and 'bald'. The other is precisely our present focus: judgements of taste and other matters of inclination. In both these cases we are antipathetic to the idea that truth has no implication of ascertainability; but in both cases we are likewise uneasy with the suggestion that claims have to be decidable, one way or the other. In the terminology I have used in earlier work, borderline cases of vague predications, and predications of concepts of taste, are, no less than mathematical statements like Goldbach's conjecture, liable to present *quandaries*: examples where we may be uncertain not merely what it may be correct to think but even whether there is any metaphysical space for knowledge, or all-things-considered *best* opinion, properly so termed. These two pressures—evidential constraint and the potentiality for quandary—squeeze out an unqualified acceptance of Bivalence over the two classes of statements in question; but they put no pressure on a continued adherence to the law of non-contradiction. So we should not, in reasoning among these statements, rely on a logic which forces us to be insensitive to the distinction between them which, it appears, had better be made.

This comparison—between statements like Goldbach's conjecture, borderline predications of vague concepts, and judgements of taste—has been misunderstood by at least one commentator[6] so further clarification may help. Undeniably, there is the following difference. While no one knows whether knowledge either of Goldbach's conjecture or its negation is metaphysically possible and—it is tempting to add—no one is really entitled to an opinion (contrast: a hunch) about the matter, borderline cases of vague predicates may quite defensibly give rise to weak, qualified opinions. And matters of taste, for their part, may give rise to

[6] Kölbel (unpublished).

strong ones. So what is the intended analogy between the three kinds of statements? What similarity is the notion of quandary meant to mark? The answer is: a similarity which is manifested by each of the three kinds of statement *as a class*. Sure, any particular statement of each of the three kinds in question is such that we cannot rule out the possibility of a competent determinate—positive or negative—view of it (though with statements about borderline cases of vague concepts we can, admittedly, rule out the possibility of a competent but *strong* view). But nor, in each of the three kinds of case, do we have any grounds for thinking that knowledge, or all things considered best opinion, has to be possible *for every example*. In particular, while I may indeed have many opinions on matters of taste, and consider them competent, or even superior, I have to acknowledge that I know nothing which ensures that a determinate knowledgeable or best opinion is possible about every matter of taste or inclination generally. That would be a guarantee that all disputes of inclination have a winner. We have no such guarantee.

There, then—in the combination of quandary and evidential constraint—is one kind of motivation for broadly intuitionistic reservations about classical logic in general, and about the (in my formulation above, implicit) final step in the Simple Deduction. If accepted, it allows us to stop short of letting the Simple Deduction conclude that someone has to be mistaken in any dispute of inclination—indeed in any dispute about a genuinely indicative content.

Maybe the foregoing train of thought is of most interest in a context in which the primary question is whether the intuitionists' ideas about the logic appropriate to mathematics can be generalized to other regions of discourse. Anything properly viewed as an extension of their ideas will have to involve *some* kind of play with evidential constraint, since that is the role, in the mathematical case, of their very *constructivism*. However we should not overlook another, simpler, and perhaps yet more compelling line of reservation about Bivalence in the cases that concern us, which puts evidential constraint to one side. Reflect that the opinion that Bivalence holds, of necessity, throughout vague discourse is a commitment to holding that each vague predicate is associated with a property of absolutely sharply bounded extension as its semantic value. But for a very wide class of such expressions—including especially predicates of Lockean secondary qualities—we have no clear idea what kinds of properties these may be. Nor, in general, do we have any clear idea how the required semantic associations might have been established. A commitment to Bivalence holding of necessity in all such cases is a commitment to postulating a kind of arcane natural history of semantic relationships for which we have absolutely no evidence. And it's just the same with predications of taste. There is just the same semantic mystery, just the same puzzlement, in a wide class of cases, about the nature of the properties that would be fit to discharge the demanded role. What *is* deliciousness if it is to be possible for normally competent speakers, like Tim and me, to go so completely astray about it in a perfectly ordinary case? The idea that there is a mandate for unrestricted Bivalence is, one way or another, a commitment to philosophical obligations—perhaps rampant realist, perhaps response-dependence realist— which we simply do not know how to meet. Surely the mere idea that Tim and I hold contradictory opinions about rhubarb ought to impose no such obligations. The *reductio* carried out in the Simple Deduction properly takes us no further than to the conclusion that our opinions cannot both be true. It is classical logic that is responsible for muddying the distinction between that and the idea that one in particular of us is missing the real fact.

4. Can the Intuitionistic Response Rescue Faultlessness and Sustainability?

As remarked, however, it is one question whether there is a well-motivated intuitionistic distinction to draw, in the service of stabilizing the Ordinary View, between the claim that Tim and I cannot both be right about rhubarb and the claim that one of us in particular must be wrong. Even if so, it is a further question whether we thereby secure the means to say something effective in stabilizing the Ordinary View of disputes of inclination. The challenge was to harmonize the three ingredients—Contradiction, Faultlessness, and Sustainability. And the point hasn't gone away that if it is insisted that a dispute can be regarded as fault-free only if it's open to us to suppose that each antagonist has a correct view, then a mere acceptance that the dispute is genuine—so involves contradictory opinions—precludes regarding it as fault-free. *Punkt.*

The question, of course, is what, in regarding such a dispute as potentially fault-free, we really intend to maintain. Well, each will have to examine their own preconceptions. But my own impression is that the principal point is to contrast the case with situations where, should attempts at resolution fail, the mere existence of a contrary opinion, no worse supported than one's own, is sufficient to put one at fault in persisting in one's view. That will be a characteristic of the rhubarb dispute once the Simple Deduction is allowed to establish the disjunctive conclusion: either Tim is mistaken or I am. As soon as it is accepted that one of us has to be mistaken, the fact that neither of us is able to make his opinion prevail ought to encourage the worry that the mistaken party could as well be him as his antagonist. And once one recognizes that, then it should seem at best pig-headed not to withdraw from one's initial opinion. If this is right, then the really important thing about the idea of fault-free disagreement in such cases is actually its implication of Sustainability—its implication of the idea that the opinions in a dispute of inclination may justifiably be persisted in, even when it is clear that it is a stalemate.

This comes close to but is not quite the same thing as suggesting that the essence of the Ordinary View can be captured just by the first and third components—Contradiction and Sustainability. But that conclusion is not right. There are readily conceivable cases where Contradiction and Sustainability are satisfied but where there is—or may be, depending on one's view—no proper comparison with disputes of inclination. Consider for instance two rival scientific theories which match in their empirical, explanatory, and other virtues, which are unsurpassed by any other extant theory, and for which we've yet to devise a crucial experiment. It is debatable whether it should be regarded as irrational for a supporter of either theory to persist in holding to it even after they become aware of the credentials of the other. After all, there is, by hypothesis, no sufficient reason to adopt the opposing view—there is, by hypothesis, parity of virtue. And merely to abandon either theory without putting anything in its place would mean restoring all the disadvantages, whatever they may be, of having no theory of the subject matter in question at all. In such a case, then, regarding the dispute as genuine and factual is quite consistent with Sustainability. If so, then even if the intuitionistic response can indeed save Sustainability—I will address that in a minute—the scientific example shows us that we need something extra, *something* to play the role of Faultlessness, if we are to explain the difference between the two kinds of case. And we are still no wiser about what that extra might be, consistently with the Simple Deduction, nor about whether the intuitionistic setting can provide it.

The difference between the two kinds of case—rhubarb and the scientific theoretical disagreement—consists in the way in which Sustainability is supported. In the scientific example, there *is* reason to accept (at least if one is a scientific realist) the disjunctive claim: one theory or the other—and perhaps both—will be false to the facts. One in particular—perhaps both—of the rival theorists will be proposing a misrepresentation of Nature. And the point is then that, notwithstanding that consideration, there are nevertheless overriding *pragmatic* reasons, grounded in the desirability of having a theory in the first place, for each to persist in their respective views—so that we have Sustainability anyway. In the rhubarb dispute, by contrast, there is—according to intuitionistic proposal— no impartial reason to suppose that one disputant in particular—Tim or me—is making a mistake; and it is *because there is no reason so to suppose* that we have Sustainability.

So the suggestion at which we arrive is this: disputes of inclination may indeed be stably characterized by ascribing to them versions of all three features proposed by the Ordinary View: they are genuine disputes in which conflicting opinions are held; they may be fault-free; and they may be rationally sustained even after it becomes clear that they are stand-offs. The refinements we need to add are, first, that in disputes of inclination Sustainability is properly seen as grounded in Faultlessness; in disputes of fact, by contrast, Sustainability, where it occurs, is grounded otherwise—in the scientific theoretical example, for instance, it is grounded pragmatically. Second, Faultlessness needs to be interpreted not as something flatly inconsistent with genuine conflict—with Contradiction—but rather as something that resides in the unavailability of any impartial reason to make (the relevant analogue of) the disjunctive claim: to insist that there is fault somewhere. What counts against rationally sustaining a dispute, once debate is exhausted without producing a winner, is the thought, roughly, that someone is mistaken here and, for all that has emerged, 'it could as well be me'. Once it is granted that someone has to be mistaken, that thought locates a concern that rationally ought to occur to each of the antagonists. The concern may still not mandate withdrawal if, as in the scientific theory case, there are overriding reasons that license retaining a view. But—the crucial point—it does not get off the ground without independent[7] reason for the disjunctive claim. It is by refusing the disjunctive claim that the intuitionistic proposal rescues Sustainability, and grounds it on Faultlessness, with the latter now understood precisely as located in the shortfall between the negated conjunction—which, it is conceded on all hands, the Simple Deduction establishes—and the stronger disjunctive claim which is what it takes to implicate error on one side or the other.

This proposed way of developing the Ordinary View and staving off the threat posed by the Simple Deduction seems to me to be stable thus far. The question is whether there is any serious additional cause for dissatisfaction with it.

5. A Problem for the Intuitionistic Rescue

The intuitionistic rescue reconciles Contradiction with Faultlessness by insisting that it is insufficient for a dispute to involve Fault merely that it be a genuine dispute—genuinely involving contrary or contradictory opinions. Conflict of opinion—it is contended—suffices for the presence of mistake only when Bivalence is guaranteed to hold for the discourse of the dispute; and that, it is argued, is something for which there is—in the cases which concern us—no guarantee.

Someone who is sympathetic to intuitionistic ideas is not likely to find this a particularly controversial application of them. And indeed I would suggest that this also makes for an argument in the opposite direction. Absent a better kind of proposal, the need to make sense of the Ordinary View, and the apparent impossibility of doing so in a classical framework, provides a powerful argument for sympathy with intuitionistic distinctions and for further work on them.

There is, however, a problem with the approach which, if we are convinced that coherent provision must be made for the Ordinary View, threatens to force us to look further afield. Simply stated, it is this: that since the Ordinary View is

---

[7] Independent, that is, of one's view of the matter in hand.

inconsistent with rampant realism, no justice can have been done to it by an account that is consistent with the possibility that rampant realism is correct. But the intuitionistic proposal merely leaves us in a position of agnosticism about that. The response to the Simple Deduction was to argue that there is no justification for the relevant transition of the form:

$$\frac{\text{Not-}(\text{Not-}A \ \& \ \text{Not-}B)}{A \vee B}$$

Even granting the proposed interpretation of Faultlessness, that is merely to say that there is no extant justification for regarding either Tim or me as having a mistaken opinion. But to say that *there's no justification* for regarding the dispute as involving a mistake is not to say that *it's not the case* that the dispute involves a mistake. Yet surely, the objection says, Faultlessness should involve the latter. Yet the latter—the negation of the disjunction—does entail, even intuitionistically, the negations of both disjuncts. And those, conjoined, are then inconsistent with the intermediate conclusion—the negated conjunction—which, everyone agrees, the Simple Deduction does establish (and indeed inconsistent in their own right).

So, a critic may contend, the intuitionistic rescue has not really saved Faultlessness in any intuitively sufficient sense. The most that has been saved is justification for our reluctance to *attribute* fault in relevant cases, consistently with acknowledging the Simple Deduction. This leaves it epistemically open that there is indeed a determinate fact of the matter in the rhubarb dispute, and indeed in such disputes in general, and hence that there is indeed a determinate fault on one side or the other. And that is exactly what we—most of us—are reluctant to believe. It is good if the intuitionistic proposal can save us from being forced to think it true just by elementary logic. But we would like to be in a position to think it *false*.

A supporter of the intuitionistic rescue may rejoin that it is no serious short-coming in the proposal that it leaves us at most unsympathetically agnostic towards the rampant realist view of the dispute. After all, that, as it may seem, just is the extent of the justified position. The rampant realist view calls for the association of the predicate 'delicious', understood as by both Tim and me, with a property that determinately applies or fails to apply to stewed rhubarb. We may not believe there is, as a matter of metaphysics, any suitable such property, much less that our linguistic practices somehow enthrone such a property as the *Bedeutung* of 'delicious'. But come on: we do not *know* that these things are not so—not if knowing requires being in a position to prove it. The honest objection to rampant realism is not that we know that its presuppositions are not met but that there is not the slightest reason to regard it as true. If the preconceptions that underwrite the Ordinary View slur that distinction, they are not to be respected to the letter. We should stick to what we can justify.

This reply, though, only partially addresses the objection. Maybe we do not, strictly, know that rampant realism is false. But at the level of analysis displayed by the Simple Deduction, even with intuitionistic distinctions superimposed, the point remains that no space is left for a coherent belief that neither Tim nor I is mistaken in the original dispute. In particular, no way whatever has been offered of recovering a content for the idea that there is no 'fact of the matter' to be mistaken about. Even if we don't know that the rampant realist's insistence that there is indeed a fact of the matter is itself mistaken, it may yet be felt as a very serious limitation of the intuitionistic treatment if it does not, so far, allow us so much as to attach content to the idea of that mistake. The worst mistake of which we have been empowered to make sense is an epistemic mistake: one of lack of warrant—the unwarranted insistence that the world and the relevant concepts are bound to conspire to render true one of the disputed opinions or the other. But nothing has been said to explain how, or in what respect, rampant realism might be incorrect, rather than merely unjustified.

The intuitionistic rescue provides theoretically respectable houseroom for our reluctance to be press-ganged into realism by the Simple Deduction. But it does not offer—and it seems has no resources to offer—any account of what it would be for (rampant) realism to be, not merely not imposed, but false: a misrepresentation in its own right. Surely, it may be felt, a satisfactory account of disputes of inclination should explain how it is possible that this might be so, even if we are forced to grant that, in the end, we are not in position to show, once and for all, that it is so.

6. The Intuitionistic Rescue Rescued?

The objection may seem convincing. But in fact it runs together two distinct complaints and arguably derives some of its force from the conflation.

One complaint is that the intuitionistic rescue treats the transition from the conjunction:

It is not the case that neither Williamson nor Wright is mistaken

to the disjunctive conclusion:

Williamson is mistaken or Wright is mistaken

merely as a *non-sequitur*, whereas someone who takes the Ordinary View will want to reserve space for the belief—even if conceded not to be a strictly *knowledgeable* belief—that the disjunctive conclusion is *incorrect*: that nobody need be mistaken. Since there is no provision within an intuitionistic framework for a coherent denial of the disjunction, it appears that the intuitionistic rescue cannot do justice to the Ordinary View. However a second, distinct complaint is that the intuitionistic rescue cannot so much as provide for a coherent belief that *rampant realism* is false—even if it were granted that such disbelief would involve a degree of presumption. Since the Ordinary View is indeed inconsistent with rampant realism, the two complaints converge on the thought that the intuitionistic rescue cannot do justice to the Ordinary View. Nevertheless the complaints are not the same—for the straightforward reason that denial of the disjunction is not required by the denial of rampant realism.

What are their relations? Well, rampant realism is—presumably—committed to the disjunction; conversely, an acceptance that the disjunction follows just from the premiss that Tim and I have contradictory views is, arguably, a commitment to rampant realism. But that is not to say that only a framework that provides for a coherent denial of the disjunction can provide for a coherent disbelief in the metaphysical and semantic postulations of rampant realism. That would be true only if disbelief in rampant realism were a commitment to denying the disjunction. But that cannot be correct: after all, both Tim and I accept the disjunction, presumably (since each thinks the other is mistaken)—but at most one of us is a rampant realist about matters of basic taste in desserts!

It is not—the point is—an acceptance of the disjunction *qua propositional content* that commits to rampant realism; it is an acceptance that its truth is ensured simply by the fact of Tim's and my respective views being contradictories. In fact, anyone with a determinate—positive or negative—view on whether stewed rhubarb is delicious should accept the disjunction; no *philosophical* commitment is entrained. A philosophical commitment is entered into only when one regards the disjunction as imposed by the nature of the subject matter and the kind of content carried by claims of the kind in dispute. One may therefore reject a rampant realist—indeed, any form of realist—view about those matters without commitment to any particular attitude to the disjunction.

The second of the two complaints is accordingly misconceived. A supporter of the intuitionistic rescue is quite at liberty to *deny* rampant realism. It is not true that they can go no further than agnosticism about the point. They thereby deny that the truth of the disjunction is guaranteed in the way rampant realism supposes. The dialectical situation is, in fact, exactly analogous to that in the philosophy of mathematics, where the intuitionist may quite coherently—if they wish—deny the Platonist metaphysics of a crystalline world of determinate mathematical structures, potentially conferring truth and falsity upon our mathematical statements in ways transcending all possibility of proof. That denial commits them to denying that Excluded Middle holds of necessity for reasons connected with that metaphysics. But it does not commit them to denying Excluded Middle itself, still less any instance of it. Rather, in the absence of justification for the principle of any other kind, they merely regard it as unacceptable.

The first complaint still stands, though: the thought that the intuitionistic rescue leaves no space for a coherent belief that neither Tim nor I is mistaken in the original dispute. The closest the intuitionistic rescue gets to this is in establishing a position from which it can be allowed that the presence of error is dictated neither by elementary logic and the contradictoriness of the attitudes involved nor—I have just argued—by the semantics and metaphysics of discourse of taste. So we save *a* negative modal claim: there doesn't have to be error for *those* reasons at least. But we don't, it seems, give sense to the idea that there doesn't have to be error *tout court*, nor therefore provide any possibility for someone coherently to believe that there *isn't* any error in the case in point. But wasn't that suggestion just the force of the Latin proverb? Recall that we initially glossed the Ordinary View with the words, 'Nobody's wrong. Tim and I should just agree to disagree.'

It is easy, of course, to dismiss the idea that there *is* any such coherent belief, stronger than any of the beliefs that the intuitionistic rescue can accommodate and still remaining to be made sense of. After all, Tim and I do disagree. So Tim must think, presumably, that my view is mistaken. And I must think that his is mistaken. So someone who thinks that nobody actually is mistaken is committed to disagreeing with us *both*—and so to regarding *everybody* as mistaken: Tim, me, and indeed themselves! If there is a way further forward, it must consist in finding the means to deny that Tim and I must, in fact, each regard the other's view as mistaken—this despite the fact that our views are genuinely contradictory. So in a certain sense, their contradictoriness notwithstanding, we have to agree that our views are not in conflict—that we do *not* disagree.

This extra step is inaccessible on the intuitionistic treatment, and it is unquestionably of interest to consider what kind of position could possibly accommodate an insistence on it while avoiding aporia. One may well think that, for all we have so far seen, the intuitionistic treatment delivers enough to rank as a satisfactory explication of the Ordinary View. But if there is a stable account which manages the extra step—which can somehow allow that while Tim and I have genuinely contradictory attitudes, neither of us need regard the other as mistaken—it may well be felt to offer progress.

7. True Relativism

That is the prospectus that what I will call the *True Relativist* exegesis of the Ordinary View aims to fill. According to true relativism, it can be the case that Tim and I are both right even though we understand the claim that rhubarb is delicious in the same way, and even though we are making incompatible judgements about it. And the reason is because there are no absolute facts about taste—what it is true to say about taste depends upon a stance, or a set of standards, or a set of affective dispositions. The very same claim can be true for Tim and false for me—and that it is so can be something that is available to us both.

Familiarly, the idea that truth is *globally* relative—that some form of relativity is of the nature of truth—has often been held to implicate dialectical incoherence, or worse. Whatever the fact about that, our questions are more specific: whether relative truth is even *locally* coherent; whether, if so, it can accommodate each of Contradiction, Faultlessness, and Sustainability at all; and whether it can do so without undue metaphysical cost, and in particular in a way which allows for a more robust understanding of Faultlessness than could be secured by the intuitionistic proposal—one which allows for a consistent profession that Tim's and my views can both be correct.

Obviously, in order to accomplish the last of these things, true relativism has to have the means to block the Simple Deduction *before* it reaches the problematical line:

It's not the case that (it's not the case that Williamson is mistaken and it's not the case that Wright is mistaken).

It is clear how the attempt should be made. The true relativist must insist that, for statements of the kind that concern us, we may no longer validly infer from the supposition that *P* that someone who holds that not-*P* is making a mistake. A mistake will be implicated only if the judgement that not-*P* is held accountable to the same standards, or perspective, or whatever, that are implicated in the (hypothetical) supposition that *P* is true. Very simply: if *P* is true by one set of standards, or whatever the relativistic parameter is, and I judge it false by another, then what makes *P* true need not be something which, in judging that it is not true, I mistakenly judge not to obtain.

That, then, will be the *shape* of the true relativist response to the Simple Deduction. The question is whether it can be made sense of. There is a temptation to think that making sense of it is easier than it really is, which we need to expose straight away. A philosopher seeking to stabilize the Ordinary View should not be interested in relativity—as a function of context of utterance, or whatever else—in the truth-conditions, and hence the truth-values, of *sentences*. The relativity that needs to be made out is relativity in the truth of *thoughts*, or *propositions*. If we identify a proposition by its truth-conditions, the relevant form of relativity is relativity in the question whether *those very truth-conditions* are satisfied. Suppose that in the course of a medical procedure, a surgeon says of a scalpel that's been poorly prepared: 'This instrument is dangerously blunt.' Later, when the instrument is about to be re-sharpened and sterilized, his assistant may warn an inexperienced orderly: 'Watch out when you handle that—it's dangerously sharp.' Granted, it would be crass to say that the surgeon and his assistant mean different things by 'sharp' and 'blunt' respectively. What is true is that there is a relativity of standard: the surgeon's needs require a much finer edge on the blade than would suffice to justify his assistant's subsequent warning.

A similar set-up is illustrated by the kind of attributer-contextualist accounts of knowledge proposed by writers such as Keith DeRose and Stewart Cohen.[8] The point to note, however, is that the kind of relativity involved in these examples—plausible in the case of the scalpel, more controversial in the case of knowledge-contextualism—is not at all to our present purpose. For while it would be crass to see them as involving anything comparable to simple ambiguity in 'sharp' or 'knows', they do involve that the truth-conditions of ascriptions of sharpness and knowledge are so affected by contextual or other relevant parameters that *there is no single content* respectively affirmed and denied by the surgeon's claim and that of his assistant, or—to cut a long story short—by G. E. Moore's claim that he knows he has a hand and the sceptical claim that he does not. These views might naturally, if perhaps a little loosely, be described as involving relativism about sharpness, or knowledge. But true relativism is relativism about *truth*. It is *not* the thesis that the content of a certain kind of ascription can vary as a function of varying standards, or contexts, or other parameters. That's a thesis that, applied to our present problem, simply gives up on the attempt to satisfy Contradiction and so holds out no comfort to the Ordinary View. True relativism is the thesis—to repeat—that *after* the truth-conditions of an utterance have been settled, there can be relativity in the question whether they are satisfied. It is a thesis that engages at the level of content, rather than at the level of speech-acts. Or if it is not, then it's merely a slightly more sophisticated cousin of the simple indexical relativist proposal I canvassed at the start—a variant which holds that while a statement on which a dispute of inclination is targeted is indeed not an ellipsis for something which explicitly mentions some parametric standard or perspective, etc., it is nevertheless something whose content is implicitly fixed by reference to such a parameter, so that—as before—Tim and I will have no genuine conflict of opinion about rhubarb. A true relativist accommodation of the Ordinary View must demand that it is the very same proposition that Tim affirms and that I deny—and at the same time that neither the affirmation nor the denial need be mistaken, with this a point which the antagonists themselves can coherently take on board. The latter point is entirely unproblematical if it is not really the same proposition that is involved. What the relativist has to explain, in contrast, is how to maintain the point alongside the claim that there is a single proposition affirmed and denied respectively. What is the relevant notion of propositional identity, and how is it possible rationally to affirm the truth of such a proposition consistently with allowing that someone else's denial of it is also true?

It is not, it seems to me, at all straightforward to see that the demanded notion of relative truth—relative truth at the level of propositions—is fully intelligible. But the difficulties are especially daunting if we essay to think of truth as

---

[8] See, for instance, DeRose (1992, 2002) and Cohen (1999).

correspondence, in a robust sense of correspondence with calls for an internal relation between a proposition, conceived as an articulated abstract entity, and some correspondingly articulated aspect of non-propositional reality. On any such picture of truth and truth-conferral, it seems impossible to make room for the additional parameter which relativism posits; the internal structural relationship between propositions and the things that make them true or false is so conceived as to be essentially dyadic. It's like the congruence in form between a head-and-shoulders sculpture and the model who posed for it. No doubt the former may be an accurate representation, or not, relative to the conventions of representation, but we are looking for something to illuminate an alleged relativity which bites *after* the conventions of representation have been fixed. And we draw a blank. The unavoidable conclusion seems to be that, while particular, such conventions may allow of degrees of accuracy in representation, the degree to which there is accuracy is something which supervenes entirely upon the respective physiognomies of the statue and the sitter. There is no place for a third term in the relation.[9]

If that is correct, the immediate lesson to draw is merely the unremarkable one that to attempt to think of truth—propositional truth—relativistically is to foreclose on thinking of it as correspondence. That's an objection to relativism only if it's impossible to think of truth in any other viable way. Suppose on the contrary that, at least in some regions of thought, truth may satisfyingly be construed as consisting in some kind of coherence relation, with coherence an internal, analytic relationship, fixed by the content of the propositions among which it obtains. Let it be proposed, for example, that the truth of a proposition consists in its participation within a maximal, coherent system of propositions incorporating some specified base class of propositions, *B*. Then depending on the choice of *B*, a proposition may be true or not—may be a member of the relevant maximal set of coherent propositions or not—even after its content is fully fixed. Such a conception of truth may only locally have any attraction at all—one might, for example, think of truth in pure set theory along such lines—but it provides at least a *prima facie* model of how a truth predicate for propositions may intelligibly be conceived as relative.[10]

No such coherentist model is presumably wanted for the notion of truth that is to engage disputes of taste and other matters of inclination. Still, the example suggests that once one begins to think of truth along the kind of pluralist lines that a number of philosophers, myself included, have canvassed in recent work,[11] it

---

[9] As J. C. Beall points out in his contribution to Greenough and Lynch (2006, p. 69ff.) this conclusion is good only if one assumes that a *single world* furnishes the facts to which the propositions at issue are liable to (mis)correspond. If sense could somehow be made of the Goodmanian figure of distinct worlds to correspond to distinct sensibilities, Tim and I could each be thinking the literal (correspondence-)truth about our respective worlds.

[10] For the credentials of coherence, so conceived, to count as truth, and for more general discussion of what it takes for a predicate to express the concept of truth, see Wright (1998).

[11] See especially Wright (1992, 1998) and Michael Lynch (2001, 2004).

may be possible to come closer to a stable working-out of true relativism than one might otherwise suspect.[12] I'll conclude by outlining one specific suggestion in that direction.

8. Relativism and Idealized Assertibility

Assertibility[13] is manifestly a relative notion: a statement may be assertible relative to one state of information and not to another. Might notions of truth arrived at by idealization of assertibility retain this, or a kindred, relativity?

There are two principal such proposed idealizations to be found in the literature. The first, in the Peircean tradition and associated with Hilary Putnam's latterly renounced 'internal realism', idealizes on the state of information: what is true is what is assertible in a state of information incorporating all possible relevant data for the proposition in question. It's obvious that this proposal, whatever we might want to say pro- or anti- the credentials of the resulting truth predicate, holds out no interesting prospect of relativism, since the whole point of the idealization involved is that it is supposed to ensure *convergence*. Either a proposition is assertible at the relevant Peircean limit of information gathering—in which case it is true *simpliciter*—or, even at the limit, its credentials are matched by a rival, in which case it is neither assertible nor—for internal realism—true.

Matters may interestingly turn out differently, however, if the idealization assumes the form proposed in the notion of *superassertibility*.[14] Superassertibility is the property not of being assertible in some ideal—perhaps limiting—state of information, but of being assertible in some ordinary, accessible state of information

---

[12] The tension between correspondence truth and relativistic truth, and indeed an implicit pluralism about truth, is actually close to the surface, it seems to me, in several of the treatments canvassed in the recent revival of sympathetic discussion of relativism within analytical philosophy. John MacFarlane, for example, in a growing series of important discussions (for instance, MacFarlane (2003a, 2005a, and 2005b) has tended to promote a conception of the conferrers of relativistic truth as consisting in ordered pairs of a world and a 'context of assessment'. Likewise Max Kölbel (2002, 2004) proposes that truth is relative to what he terms 'perspective'—where the very word conjures the idea of an argument place: something the perspective is a perspective *on*. These proposals are, of course, partly formal: what may vary with variation in the context of assessment, or the perspective, is just whatever truth is being conceived as relative to: perhaps standards, perhaps taste, perhaps information, perhaps time. But it is unintelligible what contribution a *world* is supposed to make except as providing an input of unreconstructed states of affairs, things standing thus-and-so. The very intelligibility—even *prima facie* intelligibility—of the kind of framework MacFarlane explicitly, and Kölbel implicitly, propose thus seems to call for a prior domain of circumstances—the kind of thing a 'world' contributes to the ordered pair, or what a perspective is exercised on—of which, presumably, there is no obstacle in principle to an independent self-standing statement. For such statements there will then be no need—and, on pain of vicious regress, ultimately no space—for a relativistic conception of truth.

[13] I use 'assertibility', as is customary if a little unhappy, as a shorthand for *warranted* assertibility, where the relevant notion of warrant relates just to the *acceptance* of the content asserted and has no other bearing on the justifiability of (publicly) *asserting* it.

[14] See Wright (1992, 1998).

and then remaining so no matter what additions or improvements are made to it. When superassertibility for a given class of statements is taken to be truth, then truth is held to consist not in assertibility at some ideal limit of information gathering but in enduring assertibility over indefinite improvements. Does super-assertibility offer the prospect of an interesting relativity? More specifically: can this happen—that *in a single world* one thinker, Hero, is in position to accept *P*, and another, Heroine, is in position to accept not-*P*, and that each can retain their respective situations no matter what improvements or enlargements are made to their states of information?

Well, not if Hero's and Heroine's respective bodies of information allow of *pooling*, and if it is determinate and unique what the resulting pooled state of information should be, and determinate whether it supports *P*, or not-*P*, or neither. But those conditions may not all be met. When Hero and Heroine bring their respective bodies of information together, it may be that there is more than one equally rationally defensible way for accommodating the compo-nents into a unified state, each maybe involving some discards, with none superior to the others in virtue of the number or kind of discards involved or the quality of the information remaining. It may also happen that some of the resulting enlarged states of information continue to warrant acceptance of *P*, and others acceptance of not-*P*. And once granted to be possible at all, it's difficult to see how to exclude the thought that such a situation might persist indefinitely. In that case super-assertibility would be relative to a starting point, an initial basis for acceptance or rejection. If one were satisfied there were no other obstacles to the identification of truth with superassertibility over the region of discourse in question, that would be a kind of relativity of truth.

However, the kind of case which is our main focus—disputes of taste—is marked by the following peculiarity: that the basic form of assertibility condition for statements of the relevant kind is given by a subject's finding herself in a certain type of *non-cognitive* affective state: liking the taste of rhubarb, for instance. The basic form of assertibility condition, that is to say, for the impersonal statement—about the vegetable—coincides with that for the self-ascription of a subjective state that is not conceived—at least not by anyone attracted to the Ordinary View—as a cognitive response. In that case Hero and Heroine may respectively be in a position to assert *P* and to assert not-*P*, not because they possess differing initial information bases but just by virtue of differing in their non-cognitive responses to things—and because these responses are non-cognitive, there will be no clear sense to the idea of 'pooling' their respective starting points and determining what is warranted by the result. Of course there is such a thing as enlarging one's information by the addition of the datum that others do not share a particular non-cognitive response. But if that datum is not treated *per se* as a defeater, then there will be no immediate threat to the super-assertibility of the original claim.

Much more would need to be said if a satisfying proposal in this direction is to be developed. In particular, if a content is to be associated with the impersonal statement—'Rhubarb is delicious'—contrasting with that of a subjective report, then something has to be said about how the contrast between the two is sustained. Presumably such an account will give central place to asymmetries in the conditions of defeat, with the assertibility of, for example, 'I relish eating rhubarb', surviving in circumstances where that of 'Rhubarb is delicious' is lost. It's hard to envisage how the story might plausibly go without some kind of play with intersubjective accord: what purposes could be served by our having the impersonal form of statement if one could seldom reliably encourage expectations in an audience about their own affective states and responses? Still, if one's own tastes are not too idiosyncratic—if enough of a constituency goes along with them—then that may be enough to license a claim, even if significantly many may, with the same licence, dissent from it. And in that case there may be theoretical advantages in representing the situation as one in which conflicting claims are each true relative to varying parameters of taste, with truth construed as superassertibility on the basis of a notion of assertibility grounded on the relevant non-cognitive affect.

Such a proposal looks to be promisingly placed to handle Faultlessness and Sustainability. But matters may seem less clear with Contradiction—the claim that genuinely incompatible opinions are involved: how exactly does the proposal promise a better accommodation of the Ordinary View in this respect than the kind of position, illustrated by the examples of the blunt scalpel and knowledge-attributions when construed along contextualist lines, which effectively diagnoses disputes of inclination as illusory? What can be said, in the spirit of the superassertibilist-relativist proposal, to support the idea that it is the *same* content that, as it may be, is superassertible for Tim but not for me?

To think of truth in some area of discourse as constituted by superassertibility no doubt leaves considerable latitude when it comes to theorizing about propositional content. I shall not here attempt such a theory. However, if Tim and I do have an understanding in common of the proposition that rhubarb is delicious, as it occurs in our respective affirmation and denial, it would be natural to locate the commonality in a shared conception of basic, sufficient—if defeasible—grounds for accepting the proposition (one's enjoying rhubarb, presumably) and a shared conception of the consequences of regarding it as correct. Among the latter might be, for example, the desirability of regular harvesting of one's rhubarb crop when in season, a high ranking for choosing a dessert in a German restaurant identified to one as rhubarb crumble, a high priority assigned to the rhubarb patch in the re-organization of the vegetable garden, and so on. Commonality of understanding will involve that my negative view, by contrast, will lead to corresponding low priorities and opposed choices. This is the pre-theoretic background against which it seems intuitive to say that Tim and I have genuinely conflicting views about a single proposition. An explicit theory subserving the point would be one in the broad tradition deriving from Gentzen's work on the logical constants which locates the individuation of content in canonical grounds and consequences.

Against this kind of background, it's salient that the situation contrasts with the case of the rejected scalpel. Baldly, suitable grounds for the attribution of sharpness that the surgeon denies would be quite different to those sufficient for the attribution of sharpness that the orderly affirms. When the latter asserts that the scalpel is (dangerously) sharp he is not challenging the surgeon's judgement that it is not—as indeed the surgeon is not challenging the orderly's judgement that great care is necessary in handling it and preparing it for sharpening and sterilization. But more: each can quite coherently accept and, in various ways, appropriately *act on* the other's claim while still maintaining his own—surely a conclusive consideration in favour of the point that different, and compatible, contents are involved. By contrast, that Tim and I are involved in genuine disagreement is borne out by the fact that we agree about the, loosely described, consequences of each other's views and then sustain our disagreement through our respective acceptance or rejection of those consequences and the courses of action involved. Tim orders the crumble; I don't. Tim designs his vegetable patch in a certain way; I don't.[15] Rational action on either of the views excludes rational action on the other.

So here's the package: Tim and I are in genuine disagreement about whether rhubarb is delicious. Our opinions are incompatible. And the common understanding, necessary to ground that incompatibility, is based on a common conception of the assertibility conditions of the claim—that, absent defeating considerations, it may be asserted just if one relishes eating rhubarb—and on a shared conception of a range of consequences, both analytical and practical, which attend its correctness. Our disagreement can be faultless because it can be based on our respectively perfectly proper responses to our respective non-cognitive propensities. And it can be sustainable because—precisely—neither claim has been defeated nor has to be defeasible. Finally, the Simple Deduction is blocked in exactly the way prefigured: when truth is conceived as superassertibility relative to a subject's non-cognitive responses, the supposition that P is true will be answerable to the corresponding responses of a tacitly understood constituency of subjects; and it will implicate a mistake in the opinion of one who takes it that not-P is true only if their opinion is properly held answerable to the responses of the same constituency.

---

[15] Notice that attributor contextualism—which proposes to construe 'x knows that p' as comparable to 'that instrument is dangerously sharp', rather than to 'rhubarb is delicious', understood as by the Ordinary View—has work to do with this point. A third party can accept not merely that the surgeon's and the orderly's claims are both correct in context: she can, as it were, take both claims on board—indeed the orderly does so, in effect, by replacing the knife with a better prepared one for the purposes of the surgery and then taking appropriate personal care while he sharpens and sterilizes the rejected knife. But what would it be to take on board the claims of both G. E. Moore and a Sceptic: how would one act out a simultaneous acceptance of both claims?

If all this is soundly conceived, then a relativism about truth, fashioned along the indicated lines, may be the natural companion of non-cognitivist conceptions of competence in particular regions of discourse. But here I must be content merely to have outlined the approach.

References

Cohen, Stewart (1999), "Contextualism, Skepticism and the Structure of Reasons," *Philosophical Perspectives* 13, 57–89.

DeRose, Keith (1992), "Contextualism and Knowledge Attributions," *Philosophy and Phenomenological Research* 52, 913–29.

DeRose, Keith (2002), "Assertion, Knowledge, and Context," *Philosophical Review* 111, 167–203.

Greenough, Patrick and Michael Lynch (eds.) (2006), *Truth and Realism*, Oxford: Clarendon Press.

Kölbel, Max (2002), *Truth without Objectivity*, London: Routledge.

Kölbel, Max (2004), "Faultless Disagreement," *Proceedings of the Aristotelian Society* 104, 53–73.

Kölbel, Max (unpublished), "Wright on Disputes of Inclination," available as a PDF file at: https://members.phl.univie.ac.at/koelbel/wp-content/uploads/sites/2/2017/12/Wright-on-Disputes-of-Inclination_2002.pdf

Lynch, Michael (2001), "A Functionalist Theory of Truth," in M. Lynch (ed.), *The Nature of Truth*, Cambridge, MA: Bradford/MIT, 723–49.

Lynch, Michael (2004), "Truth and Multiple Realisability," *Australasian Journal of Philosophy* 82, 384–408.

MacFarlane, John (2003b), "Future Contingents and Relative Truth," *Philosophical Quarterly* 53, 321–36.

MacFarlane, John (2005a), "Making Sense of Relative Truth," *Proceedings of the Aristotelian Society* 105, 321–39.

MacFarlane, John (2005b), "The Assessment-Sensitivity of Knowledge Attributions," in Tamar Szabó Gendler and John Hawthorne (eds.), *Oxford Studies in Epistemology*, Oxford: Oxford University Press.

Wright, Crispin (1992), *Truth and Objectivity*, Cambridge, MA: Harvard University Press.

Wright, Crispin (1998), "Truth: A Traditional Debate Reviewed," *Canadian Journal of Philosophy* Supplementary Volume 24, 31–74 (on "Pragmatism," edited by Cheryl Misak). Reprinted in Simon Blackburn and Keith Simmons (eds.) (1999), *Truth*, Oxford: Clarendon Press, 203–38.

Wright, Crispin (2001), "On Being in a Quandary: Relativism, Vagueness, Logical Revisionism," *Mind* CX, 45–98.

Wright, Crispin (2002), "Relativism and Classical Logic," in A. O' Hear (ed.), *Logic, Language and Thought*, Cambridge, Cambridge University Press, 95–118.

3

New Age Relativism and Epistemic Possibility

The Question of Evidence

1. Preliminary Remarks

What I am calling New Age Relativism is usually proposed as a thesis about the truth-conditions of *utterances*, where an utterance is an actual historic voicing or inscription of a sentence of a certain type.[1] Roughly, it is the view that, for certain discourses, whether an utterance is true depends not just on the context of its making—when, where, to whom, by whom, in what language, and so on—and the 'circumstances of evaluation'—the state of the world in relevant respects—but also on an additional parameter: *a context of assessment*. Vary the latter and the truth-value of the utterance can vary, even though the context of its making and the associated state of the world remain fixed.

New Age Relativism is interesting for at least three reasons. First, it presents as a sober, semi-technical thesis in the philosophy of language, drawing essentially on an apparatus of semantic theory fashioned in the well-tried Lewis-Kaplan tradition, and marks an attempt to articulate one of the oldest, most enigmatic tendencies in philosophy in a sharply formulated theoretical framework. This is in refreshing contrast to the rhetorical and impressionistic style of much of the writing of contemporary postmodernism. Second, its motivation, at least in some cases, is empirico-linguistic. Traditionally, relativism about truth has been a metaphysical view, driven by ideas about the limits of the objective world, or the illusoriness of any aspiration to purely representational thought. Its re-emergence as a form of semantic theory, by contrast, has been fostered in large part by considerations about the ways in which, supposedly, relevant areas of language actually work. New Age Relativism allows, it is alleged, of a solid motivation in local data of linguistic practice, rather than antecedent metaphysics or

---

[1] This discussion is in many ways complementary to—and indeed originated as part of—my (2008). While self-contained, it may be an easier read for someone familiar with the latter.

Essays on Relativism: 2001–2021. Crispin Wright, Oxford University Press. © Crispin Wright 2023.
DOI: 10.1093/oso/9780192845993.003.0004

postmodernist party doctrine.[2] Third, the framework proposed easily provides for *local* relativisms. Many of the traditional reasons for dismissing relativism have turned on singularities that erupt when it aspires to be a global doctrine (thereby applying in particular to its own very statement[3]). But the New Age framework makes provision from the start for the idea that 'context of assessment' may be an idle wheel in the determination of truth-value for some—perhaps even most—kinds of claim.

Locality of concern has been the norm in the recent literature. Besides the traditional relativistic stamping grounds of ethics, aesthetics, and taste,[4] New Age Relativistic proposals have recently been advanced in a locally specific way for indicative conditionals,[5] future contingents,[6] ascriptions of knowledge,[7] and for epistemic possibility claims.[8] The latter is the most well-developed and widely discussed example in the recent literature and will provide the main example for the discussion to follow, though our overarching concern will be equally with the general methodology of the debates—specifically, with the sufficiency in principle of the models of linguistic evidence for relativism that have been appealed to.

2. The Basic Linguistic Case for the Assessment-Relativity of Epistemic Possibility Claims

Here is what has become a stock example, given by John MacFarlane:[9]

t_1 Sue: "Bill could be in Boston"
        Ted: "Actually, I just saw him board a flight to Houston"
t_2 Sue: "Oh. Then I was wrong."

MacFarlane, for one, finds this an entirely plausible piece of dialogue, and he thinks we should take Sue's t_2 utterance very seriously, as an intended *retrospective*

---

[2] The picture is mixed. Certainly this has been the pattern of argument with epistemic modals, knowledge ascriptions, and conditionals. It is different with John MacFarlane's (2003b and 2008) attempts to provide a stage-setting for a cogent expression of the Aristotelian Open Future. And the principal spur to relativistic treatments of ethical and aesthetic discourse remains the antecedent (folk-) philosophical idea that these are areas of (potential) faultless disagreement—areas where *prima facie* genuinely contradictory opinions may be held without error on either side. See, e.g., Lasersohn (2005) on this with respect to taste and, for a similar direction with respect to predicates like "rich," Richard (2004). Wright (2006) (this volume, chapter 2) is a general discussion of the idea of faultless disagreement and ways of handling it. See also MacFarlane (2007).

[3] Thus the traditional debate following the discussion in the *Theaetetus*. The modern contributions to the *Theaetetus* debate include Jordan (1971); Meiland (1977 and 1979); Swoyer (1982); and Seigel (1986).

[4] Kolbel (2002); Lasersohn (2005); Stephenson (2005).   [5] Weatherson (2009).

[6] MacFarlane (2003b and 2008).   [7] MacFarlane (2005a).

[8] MacFarlane (2003a and 2011); Egan (2005); Egan, Hawthorne, and Weatherson (2005); Stephenson (2005).

[9] MacFarlane (2003a).

retraction. Thus interpreted, Sue's t_2 utterance contrasts with what she would be doing if, after Ted's observation, she was to affirm:

$t_2{}^*$ "Then that's wrong—he can't be in Boston,"

in which the rider suggests that what she now wants to distance herself from is merely the proposition that *would* be affirmed by a present—t_2—affirmation of a token of her t_1-utterance type. No doubt Sue is doing this in the original scenario as well. But in MacFarlane's view she is there properly understood as doing more. For it would, in his view, be "odd and unnatural" if Sue were to continue,

$t_2{}^*$ (continued) "—although when I said, 'Bill might be in Boston', what I said was true, and I stand by that claim."

MacFarlane comments,

> it seems to me that th[is] alternative continuation, on which [a speaker] stands by her original claim, *always* sounds wrong. We simply don't have the practice of standing by old claims of epistemic possibility in the face of new knowledge. We *could have* had this practice, but as things are, we just don't talk this way.[10]

Suppose for now that this suggestion is agreed. Why is the dialogue *prima facie* evidence of assessment-relativity? MacFarlane's strategy is to canvass various possible accounts of the truth-conditions of epistemic possibility claims, including an assessment-relative account, and then to argue that—with the exception of the latter—they variously stumble over the above and other aspects of the linguistic evidence. Here are three possible non-relativistic accounts he considers:

Simple: "It might be the case that P" is true as uttered by S at t iff P is compatible with everything S knows at t.

Complex: "It might be the case that P" is true as uttered by S at t iff P is compatible with everything known or knowable via some *envisaged class of methods* by any member of C's *conversational circle* at t.[11]

Universal: "It might be the case that P" is true as uttered by S at t iff (i) no-one knows that not-P at t, and (ii) there is no way in which anyone can come to know that not-P.

The problem with *Simple* is that it cannot account for Sue's self-correction in the stock example. If it were correct, then her t_1 remark would have been true just in case Bill's then being in Boston was consistent with everything she knew at the time

---

[10] MacFarlane (2003a, p. 4).   [11] This is broadly in the spirit of DeRose (1991).

of utterance. Since—we may suppose—the only thing she knows inconsistent with that is what Ted subsequently told her, *Simple* predicts that she will "stand by" the former claim. It is just that it can no longer be made using the same form of words.

The same point presumably scotches any broadly utterance-contextualist account of epistemic possibility claims—any account which holds that the truth-conditions of "It could be that *P*" vary with the context of utterance (in ways not accounted for by such variation in the truth-conditions of *P*). Any such account will struggle to explain retrospective correction phenomena of the kind illustrated by the stock example: why, on the basis of evidence which stops me from truthfully asserting a token of the sentence type *P now* should I withdraw another earlier token of the same type if the type concerned is indexical, or otherwise utterance-context sensitive, and the contents of the two tokens are correspondingly different?

Complex looks to do better with self-correction data. Ted is presumably part of Sue's conversational circle. So when Sue makes her t_1 epistemic possibility claim, what she asserts is hostage to Ted's state of information at the time. Ted knows that Bill isn't in Boston. So what Sue said was false—just as she correctly says at t_2. Moreover *Complex* will also handle the following dialogue:

t_1 Sue: "Bill could be in Boston"

Ted (Bill's PA): "Wait a minute. I'll just check his itinerary and see."

He thumbs through his Filofax, "Ah, no. He was scheduled to board a flight to Houston five minutes ago."

t_2 Sue: "Oh. Then I was wrong."

This time, Ted does not *already* know something inconsistent with the embedded content in Sue's claim. But her claim is nevertheless hostage—assuming that it is common knowledge that Ted is privy to Bill's schedule—to the information that is accessible to him in certain foreseeable ways. That it is so is confirmed by her self-correction. (Of course, this dialogue is entirely fictional. But it seems likely that someone who shares MacFarlane's intuitions about the original case will find this conversation natural and convincing as well.)

However, *Complex* cannot, it appears, account for examples like these:

(a) June is an FBI agent who is carrying out surveillance on Bill and his circle, and is using a remote listening device to monitor Sue's and Ted's conversation. She overhears Sue's t_1 remark and says to herself: "That woman is wrong: I just saw the guy board a flight to Houston"

(b) Ted is not Bill's PA. He has no known or foreseeable special (access to) information about Bill's movements. But as Sue speaks, he happens to notice a piece of notepaper in the trash can in Bill's handwriting—he picks it out and finds it is Bill's itinerary for the coming week with HOUSTON clearly marked against the present date. He immediately corrects Sue. And Sue responds with a retrospective self-correction as before.

If the patterns of discourse represented by these fables are intuitive and correct, it appears that *Complex* too gets the truth-conditions of epistemic possibility claims wrong.

Universal, for its part, has no difficulty in accommodating all these "data." According to *Universal*, an utterance of "It might be that *P*" is false whenever anyone at all, whether or not within the 'conversational circle' of the utterer, either does or can (in the actual world) come to know that not-*P*. So it predicts the appropriateness of Sue's self-correction when Ted utterly fortuitously comes to know not-*P*. And it also predicts the propriety of June's eavesdropping correction of Sue. But it is obviously independently objectionable. In effect, it demands of a justified assertion of "It might be the case that *P*" that the assertor have evidence that no-one knows, or can get to know, otherwise. This is much too strong and would outlaw many perfectly justified epistemic possibility claims. For instance, in order to justifiably assert that there could be an even number of words in this chapter, you would need to be in position to claim that no-one can know that the number is odd—and hence in position to claim that it isn't.

MacFarlane's preferred proposal, by contrast, is this:

Relative: "It might be the case that *P*" is true as uttered by *S* at *t* *and assessed by A at t′* iff *P* is compatible with everything *A* knows at *t′*.

And this seems to cope with all the "data." In each of the examples, an assessor—Sue herself after Ted's sighting of Bill boarding the Houston flight, Sue again after Bill checks his Filofax, Sue once more after Ted finds the piece of paper in the trash can, and FBI agent June—is in an information state at a relevant *t′* which empowers her to assess Sue's t_1 utterance as false if its truth-conditions are as *Relative* proposes. So the conclusion is invited that *Relative* correctly captures the truth-conditions of epistemic possibility claims, whose truth should therefore be conceived as relative to a context of assessment, understood as including a variable for shifts in information.

3. Six Sets of Issues and Misgivings

3.1 Is the Correction Datum Authentic?

Linguistic "intuition"—what we find it smooth and normal, or alternatively "odd and unnatural" to say—is notoriously slippery ground. Is the correction datum authentic? I know from experience that many (including non-philosophers) find it so in a wide range of examples. But I think there may be an explanation of that, which I will touch on shortly, which neutralizes the suggested evidential force of the datum. In any case the invited assessment-relativist interpretation of the stock example tends to stifle another linguistic 'intuition' which you may find you have—a sense that it would be perfectly proper for Sue to continue the first dialogue by saying: "But he might have been in Boston, for all I knew before." Such a response *does* seem on the face of it to amount to "standing by an old claim of epistemic possibility." So we need to be clearer what the relevant "old claims" that we allegedly don't stand by amount to.

It is a platitude that knowledge admits of growth and decay. That requires that the verb "to know" has a significant tense: it can be true that I once didn't know P but do now; and that I once knew P but don't anymore. So presumably—given that it's not *totally* wrong-headed to think of epistemic possibility as somehow intimately related to compatibility with knowledge—the same will go for epistemic possibility: the epistemic "might" or "could" will also allow of a significant tense. How, then, are the "old claims of epistemic possibility" which we allegedly don't "stand by" to be understood as tensed?

Well, if they are to be the *very same claims* as were formerly made, then the appropriate way for Sue to express her former claim at the point of the alleged retraction should presumably involve recasting it in the past tense. At t_2 Sue ought to be repudiating a claim that she can then express by saying that it *was* epistemically possible at t_1 for Bill to be in Boston. If so, my sense, at least, is that this is nothing she should want to repudiate, and indeed that it is just what she would affirm by "but he could have been, for all I knew before." It is true of course that the form of utterance, "For all I know/knew, P" is not committal to the truth of P—Sue might equally well say: "but for all I knew, he *was* in Boston." So one attracted to a relativist response to the datum might be inclined to grant the propriety of "but he could have been, for all I knew before," and then to contest whether this really amounts to an endorsement of the "old epistemic possibility claim" seemingly expressed by the words before the comma. But I think it would also be perfectly smooth and natural for Sue to say simply, "Oh, so he can't be in Boston then—but when I said what I did, he *could/might have been.*"

I alluded above to an alternative explanation of the correction datum. It is that the pattern of exchange illustrated by the stock example does not involve correction of an epistemic possibility claim at all, but of something more like a tentative assertion, or some form of placement upon the "conversational record," of the embedded proposition. There is no doubt that "it may be that P" and cognates are sometimes used to effect a tentative endorsement of P, with roughly the effect of: there is (for present purposes) a significant likelihood that P, or: we need, for present purposes, to work on the assumption that P. Think of the natural setting for remarks like "I might be late—don't wait for me," "Iran could already have nuclear weapons," "That dog looks as if it might bite," "Sri Lanka might still get that total." It does not matter for the point whether this kind of lodging, or quasi-endorsement of the embedded proposition is best viewed as a (frequent) implica-ture of the assertion of an epistemic modal, or whether it signals rather a semantically different—illocutionary—role for words and phrases which also function as epistemic modal operators.[12] The point is that a tacit familiarity with this aspect of their use would be enough to trigger a sense of the propriety of Sue's retrospective self-correction, once it turns out that Bill is not in Boston.

To screen this possibility off, we need to construct a case where it is clear that there is no kind of tentative endorsement of the embedded P and that what is being asserted really is just the epistemic possibility claim. As an approximation, try this. Ted is about to head off to the wood stack, chainsaw in hand, wearing just shorts, sandals, and a T-shirt. He is reasonably experienced, and chainsaw accidents are anyway pretty unusual but tend to be horrific when people are not wearing the proper protective clothing. Sue says, "Please don't use that without wearing the proper gear. You could get horribly injured." Insouciant, Ted replies, "I'll be fine." Later he returns, having cut many logs, pleased with himself and uninjured. He says, "See, I was just fine." Which is the more natural continuation for Sue:

"Oh, then I was wrong," or
"You are a damn fool. You could have been horribly hurt"?

Relative predicts Sue's retrospective self-correction in the stock example. But it also predicts self-correction in the chainsaw example. And here, I think, we will side, rather, with Sue's second response than with the first.[13]

3.2 Assessments Based on Ignorance and Knowledge-Loss

Richard Dietz may have been the first to place emphasis upon an apparent asymmetry illustrated by the following kind of case.[14] At t_0 Sue discovers a (genuine) proof of Goldbach's Conjecture. Later, Ted, unaware of this, says

---

[12] MacFarlane considers something like this suggestion in §§4.1–4.3 of his (MacFarlane 2011) and points up some of the obvious problems with any attempt to construe the locutions we are concerned with as force-modifiers in general (for instance, the standard Frege-Geach-type point that it is possible to subordinate the clauses in question under negation and the conditional and other operators). But my suggestion is not that what we erroneously take to be epistemic modal operators are in fact markers of illocutionary force: it is rather that the cases when the correction datum seems most intuitive are cases where the words in question *do* play that role—whether instead of or additional to (perhaps as a pragmatic implicature of) functioning as modal operators is another issue.

[13] No doubt the example allows interpretation in such a way that the modalities involved are alethic rather than epistemic. But to discount it, we would have to argue that it does *not* allow an epistemic possibility interpretation except at the cost of distortion of linguistic practice. That seems wrong.

[14] The example is from my NYU graduate seminar of Fall 2005.

t_1 Ted: "There may be counterexamples to Goldbach"

t_1 Sue, excitedly: "You are wrong: It couldn't be that Goldbach has a counter-example"

Sue's response is mandated by the consequence of *Relative* that

"It is not the case that it might be the case that P" is true as uttered by S at t and assessed by A at t' iff it is not the case that: P is compatible with everything A knows at t'.

However, later Sue accidentally throws out her handwritten notes and her hard drive crashes. Distraught, she suffers a stress-induced amnesia and forgets the whole episode. In a subsequent conversation, she says

t_2 Sue: "It might be that there are counterexamples to Goldbach."

t_2 Ted: "But you told me a while ago that there couldn't be!"

t_3 Sue: "Then I was wrong."

Sue's t_2 claim is also apparently mandated by *Relative*, given her state of information at that time. And since the information Bill then gives her, about her t_1 remark to him, leaves her total state of information still compatible with there being counterexamples to Goldbach, *Relative*—so says the objection—predicts the propriety of her self-correction at t_3. Obviously one has to correct the negation of an epistemic possibility claim if one is forced to regard the claim itself as true. Sue's t_2 claim is mandated by her t_2 knowledge and *Relative*. Since Bill's remark gives her nothing to change that mandate, the t_3 correction is forced. But, without additional information—for instance, her recollection of the proof and discovery of a flaw in it—the self-correction seems bizarre and premature.

MacFarlane agrees that this kind of case counterexemplifies *Relative*. He writes that,

> If epistemic possibility is perspectival, this data [sic] suggests, it is asymmetrically pespectival. The truth of epistemic modal claims can depend on what is known by the assessor, but only if the assessor knows more than the original assertor. Taking this asymmetry into account complicates the relativist account considerably.[15]

---

[15] Macfarlane (2011), p. 174.

However, he has a suggestion about the kind of complication that is required. What is needed, he believes, is to pool the information of assertor and assessor, so that we have a clause, e.g., like this:[16]

Relative*:   "It might be the case that P" is true as uttered by S at t and assessed by A at t' iff P is compatible with everything A knows at t' and with everything S knows at t;

or this:

Relative**:   "It might be the case that P" is true as uttered by S at t and assessed by A at t' iff P is compatible with everything A would know at t' if he added to what he actually knows at t' everything that S knows at t (and then exploited the combined resources perfectly rationally, etc.).

These proposals will certainly address the immediate problem. While Sue is still straightforwardly empowered at t_1 to correct Ted's t_1 remark just on the basis of her own knowledge at the time, her t_3 correction is premature—on either account, she needs to know more about her knowledge state at t_1, just as seems intuitive.

But now there are other, related problems. Suppose Bill thinks that he has found the first proof of Goldbach's Conjecture, and joins in the conversation at t_1:

t_1 Ted: "There may be counterexamples to Goldbach"

t_1 Sue, excitedly: "You are wrong: It couldn't be that Goldbach has a counterexample"

t_1 Bill, complacently: "Yes, it couldn't be that Goldbach has a counterexample. In fact it was I who found the proof—it is already on the way to the publisher."

Bill is wrong—his proof is a muddle—but Sue believes he has anticipated her and that she will never now get any credit. Bitterly, she later shreds her hand written notes and wipes her hard drive. Then, distraught, she suffers a stress-induced amnesia and forgets the whole episode. In a subsequent conversation, she says

t_2 Sue: "It might be that there are counterexamples to Goldbach."

t_2 Ted: "But you and Bill both told me a while ago that there couldn't be!"

t_3 Sue: "Then we were both wrong."

---

[16] The formulations following are my own gloss on MacFarlane's suggestions. (*Relative*** is less permissive than *Relative**—it will exclude possibilities that P where it takes the combined epistemic achievement of S and A to rule out P.)

It seems clear that though bizarre as before, Sue's t_3 evaluation does at least have the merit of consistency, for she and Bill intuitively made the same claim, just as Ted reports, of which competence now demands a uniform evaluation. But both Relative* and Relative** ascribe different truth-conditions to Sue's and Bill's respective t_1 claims. Both require that Sue should evaluate the two claims differently, since her t_3 knowledge pooled with her t_1 knowledge does rule out counterexamples to Goldbach, whereas her t_3 knowledge pooled with Bill's t_1 knowledge does not. So, if Relative* or Relative** is to be believed, the truthful thing for her to say at t_3 is

t_3 Sue: "Actually, I was right. But Bill was wrong."

This is obviously completely unintuitive.

There may be a temptation to think that what this shows is that a clause is wanted which allows Sue's t_3 evaluation to pool her present knowledge with both hers *and* Bill's former knowledge—an analogue of the play with "conversational circle" involved in *Complex*, but this time within the framework of assessment-relativity. However, I do not think the relativist should be tempted towards such epicycles—rather the original objection is misconceived, and MacFarlane was wrong to sustain it. For it simply isn't true that *Relative* enforces assessments based on ignorance or knowledge-loss to trump the epistemic possibility claims of agents who know or knew more. Reflect that what is *outré* about these assessments is not so much the idea that they might be true. It is not as if we want to say that the mere fact that someone knows not-P *tout court* sufficient for anyone else's claim that it could be that P to be false. What jars is rather the apparent *presumption* of the assessor—their taking themselves to be in position to correct the claim of someone who, for all they know, may be better placed. But *Relative* does not enforce such presumption. To see this, suppose a community in which, as for us, testimony is conceived as a source of knowledge, but whose members are mutually known never to make mistakes or to lie, at least on matters of the kind with which the proposition that P is concerned, and whose assessments of epistemic possibility claims are, again mutually knowledgeably, governed by *Relative*. Imagine that you are a member of this community and rightly judge that P is consistent with everything you know. Taking yourself as both speaker and assessor, you accordingly know that an utterance by you of "It is possible that P" would express a truth. Now you learn that Sue, a member of your community, has asserted, "It could not be that P."[17] By hypothesis, this will be a knowledgeable assertion, so you learn that P is not consistent with the knowledge base of another member of your community—and hence that there is something to be known, not

---

[17] —and let's prescind from any issues about ascertaining that what she intended was an *epistemic* possibility claim.

yet known to you, which rules out the truth of *P*. This existential claim is itself inconsistent with the truth of *P*. And it is now something that you know. So you are no longer in position to assess your hypothetical utterance of "It is possible that *P*" as expressing a truth, nor accordingly to correct Sue's more knowledgeable claim.

This reasoning makes idealizing assumptions about the practices of members of the community concerned. But they are assumptions that do no more than hypothesize the attainment of standards to which we actually aspire. If *Relative* is correct and tacitly accepted, then what one learns when another sincerely denies an epistemic possibility claim is that they judge their information to rule out the embedded proposition. Lacking special reason to think the denial insincere, or incompetent, one should be receptive to the idea that one has just learned that there is information to be had sufficient to rule out *P*. So one is in no position reasonably to judge that all one's knowledge is consistent with *P*.

I conclude that, whatever its other difficulties, *Relative* does not have an "ignorant-assessor" problem.

3.3 Other Counterexamples

But there are more obvious, potentially no less serious problems. Granted that there is a range of cases where the kind of correction required by *Relative* does seem intuitive—and prescinding from the explanation suggested above of these cases (that they in effect involve correction of *P*)—*Relative* seems massively to over-predict our propensities to correction of epistemic modals. Suppose Sue has just bought a £1.50 ticket in the Euro-millions Super Draw. Ted tells her she is wasting her money.

t_1 Sue: "Not at all. I might win"

Later the draw takes place. Sue does not win.

t_2 Ted: "See. I told you so"

It would be, it seems to me—assuming Sue has no further relevant information—completely inappropriate if she was to reply,

(a) t_2 Sue: "Yes, I guess I was wrong. It wasn't true that I might win"

and perfectly natural if she answered instead,

(b) t_2 Sue: "That's just hindsight. It's still true that I might have won."

MacFarlane considers this kind of example.[18] His response is not to dispute the naturalness of the kind of dialogue that ends with Sue's remark (b), but to dispute whether the modality involved is epistemic, rather than alethic. I have no space here to consider the grounds on which he tries to make this plausible, but I don't think it is. The naturalness of the dialogue depends on treating Sue's remark (b) as a re-affirmation, *modulo* an appropriate shift of mood and tense, of the possibility she affirmed at t_1.[19] So if the possibility affirmed by her remark (b) is alethic, so is that affirmed by her t_1 response to Ted. But the alethic possibilities at t_1 are presumably no news to Ted. What Sue is telling him at t_1 is that he doesn't know that she is going to lose.

But let us put the particular example to one side and step back. *Relative* requires that any epistemic possibility claim be assessed as false, no matter when it is made or from what state of information it issues, by any assessor who happens to know that the embedded claim is false, no matter what her social context. It respects no limits of distance in time and space between utterer and assessor. It is natural to suppose that as knowledge advances, the domain of epistemic possibility shrinks. Not so according to *Relative*, which mandates that we regard the space of epistemic possibilities open to our pre-Darwinian, pre-Newtonian, pre-Daltonian ancestors as no wider than ours. If *Relative* is right, we should believe that they were mistaken even in taking their various false theories of things to be epistemic possibilities. But this is not what we think.

3.4 How in Any Case Can Mere Patterns of Correction Motivate Assessment-Relativism?

Even if the correction data were solid and general, there would still be something puzzling about the relativistic response. After all, we go in for correction of *all kinds* of claims, both our own previous utterances and those of others. Is it being suggested that all of them are apt material for assessment-relative semantics? Can it really be that the mere phenomenon of change of mind under altering information already provides all that is needed to motivate the view? Presumably not.

---

[18] Cf. Ian Hacking (1967). MacFarlane responds in §8.1 of his (2011).

[19] Compare:

"Why don't you open up the barbecue to anyone who happens to be around?"
"That wouldn't be a sensible idea—strangers might cause problems."

and

"Why didn't you open up the barbecue to anyone who happened to be around?"
"That wouldn't have been a sensible idea—strangers might have caused problems."

(I intend the play with 'strangers' to grease interpretation of the modality involved in the example as epistemic.)

But then what is the difference in the present case? What is the extra datum, or background consideration, that makes the difference?

Well, the correction data disfavour—let's allow—each of *Simple*, *Complex*, and *Universal*. If *Relative* were the only other possible account, that would certainly be a relevant "background consideration." But that surely isn't so. There will be no end of accounts that, like the three MacFarlane discards, diverge from each other by variously widening and restricting, as some kind of function of the context of utterance,[20] the information base with which the proposition embedded in the claim of possibility has to be consistent if the claim is to be true. So it would need to be made plausible that *no* such account is likely to be able to accommodate the correction data before the latter could emerge as accredited by default. The strategy of motivating an assessment-relativist account by elimination thus looks a little desperate, particularly when for reasons already reviewed and some to follow, *Relative* itself looks to be in difficulty with certain of the *prima facie* data of linguistic practice.

The reason, I surmise, why MacFarlane and others have been impressed by the correction data is because they are already seeing the landscape as one in which assessment-relativism is to compete with contextualism, and because, as we remarked earlier, the correction data, unchallenged, surely are anomalous for any view on which the content of the original utterance at the time of utterance and the content of a tokening of the same type at the time of assessment are different. When Sue learns that Bill is on the flight to Houston, she comes— according to the face-value reading of the datum—to be in position to deny that it is possible that he is in Boston. But that is not to have any ground whatever to criticize her former utterance unless it claimed or implied otherwise. If, as on a standard contextualist account, the relevant information base shifts with the context of utterance, that won't in general be so.

Well and good. But the evident problem is that we—all of us, all of the time— routinely discard erstwhile-justified opinions about all kinds of subject matters in the light of altering information. In order to distinguish the case from one of that routine kind—in order for the example to provide any motivation at all to start thinking of the truth of epistemic possibility claims as context-of-assessment-re- lative—there has to be, I suggest, some kind of *additional* evidence, over and above the correction data, that Sue's claim at t_1 was *also* perfectly proper—and this not just in the sense of having been justified when she made it, but *true*. It is *truth* that has to vary with context of assessment: that thesis is the heart and soul of relativism. So unless there is manifest in our linguistic practice, even after the allegedly perfectly proper correction at t_2, some way in which speakers can give

---

[20] *Universal* can be thought of as a limiting case of this.

expression to the correctness of Sue's earlier t_1 claim, there can be—or so a critic should charge—absolutely no call for a truth-relativistic response to the alleged linguistic data. We should conclude merely that Sue simply made an epistemic possibility claim at t_1 that, at t_2, she recognizes to have been incorrect. She was just wrong before.

It is actually difficult to envisage what shape a dialogue that was assessment-relativism suggestive on this crucial point might take if the correction datum is to be part of it. The very aspect—the apparent *retrospective* self-correction—that makes the problem for a contextualist account seems, in fact, to be equally awkward for relativism. After all, Sue precisely *doesn't* merely say, "Oh, then that's wrong—he can't be in Boston." If she did, she could be interpreted merely as re-assessing the content of her previous remark from her present assessment-standpoint, and she could perhaps then add—in an assessment-relativism suggestive way—something like "But when I said he could be just now, I was right." But MacFarlane, as noted, emphatically believes that we do not speak in the latter way where epistemic modals are concerned, and he thinks that is a crucial piece of evidence against assessment-relativism's rivals. By saying, "*I was* wrong," Sue goes beyond merely re-assessing the truth-value of the content of her previous remark: she affirms it had a status when made which is inconsistent with her adding now that "When I said he could be, I was right." If she could add the latter, the case would be no different to that of this dialogue:

t_1 Sue (excitedly, on the TGV): "Look, there is an Alpine hare!"

Ted (opens his eyes slowly and sleepily looks out of the carriage window):

"Actually, there isn't any hare."

t_2 Sue: "Oh, how irritating you are—of course there is none now, but when I said that there was an Alpine hare, I was right,"

which involves nothing more mysterious than routine indexicality of content. Hence, again, the force of the correction datum against contextualism. However the latter addition is just what assessment-relativity *also* seems to predict should be acceptable. *Relative* allows that the original utterance of "Bill could be in Boston," when assessed from the same context as that of its original utterance, expressed a truth—and that what that utterance expressed is the *same proposition* as expressed by the same words on the later occasion of assessment. It is therefore actually very *bad* for relativism that Sue says that she *was* wrong. What she should be doing is somehow evincing the assessment that the content concerned is wrong now while simultaneously conceding merit to her former opinion about it in the context in which she held it—and merit, moreover, somehow contrasting with mere (defeasible) justifiability.

The simple point is that the kind of linguistic patterns which would advantage an assessment-relative account of truth in some region of discourse over both contextualist and invariantist alternatives are actually *compromised* by the stock correction data, rather than (partially) composed by it. What is required is some kind of evidence of *co-variation* of truth-value with variation of assessment-contextual parameters. That is just what is obstructed by retrospective correction, taken at face value.

3.5 What about the Eavesdropping Component in the Data?

We have so far paid no attention to one aspect of the data that has moved proponents of relativism—the intuition, apparently shared by significantly many commentators,[21] of the propriety of corrections of epistemic modal claims by arbitrary non-participants in the conversation in which they are made. Since *Universal* is hopeless, any non-relativistic account of the truth-conditions of epistemic possibility claims is presumably going to interpret them as answerable to the knowledge of some determinate but less than all-embracing population of thinkers. However this population will presumably be variable—it is not, presumably, fixed once and for all and independently of context, just who among all possible thinkers needs to be ignorant of *P* if an utterance of "It could be that *P*" is to be true. This is what makes it natural to seek a further analysis using contextualist resources. But how could any systematic account of a broadly contextualist kind possibly get the truth-conditions right if any such claim is open to proper correction by an arbitrary, fortuitously well-informed eavesdropper? The FBI agent, June, demurs perfectly naturally and properly—or so it is alleged—from Sue's claim that Bill could be in Boston. As a competent speaker, Sue should have at least an implicit understanding of the population to whose information states her remark is answerable if it does indeed allow of some contextualist or invariantist account. Yet surely she cannot plausibly have intended her claim to be answerable to June's, or any other eavesdropper's information. If it is correctly corrigible by someone who merely overhears it, that is surely strong evidence that no such account can be correct.[22]

As always, there is some room for manoeuvre. There is a thought about such cases which would reconcile them with a broad contextualism even if we treat them as normal and proper corrections of an epistemic modal: the thought that,

---

[21] See especially Egan, Hawthorne, and Weatherson (2005).

[22] Of course the point requires, once again, that the data of correction by eavesdropping is robust, and that it really is the epistemic modal claim that is corrected and not, for example, some form of qualified assertion of *P*, or its placement upon a conversational record. Notice that it would not be enough to defeat the latter suggestion that eavesdropping June is not party to Sue's conversation—she doesn't need to be to find fault with what Sue places on the record.

by eavesdropping upon a conversation, one in effect *muscles in on it*—places oneself in the relevant conversational circle—even if unbeknownst to the other participants. If that is allowed, then an account along the lines of *Complex*:

"It might be the case that *P*" is true as uttered by *S* at *t* iff *P* is compatible with everything known or knowable via some *envisaged class of methods* by any member of *C*'s *conversational circle* at *t*,

perhaps modified to include additional references to what members of *C*'s conversational circle might easily come to know, and to what they would be negligent not to come to know, will have no problem coping with any of eavesdroppers' fortuitously available bits of information in trash cans, or indeed with the range of apparent counterexamples to *Simple* (which I won't discuss further here) where an epistemic possibility claim is rebuffed on the ground that the assertor "should have known better."

More important, however, is the point that even if *Relative* predicts the propriety of eavesdropping corrections—and even supposing no otherwise not implausible invariantist or contextualist account does so—it doesn't predict the full range of endorsements and corrections that eavesdroppers, and overhearers more generally, go in for. Suppose I am an umpire during a weekend of war games. A platoon of the Blue Force is inching its way on their bellies up a slight depression in a field. Their sergeant says, "Keep down…there could be Red snipers on the ridge." I know better—they have picked the best possible line of approach and would not be visible from the actual Red positions even if they stood up and ran. But I regard the sergeant's order, and his explanation of it, as correct— he is playing well. Indeed, suppose I am the sergeant and happen to know the lay of the land and the actual disposition of the Reds. Still, I am training my men and it is important that they learn to cover all possibilities and act accordingly. So I say to one who is about to stand up, "What are you thinking of? There could be Red snipers on the ridge."[23]

Such examples illustrate a phenomenon of what we may term *assessment-deference*: sometimes an assessor of an epistemic modal claim will defer to the information of an audience, or a third party, and endorse the claim (or not) on that basis, rather than in the light of their own information. This is still consistent with a more relaxed form of assessment-relativism—one whereby an assessment offered in a particular context may be conditioned, perhaps at the discretion of the assessor, by a value of the relevant assessment-parameter other than that obtaining at the context of assessment, in deference to the situation of an audience or

---

[23] Examples of this kind were emphasized to me by Herman Cappelen in conversation in September 2006. They were also central in a talk given by John Hawthorne at an Arché Basic Knowledge workshop in November 2006.

some other salient agent(s). But it would be a bold claim that, once a proponent of *Relative* sets off on such a path of epicycles and pragmatic complication, no descendant of *Complex* is going to be able to cope as well.

Someone might be tempted to deny that the deferential assessments provide examples of literal, sincere endorsement. I might, as sergeant, just be telling my men a 'white lie' when I say, "There might be Red snipers on the ridge," with a view to enhancing the training experience. Or I might, as umpire, regard the sergeant's order as correct only in the sense that it is the order that he ought to give: what is true is not that there might be Red snipers on the ridge, but only that he and his men ought to think that there might. These are both things that a proponent of assessment-relativism can say. But *Relative* needs to be independently well entrenched before it can be acceptable methodology to dispute, or explain away as loose or misleading, those patterns of speech that seem to contradict it. There are similar ways of discounting the original correction data, after all.

3.6 Embedded Epistemic Modals

This is the final issue for the present discussion. Epistemic modal operators allow of occurrences within the scope of other operators, like tenses—as we already emphasized—and indeed other epistemic operators. Consider, for example, some effectively but tediously decidable proposition, Q—say that $10^{27} + 1$ is a prime. For all I know, you know that $10^{27} + 1$ is not a prime and hence are in position to assess "It is epistemically possible that Q" as false. Since—for assessment-relativism—there is no indexicality in that sentence, it seems that (the relativist should allow that) for all I know, you know that it is not epistemically possible that Q. We now make two plausible assumptions:

(1):   If a theory of epistemic possibility permits the competent assertion of a conjunction of the following form (the *proscribed* form)

A & EP[not-A],

   it is in trouble.

The justified admission of an epistemic possibility cannot cohabit with a justified assertion that it does not obtain. This is a feature that distinguishes epistemic possibility from metaphysical and other forms of possibility. The point is easily substantiated if assertion is subject to the knowledge rule, for in that case by asserting A one implicitly lays claim to the knowledge which, by asserting the epistemic possibility of not-A, one forswears. For those who think that warranted assertion requires less, the account offered on the right hand side of *Relative* will presumably be relaxed *in tandem*. But the crucial point is that whatever the epistemic standard required by warranted assertion, there will be a correlative epistemic modal standing to it as epistemic possibility, as we have so far been understanding it, stands to knowledge. And it would hardly be plausible that assessment-relativism be appropriate for the intuitive notion of epistemic possibility, whatever that is, but not for this modal.

Very well. The second assumption we need springs from the reflection above that some instances of

$$EP[Q] \ \& \ EP[X \text{ knows that not-}Q]$$

are acceptable and harmless. We just saw an example: from my present state of information, it is epistemically possible that $10^{27} + 1$ is a prime but also epistemically possible you, the reader, know that $10^{27} + 1$ is not a prime. Now for a particular Q and choice of method, it may be that one who verifies Q, or not-Q, by that method can normally know that they know. Plausibly, simple arithmetical propositions and arithmetical computation provide an example. So in such a case, it seems that if the relevant instance of the above schema is acceptable and harmless, so is this (our second) assumption:

(2):   Some instances of

$$EP[Q] \ \& \ EP[X \text{ knows that } X \text{ knows that not-}Q]$$

are acceptable and harmless.

But now, since someone who knows that [they] know that not-Q knows that Q is not epistemically possible, it seems to follow that the following will hold in such an acceptable and harmless case:

$$EP[Q] \ \& \ EP[X \text{ knows that not-}EP[Q]]$$

and hence that

(*Rogue*) $EP[Q] \ \& \ EP[\text{not-}EP[Q]]$

should also be acceptable and harmless (by factivity of "knows" and closure of EP). But (*Rogue*) is of the proscribed form.

There is an obvious solution, no doubt. The objection, however, is that the supporter of *Relative*—or of any similar though perhaps more complex form of assessment-relativism for epistemic possibility claims—cannot avail themselves of it;

and that it is not clear that they have any other solution. The obvious solution is that (*Rogue*), validly inferred from acceptable premises as above, must be read as having *hidden constituents*. It is to be read, very crudely, as something of the form:

$$EP_x[Q] \ \& \ EP_x[\text{not-}EP_y[Q]],$$

where the varying suffixes mark variables for states of information that can of course be bound or variously instantiated. For me, it is epistemically possible both that $10^{27} + 1$ is a prime and that for you, the reader, it is not epistemically possible that $10^{27} + 1$ is a prime. But to express this harmless case, I have to be able to instantiate the variable 'y' differently from the variable 'x', and the variables—naturally—have to be there in the logical form in the first place. So construed—surely as demanded—(*Rogue*) isn't really of the proscribed form. The problem for assessment-relativism, however, is that it has no option of such a construal. There is, for assessment-relativism, no place in the logical form of an epistemic possibility claim for a variable that ranges over states of information, and that may take instances other than the state of information of an assessor. It is no part of such claims, construed as by the relativist, to *talk about* states of information or knowledge and what is compatible with them. The state of information parameter belongs to the context of assessment, not the content of the claim assessed. This is of the absolute essence of the view. The distinction is parallel, roughly, to that between an assessment-relativist construal of ascriptions of knowledge, as MacFarlane has also advocated,[24] and the kind of *subject-sensitive* or *interest-relative* invariantist account offered by Hawthorne and Stanley.[25] On the former kind of view, the truth-value of an utterance of 'X knows that P' may vary with standards determined by the context of an assessor. But there is nothing in the semantics of the utterance as such—the proposition it expresses—to determine what those standards may be; it does not speak of an assessment-parameter that needs to be settled before it can take a truth-value. For a view of the Stanley-Hawthorne kind, however, the opposite is true: the proposition expressed does speak of the subject, X, of the knowledge ascription and—according to the view—it will be determined by X's interests at the time of ascription (so there is a modest element of contextuality of truth-conditions) what the appropriate standards are to determine whether X's evidence suffices, for its part, for knowledge that P. In any case, the proposition concerned takes its truth-value absolutely. Whatever the respective merits of this kind of view and assessment-relativism in the case of knowledge ascriptions, it seems to me that no account of epistemic modals is going to succeed unless it makes provision for embedded occurrences of an operator of epistemic possibility to involve reference to information states of a

---

[24] MacFarlane (2005a).   [25] Hawthorne (2004); Stanley (2005).

subject distinct from that of an assessor of the embedding context. Since—in contrast to the case of knowledge ascriptions—no such reference is generally explicit in the overt grammar of the sentence, a developed, subject-sensitive account of epistemic modals, analogous to the Stanley-Hawthorne view about knowledge, will have to traffic in special hypotheses about covert logical form, or even in 'unarticulated' constituents. Fare that approach as it may, it remains, to repeat, a cardinal feature of assessment-relativism about epistemic possibility that "EP[Q]" involves no such tacit reference—that it expresses the *same proposition* in all occurrences—and that all that is permitted to vary is the context of assessment in which an embedding statement is considered. So shackled, the relativist has no way of making out that (*Rogue*) is not of the proscribed form.

4. Summary of Conclusions

New Age Relativist treatments have been proposed for a variety of reasons in different regions of discourse. In a wide range of cases these reasons have been metaphysical. What is particularly interesting about the case of the epistemic modalities is that the proposal is offered as assisting the provision of a systematic *semantic* theory in the light of certain allegedly otherwise recalcitrant aspects of the linguistic practices concerned—specifically, data of retrospective self-correction, and 'correction by eavesdropper'.

Our review of the issues, though unavoidably incomplete, suggests pessimism whether assessment-relativistic semantics is likely to make best sense of these data. In many cases, it is a competitive thought that what is corrected is not the epistemic possibility claim itself but the embedded proposition, understood as having been tentatively endorsed or entered into the reckoning for some practical purpose by the making of the original (apparently) epistemic modal claim. In any case, both relevant kinds of corrective pattern are partial—there is a very significant range of cases in which they are not upheld, and in general there seem to be no fewer counterexamples to *Relative*—the simplest natural way of assigning relativistic truth-conditions to epistemic possibility claims—than to its non-relativistic competitors. Additional difficulties for the assessment-relativist direction include providing the resources to handle certain kinds of embedded epistemic possibility clauses, and the fact that the retrospective correction data seem to be at odds with the admission, presumably integral to relativism, that the criticized claim may have been correct in its original assessment-context.

Perhaps most important, our discussion has indirectly raised doubts about whether, whatever one thinks about epistemic possibility in particular, there is at present any extant clear model of the patterns that linguistic data in any region of discourse should *in principle* assume if they are to provide compelling grounds for preferring an assessment-relativist style of semantic theory. While that lack remains, we should regard the jury as out on whether the New Age 'linguistic turn' to relativism—as opposed to the more traditional metaphysical lines of entry—can in principle be made cogent at all.[26]

References

DeRose, K. (1991), "Epistemic Possibilities," *Philosophical Review* 100 (4), 581–605.

Dietz, Richard (2008), "Epistemic Modals and Correct Disagreement," in M. García-Carpintero and M. Kölbel (eds.), *Relative Truth*, Oxford: Oxford University Press, 239–64.

Egan, Andy (2005), "Epistemic Modals, Relativism and Assertion," in J. Gajewski, V. Hacquard, B. Nickel, and S. Yalcin (eds.), *New Work on Modality*, MIT Working Papers in Linguistics, v. 51, 35–61.

Egan, Andy, John Hawthorne, and Brian Weatherson (2005), "Epistemic Modals in Context," in G. Preyer and P. Peters (eds.), *Contextualism in Philosophy*, Oxford: Oxford University Press, 131–69.

Gajewski, Jon, Valentine Hacquard, Bernhard Nickel, and Seth Yalcin (2005), *New Work on Modality*, MIT Working Papers in Linguistics, v. 51.

García-Carpintero, Manuel and Max Kölbel (eds.) (2008), *Relative Truth*, Oxford: Oxford University Press.

Hacking, Ian (1967), "Possibility," *Philosophical Review* 76, 143–68.

Hawthorne, John (2004), *Knowledge and Lotteries*, Oxford: Oxford University Press.

Jordan, James (1971), "Protagoras and Relativism: Criticisms Bad and Good," *Southwestern Journal of Philosophy* 2, 7–29.

Kaplan, David (1989), "Demonstratives: An Essay on the Semantics, Logic, Metaphysics, and Epistemology of Demonstratives and Other Indexicals', in J. Almog, J. Perry, and H. Wettstein (eds.), *Themes from Kaplan*, Oxford: Oxford University Press, 481–566.

Kölbel, Max (2002), *Truth without Objectivity*, London: Routledge.

Lasersohn, Peter (2005), "Context Dependence, Disagreement, and Predicates of Personal Taste," *Linguistics and Philosophy* 28, 643–86.

Lewis, D. (1980), "Index, Context, and Content," in S. Kanger and S. Ohman (eds.), *Philosophy and Grammar*, Dordrecht: Reidel, 79–100. Reprinted in D. Lewis (1998), *Papers in Philosophical Logic*. Cambridge: Cambridge University Press, 21–44.

MacFarlane, John (2003a), "Epistemic Modalities and Relative Truth," available at https://johnmacfarlane.net/epistmod-2003.pdf

---

[26] Thanks for valuable critical comments and suggestions to colleagues in the Arché Contextualism and Relativism seminar over the last two sessions, to participants in my NYU seminar on Relativism in Fall 2005, and at the workshop on Epistemic Modality and Relativism organized by Philipp Keller in Geneva in April 2006; and to Jessica Brown and Herman Cappelen for informal discussion of the issues.

MacFarlane, John (2003b), "Future Contingents and Relative Truth," *Philosophical Quarterly* 53, 321–36.

MacFarlane, John (2005), "The Assessment-Sensitivity of Knowledge Attributions," in Tamar Szabó Gendler and John Hawthorne (eds.), *Oxford Studies in Epistemology*, Vol. 1, Oxford: Oxford University Press, 197–233.

MacFarlane, John (2007), "Relativism and Disagreement," *Philosophical Studies* 132, 17–31.

MacFarlane, John (2008), "Truth in the Garden of Forking Paths," in M. García-Carpintero and M. Kölbel (eds.), *Relative Truth*, Oxford: Oxford University Press, 81–102.

MacFarlane, John (2011), "Epistemic Modals Are Assessment Sensitive," in A. Egan and B. Weatherson (eds.), *Epistemic Modality*, Oxford: Oxford University Press, 144–78.

Meiland, Jack W. (1977), "Concepts of Relative Truth," *The Monist* 60, 568–82.

Meiland, Jack W. (1979), "Is Protagorean Relativism Self-Refuting?," *Grazer Philosophische Studien* 9, 51–68.

Richard, Mark (2004), "Contextualism and Relativism," *Philosophical Studies* 119, 215–42.

Seigel, H. (1986), "Relativism, Truth, and Incoherence," *Synthese* 68, 295–312.

Stanley, Jason (2005), *Knowledge and Practical Interests*, Oxford: Oxford University Press.

Stephenson, Tamina (2005), "Assessor Sensitivity: Epistemic Modals and Predicates of Personal Taste," in J. Gajewski, V. Hacquard, B. Nickel, and S. Yalcin (eds.), *New Work on Modality*, MIT Working Papers in Linguistics, Vol. 51, 179–206.

Swoyer, Chris (1982), "True For," in M. Krausz and J. W. Meiland (eds.), *Relativism: Cognitive and Moral*, Notre Dame: University of Notre Dame Press, 84–108.

Weatherson, Brian (2009), "Conditionals and Indexical Relativism," *Synthese* 166, 333–57.

Wright, Crispin (2006), "Intuitionism, Realism, Relativism and Rhubarb," in P. Greenough and M. Lynch (eds.), *Truth and Realism*, Oxford: Oxford University Press.

Wright, Crispin (2008), "Relativism about Truth itself," in M. García-Carpintero and M. Kölbel (eds.), *Relative Truth*, Oxford: Oxford University Press

4

Relativism about Truth Itself

Haphazard Thoughts about the Very Idea

πάντων χρημάτων μέτρον ἐστὶν ἄνθρωπος,
τῶν μὲν ὄντων ὡς ἔστιν, τῶν δὲ οὐκ ὄντων

ὡς οὐκ ἔστιν[1]

(Protagoras DK80b1)

The setting of relativistic ideas about truth in the general style of semantic-theoretic apparatus pioneered by Lewis, Kaplan, and others has persuaded many that they should at least be taken seriously as competition in the space of explanatory linguistic theory, a type of view which properly formulated, may offer an at least coherent—and indeed, in the view of some, a superior—account of certain salient linguistic data manifest in, for example, discourse about epistemic modals, about knowledge and about matters of taste and value, and may also offer the prospect of a coherent regimentation of the Aristotelian "Open Future" (along with, perhaps, the Dummettian 'anti-real' past.) My main purpose here is enter a reminder of certain underlying philosophical issues about relativism—about its metaphysical coherence, its metasemantic obligations, and the apparent limitations of the kind of local linguistic evidence which contemporary proponents have adduced in its favour—of which there is a risk that its apparent rehabilitation in rigorous semantic dress may encourage neglect.

1. Relativism Intuitively Understood

Relativism, as a view about some discourse or subject matter, is one of the oldest of philosophical stances. Many, not merely in the academy but more widely, would be willing to describe themselves as "relativists" about certain selected subject matters: about matters of taste or, more generally, about the substance of what

---

[1] "Of all things the measure is man: on the one hand of things that are, that they are; on the other of things that are not, that they are not."

Essays on Relativism: 2001–2021. Crispin Wright, Oxford University Press. © Crispin Wright 2023.
DOI: 10.1093/oso/9780192845993.003.0005

I have elsewhere called "disputes of inclination."[2] Post-Einsteinian physics has made a received view of relativism about motion and simultaneity. Is there a common idea between, say, ethical relativism and motion relativism? A widely acknowledged manifestation of an intuitive relativistic tendency is a willingness to take seriously the idea of faultless disagreement—disagreement about a shared content where not merely need there be no flaw of evidence or procedure on the part of the disputants but where, as it is supposed, *nobody need be wrong*.[3] I do believe that this is an ineliminable aspect of anything plausibly purporting to be relativism in the Protagorean tradition. However it is, I think, more illuminating to place initial emphasis on a different and, I suggest, more basic indicator of 'folk-relativism', and then work upwards, so to speak, to try to make space for faultless disagreement.

The more basic indicator of folk-relativism is its characteristic expression in ordinary discourse in cognates of the idiom: "There is no such thing as simply being Φ." After Einstein, there is, for example, no such thing as simply *being in motion*: things move, or not, in relation to each other (or, more sophisticated, in relation to a frame of reference). More intuitively, there is no such thing as an object's simply *looking red*: something looks red, or not, in particular viewing circumstances. Indeed there is presumably no such thing as simply *being useless*: something is useless or not in relation to a particular purpose. More controversially, there is no such thing as simply *being beautiful*: things are beautiful or not in (relation to) 'the eye of a beholder'. There is no such thing as its simply *being four o'clock*—it is four o'clock or not in relation to a time zone (that is, a set of places). Note that it doesn't go with the "no such thing as simply being Φ" rubric that in all cases there is no content to the idea of something's being *absolutely* Φ—say absolutely useless. But the sense of "absolutely" involved will involve quantification through the latter place of the relation (useless for *every* purpose), not a genuine drop in degree (useless *simpliciter*).

I suggest we think of the "no such thing as simply being Φ" idiom as gesturing at a kind of proto- or ground-level relativism. The underlying idea is that the circumstances that confer truth or falsity on a predication of Φ tacitly involve a *further parameter* of some kind—a parameter that goes unreflected in the surface syntactic structure of the relevant predication. In such cases, what makes a predication of Φ on *x* correct or not is actually *x*'s standing in a certain relation to certain relevant items that is more complex than the surface expression reveals. The ground-level relativistic idea is that the satisfaction-conditions of a certain property or family of properties, though superficially presenting as unary, are

---

[2] See Wright (2001).

[3] That is, where neither of two irreproachably generated but (apparently) mutually inconsistent opinions need involve error. As is familiar, this idea is not easy to stabilize. For a developed discussion of the issues, see my (2006) and (2021)—this volume chapters 2 and 10.

actually implicitly relational—or more generally, are of a *higher degree* of relationality than is apparent in the surface syntax of the predications and other
characteristic forms of locution in the relevant discourse. Proto-relativism is thus
a thesis about *tacit additional relationality.*

Such a thesis is often advanced in a critical spirit, or as a reminder: ordinary
thinking is alleged to make a mistake about, or to be unaware of, or to be aware of
but fail to pay due heed to, the real degree of a certain characteristic (or family of
characteristics; say, the values). One issue for such a critic, naturally, is where
exactly to locate the putative error or oversight in ordinary thought. Is it that the
discourse in question calls, by virtue of its *literal sense*, for a characteristic of a
certain degree when all that is available is something more complex—so that,
strictly, there is sweeping untruth across the discourse? Or is it that, when
speaking literally, we do succeed in referring to the more complex properties,
but misunderstand their nature (and hence the content of our discourse)? I'll
return to this briefly below.

In sum: one root relativist idea as applied to a given region of discourse is that
its distinctive vocabulary is somehow associated with characteristics of higher
degree than manifest on the syntactic surface. But this is just the start. How do we
move from here to something more recognizably Protagorean? There are no less
than, arguably, five further moves to make.

As remarked, a tacit relationality thesis need not be to the effect that a certain
apparently unary property is in fact binary. It may be to the effect that a certain
apparently *n*-ary relational property is in fact $n + k$-ary, $k > 0$. We need a
distinction here. To fix ideas, let's consider whether the kind of *subject-sensitive*
or *interest-relative invariantism* about knowledge proposed by writers such as
Hawthorne and Stanley should be counted as a form of relativism, intuitively
understood.[4] Everyone accepts that knowledge consists in some kind of relation
involving a thinker and a true proposition. What Hawthorne and Stanley are
naturally viewed as proposing is that the relation in question is more complex
than traditionally supposed: that it involves an additional kind of parameter—one
of needs, purposes, interests, or saliences—variation in whose values between two
same-world subjects can make the difference between one being knowledgeable
that *P* while the other is not, even though their evidential achievements are
otherwise exactly the same. It may seem not unnatural to propose a relativistic
caption for this kind of view—that "knowledge is relative to need," or to saliences,
or whatever. Still, I expect that the theorists in question would scorn the description of their proposal as "relativist," and for good reason. For while *X*'s knowing
that *P*, on such a view, is indeed constituted in a complex relationship involving *X*
and the proposition that *P*, in which *X*'s needs, or interests, or whatever, are an

---

[4] Hawthorne (2004); Stanley (2005).

additional, traditionally unrecognized relatum, that point is not enough to motivate a relevant instance of the "no such thing as simply being Φ" rubric. There is no sufficient motive yet for the claim that there is no such thing as (X's) simply knowing that P. There is, in fact, no difficulty at all, for subject-sensitive invariantism, in the idea of X's simply knowing that P. True: what *determines* whether or not X knows that P may involve additional relational complexity, at least in comparison with traditional accounts. But the upshot—prescinding from other possible sources of indeterminacy—is still that X does, or doesn't, know that P, *tout court*.

So: what is it about the original examples that we gesture at by the "no such thing as simply being Φ" locution, and which goes missing in knowledge as conceived by subject-sensitive invariantism? The difference is this. The truth-conditions of judgements of the form, X knows that P, proposed by Hawthorne and Stanley do indeed involve an additional parameter, unreflected in the surface syntax of the judgement. But settlement of the semantic values of certain of the (surface) syntactic constituents of such a judgement is *itself sufficient* to settle the value(s) of the relevant additional parameter(s). Merely settle, that is, who X is, and what point in his/her history is being spoken about, and you presumably have enough to determine a specific fact about what his/her relevant needs and purposes, etc., are. In the "no such thing as simply being Φ" cases, by contrast, this—the settlement of the semantic values of other syntactic constituents of the judgement—is, precisely, not enough. In these cases, determination of the value of the extra parameter requires a contribution from factors lying outside anything settled by the semantics of the judgement concerned. There is no semantic constituent of "The Sun is moving" which denotes a frame of reference, nor are the semantic values of the constituents of that sentence, on a particular occasion of use, themselves collectively sufficient to determine a frame of reference (though other aspects of the context of use may be). Likewise, *mutatis mutandis*, for an utterance of "This screwdriver is useless." There are no semantic constituents of that sentence such that, once their semantic values—for a particular context of utterance—are determined, that must suffice to determine the relevant value of a purposes parameter, relative to which the instrument's uselessness is claimed.[5]

---

[5] Here is an opportune place to begin to emphasize the contrast between relativity of truth-value of the kind encompassed by the proposals so far made and contextuality (including indexicality) of *content*. Contextuality of content has to do with the mechanisms whereby the semantic values of the constituents of a token sentence are determined. The semantic value of a context-sensitive expression is determined as a function of its semantic character and, precisely, a context (normally, the context of an embedding sentence's use.) Relativity of truth-value, of the kind we are concerned with, also has to do with the presence of a parameter that needs to receive a specific value before any truth-evaluable claim can be entered by a use of the sentence. But the difference is that the determination of the value of this parameter is precisely independent of that of the semantic values of the constituents of the sentence, whether or not *they* are determined as a function of context (of use).

The salient next question is: what *does* determine the value of such alleged, additional parameters in relativistic cases? Of course we are hampered by the lack of uncontroversial relativistic cases—that is, examples where the operation of such a parameter, and the values it takes, can be uncontroversially agreed to be independent of the semantics of the form of sentence concerned. But there is no shortage of examples where such a view has been seriously proposed, or might at least be. And in many of these, the answer is, broadly: the intentions of the speaker. Suppose, for example, we are relativists about motion. Asked whether an overtaking car was travelling quickly, we may properly answer affirmatively even though its speed exceeded that of the car in which we are travelling by no more than five miles per hour—the 'frame of reference' is supplied by the conversational intention rather than the physical circumstances of the conversants. A little reflection, however, discloses that, at least in the kind of case most often connected with intuitively relativist ideas, it is not the situation of a speaker, qua speaker, that matters. What matters is the situation of a *judge*. Often speaker and judge are one. But when they are not, it is often in the situation, broadly construed, of the judge that the factors determining the additional parameter are to be found. Not always. If I report John as having asserted that it was raining, and you ask me if he was right, it would be expectable that your question is asking after the probity of John's assertion relative to the place of *his asserting* it.[6] But if I report him as having asserted that stewed tripe is delicious, and you ask me if he is right, it is natural to hear you as asking after a judgement of the matter by *my standards*; so here the determination of the relevant parameter goes with the judge, not the assertor. This is the point that underlies the organization of the modern debates around a conception of truth as relative to *a context of assessment*.[7]

To take stock. So far, we have diagnosed an intuitive relativism about the characteristic claims of a given discourse as involving three components: first, that the truth or falsity of such claims is constituted in states of affairs whose fully explicit characterization involves an additional degree of relationality as compared with what their surface syntactic structure would suggest. Second, the determination of the value of the extra parameters involved in this additional relationality is not a function of the determination of the semantic values of the syntactic constituents in (a tokening of) the claim. Third, what does determine their value belongs with the properties of an assessor of the claim. The result is that whether

---

[6] I am not suggesting that we are intuitively inclined to a kind of Protagoreanism about the weather. (In fact, we'll look at the example in more detail later.) Remember that at this stage we are merely working with the "no such thing as its simply being Φ" rubric. "It is snowing" and its kin at least comply with this rubric: there is indeed no such thing as it's simply snowing—it depends on *what place* is considered.

[7] My impression is that this turn is more or less wholly owing to the influence of John MacFarlane's writings.

such a claim is true will depend not just on its content, and the state of the world in other respects, but on who judges it and *their* state at the point of judgement.

This is still not Protagoreanism, however. For all the conditions so far imposed, it can happen that, for claims of a particular kind, the factors determining the values of the additional parameters are such as to settle the *same* values for all participants in any particular conversation (in however broad a sense of 'conversation'). Should that be so, there will be no possibility of intra-conversational fault-free disagreement—or at least, none occasioned purely by the relevant form of relativity. In order to provide for faultless disagreement (if indeed it is possible to make coherent provision for it), whatever settles the values taken by the extra parameters must allow them to take on distinct values for distinct assessors of a single claim—thereby generating the possibility of disagreement occasioned just by differences in the values taken. And if, in addition, disagreement is to be possibly *faultless*, the distinct values assumed for different thinkers must likewise be determined in a manner that provides no grip for the idea of fault—that is, in a fashion that does not involve bringing the assessors into liability of reproach nor underwrite any disadvantageous comparisons between the values taken (as when, for example, although X and Y are both right by their respective standards, X's standards are properly adjudged superior to Y's).

We thus arrive at the following proposal about what an intuitive, full-blown, Protagorean relativism about a property Φ—goodness, beauty, justice, obscenity—may, as it were incrementally, consist in. (We restrict attention, for simplicity's sake, to the range of atomic predications schematized by 'Φa'.)

(i) The circumstances conferring truth or falsity on any single token of 'Φa' involve an additional parameter, V, unreflected in the overt syntactic structure of the sentence.

(ii) The value taken by V is not settled by determining the semantic values (in the context of use) of the syntactic constituents of the sentence.

These first two clauses secure a basis for the "no such thing as simply being Φ" idiom.

(iii) The value taken by V is determined instead by characteristics of one who assesses the token of 'Φa', at the point of assessment.

(iv) These characteristics may vary between distinct assessors, for whom accordingly, as a result of different values taken by V, differing assessments may be appropriate of the token in question.

The latter two clauses secure a minimal Φ-relativism, involving the possibility of correct but conflicting judgements about its application in different contexts of assessment. However they do not ensure the possibility of faultless disagreement, for which we require in addition:

   (v) The variation in values taken by V may afflict participants in a single conversation.

  (vi) There is, or need be, no sense in the idea of the superiority of the assessments constrained by one value of V over those of any other.

2. Truth-Relativism

So much for relativism about Φ. Our topic, though, is relativism about *truth*. We can, of course, apply the successive steps in the foregoing more or less mechanically to the idea of truth itself. The resulting truth-relativism will hold, in the first instance, that '*is true*' (i) ascribes to a statement S a property of tacit relationality, involving (ii) an additional parameter whose values are independent of—i.e., left unsettled by determining—the semantic values of the constituents of S. Since— apart from those (deflationists) who do not reckon it to be a property at all— anyone will view being (contingently) true as implicating at least a binary relationship of some kind—viz. being *made true* by relevant circumstances— something worth describing as truth-relativism ought to involve the view that truth is at least *ternary*, with the values of the additional parameter fixed (iii) by certain of the characteristics of an assessor of S's truth. We can then escalate up through clauses (iv) to (vi), arriving eventually at the view that S's truth-value may vary with certain properties of its assessors—properties that in turn may vary irreproachably among the protagonists in a single conversation.

    That may seem more or less like the kind of thing one would want truth-relativism to be. However two issues require immediate note. First, there is the question, what exactly is truth being proposed to be ternary property *of*? What is the schematic range of 'S'? The claim of tacit additional relationality is nothing terribly startling if restricted to truth-bearers whose *content* is variable (e.g., type-sentences). It is the merest platitude that truth is relative to (varies with) content. Truth-relativism becomes potentially interesting only when the truth-value bearers are conceived as *beliefs*, or as *thoughts* (one use of "proposition," which I shall stick by here), or—as more commonly in the contemporary literature—as *utterances*, but where the historical context of the utterance (by whom, when, and where it is made, and in what collateral circumstances), and the semantics of the language, are fixed; in short, when everything is fixed which is normally conceived as sufficient to fix an utterance's content.

    This reflection—that any interesting truth-relativism operates *after* content is fixed—signals one major strategic line of resistance to it: that of (what I propose we here and now decide standardly to call) *Contextualism*.[8] Contextualism, where

---

[8] The terminology in the literature is already getting horribly tangled, and matters have not been helped by the choice of "non-indexical contextualism" by John MacFarlane to denote a type of view that is actually a variety of truth-relativism. (I'll say a little bit more about this later.)

philosophically contentious, is the thesis of some (interesting and unobvious) form of relativity of *content*. Whenever there is a case for truth-relativism—whatever form such a case may assume—there has to be theoretical space in principle for a corresponding and opposed contextualism: a thesis to the effect that the additional parameter to which the truth-relativist contends that truth is relative, is actually something variation in which leads to variation in *truth-conditional content*, with the resulting variable propositions then taking their truth-values in some unremarkable, non-relativistic manner. Thus it may be suggested, for example, that it is not that the truth of the proposition that stewed rhubarb is delicious varies as a function of the standards of taste of different linguistically competent English consumers, but rather that the *propositions* they respectively express by tokens of the sentence, "Stewed rhubarb is delicious," may so vary, and that these propositions may then take different truth-values in a straightforward, non-relativistic manner. Strategically, it is expectable that what may look like evidence for relativity of truth-value may always be *explained away* by a content-relativity thesis.[9]

It might be thought that this might be challenged as follows. Have we not in effect excluded any such diagnosis by requiring that S's apparent relativity in truth-value should manifest as a function of variation of features of assessors, or more generally of *assessment-context*? For by contrast the features that characteristically determine the content of an indexical, or otherwise context-sensitive judgement are standardly part of the *context of its making* (the context of its utterance, if it is made out loud, or of its inscription if made on paper), rather than a context of assessment. Surely, then, there will not in general be an option of explaining the kind of relativity in truth-value characterized by our clauses as turning on context-driven shifts in content.

Not so. The correct point is rather that the form of contextualism that always potentially stands opposed to truth-relativism is a *non-standard* contextualism. Any data that suggest that judgements of a certain kind do admit of variations in truth-value in the manner characterized by the clauses we listed will allow in principle of a contextualist, rather than truth-relativist explanation provided the contextualism in question is one that allows that the *content* of a single token statement need not be something unique but may vary as a function of the properties of an assessor—in other words, that what someone literally says is not determined just by standing semantic properties of the type-sentence and the circumstances of the saying but has its own relativity to parameters whose values may vary among assessment-contexts. Far from being unheard of, such a view belongs with a long 'hermeneutic' tradition in philosophical semantics.[10] An important point for our present purposes is therefore that truth-relativism is heavily invested in a conception of content that requires this tradition to be

---

[9] This reinforces Williamson's (2005) slogan that "Contextualism is relativism tamed" (though the point is not quite what Williamson had in mind).

[10] Most recently represented by the "interpretationism" of Davidson.

misguided, for the two kinds of view promise to be co-predictive in crucial cases otherwise. I'll say more about this below (Section 5).

The second salient matter is that if the general account proposed of relativism about an arbitrary property, Φ, is accepted, at least in outline, then it is, in a way, confused to seek an account of what specifically relativism about *truth* might consist in—since there is no specific such thing. For, providing that the so-called Equivalence Schema:

It is true that *S* if and only if *S*

is not called into question, the import of truth-relativism for a range of admissible substituends for '*S*' is always going to reduce to relativism about their proper subject matter, whatever it is. In the presence of the Equivalence Schema, relativism about truth for ascriptions of beauty is just relativism about beauty. And in general, relativism about truth for ascriptions of the property Φ is just relativism about Φ.

Although this is apt to impress as a point of some significance, I doubt that it is so. Certainly it would be a mistake to conclude that there is nothing for relativism about truth to be, or anything of that sort. The right conclusion is only that relativism about truth is always relativism about something else. You can be a relativist about beauty and about no other subject matter. But you cannot be a relativist about truth and about no other subject matter. Still if you are a relativist about beauty, you are a relativist about the truth of ascriptions of beauty, and some of the implications of your view—for instance its implications for content—may be easier to bring into focus when it is taken in the latter guise.

A final point of emphasis. According to the preceding perspective, truth-relativism comes by incremental stages, the earlier among which need not involve that the postulated extra parameter(s) should implicate any kind of subjectivity or anthropocentricity. Of course many of the proposals that make up the 'usual suspects'—perspective, point of view, sensibility, standards of taste—explicitly do so. But that doesn't have to go with assessment-relativity as such: one possible counterexample (to be reviewed later) is provided by Aristotelianism about the future. Here the additional element of relativity is merely time: no subjectivity need be involved in the idea that a proposition depicting a sea fight at *t* is true at *t*—if a sea fight occurs—but is untrue at any time before its occurrence. The metaphysical view in question would equally apply to future contingents at a world altogether free of human agency or perspective. In general, the connections between truth-relativism and the 'pluralism' or 'perspectivalism' of the Protagorean tradition are not straightforward: the former is neither sufficient—nor, I would argue, necessary[11]—for the latter.

---

[11] I have it in mind that the notion of a discourse's failing to exert Cognitive Command, in the sense of my (1992), is an adequate vehicle for a sober pluralism, and that its characterization requires no use of a relative truth-predicate. But I cannot elaborate this thought here. Cf. Wright (2006).

3. The Traditional Misgiving

There has always been a major question whether any interesting form of relativism about truth is so much as coherent. Everyone knows one classic kind of argument why not: if truth is relative, then the thesis that truth is relative is itself at best only relatively true, and that—for reasons which are seldom clearly stated—supposedly somehow makes it abrogate its own cogency, or dialectically undermine the position of one who advocates it. This is one form of (what we may call) the *traditional misgiving*.[12] Is it compelling?

Perhaps the most immediate observation is that the objection seems to presuppose that the relativity in relativism must be to something optional, so that the relativist may always be confounded by shifting the value of the parameter involved in such a way that the very relativistic thesis is itself incorrect. The idea seems to be that if the thesis of truth-relativism is itself only relatively true, then an opponent can always deflect the thesis by judicious parameter selection, as it were. We have already noted that this need not be so. The extra parameter(s) may be something whose values are settled independently of any contingencies of anthropology or personality. And even if not, the upshot need only be, at worst, that that truth of relativism would itself be somehow dependent on contingencies of human perspective. Such a result need no more "optionalize" the acceptability of the view than—supposing it is so—the relativity of colour to human sensibility makes it optional what to think about the colour of the sky.[13]

There are other pressures worth reviewing, distinct from the traditional misgiving, to think that global truth-relativism is incoherent. Two of them I'll label, in a Quinean spirit, 'from above' and 'from below'. Both can be elicited just by reflection upon the general form of the idea that truth is relative to a 'context of assessment'—that it is, so to speak, 'in the eyes of an assessor'—without troubling to enquire how exactly the idea of a context of assessment is to be understood, what variables it encompasses.

---

[12] Its *locus classicus* is of course Socrates' dissection of Protagoras' ideas in Plato's *Theaetetus*. The modern discussion includes Jordan (1971); Meiland (1977 and 1979); Swoyer (1982); and Siegel (1986).

[13] There is a subtler response to this form of the traditional misgiving. Reflect that the assumption that relativism is committed to regarding its own proper statement as only relatively true is unfounded in any case unless it is taken that relativism is a global thesis, extending to *all* truth-evaluable contents. However the thought that if the thesis of relativism is merely relatively true—true relative to the particular value of some relevant parameter which the relativist instantiates—then it may be seen off by calibrating oneself, as it were, to instantiate a suitable different value, seems to presuppose that what is true once such a value is settled is itself an *absolute* matter; that is why the deflection requires a different selection. Whereas a global relativism must also embrace judgements of the form that the relativistic thesis is true relative to v_i, for variable values $v_1, \ldots, v_n$, of the relevant parameter V. In that case, the contention that relativism is incorrect relative to some v_i will itself be merely relatively true. So when the anti-relativist triumphantly announces that he has so calibrated himself that, relative to his value of V, the thesis of relativism is incorrect, he is open to the rejoinder that such a claim is itself at most relatively correct and cannot therefore be presumed to hold in an arbitrary context of assessment—in particular, not that of his relativist opponent. I leave the further prosecution of this dialectic to the reader!

The pressure from below emerges like this. There is among modern proponents no suggestion that truth depends *only* on the standards of an assessor, or other aspects of a 'context of assessment'. It will also depend on an *input*: the material to be assessed (the 'circumstances of evaluation', a *world*). This input must presumably allow of propositional articulation in turn, so the question arises how the truth of *these* propositions—those that characterize the worldly input—is to be conceived. If it is conceived non-relativistically, then we are not after all dealing with global relativism. But if it too is conceived relativistically, then a regress is launched: the truth (in a context of assessment) of each relativistic proposition depends on the truth of another proposition articulating the relevant circumstances of evaluation—and when relativism is global, this too is in each case a relativistic proposition. Note, however, that this regress ascends through an infinity of types of *logically independent* proposition; for nothing follows just from the description of the circumstances of evaluation—from the input propositions—at any particular stage about which among the relevant truth-relativized propositions are true; and conversely, or so one would suppose, nothing follows just from the true relativistic propositions at each stage about exactly which of the relevant input propositions are true. The result is an epistemological problem. Mastery of the relativistic truth-conditions of propositions at each level in the regress will presumably require grasp of the truth-conditions of propositions describing the relevant kind of circumstances of evaluation, or worldly input, for them; so the threat is that mastery of the former will involve an implicitly infinitary range of propositional understanding, not in the benign sense of something recursive with a finite base but in a sense that makes it unattainable.

The pressure from above is this. In general, that P is true relative to circumstances C and parameter V looks like an *absolute* claim, whereas global truth-relativism will have to construe the truth of such claims as relative in turn. So parameters will have to be identified to which the truth of these absolute-seeming claims will itself be relative. This is very implausible in most cases, and will be additionally so if the very same parameter is just repeated. Claims, for instance, about what is true relative to certain ethical standards, if they themselves have some implicit relativity, are at least, presumably, not relative to *ethical* standards. What coherent account can be given of such an ascending hierarchy of invoked standards, or other relativistic parameters? Does it stabilize in some one Master Parameter, to which all truths above a certain level are relative? Or is there a literally endless variety?

I don't know whether either of these misgivings, or others, can be developed to the point of conclusiveness. It would be of interest finally to resolve the question whether a global truth-relativism can be a coherent stance. But I do not think it is important to do so. Even if the global thesis is incoherent, the fact is that the relativist views in contemporary debate are typically local—to epistemic modals, morals, knowledge ascriptions, or conditionals, for instance. As far as I am aware, each of the relativist positions in these local debates is quite comfortable alongside an absolutist view of the philosophical thesis that truth for the relevant locality is relative. (Indeed, as a limiting case, one might hold that truth in philosophy is absolute but relative everywhere else!)[14]

4. Truth-Relativism and Representation

We are entertaining the idea that for certain kinds of proposition, P, truth is to be thought of as fixed not merely by a world—a set of circumstances of evaluation—but by a world-cum-context-of-assessment. Call this the *ternary model*. Thus it may happen, one would suppose, where standards, say, are the relevant variable within contexts of assessment, that P is true by S_1 in w_A, but false by S_2 in w_A. Considerations not far from the territory just reviewed now suggest that the ternary model is inconsistent with P's possession of *representational* content. For what state of affairs might we think of P as representing? Nothing, presumably, that might be mentioned in a compendious description of w_A—since those matters are all, as far as they go, neutral on the question of the truth of P, whereas the obtaining of a state of affairs of a kind represented by P would have to suffice for its truth. But nor are we at liberty to think of P as representing some state of affairs of the form: *by standard so-and-so, such-and-such is the case*—for that would be to misrepresent its content. As noted, facts about standard relativity are not in general plausibly taken to be themselves standard-relative; and even when they are, they are not plausibly taken to be relative to the same standards. But what other candidate type of state of affairs is there for P to represent? It looks as though the ternary model excludes representationality.

This is hardly surprising if, as I think is so, representing is an essentially binary relation holding between a *representans* and the matter (if any) that it represents. In saying that, I am not overlooking that whether something successfully pictures, or encodes, or in some other way represents something else, may depend on conventions of representation, or a 'method of projection', variation in which may lead to the question of successful representation getting a varying answer. But of course that's an irrelevant consideration. Varying the 'method of projection' is to be compared with varying the *content*—and our interest all along has been in the nature of representation (and truth) *after* content has been fixed. That is why we

[14] An arresting argument against the coherence even of certain *local* forms of truth-relativism is offered by Paul Boghossian in his (2008). It applies to any form of truth-relativism where the claimed relativity is to standards and where standards are thought of—as seems most natural and intelligible—as consisting in a set of general propositions informing the assessment of particular cases. Considerations of space prevent me from including here the discussion of it that I offered in my presentation at the Barcelona workshop.

are focused on truth for propositions. Representation, once the conventions of representation have been fixed, surely *is* essentially a binary relation. So having the kind of content fit to represent something is—in the case of propositions—having the kind of content that fits a bearer to stand in a binary *true-of* relation. Propositions for which the ternary truth model is appropriate cannot, on that account, have that kind of content.

I do not want to belabour the point, but maybe it is worth pausing over. Cannot representation, it might be objected, be *perspectival*? Indeed, it is suggestive that at least one writer in the vanguard of the recent surge of interest in relativism uses exactly the term, "perspective," as a catch-all to denote the kind of parameters to which relative truth is supposedly relative *to*.[15] Perhaps only perspective-free representation is essentially binary. But clearly the fidelity of, say, a visual representation—a diagram, or a photograph—to the shape of an object can depend upon settling a notional perspective. For example, Figures 4.1 and 4.2 are potentially both adequate representations of one and the same solid object once it is specified that the respectively implied angles of view are such that first the point *A*, and then the point *C*, are to be thought of as representing that part of the object that is closest to an observer; but not if it is given that the closest points are *A* and *D*. Successful representation can be and often is perspectival—that is, in the present kind of example, relative to an implied angle of view—in this kind of way. So, it may be thought, it does *not* go with the very idea of representation that it be a purely binary relation; and there is, correspondingly, no reason why a theorist who thinks of the truth of propositions in some region of discourse as involving relativity to an assessment parameter should thereby foreclose on their representationality either.

The analogy has the additional feature, attractive for the relativist purpose, that there is a sense in which the two figures are *incompatible*: they cannot both be accepted as accurate representations of one and the same figure from any single perspective (implied angle of view). On the other hand, they can both be accurate from a suitable pair of perspectives, and a pair of thinkers, occupying those perspectives can, in respectively endorsing their accuracy, both be right.

Is it along the lines of this analogy that we should try to fashion our thinking about truth-relativism about propositions and the idea of faultless disagreement? Well, only if we can think of the 'contents' carried by such figures as comparable to propositions. We have an analogue of the sought-after idea—that of a species of proposition which is representational in content all right, but where the fact of actual representation turns on perspective, or point of view—only if we suppose that the content of the figures is invariant under changes in perspective or point of view. It is here, obviously, that the analogy breaks down. Of course *something* is

<hr>

[15] Kölbel (2002).

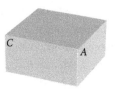

Figure 4.1.

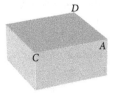

Figure 4.2.

invariant under changing perspective. The diagrams don't change shape, and the lines continue to represent edges, and so on. But it is clear that what is unchanging is not representational content: i.e., how the object is being represented as shaped. Suppose you are told that Figure 4.1 *is* an accurate representation of an aspect of some solid object; what do you thereby learn about the object's shape? The answer *varies with perspective*. If you are also told that the implied angle of view is such that point *A* on the diagram represents the nearest point of the object to the observer, you learn that three of its sides are configured in a way consistent with its being a cuboid. If you are told only that point *A* on the diagram does not represent the nearest point of the solid to the observer, you do not learn that and then there are any number of other possibilities. Perspective—the implied angle of view—in such cases is accordingly first a parameter in the determination of *representational content*, and only secondarily in the determination of whether the figure successfully represents. Whereas—to stress again—truth-relativism at the level of propositions sees truth-value as variable in tandem with variation in some relevant parameter *after* content has been fixed.

There is no doubt a lot more to be said, but—with a qualification to follow—I think we can reasonably take it that further reflection should be constrained by the following *Non-Representationality Conjecture*:

Truth-relativism, construed along the lines of the ternary model, excludes the representationality of the propositional contents concerned.

A number of questions are pertinent if the Conjecture is accepted. First, any good argument for a (local) truth-relativism at the level of propositions should implicate grounds for denying that the contents in question are representational. One crux for representational content for which I have argued elsewhere is the constraint of *Cognitive Command*: a constraint which a discourse satisfies just in case it's *a priori* that differences of opinion within it—where they do not fall among certain admissible exceptions: difference of opinion due to vagueness, for instance, or idiosyncratically varying thresholds of evidence—will turn on something properly viewed as a *cognitive shortcoming*. If, as I have argued,[16] Cognitive Command is a necessary condition for representationality, then one natural channel for argument for truth-relativism will be to make a case for a failure of Cognitive Command. It may not be the only possible channel. However, whatever argument is advanced if informed by the ternary model, must—in the presence of the Non-Representationality Conjecture—somehow carry the conclusion that the discourse in question is not representational.

There is also a good question about why, if the Non-Representationality Conjecture is correct, anyone should want to propose truth-relativism for any of the broadly anti-realist reasons that have been traditional.[17] For if there is a solid case that a particular discourse is not representational in content, that *already* undermines the realism associated with absolutism. If ethical discourse, for instance, is not representational, we already have the conclusion that there are no absolute moral facts, since if there were such facts, they would have to allow of representation by moral thought. What need, then, to claim an additional relativity in the notion of moral truth? Some deflated or minimalist line of goods will serve all purposes worth serving.

The connections between relativism and representationality are complicated, however, by the realization that not everything that's been presented as an example of truth-relativism is happily thought of in terms of the ternary model. Consider, for example, the Aristotelian view of future contingents, recently argued by John MacFarlane to provide an example of a view which calls for the kind of truth-relativism he thinks may be coherent and stable.[18] Suppose at t_0 that X asserts that there will be a sea fight at t_2, $= P$. According to the Aristotelian, it will be correct for an assessor, Y, at t_1, $< t_2$, to assert that X's assertion that P was untrue. It will be correct because there is nothing at t_0 or at t_1 to render P true—the future is open. But at t_2 it will be appropriate for Y to assert that X's assertion that P was true if—as we may suppose—a sea fight is then in full swing. So the very same content—that of X's assertion at t_0—is correctly assessed as untrue at t_1 but true at t_2.

Now it is of course perfectly true that we *can* cast the example in the form of the ternary model, with *time of assessment* in the slot occupied by 'perspective', or 'standards', in the other kinds of case. We can, if we like, include time of

<hr />

[16] Wright (1992, p. 88 and *passim*).
[17] Of course these contrast with the putative empirico-linguistic reasons prominent in MacFarlane's writings and those of other recent authors in the field.
[18] MacFarlane (2003 and 2008).

assessment as one more variable under the umbrella of 'context of assessment' in the ternary model. But it seems to me that this is a bad idea if we want to avoid confusion. It's certainly a bad idea if we are persuaded of the correctness of the Non-Representationality Conjecture, since the Aristotelian does not at all mean to contest the representationality of ordinary tensed discourse about mundane events like sea fights. What he means to contest, rather, is the ordinary *static metaphysics* of the being of such events: his view is that the future unfolds not in the sense of *revealing* itself as we reach it in time, but in the sense of, literally, *becoming*.

Aristotelianism is not at all a view about the *degree* of utterance/propositional truth—it is, for example, consistent with the most robustly correspondence conception of truth. On the contrary, it's a view about the metaphysical behaviour of the *truth-conferrers*. We can, if we like, caption it by saying that it holds that truth is relative to time—but what it really holds is that the *population of facts that constitutes the actual world* changes with time. The ternary model, properly understood, fixes the worldly parameter and *then* allows truth to vary as a function of 'context of assessment'. By contrast, what's happening in the Aristotelian metaphysics of time is that the *world itself* is varying with time, and truth at a time is varying accordingly. There is no genuinely additional parameter of context of assessment. Aristotelian truth-relativism is a kind of Fool's truth-relativism: a thesis about the nature of the world misconceived as a thesis about the degree of the truth-relation.

Once that distinction is in the open, it's salient that the Aristotelian model could also be extended to the standards-and-taste varieties of truth-relativism. What, in effect, the Aristotelian view provides for is a plurality not merely of possible but of *actual* worlds, as indexed by the class of propositions that are true at them. The world at t_1 and the world at t_2 are both actual—that is why P changes its truth-status as the passage of time takes us from one to the other. But once we have the prototype of time supplying different locations for actual worlds, what is to stop us allowing other forms of locality as well? We might for example permit the actual world *at Williamson*—that is the actual world as reflected in Timothy Williamson's gustatory standards—to exist simultaneously with the actual world *at Wright*, that is, the actual world as reflected in Crispin Wright's gustatory standards. The proposition that stewed rhubarb is delicious can then be true at the one aesthetic location, so to say, and untrue at the other, just as the proposition about the sea fight can be true at t_2 but untrue at t_1. No need, in this case, to resort to a context of assessment parameter in order to accommodate the truth-relativist impulse—truth can be old-fashioned truth-at-a-world, *simpliciter*. The relativism surfaces, rather, in the thought that there is no single actual world but a plurality of them.

No doubt these worlds may substantially overlap. The thought that truth-relativism can plausibly only be a local doctrine can be accommodated within this framework by insisting that some denizens of any actual world will be denizens of all. Much of each actual world, perhaps, is made for us, but—the picture will be—we, each of us, individually and collectively, by our sensibilities, tastes, and perspectives, give rise to locally variable actualities, partially creating our own domains of truth-conferrers.

Maybe the right conclusion is that we need to distinguish two utterly different forms of propositional truth-relativism. One offers a package of the ternary model of truth for selected regions of thought and discourse, together with non-representationality of content, an implicit distinction from non-relativistic areas of thought and talk, and a single actual world fit for representation. The other says nothing unorthodox about truth or content; it is, for example, consistent with both correspondence and deflationist accounts as holding across the board. But it abandons the idea of a single, comprehensive Tractarian world—a totality of all facts.

No doubt this distinction complicates the question of motivation. It also complicates the question of obligation: a good argument for truth-relativism about some class of propositions must, it appears, either enforce the thought that they lack representational content—so some other conception of their content will be owing—or it must enforce a pluralistic conception of the actual. Again, we should keep these points in mind when reviewing the considerations marshalled by those who are sympathetic towards (local) truth-relativism.

5. Weather-Report Relativism and Non-Representationality

The point still stands, it seems, that a theorist who is drawn to relativism about some region of discourse but wants no traffic with a pluralistic conception of the actual, is committed to thinking of the contents with which the discourse in question characteristically trades as non-representational. Call such a content an NRP (non-representational proposition). It is clearly an obligation on the relativist to say more about this species of content. We already remarked on the relativist's obligation to make a case that these contents are genuinely shared across disputes in which the protagonists differ merely in the values taken by relevant parameters in their respective assessment-contexts; equivalently, to argue against any form of opposed contextualist suggestion that it is *content* that varies across such disputes. An account is also owing of the aptitude of such contents for all the usual propositional-logical and attitudinal constructions: they must be negatable, conditionalizable, believable, supposable, doubtable, and so on, and a story must be told about the commitments of one who takes any of these attitudes to an NRP. It is my impression that much more needs to be said to address these issues. But I will not try to explore them further here.[19]

---

[19] Those who assert a relativistic proposition presumably commit themselves to its correctness in the assessment-context that coincides with the context of its assertion. The crucial question is what commitments are undertaken with respect to other contexts of assessment. MacFarlane has proposed that such an assertor commits to the continuing assertibility of the proposition in question in *any*

What I want to canvass in this section is one, in some ways disappointingly deflationary account of what NRPs could turn out to be. Consider again the example of reports of the weather of the type, "It is snowing," "It is windy," etc. For reasons to be outlined shortly, these do not seem promising as candidates for truth-relativistic construal. But they certainly pass the most basic of our intuitive tests: there is indeed, plausibly, no such thing as its simply being the case that it is snowing or not—there is the possibility of a true or false verdict whether it is snowing only when the issue is understood to pertain to a particular location. So while no one has, to the best of my knowledge, seriously proposed a relativistic account of weather reports, it is very easy to envisage the beginnings of one. The relevant assessment-contextual parameter would simply be place: "It is snowing" as uttered by T would be correctly assessed by A as true just in case there is snow falling at the place and time of A's assessment.

It will, of course, be immediately objected that this gets the truth-conditions of such utterances grossly wrong: that what, for competent judges, determines whether or not T speaks truly is not *their* meteorological predicament, at the time and place of assessment, but that of T at the time and place of the utterance. But that claim is certainly not exceptionless. Invited while in St. Andrews to express an opinion on the weather currently in New York, I may venture simply, "It is mild and raining." So the immediate objection was only a first approximation. A better formulation would be that what determines the place with respect to which an utterance of "It is raining" is to be assessed is the intention of the speaker, not the context of an assessor.

Even this, however, is not the real objection to weather-report relativism. The point about speaker intention can be conceded consistently with the broader spirit of relativism. That broader spirit requires only that "It is raining" and its family be viewed as expressing propositions whose truth-evaluability then depends upon settling a place. This place is left to be determined as *some* kind of function of context of assessment. But there is no particular reason why that function should require it to coincide with the place of assessment. It can be that the way in which context of assessment determines the relevant place is, sometimes or normally, via interpretation of the intentions of an utterer. This is still relativism: one and the same proposition is still conceived as expressed by utterances of "It is raining" in different locations and its truth-value is still conceived as relative to place. It is just that (the rules of assessment determine that) the relevant places are the places that the respective utterers intend.[20]

assessment-context, no matter what the value of the relevant parameter in that context. There are theoretical pressures towards this proposal but it seems like an extravagant, even an irrational commitment to undertake. See MacFarlane (2005a, §5).

[20] This is actually an example of the extended form of relativism rather unhappily termed "non-indexical contextualism" by John Macfarlane. See especially his (2005b).

Nevertheless, this whole direction stands opposed to what may seem like utter commonsense on the matter. According to commonsense, when you truly utter (A) "It is raining" in New York and at the same time I truly utter (B) "It is not raining" in St. Andrews, it is not that we disagree faultlessly—rather, we do (or need) not disagree *at all*. According to the extended relativist proposal, we respectively affirm and deny the same content—hence the disagreement—but that content requires assessment with respect to different places—hence faultlessness. And against this, it would be normal to deny the first: to report us instead as having been *speaking of* different places, the lack of any overt reference to place in the uttered sentences notwithstanding. The relativist treatment mislocates the parameter of place when it leaves it to be settled by assessment-context, whatever the proposed mechanism of settlement. Rather, it belongs in the *content* of the propositions respectively expressed and is settled by that.

That's the respect in which weather-report relativism essentially offends commonsense intuition. Naturally, the commonsensical view engenders theoretical obligations. If it is right, then in uttering the weather reports (A) and (B), we speak of different places using forms of words that explicitly contain no vocabulary of place. An account needs to be given of how this is achieved. Familiarly, the matter is contentious. One proposal is that a reference to place is an *unarticulated constituent* of the propositions expressed.[21] Another is that the reference to place occurs at the level of the deep syntax of the uttered sentences—that there is, so to say, a hidden indexical expression for which context of utterance serves to supply a reference in the normal kind of way. There is much to say about the content of these contrasting proposals and their respective advantages and problems.[22] But on both of them, the contents respectively affirmed by utterance (A) and negated by utterance (B), when identified with the propositions expressed, are not the same.

A serious relativistic proposal about weather descriptions will hold that the content affirmed by (A) and negated by (B) *is* the same, but that it is a content which is truth-evaluable only when relativized to a place. However, this proposal stands opposed to both those just adumbrated only when the mention of contents is construed as a reference to *propositions*; that is, to complete, truth-evaluable thoughts. The relativist proposal takes it that tokens of "It is raining" and its ilk express fully articulated, complete propositions, albeit propositions whose truth-values vary with a parameter which is unrepresented in their logical form. So there is an evident question: why assume that tokens of those sentences express any such *fully articulated* propositions? The alternative is to think of the assignment of a value to the place parameter as serving to *complete* the propositions, rather than

---

[21] See Perry (1998).
[22] For further discussion, see Perry (1998); Stanley (2000); Recanati (2002); and Cappelen and Lepore (2007).

set up the means to assess it—completing it, for example, by assigning a referent either to an unarticulated constituent or to a hidden indexical for place.

The exact details of the opposing view do not matter. The crucial point is that the relativist is making an assumption in taking his distinctive direction against such views. For the case of weather reports, it is the assumption that "It is raining" and its ilk provide a fully articulate and explicit expression of the logical form of the relevant, allegedly truth-relativistic propositions. In this case, it is, as noted, most people's inclination to regard the assumption as false. But the crucial point is that this general form of theoretical dispute must arise *in every instance*—every region of discourse—where some kind of case for assessment-relativity can be made. For wherever there is such a case, there will be the option of supposing either that the propositions expressed by the targeted sentences contain unarticulated constituents referring to values of the assessment-contextual parameter which features in the relativist account, or that they contain hidden indexicals with the same range of reference, whose values are settled by features of an assessment-context. The latter would, admittedly, be an unusual kind of indexical. But perhaps it is to the existence of such unusual indexicals that linguistic data that might otherwise seem to support relativism would be best construed as pointing.

To fix ideas, suppose we are inclined to a relativistic account of taste evaluations like "Stewed rhubarb is delicious," according to which a single proposition thereby fully explicitly expressed is correctly evaluated as true by Tim Williamson's gustatory standards but false by mine. According to the "hidden indexicals" proposal, there is no such single proposition so evaluated. Rather the proposition expressed is of the deep syntactic form: [stewed rhubarb is delicious by x], where 'x' marks a place for an indexical for standards, whose value is normally[23] fixed as the standards of one assessing the claim. So Tim and I evaluate different propositions, one making mention of his gustatory standards and the other making mention of mine. And it is the same on the unarticulated propositional constituents proposal; the difference is merely that the references to standards respectively effected by the propositions concerned correspond to nothing in the syntactic structure, even the deep syntactic structure, of the sentence but are supplied by pragmatic factors which vary in the two assessment-contexts.

It is this latter train of thought that promises the "disappointingly deflationary" account of NRPs advertised at the start of this section. On this proposal, "Rhubarb is delicious" expresses *no* complete, truth-evaluable proposition. The content common to "Tim thinks that rhubarb is delicious" and "Crispin doubts that rhubarb is delicious" is indeed non-representational. But it is also non-truth-evaluable. What are truth-evaluable are the propositions that uses of the above

---

[23] Evidence: suppose you have never tasted rhubarb and ask whether Tim spoke truly when he said that rhubarb is delicious. Your interest is unlikely to be in whether he spoke truly by *his* standards.

sentences pragmatically convey as the respective contents of Tim's and Crispin's attitudes. But these are not NRPs: they are regular relational propositions about what passes muster by standards they mention; they represent, and—we may presume—they take their truth-values absolutely. On this view, there are no NRPs. The forms of words that seem to express them do not, semantically, express propositions at all. Rather they are, so to speak, sawn-off expressions of proposition radicals—as it were, propositional *amputees*—whose completion is accomplished by the pragmatics of assessment, and whose completed products are regular propositions, true or false in regular ways.

6. Can Truth-Relativism Be Motivated by Purely Linguistic Data?

Let us nevertheless persist with the idea that there are genuine NRPs—full-fledged propositions for which truth is relativistic in some parameter, V, of assessment-context. To each such proposition corresponds a range of explicitly relational propositions (ERPs), each of the form: it is true that P relative to value v of V ("That rhubarb is delicious is true relative to Tim Williamson's gustatory standards," "That there could be snipers over the rise is true relative to the information possessed by the platoon commander"). ERPs, it is natural to think, will not in general themselves be candidates for relativistic truth, and indeed there are worries, some canvassed earlier, one to be outlined below,[24] about the coherence of views that allow otherwise. However they will all be associated, naturally, with possible assessment as true or false. So here is a question we can ask about a given species of (putative) NRPs and the corresponding range of ERPs: must any context in which it is possible competently to assess an ERP in the latter range itself supply a value, v, for each assessment parameter, V, relative to which the relevant NRPs take their truth-values? In other words, if you are in position competently to assess a claim of the form

P is true relative to value v of parameter V,

must your situation itself incorporate a value for V, and so commit you to your own assessment of the truth-value of P?

A quick review of the types of discourse for which modern truth-relativists have proposed the view shows a mixed picture. There is, for example, no particular reason why a subject with no gustatory standards or predilections—perhaps someone born with no taste buds—should be hampered when it comes to assessing "Stewed rhubarb is delicious by Tim Williamson's standards"; she can

---

[24] In the Postscript (Section 7).

have exactly the same evidence—Tim's sayings, actions, and reactions—as the rest of us. Similarly, there seems no reason why an utterly amoral subject—one party to no moral standards whatever—should be hampered when it comes to the assessment of claims of the form, "Incest is wrong by Western standards," or "Welfare-maximizing punishment of the innocent is permissible by strict utilitarian standards." But suppose we take a relativistic view of, say, logic, holding that, notwithstanding a uniform understanding of its logical vocabulary, one and the same propositional schema, e.g. Peirce's Law, is valid by classical standards but invalid by intuitionistic ones. Here the assessment of the relevant ERPs itself demands propositional inference, and hence implicates a set of rules of inference. So there has, presumably, to be an answer to the question whether Peirce's Law may be validated by just those rules. Whether that commits an assessor to a view about Peirce's Law depends, of course, on what the answer to that question is. If the answer is "no," the matter will turn on whether the assessor takes it that the rules he is using to assess the two ERPs are the strongest sound such rules. So logical relativism offers a kind of intermediate, *partially committed*, case, lying between *neutral* cases like, seemingly, ethics and aesthetics, where competent second-order assessment—assessment of an ERP—need involve no commitment to any particular first-order assessment—assessment of the associated NRP—and cases where there always has to be such a commitment. It is the latter that I am calling *fully committed* cases. Are there any examples of this kind?

Certainly, at least according to proposals made by contemporary relativists. Suppose, for example, that epistemic possibility claims, "It might be that *P*," take their truth-values relative to the state of information of an assessor.[25] The relevant ERPs then take the form, "It is true that it might be that *P*, relative to state of information *I*." But to assess any such claim, you have of course yourself to be in *some* kind of state of information; and that, whatever it is, will itself presumably mandate a verdict about the epistemic possibility of *P*. So if truth for epistemic possibility claims is assessment-relative in this way, then they provide an example of a fully committed case.

It will presumably be similar with the view that knowledge-attributions are assessment-relative[26]—that whether *X* knows that *P* depends upon the standards of an assessor. Suppose you are in position to assess whether *X* knows that *P* relative to certain demanding standards for knowledge. Then your situation will presumably both involve awareness of what comprises *X*'s relevant information

---

[25] They don't always—there are apparent cases of *deferential* uses, where an assessor reports, or colludes in a possibility for an audience or third party: a Red platoon commander may order his trainee soldiers to "Keep down: there could be snipers on the hill," even though he knows there are no Blue positions in the area. For sympathetic proposal of assessment-relativism for epistemic modals, see MacFarlane (2003a and 2011); Egan, Hawthorne, and Weatherson (2005); Egan (2005); and Stephenson (2005). Critical discussions of epistemic possibility relativism include Dietz (2008) and Wright (2007). We will focus on this example in a moment.

[26] See MacFarlane (2005a).

and cognitive state and a set of standards—perhaps less demanding—of your own for the ascription of knowledge that P to X. So you will be committed to a view about whether X does know that P.

There is a third very salient example: precisely the (putatively) Aristotelian view that the truth-value of contingent propositions concerning singular events is relative to *time* of assessment. We are, ineluctably, stationed in time. So an Aristotelian thinker called upon to assess the truth-value of a proposition of the form, 'What Aristipides asserted at t_0 by saying, "There will be a sea-battle tomorrow," is (tenseless) true at t_1', will himself occupy a station in time relative to which Aristipides' prediction will have or will not have (yet) come to fruition; and so will be committed to his own assessment of that prediction.

What is the interest of the notion of a fully committed case? That there is an interesting difficulty about characterizing what, in principle, would constitute good linguistic evidence for a truth-relativistic semantic treatment of any region of discourse where it would have the effect that the discourse in question was fully committed. Consider for example, the way that John MacFarlane and others have actually tried to motivate relativism about epistemic possibility claims. MacFarlane writes

> Here's the puzzle. When we claim 'It might be the case that p' and later come to know that not-p (for example, by being told this by a trusted authority), we tend to *withdraw* our earlier assertion and regard what we said as false. That is, we tend to assess past assertions containing epistemic modals against our *current* epistemic situations, rather than the epistemic situations in which they were made. Consider the following dialogue:

Dialogue 1

Sally: Joe might be in Boston. (= It might be the case that Joe is in Boston.)

George: He can't be in Boston. (= It is not the case that it might be the case that Joe is in Boston.) I saw him in the hall five minutes ago.

Sally: Oh, then I guess I was wrong.

> This is not what one would expect if the standard semantics for epistemic modals were correct. If the truth-conditional content of Sally's original claim is just that she does not (at the time) know that Joe is not in Boston, then she should not retract this claim upon learning that Joe is not in Boston. What she said is still true, even though she could not *now* truly say "Joe might be in Boston." So if the contextualist semantics is correct—the Simple version, at any rate—then we should expect the last line of the dialogue to be:

Sally: Oh, okay. So he can't be in Boston. Nonetheless, when I said "Joe might be in Boston," what I said was true, and I stand by that claim.

I hope you'll agree that it would be odd and unnatural for Sally to say this.[27]

Let's grant—although I think the point is questionable—that it would be "odd and unnatural" for Sally so to speak. Then that is evidence that we do not understand Sally's original assertion, "Joe might be in Boston," as making a claim about the limitations of her then current state of information, and hence also, if the standard semantics implies otherwise, evidence *against* the standard semantics. But how exactly is this evidence *for* a relativistic semantic treatment? The pattern of the exchange is simply

A: P
B: [new info]
A: I was wrong.

together with an impression that it would be "odd and unnatural" for *A* to replace his second remark with

A: OK, not-*P*. Nevertheless when I said '*P*', what I thereby said was true and I stand by it.

If the latter is incongruous, that does indeed tell against imputing utterance context-sensitivity to the content of tokens of '*P*'. Nevertheless: how could data as austere as this motivate any form of relativism? What is schematized is merely something that fits the withdrawal of any defeasibly grounded, non-context-sensitive assertion.

If a propensity to exchanges of the kind MacFarlane illustrates is to provide any motive at all to start thinking of the truth of epistemic possibility claims as context-of-assessment-relative, it has to be supplemented. And what it needs supplementation with, if relativism is to be the right way to go, is evidence of some kind that, her withdrawal of it notwithstanding, Sally's initial claim is also regarded by competent speakers as having been in some way *perfectly proper*—and this not just in the sense of having been justified though incorrect when she made it. Correctness varies with context of assessment: that claim is the very heart and soul of truth-relativism. So that is what we need to see evidenced in linguistic practice if linguistic practice is to provide evidence for relativism. We have to identify some feature of what strikes us as acceptable linguistic practice which would somehow evince practitioners' recognition of the propriety of Sally's initial claim consistently with that of her subsequent retraction of it. Absent any such feature, there is, so far as I can see, absolutely no call for a truth-relativistic response to the (alleged) linguistic data adduced by MacFarlane. We should

---

[27]   MacFarlane (2003a).

merely conclude that Sally made an epistemic possibility claim at t_1 that, at t_2, she recognizes to have been incorrect. She was just wrong before.

The point is simple and general: impressive evidence for the assessment-relativity of truth in some region of discourse has to include some kind of evidence of co-variation of truth-value with the values of an assessment-contextual parameter. You can't make a case based purely on patterns of *correction*. There has also to be some kind of evidence of *concession* to the propriety of claims made in other assessment--contexts—a manifestation of relativistic *even-handedness*. The pattern of linguistic practice—again, I am not, for the sake of argument, challenging its reality—adduced by MacFarlane is merely one-sided, and accordingly unconvincing.[28]

Very well. So now we need to ask what in principle could amount to such even-handedness suggestive evidence. What is needed is some characteristic means whereby speakers can express an appropriate kind of equality of respect for contrasting opinions which originate in differences in the values taken by relevant parameters of assessment. But the problem is that if the discourse in question is *fully committed*, any assessor of such an opinion is liable to be stuck with an opinion of his own on the matter in question. Sally has no option, after George's intervention, but to regard her initial claim, that Joe might be in Boston, as false. So the strongest thing she could say by way of respect for it is that she was right to endorse it in the informational state she occupied when she made it. Unfortunately, that kind of endorsement does nothing to distinguish it from any claim that is appropriately advanced on the basis of certain evidence and subsequently withdrawn on the basis of altered evidence. It is, to repeat, no evidence of truth-relativity. Moreover—the crucial point—because discourse of epistemic possibility is fully committed, no other assessor of her claim is going to be able to do any better. Anyone in a position to judge that she spoke correctly on the basis of the information originally available to her will be mandated in an opinion of their own about Joe's possible whereabouts at the time. If it conflicts with hers, they too will be restricted to the form of endorsement of her claim—viz. that she was right to say what she did in the informational state she occupied at the time—which she herself can offer after George's intervention. That's of no inter-est, as emphasized. But if it coincides with hers, it is of even less interest, from the point of view of one seeking evidence for relativism.

Things look somewhat better if the discourse is neutral. In a neutral discourse, it is still true that a thinker, T, for whom a relevant assessment parameter shifts to a different value will be in no position to endorse a now discarded proposition in any way that evinces the distinctive form of concession to its former relative correctness that we are looking for. But what may be possible is for a third party,

---

[28] Indeed, it is not merely one-sided. It is actually an *awkwardness* for the relativist that Sally corrects her former self—"Oh. Then I guess I was wrong"—and is not content merely to revise her verdict: "Oh. Then I guess that is wrong." I discuss this further in Wright (2007).

U, whose own assessment-context takes no value for the relevant parameter, correctly to judge both that each of T's verdicts is correct in the context of assessment in which it is made and—the crucial extra—that neither of T's verdicts is superior in any respect to the other; or superior, at least, in any respect assessable by U. It is the unavailability of the latter claim in fully committed discourses that sets up the obstacle to the relevant kind of even-handed evidence.

However we need a final pair of cautionary distinctions. First, notice that even in such neutral cases, it will take collateral philosophical work to build a case out of the accepted propriety of the relevant kind of even-handed third-party assessments that a relativistic conception of truth operates in the discourse in question. The evidence will be just that a competent neutral assessor, U, can encounter cases where they can recognize first, that each of two conflicting verdicts is sanctioned by differing values of the relevant parameter, V—different standards, let's suppose—operating in the respective contexts of their authors; and second, that neither verdict is based on any shortcoming that U can detect from her position of standard neutrality. That is perfectly consistent with U's position of standard neutrality being conceived by practitioners of the discourse as one of *cognitive limitation*; more abstractly, it may be that assessment-contexts which are neutral on the parameter V are, just for that reason, thought of as contexts from which the fact that makes one or other of a relevant pair of conflicting verdicts absolutely correct is *invisible*.

Second, it is in any case—surely—not for *linguistic* evidence to decide whether or not a relativistic view of, say, epistemic possibility claims is appropriate. The most that might be manifest in features of our linguistic practice involving such claims is that *we understand them* as trafficking in assessment-relative contents. We are some considerable way short, I have been suggesting, of a model of the kind of linguistic data that might distinctively manifest even that. But even if we had such a model, and found it exemplified in speakers' practice, that would indicate no more than that they *implicitly conceived* of truth in the region of discourse in question as assessment-relative. That conception could still be philosophically completely unmotivated, or utterly mistaken.[29]

7. Postscript

As emphasized, once any global Protagorean ambition is abandoned, and truth-relativism is viewed as an at most locally appropriate view, ERPs, it is natural to

[29] Thanks to participants at the Barcelona workshop and to members of the Arché 2005–6 Pilot seminar on Contextualism and Relativism for comments and questions on earlier drafts. Special thanks to Paul Boghossian and Sven Rosenkranz for detailed critical discussion and to John MacFarlane for generous written comments.

expect, will in general be regarded as absolute. But there is one striking exception. The metaphysics of the Open Future is *prima facie* in tension with the so-called Truth-Value Links—the principles which articulate certain necessary connections of truth-value between variously tensed utterances conceived as made at different times. Consider for instance

"There is a Cup Final today" is true at Day_2 if and only if "There will be a Cup Final tomorrow" was true at Day_1.

At first blush, it looks as though this must fail left to right on the Aristotelian view—for isn't the whole point that the left-hand side can be true today while the quoted sentence on the right was not true but *indeterminate* yesterday? Yet a willingness to swallow that upshot appears incompatible with acknowledging the existence of a systematic link between the truth-values—and hence the contents— of differently tensed statements uttered at different times,[30] and hence puts in jeopardy the entire basis of our understanding of tense. So what Aristotelians tend to say is that properly to absorb the idea of the Open Future and of the truth-conferrers for future contingents as subject to becoming must involve subjecting truth-conferral to the very constraints expressed by the truth-value links. Thus if "There is a Cup Final today" is true today, then it is also true that "There will be a Cup Final tomorrow" was true yesterday—but the latter is *itself* something that has only *become* true today, with the actual occurrence of the game. What *was* the case is likewise subject to becoming as the future unfolds.

   Set this proposal in the context of a truth-relativistic treatment of contingent propositions about singular events, where the relevant assessment-contextual parameter is just time of assessment. We already noted that, so conceived, the discourse in question is fully committed. Now in addition, we are introducing second-order relativity. The ERPs for this discourse take the form:

"*P*" is (tenselessly) true at *t*.

And what, it is being suggested, goes with saving the intuitive semantics of tense in conjunction with proper absorption of the Open Future is to hold that the truth-values of these ERPs are *themselves* relative to time of assessment. So while we can truly say *now* that it is true that

(I)   "There will be a Cup Final tomorrow" was true yesterday,

---

[30] Dummett (1978, pp. 366–7).

the proper assessment *yesterday* of the same content, viz. that then expressed by a token of

(II)   '"There will be a Cup Final tomorrow" is true today',

would have rated it false; for "There will be a Cup Final tomorrow" was then indeterminate.

Well, this is a simple contradiction. For if "There will be a Cup Final tomorrow" was true yesterday, so was "'There will be a Cup Final tomorrow' is true today." So in endorsing (I), we commit ourselves to saying that (II) was true yesterday. So we cannot consistently go on to say that it wasn't!

This is a reinforced version of the predicament of the epistemic possibility relativist latterly reviewed. There, the fully committed nature of the discourse meant that when a pair of thinkers in distinct assessment-contexts correctly return conflicting verdicts on an epistemic possibility claim, there is no way that a third party can avoid disagreement with one of them, so no possibility of the kind of even-handed assessment of their disagreement that relativism ought intuitively to make possible. What the third party can at least do, in that case, is to endorse each of the corresponding ERPs. In the present case, however, even this is not possible. Whatever my station in time, D_1, it will enjoin not only a view—indeterminate if $D_1 < D_2$; or true, let's suppose, if $D_1 \geq D_2$—of the truth-status enjoyed by "There will be a Cup Final tomorrow" at D_1 but also a view—likewise indeterminate so untrue if $D_1 < D_2$; or true if $D_1 \geq D_2$—of the truth-status of "'There will be a Cup Final tomorrow' is true at D_1." Accordingly, the Aristotelian relativist—at least so long as he determines to preserve the letter of the truth-value links—not merely lacks the resources for an even-handed evaluation of conflicting but respectively context-relatively correct claims about contingent events. He cannot so much as give consistent expression to their being context-relatively correct.[31]

References

Boghossian, Paul (2008), "What is Normative Relativism?," in Manuel García-Carpintero and Max Kölbel (eds.), *Relative Truth*, Oxford: Oxford University Press.

Cappelen, H and Lepore, E (2007), "The Myth of Unarticulated Constituents," in M. O'Rourke and C. Washington (eds.), *Essays in Honor of John Perry* Cambridge, MA: MIT Press, 199–214.

Dietz, Richard (2008), "Epistemic Modals and Correct Disagreement," in in M. García-Carpintero and M. Kölbel (eds.), *Relative Truth*, Oxford: Oxford University Press, 239–64.

---

[31] This point is elaborated in Wright and Moruzzi (2008).

Dummett, Michael (1978), "The Reality of the Past," in *Truth and Other Enigmas*, London: Duckworth, 358–74.

Egan, Andy (2005), "Epistemic Modals, Relativism and Assertion," in J. Gajewski, V. Hacquard, B. Nickel, and S. Yalcin (eds.), *New Work on Modality*, MIT Working Papers in Linguistics, vol. 51, 35–61.

Egan, Andy, John Hawthorne, and Brian Weatherson (2005), "Epistemic Modals in Context," in G. Preyer and P. Peters (eds.), *Contextualism in Philosophy*, Oxford: Oxford University Press, 131–69.

Gajewski, Jon, Valentine Hacquard, Bernhard Nickel, and Seth Yalcin (2005), *New Work on Modality*, MIT Working Papers in Linguistics, v. 51.

Hawthorne, John (2004), *Knowledge and Lotteries*, Oxford: Oxford University Press.

Jordan, James (1971), "Protagoras and Relativism: Criticisms Bad and Good," *Southwestern Journal of Philosophy* 2, 7–29.

Kölbel, Max (2002), *Truth without Objectivity*, London: Routledge.

MacFarlane, John (2003a), "Epistemic Modalities and Relative Truth," available at https://johnmacfarlane.net/epistmod-2003.pdf

MacFarlane, John (2003b), "Future Contingents and Relative Truth," *Philosophical Quarterly* 53, 321–36.

MacFarlane, John (2005a), "The Assessment-Sensitivity of Knowledge Attributions," in Tamar Szabó Gendler and John Hawthorne (eds.), *Oxford Studies in Epistemology*, Vol. 1, Oxford: Oxford University Press, 197–233.

MacFarlane, John (2005b), "Semantic Minimalism and Nonindexical Contextualism," in G. Preyer and G. Peter (eds.), *Content and Context: Essays on Semantics and Pragmatics*, Oxford: Oxford University Press.

MacFarlane, John (2008), "Truth in the Garden of Forking Paths," in M. García-Carpintero and M. Kölbel (eds.), *Relative Truth*, Oxford: Oxford University Press, 81–102.

MacFarlane, John (2011), "Epistemic Modals Are Assessment Sensitive," in A. Egan and B. Weatherson (eds.), *Epistemic Modality*, Oxford: Oxford University Press, 144–78.

Meiland, Jack W. (1977), "Concepts of Relative Truth," *The Monist* 60, 568–82.

Meiland, Jack W. (1979), "Is Protagorean Relativism Self-Refuting?," *Grazer Philosophische Studien* 9, 51–68.

Perry, John (1998), "Indexicals, Contexts and Unarticulated Constituents," *Proceedings of the 1995 CSLI-Amsterdam Logic, Language and Computation Conference*, Stanford, CA: CSLI Publications.

Preyer, Gerhard and Georg Peter (2004), *Contextualism in Philosophy*, Oxford: Oxford University Press.

Recanati, François (2002), "Unarticulated Constituents," *Linguistics and Philosophy* 25, 299–345.

Siegel, Harvey (1986), "Relativism, Truth, and Incoherence," *Synthese* 68, 295–312.

Stanley, Jason (2000), "Context and Logical Form." *Linguistics and Philosophy* 23, 391–434.

Stanley, Jason (2005), *Knowledge and Practical Interests*, Oxford: Oxford University Press.

Stephenson, Tamina (2005), "Assessor Sensitivity: Epistemic Modals and Predicates of Personal Taste," in J. Gajewski, V. Hacquard, B. Nickel, and S. Yalcin (eds.), *New Work on Modality*, MIT Working Papers in Linguistics, Vol. 51, 179–206.

Swoyer, Chris (1982), "True For," in M. Krausz and J. W. Meiland (eds.), *Relativism: Cognitive and Moral*, Notre Dame: University of Notre Dame Press, 84–108.

Williamson, Timothy (2005), "Knowledge, Context and the Agent's Point of View," in G. Preyer and G. Peter (eds.), *Content and Context: Essays on Semantics and Pragmatics*, Oxford: Oxford University Press.

Wright, Crispin (1992), *Truth and Objectivity*, Cambridge, MA: Harvard University Press.

Wright, Crispin (2001), "On Being in a Quandary: Relativism, Vagueness, Logical Revisionism," *Mind* 110, 45–98.

Wright, Crispin (2006), "Intuitionism, Realism, Relativism and Rhubarb," in P. Greenough and M. Lynch (eds.), *Truth and Realism*, Oxford: Oxford University Press.

Wright, Crispin (2007), "New Age Relativism and Epistemic Possibility," *Philosophical Issues* 17, 262–83.

Wright, Crispin and Sebastiano Moruzzi (2008), "Trumping Assessments and the Aristotelian Future," *Synthese* Special Issue (on "Relativism," edited by Berit Brogaard).

Wright, Crispin (2008a, this volume chapter 5), "'Fear of Relativism?', Contribution to a Book Symposium on Paul Boghossian's *Fear of Knowledge* in *Philosophical Studies*."

5

Fear of Relativism?

1

To many in or on the edges of the Academy, "Relativism" is a word with overtones of sinister iconoclasm, representing a kind of intellectual and ethical free-for-all in which the traditional investigative virtues of clarity, rigour, objectivity, consistency, and the unbiased pursuit of truth are dismissed as illusory and the great scientific constructions of the last 200 years, together with our deepest moral convictions, rated merely as 'our way of seeing' the world, more elaborate and organized but otherwise on all fours with the cosmology and customs of primitive tribes.

In his short book, Paul Boghossian aims to address, and to expose as bankrupt, the idea that there is even a coherent, let alone defensible, philosophical stance about truth and knowledge that can underwrite these 'pluralist' or 'postmodernist' tendencies. But since it is crucial to his project that his style of discussion makes it available to non-specialists, much of the recent more technical, less emotional debate *within* analytical philosophy about relativism's renaissance as a particular form of semantic theory is passed over unmentioned. Part of my aim in what follows is to illustrate how Boghossian's discussion connects quite straightforwardly with relativism in its contemporary analytical philosophical livery—what I have elsewhere called New Age Relativism[1]—and how some of his critical arguments may be presented in that setting. My main contentions will be, first, that when relativism about epistemic justification, and about morals, are couched in the currently canonical sort of form, they still remain in range of artillery that Boghossian positions in chapter 6 of his book;[2] second, that there is evasive action that they can take; but, third, that when they take it, they effectively have nothing to offer over other well-established forms of—broadly speaking—anti-realism, and that the play with specifically *relativist* ideas becomes nugatory. New Age Relativism, about morals and epistemic justification at least, is nothing

---

[1] See Wright (2007).
[2] Boghossian's discussion here needs to be taken in association with his (2006b).

Essays on Relativism: 2001–2021. Crispin Wright, Oxford University Press. © Crispin Wright 2023.
DOI: 10.1093/oso/9780192845993.003.0006

distinctively to be afraid of. If concern is fitting, it is centred on the capacity of our aspirations to epistemic and moral objectivity to withstand attacks that neither need nor prosper under the flag of relativism but are best articulated differently.

2

There are, of course, certain differences among the forms of the various proposals made by contemporary analytical relativists.[3] It will be convenient for our purposes to work with a simple *assessment-relativism*. This can be characterized as the doctrine, for some or a number of regions of discourse, that in a single world the very same token claim can take different truth-values when considered in different *contexts of assessment*.[4] The root semantic idea proposed is already present in Lewis's (1980), where an utterance of a sentence like "It is raining" is conceived as receiving a truth-value only when the value of a parameter of place— an 'index'—is fixed to which there is no semantic reference (not even by a 'hidden indexical') within the claim in question. Assessment-relativism for a region of discourse is what results when you construe the semantics of its claims as relevantly like that of "It is raining" on the Lewis treatment—but then incorporate the idea that the truth-values of utterances of *these* claims are dependent upon a new kind of index whose value is not settled once and for all by the context of utterance—the circumstances and occasion in which the claim takes - place—but varies with certain variable characteristics of (hypothetical) assessments.[5]

Proposals following this broad model have been made recently for quite a diversity of regions of discourse, and have postulated a variety of relevant kinds of assessment-contextual parameter. These include:

---

[3] The lion's share of the work of developing the broad approach has of course been carried out by John MacFarlane (2003a, 2003b, 2005a, 2005b, 2007, 2008, 2011), but significant, and significantly different, developments have also been made by, for example, Max Kölbel, Mark Richard, and Peter Lasersohn in the researches cited in the list of References. For misgivings about the underlying semantic assumptions, see Cappelen and Hawthorne (2009). For various specific difficulties with the approach, both local and general, and misgivings about its motivations, see Hawthorne (2007); Wright (2006, 2007, 2008); and Moruzzi and Wright (2009).

[4] It is, of course, a crucial issue whether the contents of utterances that are the bearers of assessment-relative truth-values in a given region of discourse could be anything very like *propositions* as traditionally conceived—whether, for example, there is any good sense in which a pair of thinkers in different assessment-contexts who each comprehendingly accept a particular such claim as true can be said to *agree*. The issues here are absolutely central to the interpretation and evaluation of truth-relativism in general. For discussion in depth, see Cappelen and Hawthorne (2009).

[5] You *could* so conceive of utterances of "It is raining." The result would be a conception of the truth-conditions of weather reports where the parameter of relevant place was determined by properties of an assessor, rather than the utterer. How bizarre that might be would depend on *which* properties of the assessor were supposed to do the job.

- *Time* of assessment—for the application of assessment-relativist ideas to future contingent statements and the problem of the 'Open Future',[6]
- *Information state* of the assessor—for the case of epistemic modals and conditionals,[7]
- *Saliences* to and/or *stakes* for an assessor—in the case of ascriptions of knowledge,[8] and
- *Standards* of an assessor—in the case of judgements of taste, aesthetic statements more generally, moral judgements, judgments of epistemic justification, and knowledge ascriptions again.[9]

Of special interest—and at centre stage, in effect, in chapter 6 of Boghossian's book—is the last: the idea that the truth-values of certain classes of claim may be sensitive to assessors' *standards*, and vary in tandem with those even though all other relevant circumstances remain the same.

However we need to make a distinction here. We speak quite loosely of standards, and of differences among different people's standards, in a large number of areas of preference- or aversion-expressive judgement—taste in food and drink, humour, obscenity, sexual attractiveness, appreciation of popular music, for instance—when what are really involved are, in the broadest sense, mere variations in dispositions of evaluation. You and I may have different standards in Asian cuisine, you preferring fiery Indian curries while my taste is for the subtler flavours of the Thai tradition. But we do not judge *by* these 'standards'. They are not objects of possible consultation to which we might in principle appeal, or actually do tacitly appeal, to determine our appraisal of the dishes in front of us. Any general statement of them, if such a thing is possible, will stand to our actual patterns of appraisal as a codification of regularities rather than a normative constraint. How exactly the notion of truth as relative to standards should be made out in this kind of case, is something that would merit independent investigation.[10] But in any event, such cases contrast with those on which Boghossian's discussion bears. Boghossian's cases are exactly those where standards *do* potentially inform judgement and provide norms for its appraisal. And two cardinal examples are exactly expressions of moral and epistemic evaluation. It is a paradigm of the most traditional relativistic thinking to hold that there are indeed no defensible absolute notions of morally justified action, or of evidentially justified belief, in exactly this sense: that whether an action, or a belief, is justified

---

[6] MacFarlane (2003a, 2003b, and 2008). (Actually, as Paula Sweeney reminded me, the relativization proposed by MacFarlane (2008) is to *moments*, rather than times—i.e., to nodes which may be positioned at the same time but on different paths through a branching structure of possible histories.)

[7] See MacFarlane (2003b and 2011); Egan et al. (2005); Weatherson (2009).

[8] See Richard (2004); MacFarlane (2005a).

[9] See Richard (2004 and 2008); MacFarlane (2005a); Lasersohn (2005).

[10] For one suggestion, see Wright (2006, §§7, 8).

depends on one's standards, where the standards concerned are conceived as *principles governing* evaluation, rather than *projections of actual patterns* of evaluation, and as subject to no objective notion of correctness.

This important kind of relativism—relativism, I venture to suggest, pretty much as generally and traditionally understood—is clearly easily assimilated to the New Age template. One has merely to take principles of moral and epistemic evaluation as a relevant kind of assessment-contextual parameter. Accordingly, should Boghossian's objections to its coherence prove successful, that will be both a historically important finding and a significant limitation on the range of interesting applications of relativism as it is conceived in the modern debate.

3

That said, Boghossian's own characterization[11] of epistemic relativism is, admittedly, more elaborate than these reflections anticipate. It amalgamates three claims:

A. There are no absolute facts about what belief a particular item of information justifies (Epistemic non-absolutism)
B. If a person, S's, epistemic judgements are to have any prospect of being true, we must not construe his claims of the form

"*E* justifies belief *B*"

as expressing the claim

E *justifies belief* B

but rather as expressing the claim:

According to the epistemic system C, that I, S accept, information E *justifies belief* B (Epistemic relationism)

C. There are many fundamentally different, genuinely alternative epistemic systems, but no facts by virtue of which one of these systems is more correct than any of the others. (Epistemic pluralism)

What is the rationale for including component *B*—"Epistemic relationism"? Here is what Boghossian says:

---

[11] Boghossian (2006a, p. 84).

Lets begin by looking at particular unrelativised epistemic judgements, such as:

1. Copernicanism is justified by Galileo's observations.

The relativist says that all such judgements are doomed to falsehood because there are no absolute facts about justification. If we are to retain epistemic discourse, the relativist urges, we must reform our talk so that we no longer speak simply about what is justified by the evidence, but only about what is justified by the evidence according to the particular epistemic system that we happen to accept, noting, all the while, that there are no facts by virtue of which our particular epistemic system is more correct than any of the others.[12]

We can envisage an epistemic relativist feeling very distant from this characterization and of its implicit perception of the situation. Boghossian is taking it that the truth of unrelativized claims such as (1), straightforwardly construed, is intelligible only if supported by absolute facts about justification. Since—for the relativist—there are no such facts, sentences like (1), if they "are to have any prospect of being true," have to be construed as making some other kind of claim, whose truth can be supported by facts of a kind that relativism can consistently countenance; and then the only salient candidate facts are the explicitly relational ones invoked by the epistemic relationism clause, B. But this is simply tantamount to the insistence that if relativism is to be in any position to regard claims such as (1) as true at all, then it is obliged so to construe their content as to enable them to be made *absolutely* true or false by some class of facts that it countenances. That is just to fail to take seriously the thesis that claims such as (1) can indeed be true or false, albeit *only relatively so*.

In fact it is clear that any attempt to construe claims of type (1) in accordance with the broader strategy proposed in clause B—i.e., as in effect elliptical expressions of certain neighbouring explicitly relational claims—is completely unworkable. To begin with, it involves a confusion between making a judgement *in the light of* certain standards and judging that those standards mandate that judgement. A judgement of the latter kind may be perfectly rationally endorsed by a thinker who is not at all inclined to the original judgement—because they do not share the standards in question. If it is rejoined that, according to Boghossian's formulation, the judgement concerned involves a hidden indexical reference to the thinker, so that actually they will accept the standards concerned, then we get instead the no less awkward result that when you endorse the claim that E justifies belief B, and I reject it, we each make an indexical judgement concerning what is properly judged *by our own* respective standards—whereas it was supposed to be a major point for assessment-relativism that it allegedly provides a way of *preserving content* across variable assessments of truth-value.

Worse follows. If we now try to combine the idea that the truth-value of claims of type (1) is standard-relative with the suggestion that their content is that of the

---

[12] Boghossian (2006a, p. 84).

kind of explicitly relational formulation that epistemic relationism proposes, then we commit ourselves to saying, incongruously and probably incorrectly, that the truth-value of the latter kind of claim is in turn relative to the same standards. The misery is merely compounded by the reflection that, according to clause B, the words "E justifies belief B" recur as a proper part of the unpacking of their content—how can a content be a proper part of itself?—and indeed will regressively continue to do so no matter how many times the unpacking is iterated.

The moral seems unmistakable: assessment-relativism, if it is to be anything coherent, must insist on a sharp separation between the making of a claim that is apt merely for relative truth and the making of the (potentially) absolute claim of the obtaining, in a particular case, of the relative truth constituting relationship. Epistemic relativism, on Boghossian's formulation, fails to make this separation and indeed winds up with no coherent story to tell about the content of the claims about justification for which its trademark thesis is that truth is standard-relative. Indeed, in casting about for acceptable, potentially absolute truth-conditions for them to take, it effectively loses sight of the very relativism that it intends to propose. All this would be grist to Boghossian's mill if something along the lines of clause B were indispensable to the epistemic relativist view. But the more plausible assessment is that these are the troubles of an avoidable misformulation.

4

It merits emphasis next, however, that Boghossian's own discussion actually doesn't really capitalize on the infelicities of clause B: his central objections remain pertinent even when that clause is dropped and the relativist thesis is pared down to an endorsement of a suitable instance of the New Age template,[13] together with something corresponding to the pluralist clause C. Simply stated, it is the thesis that the truth of statements about epistemic justification is assessment-relative, with systems of standards providing the relevant assessment-contextual parameter, together with the contention that alternative such systems are possible and nothing enforces the choice of any one of them as uniquely correct or best. At least some of the problems that Boghossian's discussion points up still engage this sparser view.

The problems concerned result from pressing three questions:

(i)   What exactly is a (moral or epistemic) *standard*?
(ii) When standards supply the relevant assessment-contextual parameter, what does the assessment-relativity of the truth of claims expressing judgements of epistemic, or moral, justification *consist in*?
(iii) What is it to *accept* a standard?

---

[13] —which effectively covers clause A.

There are three very natural answers:

  (i) A standard is a *general proposition*, stating—to fix on just one, salient, rubric—that certain kinds of judgement/action are (epistemically, or morally) justified/unjustified in certain specified kinds of circumstance—typically, in the epistemic case, the possession of certain kinds of evidence.

  (ii) Where standards, so conceived, supply the relevant parameter, the assessment-relativity of an utterance expressing a claim of type (1) (or an analogous moral claim) consists in its having a content that opens it to *entailment* by some such general propositions, when taken in conjunction with relevant collateral data, but to *incompatibility*, modulo the same collateral data, with certain other such general propositions which in some way compete with the first for regulation of the relevant range of claims.[14]

These ideas could no doubt stand further clarification. But the crucial point for our purposes is that the notion of assessment-relativity is here cashed out in terms of *entailment* by general propositions and collateral data. Finally

  (iii) To accept a standard is to believe the general proposition articulating it—i.e., to take it to be true.

One way of viewing the critical thrust of Boghossian's discussion is that these natural answers prove to be out of reach of the relativist, and that there are salient no other acceptable answers that are available instead.

Why should this be? Consider again the initial claim in the passage from Boghossian's chapter 6 (quoted above) about claims of type (1):

1.   Copernicanism is justified by Galileo's observations.

Boghossian remarked:

The relativist says that all such judgements are doomed to falsehood because there are no absolute facts about justification.

We already observed that it does the relativist gratuitous disservice to saddle the contention that there are no *absolute* facts of the type in question with the consequence that all claims of the relevant genre are *false*. But let us run with it

---

[14] There are issues about whether this genre of alleged assessment-relativity should be formulated, as here outlined, in terms of entailment and inconsistency, or whether it would not be better to work with entailment and independence. Nothing in that distinction will affect the discussion to follow, however, so I will not press the matter here.

for a moment. Standard-relativity, on the model we are working with, is a matter of entailment: standard-relative claims are entailed by some sets of propositions articulating relevant general standards, together with collateral information, but not by others. Clearly, if we suppose, as we may, that the collateral information is, for its part, good, but allow that the entailed type (1) proposition is, strictly speaking, false, then we will have to suppose the same about at least some of the relevant general propositions which entail it. A relativist who allows that type (1) claims are literally false, as Boghossian suggested, is therefore adopting a philosophical view which implicitly discredits the very standards to which it is averred that the acceptability of claims in the relevant discourse is relative. The account of assessments of epistemic justification (and moral justification) being advanced thus emerges as in effect an error-theory of the judgemental practices concerned, and therefore in tension with their continuation with any intellectual integrity. What are we doing judging in accordance with a set of general precepts that are no better than a tissue of untruth? Error-theoretic proposals about a region of discourse do, of course, sometimes involve a kind of extenuating story, consistent with massive untruth, to sanction its continuing practice.[15] But such manoeuvring would hardly be consistent with an intentionally *relativist* stance; the whole point of such a stance was supposed to be to explain and vindicate a sense in which the characteristic claims are *true*, just not absolutely so.

For relativism's purposes, the suggestion that type (1) claims are strictly false is accordingly just as untoward as the suggestion that they be construed as judgements of explicitly relational truths. And it is, indeed, open to the same complaint that it simply fails to take seriously the mooted idea of *relative truth*.

Boghossian canvasses a third construal of the content of type (1) claims—the suggestion that the characteristic expressions of type (1) claims are *semantically incomplete*; that when someone says "The judgement that P is justified by evidence E," this is a remark that stands comparison with: "John is taller"—said in a context where the question has arisen whether either of the twins, John and Jim, has a height advantage over the other, and I've just measured up—or with "The Sheikh of Dubai is richer"—when the question has arisen about the relative wealth of Liverpool Football Club's American owners and their principal competitor in the acquisition of the club. In such cases one and the same form of words may, without any shift in the semantic value of any explicit constituent, effect a true claim in one context and a false claim in another. But that is because the contexts concerned determine differing completions that are not fully explicit in the semantics of the overt claim. This seems agreeably unmysterious. Moreover the assessment-relativity of the claims concerned is unreflected at the level of

---

[15] The prototypical such account is Hartry Field's attempt to rehabilitate the (in his view) literally false theories of classical mathematics in terms of the virtue of inferential conservativeness. The *locus classicus* is Field (1980).

the contents they are being used to convey—this third construal involves no relativity of truth at the level of propositional content.

The proposal amounts, in effect, to a pragmatic, rather than semantic, version of epistemic relationism—Boghossian's clause B—that I claimed above is hopeless. I leave it to the reader to ponder whether the drawbacks outlined earlier are to any significant degree mitigated by its now taking a pragmatic form. As Boghossian quickly observes, however, it is anyway no good in the present context. The immediately foreseeable problem is that the inexplicit standard, mention of which would need to be made to recover the relevant complete proposition, would itself simply be a general statement similar in essential respects to the targeted incomplete statement. If

Judgment P is justified by evidence E

is incomplete in the relevant kind of way, then so, presumably, must be any expression of a sponsoring general standard:

Whenever you have evidence of type K (and no other relevant evidence), a judgement of type L is justified by that evidence

—supposing that P is a judgement of type L, and E is evidence of type K. The proposal to construe the expression of type (1) claims as incomplete, with a gap calling for completion by an expression for a standard, or set of standards, cannot avoid construing the very statement of the relevant standard(s) as itself likewise incomplete. That is going to make an utter mystery of what it is to accept such a standard and of how doing so might normatively constrain ones evaluations.

This, in effect, is where Boghossian leaves the discussion of the content of type (1) claims in chapter 6 of *Fear of Knowledge*, apparently satisfied that the relativist has no playable construal of them. Three construals of the content of such claims—the explicitly relational construal of clause B, their construal as literal falsehoods, and their construal as literally semantically incomplete—have been reviewed and each accomplishes nothing but trouble for the relativist. But we need to push the discussion further. For all three are open to the charge of failing to take relativism seriously—of failing to reckon with the idea of contents which require no semantic completion before they are capable of truth-value, but are capable only of *relative* truth-value.[16]

---

[16] A fourth proposal, anticipated by Boghossian and (grudgingly) elaborated and defended by Rosen (2007) is to construe epistemic/moral standards as general (conditional) *imperatives* mandating or prohibiting specific judgements/actions in specific circumstances. Boghossian develops further reasons for discounting this direction in his (2007). For reasons of space I must here set aside consideration of it in any detail. One immediate concern about it, unparalleled by the general propositional account of standards, is that any instruction to accept the judgement [that P is justified] is, *ceteris paribus*, an

5

To try to take it seriously is to confront hard questions which New Age Relativists have, so far, rather tended to avoid. How are we to understand the notion of relative truth at the level of *content*? What kind of construal of the content of the relevant claims is required if the problems we have been reviewing are to be finessed? It is well beyond the scope of this discussion to try to take on this cluster of issues, which arise for assessment-relativism about any region of discourse. What I want to argue to conclude is that whatever might best be said about them, the distinctive peculiarity of the present kinds of case—where truth is purportedly relative to standards understood as general propositional norms of assessment— has the effect that the application of assessment-relativism to them is going to be *pointless.*

Take it, then, that the epistemic relativist insists that type (1) claims are complete, truth-evaluable judgements, whose content is fully explicit in the sentences we use to express them, and that the kind of truth or falsity they are apt for is relative truth and falsity—that their truth-values vary as a function of the standards brought to bear upon them. So type (1) claims are both semantically fully explicit and capable of being true. The same must therefore go, presumably, for the statements of the general standards by reference to which the acceptability of type (1) claims is judged, and to which their truth is allegedly relative. The question, therefore, immediately arises how the truth of these general statements is itself in turn to be conceived? Clearly they cannot be conceived as absolute truths—that would not be consistent with the epistemic pluralist clause *C* in Boghossian's characterization and would anyway enforce the absolute truth of their type (1) consequences (assuming the absoluteness of the collateral data.) So should the statements of the general standards be conceived as themselves assessment-relative? Well, what other option is on the table? But what, in that case, are their truth-values relative *to*? It would be potentially regressive to propose that it is always to further standards, somehow determining the acceptability of standards—the same question will simply arise about the next tranche of stand- ards, and so on after that. But if relativity there must in general be, the only other available answer appears to be a reflexive one: that ultimately, (some) statements of general standards take their truth-values relative just to themselves!

That may seem immediately to induce a crisis: if the truth of the statement of a general standard is conceived as consisting in its acceptability relative to the very

instruction to accept the judgment [that *P*]. So a theorist who conceives of the acceptability of type (1) judgements as relative to systems of groundlessly accepted imperatives, and offers that as sufficient for thinking of their truth as assessment-relative, will need to explain what, if anything, will prevent the account ramifying to encompass *every* species of judgement [that *P*] that is suitable for embedding in a type (1) judgement. Such a ramification might be grateful to the Protagorean spirit. But global relativism was not supposed to go with the very territory of *epistemic* relativism.

standard concerned—i.e., in effect, as self-entailment—then every such statement should be accepted as true.[17] That is manifestly hopeless.

But it is also too fast, of course. Someone who is trying to conceive of the truth of statements of general standards as itself standard-relative should invoke the distinction, adverted to earlier, between judging *by a standard* and judging *what a standard requires*. Judging by a standard issues in an evaluation with which the assessor identifies: it involves both a judgement of what the standard requires—a judgement about an entailment—*and* an acceptance of the standard concerned. It is only when particular standards are accepted that the relevant assessment-contextual parameter takes on a value and the extension of the truth-predicate in the assessment-context concerned becomes determinate. So one who is trying out the idea that the truth of statements of general standards can be itself reflexively standard-relative may properly insist that more than self-entailment is needed for truth: such statements will take truth-values only relative to the standards actually accepted in the relevant range of assessment-contexts.

This is the right reply. But its effect is to shine a spotlight on a range of difficulties that relativism encounters with the third of the questions we originally distinguished—the question of what it is to *accept* a standard in the first place. There are a number of issues but here, in particular, is a wrinkle about truth. We are thinking of standards as general propositions. So to accept one, you would suppose, ought to be to believe it, or anyway to take it as true—in some sense of 'true'.[18, 19] But something coherent needs to be said about what conception of truth can be involved here when, for example, one is considering such a proposition for the first time and wondering whether to accept it. Let the context be one in which one is so far committed to no view—a case where the epistemic pluralist component in relativism permits one to 'go either way'. So one is rationally free to accept the standard, i.e. to accept the truth of the proposition concerned. But this precisely cannot be understood as a permission to accept that it is true relative to one's present context of assessment. That claim is, by hypothesis, false. If that is the only notion of truth the relativist has to work with, then relativism cannot after all make sense of its pluralist—clause *C*—component. Clause *C* requires that there are general propositions about epistemic, or moral justification, whose basic place in one's epistemic, or moral, system goes with their acceptance being effectively rationally or cognitively unconstrained. But if all truth in the region of discourse in question is standard-relative truth, then the question whether to accept a

---

[17] Cf. Boghossian (2007, pp. 62–3).

[18] The point will go through no matter what attitude we take acceptance to be. In general, it is a consequence of the platitude that propositional attitudes generally are attitudes to truth: that to doubt, fear, wonder, intend, etc., that *P* is to doubt, fear, wonder, intend that *P* is true.

[19] Such an attitude need not be explicit or fully self-conscious. But we may take it that the ascription of a tacit attitude only makes sense if it *could* be self-conscious. That will be enough to set up the issues now following.

standard—i.e., to accept its general statement as *true*—will be tantamount to the question whether to take it that its acceptance is mandated in one's present assessment-context. Since it is of the essence of epistemic, or moral, relativism that a freedom is operative which is inconsistent with the question invariably being so understood, we may conclude that the notion of truth that goes with the acceptance of general standards cannot always—consistently with relativism—be relative truth. So standard-relative truth cannot be the *only* notion of truth operative throughout discourse of epistemic and moral evaluation.

If this is correct, however, then the whole motivation for the New Age template as a vehicle for the general philosophical spirit expressed in clause *C* disappears. The kind of standards-relativism on which we have been focusing cannot avoid admitting a notion of the truth of statements of general standards which is not to be recovered in terms of their truth relative to an accepted standard. This notion need not, of course, be cashed out in terms of their *absolute* truth—at least, not if absolute truth is to carry the realist import that relativism opposes. It need be no more than a deflationary, or minimalist, notion of the kinds that have long figured prominently in the philosophical debates about realism and objectivity. But once such a notion is brought into play, and includes in its range of application statements of the primitive standards whose acceptance defines an assessment-context, there is no longer any need for another, relativistic notion to apply to their type (1) consequences. The same notion will serve in both cases.

The crucial, load-bearing idea in the views about moral and epistemic justification that Boghossian is attacking is that of the rationally unconstrained acceptance of (propositions articulating) basic moral and epistemic standards. This—effectively the thrust of clause *C*—has long been explored and debated under various 'non-cognitivist', 'non-factualist', and 'minimalist' rubrics. The main point I have been arguing here is that these debates are not furthered at all by superimposing the New Age Relativist semantic template onto the discourses concerned. If it is insisted that assessment-relative truth is the only notion of truth that engages those discourses, the effect of the template is to throw a spanner in the works when we seek to say something coherent about applications of the truth-predicate to statements of general standards. If it is not so insisted, the effect is to construct an idle wheel.[20]

References

Boghossian, Paul (2006a), *Fear of Knowledge*, Oxford: Clarendon Press.

Boghossian, Paul (2006b), "What is Relativism?," in P. Greenough and M. Lynch (eds.), *Truth and Realism*, Oxford: Clarendon Press.

[20] Published online: 18 November 2008 © Springer Science+Business Media B.V. 2008.

Boghossian, Paul (2007), "The Case against Epistemic Relativism: Replies to Rosen and Neta," *Episteme* 4, 49–65.

Boghossian, P. (unpublished), *Can We Make Sense of Normative Relativism?*

Cappelen, H. and J. Hawthorne (2009), *Relativism ad Monadic Truth*, Oxford: Oxford University Press.

Egan, Andy, John Hawthorne, and Brian Weatherson (2005), "Epistemic Modals in Context," in G. Preyer and P. Peters (eds.), *Contextualism in Philosophy*, Oxford: Oxford University Press, 131–69.

Field, Hartry (1980), *Science without Numbers*, Oxford: Basil Blackwell.

Hawthorne, John (2007), "Eavesdroppers and Epistemic Modals," *Philosophical Issues* 17, 92–101.

Kölbel, Max (2002), *Truth without Objectivity*, London: Routledge.

Kölbel, Max (2004), "Faultless Disagreement," *Proceedings of the Aristotelian Society* 104, 53–73.

Lasersohn, Peter (2005), "Context Dependence, Disagreement, and Predicates of Personal Taste," *Linguistics and Philosophy* 28, 643–86.

Lewis, D. (1980), "Index, Context, and Content," in S. Kanger and S. Ohman (eds.), *Philosophy and Grammar*, Dordrecht: Reidel, 79–100. Reprinted in D. Lewis (1998), *Papers in Philosophical Logic*, Cambridge: Cambridge University Press, 21–44.

MacFarlane, John (2003a), "Future Contingents and Relative Truth," *Philosophical Quarterly* 53, 321–36.

MacFarlane, John (2003b), "Epistemic Modalities and Relative Truth," available at https://johnmacfarlane.net/epistmod-2003.pdf

MacFarlane, John (2005a), "The Assessment-Sensitivity of Knowledge Attributions," in Tamar Szabó Gendler and John Hawthorne (eds.), *Oxford Studies in Epistemology*, Vol. 1, Oxford: Oxford University Press, 197–233.

MacFarlane, John (2005b), "Making Sense of Relative Truth," *Proceedings of the Aristotelian Society* 105, 321–39.

MacFarlane, John (2007), "Relativism and Disagreement," *Philosophical Studies* 132, 17–31.

MacFarlane, John (2008), "Truth in the Garden of Forking Paths," in M. García-Carpintero and M. Kölbel (eds.), *Relative Truth*, Oxford: Oxford University Press, 81–102.

MacFarlane, J. (2011), "Epistemic Modals Are Assessment Sensitive," in A. Egan and B. Weatherson (eds.), *Epistemic Modality*, Oxford: Oxford University Press, 144–78.

Moruzzi, S. and C. Wright (2009), "Trumping Assessments and the Aristotelian Future," *Synthese* 166 (2), 309–31.

Richard, Mark (2004), "Contextualism and Relativism," *Philosophical Studies* 119, 215–42.

Richard, Mark (2008), *When Truth Gives Out*, Oxford: Oxford University Press.

Rosen, Gideon (2007), "The Case against Epistemic Relativism: Reflections on Ch. 6 of *Fear of Knowledge*," *Episteme* 4, 10–29.

Weatherson, Brian (2009), "Conditionals and Indexical Relativism," *Synthese* 166, 333–57.

Wright, C. (2006), "Intuitionism, Realism, Relativism and Rhubarb," in Patrick Greenough and Michael Lynch (eds.), *Truth and Realism*, Oxford: Clarendon Press, 38–60.

Wright, C. (2007), "New Age Relativism and Epistemic Possibility," *Philosophical Issues* 17, 262–83 (special number on "The Metaphysics of Epistemology," edited by E. Sosa and E. Villanueva).

Wright, C. (2008), "Relativism about Truth Itself: Haphazard Thoughts about the Very Idea," in Manuel García-Carpintero and Max Kölbel (eds.), *Relative Truth*, Oxford: Oxford University Press.

6

Trumping Assessments and the Aristotelian Future

Co-authored with Sebastiano Moruzzi

"Can I get a witness? I want a witness."
—Marvin Gaye (Tamla Records 1963)

1. Truth-Relativism

For our purposes, truth-relativism can be characterized as the doctrine that in a single world the very same token utterance[1] can take different truth-values when considered in different contexts of assessment. The root semantic idea is already present in Lewis (1980), where an utterance of a sentence like "It is raining" is conceived as receiving a truth-value only when the value of a parameter of place—an 'index'—is fixed to which there is no semantic reference (not even by an 'unarticulated constituent') in the utterance in question. Truth-relativism is what you get for a region of discourse when you construe its utterances as dealing in contents relevantly like that of "It is raining" on the Lewis treatment—but then add in the idea that the truth-values of utterances of *these* contents is dependent upon a new kind of index whose value is not settled once and for all by a context of utterance, but varies with certain variable characteristics of (hypothetical) assessments.[2] If truth-relativism so defined holds for a certain utterance, the utterance is *assessment-sensitive*.

The doctrine is widely regarded as providing one way to underwrite the (alleged) possibility of *faultless disagreement* (Kölbel 2004; Wright 2006, 2008).

---

[1] We here set aside the issue whether the contents of utterances that are the bearers of relative truth in a given region of discourse can be anything very like *propositions* as traditionally conceived—whether, for example, there is any good sense in which a pair of thinkers, each of whom comprehendingly accepts a particular such utterance as true, can be said to *agree*. The issues here are of course absolutely crucial to the interpretation and evaluation of truth-relativism in general but they are off the agenda of the present discussion. For discussion in depth, see Cappelen and Hawthorne (2009).

[2] You *could* so conceive of utterances of "It is raining." The result would be a conception of the truth-conditions of weather reports where the parameter of relevant place was determined by properties of an assessor, rather than the utterer. How bizarre that might be would depend on *which* properties of the assessor did the job.

Essays on Relativism: 2001–2021. Crispin Wright, Oxford University Press. © Crispin Wright 2023.
DOI: 10.1093/oso/9780192845993.003.0007

Consider a sommelier with a preference for Cabernet grapes who holds that Sassicaia is superior to Barolo and another sommelier who, on the contrary, favours the Nebbiolo grapes and (apparently) denies what the other sommelier has asserted. Can the two genuinely disagree without implication of fault on either side? Truth-relativism offers an apparently easy answer: while both of them are (or can be) expressing judgement on the same utterance, viz. the first sommelier's assertion of "Sassicaia is superior to Barolo," they (may) rightly evaluate it in two different ways from their respective contexts of assessment if standards of taste in wine are taken as the relevant index.

In recent debates, the idea that there are assessment-sensitive utterances has been advanced to vouchsafe possibilities of faultless disagreement over a variety of types of subject matter—taste, aesthetics, and morals, epistemic modals and knowledge-ascriptions, and the case of future contingent statements, for example. In a series of connected publications,[3] John MacFarlane in particular has covered remarkable ground in elaboration and defence of the coherence of the idea in a number of these regions—though his motivations have not in general been focused on faultless disagreement. Much of the debate has rightly been located in the philosophy of language, preoccupied with the assessment-relativists' hostages to the theory of content and the force of the linguistic evidence adduced in support of their proposals. In this chapter, however, our concern will be less with the evaluation of particular recent relativist proposals and debates than with a certain class of more general, structural issues about truth-relativism that seem overdue for attention.

In the following we will make use of a dyadic metalinguistic truth-predicate, "$T(\ldots,\ldots)$" taking as its arguments utterances and contexts of assessment respectively. It will be important to keep in mind that the focus of the chapter is on this kind of *metalinguistic* statement, and not on truth-ascriptions within an object language. The main issues we want to consider concern the theoretical expression of the relativist thesis itself. We will not, except in one place,[4] be directly concerned with issues concerning the use of "true" and its cognates within an object language in which assessment-sensitive utterances are notionally made.[5]

---

[3] See list of References.   [4] See Section 7.

[5] What about relativism about the truth of *propositions*? Well, the idea of the assessment-sensitivity of utterances and the related idea, of the assessment-sensitivity of propositions, coincide if one assumes first that something worth calling a proposition is expressed by an assessment-sensitive utterance; and second that what proposition is so expressed is settled wholly by the context of the uttering—the context of use. So focusing our attention on utterances will not divest our discussion of bearing upon truth-relativist theses about propositions, or whatever the associated contents are, provided variation in the content expressed by a sentence can occur only via variation in the indices of the context of use. (In fact, whenever we consider variations in assessment context in the sequel, either the same token utterance will be under assessment, or we will be dealing with utterances of sentences that are presumed to have no indexical element.)

2. Attestability and Orders of Relativism

Truth-relativism, it hardly needs to be said, is a controversial view in any region of discourse. The truth-relativist needs to justify his theory. That means, we will take it, that he has to be able to formulate and then support, at least to his own satisfaction, the claim that a certain (type of) targeted utterance is assessment-sensitive. A canonical way to express that claim is presumably this:

$$(Rel) \quad (\exists U,\ ca_1,\ ca_2)\,(T(U,\ ca_1)\ \&\ \sim T(U, ca_2)),$$

where 'U' ranges over utterances of the type in question, 'ca_1,' 'ca_2', etc., range over the kind of assessment-contexts to which the relativity in question is being claimed, and '$T(U, ca_k)$' says that U is true relative to ca_k.

A number of questions arise immediately to which the relativist in any particular case owes (seldom provided) answers. Is (Rel) itself an absolute claim? Should philosophy generally be thought of as trafficking in absolute claims? If not, what are the relevant assessment-contextual parameters for philosophical claims? If so, does it follow—letting 'CA_1', 'CA_2', etc., denote specific assessment-contexts—that any putative *witness* of (Rel):

$$T(U, CA_1)\ \&\ \sim T(U, CA_2),$$

is also an absolute claim? Or could one coherently combine the thesis that (Rel) is an absolute truth with respect to a given region of discourse with the view that all *specific* witnesses for it with respect to that discourse are themselves assessment-sensitive: that while it is an absolute truth that truth is assessment-sensitive in the region of discourse in question, it is an assessment-sensitive matter how exactly this absolute truth is witnessed? If that is not a coherent combination and witness claims like the above are absolute, then so are their conjuncts. So in that case there is no question of *higher-order* relativism—relativism about the truth-status of claims of the form, "$T(U, ca_k)$," where 'U' ranges over utterances that already provide the subject matter of a proposed relativism. But as we shall see, while relativism about some range of utterances, U, cannot presumably of itself *require* extension to higher orders, the main focus of the present discussion—the attempt to harness relativistic ideas to stabilize a certain broadly Aristotelian conception of the future[6]—must make precisely such an extension if it is to accommodate all the ingredients in the intuitive view whose stabilization is aimed at.

---

[6] We intend no more than to caption a certain kind of view by this term. The view in question is excellently laid out in MacFarlane (2003b). We make no suggestion either that Aristotle himself was in any way at all a forerunner of assessment-relativism—"Aristotelian" relativism is surely no more

In general, it is open, and under-investigated, what combinations of simultaneous, multi-order relativisms are coherent, and what are the conditions for their coherence. Here of course it matters whether the higher-order relativisms involve just the same assessment-contextual variables, or whether they change—so that, for instance, it is moral standards that supply the assessment-contextual parameter at first-order and, say, logics (!) that do so at second. Another major issue is whether relativism's traditional *even-handedness*—the idea that conflicting assessments of utterances in the range of U may not merely be mandated under differing assessment-contexts but can be, in some sense, equally valid or good—can be serviced unless the theorist goes absolute with respect to claims of the form, $T(U, ca_k)$. In the present climate of renaissance of interest in truth-relativism, all these neglected questions demand attention. The discussion to follow will take some initial steps towards the development of a framework for thinking about them by working through an aspect of the Aristotelian example in detail.

Let a relativism for a particular region of discourse count as *attestable* just in case a proponent can coherently adduce a witness for its characteristic instance of (*Rel*); that is, to repeat, a claim of the form

$$T(U, CA_1) \,\&\, \sim T(U, CA_2),$$

where CA_1 and CA_2 are assessment-contexts varying in the value they assign to the parameter which the relativism in question claims that truth in that region is relative to. Our thesis will be that aristotelian relativism—assessment-relativism harnessed to the specific project of providing a coherent platform for a broadly Aristotelian conception of the contingent future as unsettled (as long as it is future)—*cannot attest to itself.* Specifically, although the proposal can of course formulate witnesses of the relevant instance of (*Rel*), it is not consistent with other aspects of the view that an assertion of them can ever be justified, no matter what the assessment-context in which justification is attempted.[7]

Aristotelian than Hume's Principle is Hume's—or that he embraced all the components of the broad view of the future that the form of relativist proposal we shall consider is aimed at stabilizing. In what follows we shall use the lower case "aristotelian" whenever no historical claim is intended.

[7] A disclaimer. In advancing this thesis, our primary concern is with the development of the apparatus by means of which the problem is elicited, and the general agenda of issues which it brings into focus, rather than with whether it provides the means to nail particular actual relativist proposals—in particular, of course, those of MacFarlane himself—concerning the metaphysics of the future. Our thesis is that assessment-relativism cannot stabilize the view we will outline save by making a serious problem for itself. But the target 'aristotelianism' can of course be modified. It would be for a sequel investigation to determine what revision of the crucial features of that view, still in the same spirit, might be well motivated, or whether extant relativist treatments are required, or can succeed, in providing a platform for such variant views.

3. Trumping

Second-order absoluteness with respect to a region of discourse is the thesis that any two relativistic truth-ascriptions to one of its utterances—say, $\sim T(U, CA_1)$ and $T(U, CA_2)$—are themselves assessment-*in*sensitive: no matter what the context in which they are assessed, their respective assessments should be the same. A source of potential conflict with second-order absoluteness, in the presence of first-order relativism, are certain kinds of dependency relations between ascriptions of truth to U and ascriptions of truth to other ascriptions of truth to U. If the facts as assessed relative to one assessment-context determine, from that context or another, their proper assessment relative to a second, we say that the former assessment-context *trumps* the latter.

Among the possibilities for such a dependency, we want to draw attention to two cases where the relevant truth-ascriptions are of the respective forms, $T(U, ca_1)$ and $T(T(U, ca_2), ca_1)$. They are these. We have *inward trumping* with respect to an utterance U if whenever U is true relative to a context of assessment, ca_1, it is thereby true from that same context of assessment that U is true relative to *any other* context of assessment. That is:

(Inward trumping) $(\forall ca_1, ca_2)\,(T(U, ca_1) \supset T(T(U, ca_2), ca_1))$

We term this "inward trumping" because the direction of determination goes from the outer assessment-context in the consequent—ca_1—to the inner. Inward trumping involves that any assessment-context of U behaves as an *inclusive perspective*: from the perspective of that assessment-context, any other assessment-contexts is viewed as mandating the same evaluation of U as is mandated by it.

By contrast, we have *outward trumping* with respect to an utterance U if whenever it is true from a context of assessment ca_1 that U is true relative to some other assessment-context, U is true relative to the context of assessment ca_1. That is

(Outward trumping) $(\forall ca_1, ca_2)\,(T(T(U, ca_2), ca_1) \supset T(U, ca_1))$

This, correspondingly, is termed "outward trumping" because the direction of determination goes from the inner assessment-context of the antecedent—ca_2—to the outer. Outward trumping involves that any assessment-context ca_2 for an utterance of U behaves as an *exporting perspective*: to sanction the correctness of a truth-ascription, $T(U, ca_2)$, relative to ca_1 commits one to the truth of U relative to ca_1 itself.[8]

---

[8] We have stated the two trumping principles in full generality. Obviously there is conceptual space for more local cases. It may be, for example, that—in a particular region of discourse—trumping, in one

It is salient that a relativist about some discourse who regarded both trumping principles as good would thereby commit himself to second-order relativism. For suppose $T(U, CA_1)$ and $\sim T(U, CA_2)$. Then from the former, by inward trumping, we may infer $T(T(U, CA_2), CA_1)$ while from the latter, taking 'CA_2' for both 'ca_1' and 'ca_2', we have by contraposition in outward trumping that $\sim T(T(U, CA_2), CA_2)$.

The latter move, where outward trumping is specialized to a single assessment-context:

$$(\forall ca_k)\,(T(T(U, ca_k), ca_k) \supset T(U, ca_k)),$$

is worthy of remark. Taken in conjunction with the corresponding specialization of inward trumping:

$$(\forall ca_k)\,(T(U, ca_k) \supset T(T(U, ca_k), ca_k))$$

it provides something tantamount to a kind of disquotation principle for the metalinguistic relative truth-predicate,

$$(\forall ca_k)\,(T(U, ca_k) \equiv T(T(U, ca_k), ca_k)),$$

requiring that assessment-contexts should be constrained to provide for *accurate self-assessment*. That may seem to be a principle that any coherent assessment-relativism should want to endorse. If so, we may conclude that any coherent assessment-relativism at nth order which allows inward trumping will need to extend to the $n+1$th order as well.[9, 10]

4. Why Might a Relativist Endorse Some Form of Trumping?

Neither form of trumping seems to draw any general support simply from the broad framework of truth-relativism *per se*. Indeed, as the reader will speedily see, each is a consequence of a generalized absolutism and to that extent, it might

---

or both directions, obtains only for assessment-contexts meeting certain conditions, or even that one particular assessment-context (God's?) is unique in trumping others. There are potentially interesting complications here, but they will not be further explored in the present discussion.

[9] What about the converse? Does the existence of witnesses for higher-order relativism—of the form, say, of $\sim T(U, CA_2), CA_1)$ & $T(T(U, CA_2), CA_2)$—impose instances of either of the trumping principles? We conjecture not, or at least not on any plausible collateral assumptions. But the matter awaits further investigation.

[10] It's natural to think of the operation of principles of trumping as enforcing patterns of *deference* among assessors. But the thought is not quite right. To defer is to accept the mandates of another perspective in place of what is mandated by one's own. Being trumped, by contrast, involves that another perspective gets, not to *override* the mandates of one's own perspective, but to determine what they are.

seem, a compromise of relativism—a principle from the camp of the enemy, as it were.[11] In any case, it seems to be a question to be determined locally for each area of (allegedly) relativistic discourse in turn whether or not either (or both) of the trumping principles are motivated.[12]

They certainly seem completely untoward in the basic case—that of assessment-relativism about taste. Let's suppose that Paul and Barry are the two sommeliers, and that Paul affirms "Sassicaia is superior to Barolo"—let's call this utterance SB. Consider the following sentences:

(1) $T(SB, CA_{Paul})$

(2) $T(T(SB, CA_{Barry}), CA_{Paul})$,

where CA_{Paul} and CA_{Barry} are the contexts of assessment that Paul and Barry respectively occupy in evaluating SB—contexts which select the operative standards for evaluating a wine.

Consider the case where Paul's operative standards do indeed assess SB as true, so (1) is true. If inward trumping held, that would entail the truth of (2). Hence, Paul's standards would mandate not merely his own favourable verdict on Sassicaia but the judgement that Barry's standards too mandate that verdict. Such a suggestion looks bizarre: how can a truth-ascription involving in its content reference to one standard of taste (Barry's standard)—i.e., that SB is true relative to Barry's standards—be deemed to be correct on the basis of different standards (Paul's standards) of *taste*? For one thing, one would suppose, SB may actually be false by Barry's standards—as he himself takes it to be. For another, standards of taste, while they may mandate one or another verdict about a wine, surely have no bearing on the question whether the wine is good, and an appropriate utterance correspondingly true, *relative to other standards of taste*. The latter question is not, intuitively, a matter of taste at all.

Trumping, in either direction, empowers acceptances of the claim that Paul's 'oenological perspective' includes Sassicaia in the extension of "superior wine" to boss the facts as assessed from Barry's oenological perspective.[13] Why should a

---

[11] For proof, see the Appendix, Thesis (III).

[12] It is plausible (thanks here to Elia Zardini) that the two forms of trumping principle are interderivable in the presence of principles of the form:

$$(\forall ca_k)(\sim T(U,\ ca_k)) \equiv T(\neg U,\ ca_k),$$

where 'U' ranges over both utterances in the base discourse and nth-order assessments of them, '$\sim$' is regular negation in the metalanguage, and '$\neg U$' is an object-language utterance expressing the broad negation of the proposition expressed by U (that is, the claim that that proposition is not true.) Since nothing of philosophical interest in the context of the present discussion hangs on the matter, we defer further investigation of the relations between the two forms of trumping to another occasion.

[13] If Barry learns that (1) is true, the appropriate instance of outward trumping will force him to conclude that SB is true from his own perspective. And inward trumping will force Paul to regard Barry as misassessing Sassicaia from Barry's own point of view if Barry takes a different view.

taste-relativist want anything to do with that? Intuitively, the heart and soul of the relativistic point about this kind of case is that the standards that contrive to generate a disagreement may simply respectively determine *each* of the conflicting classifications as correct. It seems clear that trumping must be disowned when relativism is harnessed to this traditional even-handed kind of thought.

But does, or ought, trumping to hold in others of the areas of discourse where truth-relativism has been proposed? We will suggest that aristotelian relativism supplies a case in point. Specifically, that—by the lights of the aristotelian view—a form of inward trumping seems to be mandated for future contingent statements, with consequences that we will develop.

5. Future Contingents

Consider a future contingent statement such as:

(*Peace*)   There will be peace in Middle East in 2030.

The form of aristotelian view we will consider incorporates two crucial claims. The first is an *Indeterminacy claim*: that the contingent future is unsettled in the precise sense that there are, while it is still future, no truths about it: no truths about what will contingently be. The traditional motivation for this line, familiarly, is the notion that otherwise we must accept a repugnant form of determinism.[14] If a full repertoire of propositions about how the future will turn out are *already* true, then they have been so since time immemorial, indeed always, and hence the circumstances in virtue of which they are true must somehow already be in place, before the relevant aspects of the future unfold. What scope, then, for human intervention and influence?[15]

So, to assert a token of (*Peace*) at the present time is, in the view under consideration, to make a claim with no truth-value. But what about the situation when 2030 comes? Everyone will agree that when relevant matters are assessed in 2030, there will then be a mandate—prescinding from any material vagueness in

---

[14] The modern *locus classicus* for this line of thought is of course Lukasiewicz's "On Determinism." See his (1970).

[15] It is, to stress, quite outside the scope of the present discussion to take any stand on this train of thought—which seemingly *is* one that Aristotle had—or even on its plausibility. Our interest is wholly in the question whether *if* it is accepted, along with the Determinacy claim about to be outlined, truth-relativism provides a way of stabilizing the resulting package. We cannot forbear to observe, however, that all the pressure towards the Indeterminacy claim rests on the presupposition that no viable distinction can be made between *eternal* truths—truths that always were and always will be true—and *timeless* truth: truth expressed by a tenseless predicate, "is true." It is the idea that one of the disjuncts of the Sea-fight disjunction is *already* true that sets up the anxiety. That is a consequence of conceding that one of them has to be eternally true. Timeless truth, by contrast, will entail nothing about truth-at-a-time, understood so as to require that the facts conferring truth are, so to speak, already in place. We briefly return to this thought in Section 8 below.

(*Peace*)—to affirm, or deny the proposition that an utterance of (*Peace*) now expresses, since relevant matters will have been settled. But there is an additional, very intuitive claim: that when 2030 comes, the prediction made by the contemporary utterance will then be shown *to have been* true, or false—that the mandate conferred by the events up to and including 2030 will extend to a *retrospective* verdict on the contemporary utterance of (*Peace*), so that someone who affirms it now will then (2030) properly be said to have spoken truly, or falsely, as the case may be, *at the time of speaking*. Call that the *Determinacy claim*: it says, in effect, that when the future is settled, it will also settle aspects of the (present) present, that is, the future past. Of what in fact proves to have transpired it will truly be affirmable that it *was going to* transpire, so that it is true to say that one who predicted the actual course of events spoke truly at the time of her prediction, even though this cannot truly be said before what she predicted "comes true," as we are wont to say.

It is a nice question what drives the Determinacy claim. Certainly it is entrenched in our linguistic habits. I make a prediction. Things turn out as I predicted. And I say, "See, I *was* right." More generally, the Determinacy claim is enshrined in the truth-value links—the network of principles that link the truth-conditions of utterances at different times of sentences that differ in their contents only in respect of tense. One such link precisely affirms that, for t_0 earlier than t_1,

'P will be true at t_1' was true at t_0 if and only if 'P is true at t_1' is true at t_1.

However there are obvious concerns about the coherence of the combination of the Indeterminacy and Determinacy claims. The aristotelian says that a token utterance now, of (*Peace*) is lacking in truth-value. And he agrees that one who in 2030 affirms, in some form of then appropriate words, the proposition it expresses will say something determinately true or false. So far there is no internal tension. But when he also agrees that it will then be determinately true, or false, to say that the contemporary—the present—utterance of (*Peace*) *was* determinately true or false when made, he appears to set up an antinomy. For he thereby allows that someone speaking then will be able correctly to describe the contemporary utterance as determinately true, or false, at the time of its making even though now—that is, at the time of its making!—it is correctly described as neither true nor false. It thus appears that the respective contemporary and 2030 assessments of the contemporary utterance of (*Peace*) are in simple contradiction, and that the aristotelian, in attempting to allow both claims—Determinacy and Indeterminacy—to stand, has committed himself to absurdity.[16]

How might truth-relativism help? Well, it may seem obvious. Once relativism is on the scene, a contradiction is aporetic only when each of its limbs is grounded in

---

[16] Greenough (n.d.) terms this the Perspective Paradox and offers an examination in depth of two non-relativistic way of dealing with it.

the same assessment-parameter. One who believes in the open future, the merchant of relativism may suggest, should accordingly view the truth of future contingent utterances as assessment-sensitive, with *time of assessment* itself constituting the relevant assessment-contextual parameter. Once that step is taken, the tension between the two claims is apparently relieved. The assessments of the contemporary utterance of (*Peace*) made respectively now and in 2030 are indeed mutually inconsistent. But when truth is assessment-sensitive, that can just be a case of faultless disagreement.

We need, however, to take some care with this point. It is no good just venturing that an utterance now of (*Peace*)—call it PM—can be untrue as assessed at the present time but—let's optimistically suppose—true as assessed in 2030. The proposal cannot be merely that utterances of (*Peace*) are assessment-sensitive, with time the relevant assessment-contextual parameter. That thought, by itself, is helpless to accommodate Determinacy. It allows that PM is untrue as assessed now and, let's say, true, as assessed at 2030. And that seems to be exactly what is wanted for Indeterminacy. But suppose you are reading this in 2024. A simple first order relativism here does nothing to help with the idea that 'PM is true at 2024' *itself* receives differential evaluation at 2024 and at 2030. For that we need precisely to take the relativism up to second-order. The truth-value not just of PM but also of an utterance of the first-order assessment, '$T(PM, CA_{2024})$', must both be time-of-assessment relative.

So the proposed relativist accommodation of the Indeterminacy and Determinacy claims must enter the territory of *multi-order relativism*—territory that is little explored and may well contain uncharted hazards. What we want to observe now is that, in sharp contrast to, for example, the situation with the (putative) assessment-relativity of expressions of judgements of taste, the proposed harmonization of the two essential ingredients in the aristotelian view enforces more than multi-order relativism. It enforces trumping—more specifically, conservation of the Determinacy claim enforces inward trumping:

$$(\forall ca_1, ca_2)\,(T(U, ca_1) \supset T(T(U, ca_2)), ca_1)$$

Let's think that through. The Indeterminacy claim has it that now—assuming you are reading this before 2030—we should assess PM as untrue; thus

(3) $\sim T(PM, CA_{2007})$

But suppose again that by 2030 the Middle East has become a region of peace. Looking back, we will assess the 2024 prediction, PM, as correct both now (in 2030):

(4) $T(PM, CA_{2030})$

and—by the Determinacy claim—at the time it was made:

(5) $T(T(\text{PM}, CA_{2024}), CA_{2030})$

Indeed, the Determinacy claim, together with (4), enforces a similar verdict about how PM should be assessed in *any* assessment-context ca_2:

(6) $(\forall ca_2) T(T(\text{PM}, ca_2), CA_{2030})$

Moreover, this would apply not just to CA_{2030} but to any assessment-context ca_1, for which

(7) $T(\text{PM}, ca_1)$

is correct. So we have a validation of inward trumping in full generality for PM:

$$(\forall ca_1)(\forall ca_2)(T(\text{PM}, ca_1) \supset T(T(\text{PM}, ca_2), ca_1))$$

and hence—since PM typifies any relevant example—of inward trumping in full generality for future contingents *tout court*. The Determinacy claim is exactly a thesis of cross-temporal inward trumping.

6. Aporia

It is a large question whether, if there were no further difficulty, this multi-order version of truth-relativism would indeed offer a satisfactory accommodation of the Determinacy and Indeterminacy components in an aristotelian view—or indeed whether any satisfactory view *should* aim to accommodate them both.[17] We resolutely set aside such issues here. Our point is that there *is* a further difficulty. The difficulty is that given certain other special features of the situation, trumping is inconsistent with the ability of the relativist to attest to their relativism.

To elaborate. In order to attest to their view, the relativist has to be able to advert to the possibility of witnesses—so, at the very least, they must not be constrained to regard as false, or unjustified, any candidate for being a witness that anyone might produce. The relevant kind of witness, recall, is a statement of the form,

(Witness) $T(U, CA_1) \; \& \sim T(U, CA_2)$

---

[17] Or even, again, whether the whole project of trying to stabilize the Open Future is not metaphysically entirely misguided. We are taking no stand. But see Zimmerman (2007) for a reminder of some very immediate, serious-seeming misgivings.

where CA_1 and CA_2 are in the present case specific assessment-contexts of which one is earlier than the other. Clearly there is no chance of producing such a witness when both contexts respectively antedate or post-date the events that determine the truth-value of U. So we can take it—given the way we have formulated the witness statement—that CA_2 antedates those events but CA_1 does not.

Here is the first of the 'special features' referred to a moment ago. *The theorist themself has to occupy some assessment-context of the relevant kind.* In the parable of Paul and Barry, there is no particular reason why the relativist theorist should have *any* relevant standards of taste. Maybe they cannot taste wine at all. Their own situation may simply not deliver any value for the relevant assessment-contextual parameter. But not so with time. The theorist has to be stationed in time—at least if we are speaking of a normal flesh-and-blood, human theorist. So they themselves will be (perhaps unknowingly) invested in a particular assessment of U. Call this feature *immersion*. A truth-relativist proposal is immersive just in case the assessment-contextual parameters it relativizes truth to are one's for which the theorist's own situation necessarily supplies values.[18]

Because the theorist is immersed, there are two cases:

Case 1   The theorist is at or later than CA_1. Then if $T(U, CA_1)$ is good, inward trumping will require her to allow that $T(T(U, CA_2), CA_1)$; that is, that $T(U, CA_2)$ holds good from her present assessment-context. So she cannot deny $T(U, CA_2)$ and thus has no witness. *Mutatis mutandis,* if $\neg U$ is good at CA_1.[19]

Case 2   The theorist is at some CA_2, before CA_1, and $\sim T(U, CA_2)$ is good. Here is the second of the 'special features' announced above. This is *partial blindness.* A truth-relativist proposal involves partial blindness just in case the assessment-contextual parameters it relativizes truth to are such that from the standpoint of at least some of them, there is no knowing what is true, or false, from the standpoint of (some) others. By Indeterminacy, a thinker at the earlier of two assessment-contexts is partially blind—he is blind with respect to the assessments mandated by the later context of utterance which are not yet true or false but will be so by the time of the later context. This is the situation of the relativist theorist at CA_2. There is no knowing what will be the situation as assessed at CA_1 and so the theorist is in no position to affirm $T(U, CA_1)$. So again, he has no witness of his relativism. QED

This may seem disarmingly simple. And there is indeed scope for a wriggle. Indeterminacy provides both $\sim T(U, CA_2)$ and $\sim T(\neg U, CA_2)$. But setting aside irrelevant complications to do with vagueness, it may seem that it may still be known at CA_2 that either U or $\neg U$ will be true as assessed at CA_1. That is

---

[18] Wright this volume, chapter 4, calls discourses for which truth-relativism is immersive "fully committed."

[19] We write '$\neg U$' to denote an utterance of the negation of the proposition expressed by U (Cf. note 12).

(D) $T(U, CA_1) \lor T(\neg U, CA_1)$

And if so, the theorist is in position to reason that the disjunction:

$$[\sim T(U, CA_2) \& T(U, CA_1)] \lor [\sim T(\neg U, CA_2) \& T(\neg U, CA_1)]$$

is true at CA_2, even if he cannot say which disjunct is good. There is, then, an *unidentified* witness. Isn't that good enough?

In fact, it is confused. Since U concerns events at the time of CA_1, 'U' and "$T(U, CA_1)$" are equivalent. Likewise, '$\neg U$' and "$T(\neg U, CA_1)$." So the theorist is actually in no position at CA_2 to endorse (D) unless he is then in a position to endorse the simple instance of the law of excluded middle,

$$U \lor \neg U$$

How is that consistent with Indeterminacy?

It may be replied that the theorist may be proposing some supervaluational or other treatment of disjunction that would allow endorsement of the law of excluded middle to be consistent with rejection of the determinate truth of either disjunct.[20] Obviously, however, the same must then go with the supposed disjunction of witnesses,

(DW) $[\sim T(U, CA_2) \& T(U, CA_1)] \lor [\sim T(\neg U, CA_2) \& T(\neg U, CA_1)]$

with the result that it may be accepted in a particular context of assessment without commitment to either disjunct in particular being true at that context. But it is only if one in particular *is* true that we have an unidentified witness.

Here is another way of bringing out the confusion. The existence of an unidentified witness is supposed to be affirmed from the standpoint of CA_2. So what is wanted is that one of the disjuncts of (DW) is true at CA_2, even if there is no saying which. But the premise for the argument is that (D) is true at CA_2, i.e.,

$$T((T(U, CA_1) \lor T(\neg U, CA_1)), CA_2),$$

in which truth at CA_2 is undistributed across the disjuncts of (D). It is only after it is distributed that we have something suitable to serve as the premise of an inference to (DW). But to distribute it so would be in flat contradiction of Indeterminacy.

---

[20] Thus Thomason (1970) and MacFarlane (2008).

7. Another Example?

It is not of course simply the involvement of second-order relativism that makes for the difficulty. In fact second-order relativism is involved only epiphenomenally, as it were, as a consequence of the mix of first-order relativism and inward trumping. And that mix too is, by itself, insufficient to underwrite an attestability problem (at least it is so for all that we have shown.) The crucial additional features are immersion, partial blindness, and one more: that in the particular case, any witness to first-order relativism has to straddle, so to speak, a pair of assessment-contexts *one of which trumps the other while the other is blind to the first*. The last point is crucial: if the trumped assessment-context were not blind to the trumping assessment-context, there would be no general obstacle to the production of a witness from within the former.

So it may seem to be a rather *outré* brew of ingredients that's needed to make the trouble. It therefore merits observation that there is at least one other discourse singled out for relativistic treatment in the modern debate which—so long as its principal proponent is right about one important aspect—would also appear to trigger the mix. This is discourse of epistemic modality—specifically, of epistemic possibility. John MacFarlane has famously suggested that an assessment-relativist conception of the truth-conditions of claims of the form:

It might be that *P*,

where the "might" is understood as referring to what is consonant with some body of information, rather than to any form of ontological (metaphysical) possibility, makes sense of a variety of linguistic data that otherwise appear anomalous and cannot, in particular, easily be explained by any contextualist or 'invariantist' account.[21]

The leading idea is that an utterance of "It might be that *P*" expresses a truth, or a falsehood, according to whether *P* is or is not consonant with the information possessed not by the speaker, or some utterance-contextually determined circle, but by an assessor of the utterance. One and the same such utterance can be true for one assessor and false for another, depending on variation in their respective collateral knowledge. That much is the basic, first-order relativism about the case. What about blindness? Well, whenever CA_1 and CA_2 are such that one incorporates more knowledge than the other, an occupant of the inferior will not know all that is known by the superior, so will not be able to assess what is epistemically possible as determined by the latter. As for immersion, the theorist is of course bound to be immersed, since she will have her own body of knowledge mandating

---

[21] MacFarlane (2003a and 2011). The proposal has been widely discussed. An assessment of some of the issues is offered in Wright (2007). This volume, Chapter 3.

a view about the epistemic possibility, or otherwise, of any particular targeted claim.

Now, if blindness is not to block the knowledgeable citation of a witness, the theorist has to know everything known in either of the two assessment-contexts that the witness mentions. And as far as the target utterance is concerned, he will therefore be constrained to agree with the assessment of the more knowledgeable of the two.[22] So the crux is simple inward trumping: if inward trumping holds, the theorist will not only affirm the opposite of the assessment of U—say, that mandated in CA_1—with which he disagrees: he will affirm that the CA_1 assessment of U is not true in its original context of assessment, CA_1. But then he has contradicted one component in his prospective witness.

So everything hangs on this: if one is relativist about epistemic possibility claims, why should—or why might—one think that inward trumping holds? Well, there is a case for thinking so on the basis of the very linguistic 'data' that MacFarlane regards as impelling us towards relativism about epistemic modals. Here is a version of what has become a stock example, original to his (2003a):[23]

t_1 Sue: "Bill could be in Boston"
    Ted: "Actually, I just saw him board a flight to Houston"
t_2 Sue: "Oh. Then I was wrong."

MacFarlane, in that discussion and later, finds this an entirely plausible piece of dialogue, and he thinks we should take Sue's t_2 utterance very seriously, as an intended *retrospective retraction*. She is saying that what she said was mistaken when she said it. Thus interpreted, Sue's t_2 utterance contrasts with what she would be doing if, after Ted's observation, she were merely to affirm:

t_2^* "Then that's wrong—he can't be in Boston,"

in which the rider suggests that what she now wants to distance herself from is merely the claim that *would* be made by a present—t_2—affirmation of a token of her t_1-utterance type. No doubt Sue is doing that in the original scenario as well. But in MacFarlane's view she is there properly understood as doing more. For it would, in his view, be "odd and unnatural" if Sue were to continue,

---

[22] More specifically, suppose CA_1 and CA_2 are the two contexts, respectively inferior and superior, concerned. It cannot have been that the latter reinstates a possibility claim that the former discounts, since anything inconsistent with the former must be inconsistent with the latter too. So CA_2 must discount a possibility claim which CA_1 affirms. But in that case the theorist's context, CA_3, must share CA_2's assessment, since it incorporates all CA_2's knowledge.

[23] The example and discussion are repeated in all essentials in MacFarlane (2011).

"—although when I said, "Bill might be in Boston," what I said was true, and I stand by that claim."

MacFarlane comments,

> it seems to me that th[is] alternative continuation, on which [a speaker] stands by her original claim, *always* sounds wrong. We simply don't have the practice of standing by old claims of epistemic possibility in the face of new knowledge. We *could have* had this practice, but as things are, we just don't talk this way.[24]

The point is crucial for MacFarlane because it blocks the assimilation of the case to one in which there is a context-of-use determined change of content. If Sue's "odd and unnatural" continuation would in fact be perfectly acceptable normal practice, then the obvious construal to place upon her original self-correction would be *contextualist*—that she had no quarrel with what she had said (that is, with the content affirmed) before but only with what a token of the very same sentence type would affirm at t_2. Whereas if Sue's correction is taken as MacFarlane seems to want to suggest, as implying that what she said was wrong in the original context in which she said it, then—given that the content in question is, in his view, the same—the correction is tantamount to an act of trumping.

Note that there is no space for the intermediate interpretation, so to speak, that while, *pace* contextualism, the content in question is the same, Sue's apparently retrospective correction is retrospective only with respect to the saying, as it were; i.e., that it is tantamount to "What I said back then *is* wrong." If that were the right account, there would be no obstacle to the addition, "though it was correct in the context in which I said it"—exactly the practice that MacFarlane is anxious to insist we just don't have. So it seems we should conclude that if the illustrated pattern of correction *is* indeed our standard practice, to be respected by any good theoretical account, then any such good account will incorporate trumping. Accordingly—in the light of the other circumstances noted—it will not be an attestable relativist account.

A qualification is needed. We remarked at the end of Section 1 that, with one exception, our focus would be on the relativist's dyadic metalinguistic truth-predicate, rather than on the behaviour of "true" and its cognates within an object language for which an assessment-relativist semantics is proposed. The exception is the present issue: how the pattern of correction illustrated by Sue's "I was wrong" needs to be interpreted if it is to support MacFarlane's proposal. Since it employs no overtly metalinguistic truth-predicate, or cognate of such, it cannot be said that the pattern of correction in question is one of explicit trumping. The

---

[24] MacFarlane (2003a, p. 4).

question is whether it is best construed as carrying a content which would naturally be expressed in a way tantamount to an act of explicit trumping *if* the necessary metalinguistic resources were available. The point is then that if MacFarlane is right that contextualism cannot handle the datum, and if, as seems clear, the intermediate interpretation just canvassed will not marry with a practice of not 'standing by old claims of epistemic possibility in the light of new knowledge', there is no other salient construal.

So the dilemma, in brief, is this: if MacFarlane is wrong about either the reality or the interpretation of the pattern of correction illustrated, the relativist proposal is unmotivated by it; but if he is right, inward trumping is mandated for epistemic possibility claims just as soon as the appropriate metalinguistic resources are available, and—in circumstances that satisfy the other conditions in the "outré brew"—the proposed relativism is then not attestable.

8. The Determinacy Claim Again

There is a further, connected issue about aristotelian relativism and the Determinacy claim which is worth noting. We said little to uncover any very deep motivation for the latter, referring merely to its entrenchment in our linguistic practice. So, at least as far as the present discussion is concerned, it is entirely open that the Determinacy claim *as we have understood it* is something that the proponent of the open future should simply jettison. One thought tending in that direction reflects that it is not clear what the truth-predicate is that features in the relevant entrenched aspects of our practice. We explained at the outset that our argument was concerned with the metalinguistic, dyadic truth-predicate on utterances. But is that the right predicate in terms of which to try to articulate the linguistic intuitions, or habits, that suggest the Determinacy claim?

One might, on reflection, think not. An area of discourse for which utterance truth was assessment-sensitive would be likely in any case to feature a regular object-language truth-operator on (apparent) propositional contents, "it is true that...," for which no significant tense need be defined, and whose application would accordingly be timeless.[25] Is it so clear that it is not its interpretation in terms of such an operator that makes the Determinacy claim seem nigh on platitudinous? What stands in the way of interpreting my "See, I was right," applied to an earlier prediction, as an expression to the effect that what I said— the proposition I affirmed—is timelessly true in this metaphysically lightweight sense? And what blocks the corresponding interpretation of the truth-value link earlier cited:

---

[25] See §8 of MacFarlane (2008) for a semantics for such a propositional operator for the very case of tensed discourse.

'P will be true at t_1' was true at t_0 if and only if 'P is true at t_1' is true at t_1,

as merely identifying the conditions of metaphysically light-weight, timeless truth of the proposition expressed by an utterance of 'P will be true at t_1' at t_0 with those of the proposition expressed by an utterance of 'P is true at t_1' at t_1?

The question is pointed. Here we merely observe that if this is indeed the right way to, so to say, neutralise the sting of the Determinacy claim—so that the retrospective affirmations of truth sanctioned by Determinacy no longer stand in any conflict with the putative indeterminacy of future contingent utterances— then it also provides a splendid way to deconstruct the Indeterminacy claim as a proper expression of the belief in the open future in the first place. The Indeterminacy claim is to the effect that future contingent utterances carry no truth-values, and that to think otherwise is perforce to allow the character of the future to be settled before it comes to be. The reply can now be, to the contrary, that to concede truth-value to future contingent utterances need be no more than to concede metaphysically lightweight, timeless truth-values to the propositions they express: truth-values whose possession, understood in the terms proposed in order to defang the Determinacy claim, is nothing that implies anything about date of settlement. So Indeterminacy is defanged too. The belief that the future is open, whatever exactly it may now amount to, will be nothing to motivate a denial of truth-value to future contingents. So there will be no phenomenon of variability in truth-value for a relativist proposal to assist in stabilizing.

9. Unattestable but Respectable Relativism?

(*Rel*), the canonical form of the relativistic thesis for a discourse, is an existential claim. There are constructivistically minded philosophers who would argue that any justification to regard an existential claim as true is abrogated by a demon- stration that no witness to it can justifiably be taken as true. We have some sympathy for some suitably qualified version of that claim.[26] But even if it is repudiated, there are still very awkward consequences for the would-be proponent of an unattestable relativism. One is that the relativistic apparatus is straight away precluded from the substantiation of any faultless disagreement claim, since to identify a specific type of disagreement as faultless will precisely be to attest to the

---

[26] Note, by the way, that it needs no qualification in the light of Preface Paradox type examples. These are cases where an existential is reasonably believed even though each of its instances is reasonably doubted: there is no suggestion that none of them *can* be reasonably believed but only that, in the evidential context in question, they are not. In such cases, one reasonably believes that a witness can, by some appropriate procedure, be found, and the challenge is to explain why this belief is not defeated by one's justified confidence in the falsity of each of the possible witnesses. This is not the predicament of the exponents of unattestable relativisms.

relevant relativism. Another is to put great pressure on the question of *evidence* for adopting a relativistic account of the discourse in question in the first place. What could such evidence be in the presence of a proof that no witness to the relevant instance of (*Rel*) could rationally be affirmed by any participant in the discourse? It is true that the linguistic 'data' cited by relativists are in general much more indirect than would be provided simply by speakers making witness claims—and, as we have in effect already reflected, that is as it had better be since speakers need not in general have the resource of a metalinguistic relative truth-predicate in terms of which to formulate such claims. But the putative linguistic evidence ought at least, surely, to suggest that such claims *would* be endorsed, once speakers are provided with the means to express them. Yet where relativism is unattestable, the evidence cannot possibly have that character. How might it manage to bear on the appropriate instance of (*Rel*) nevertheless?

Another conceivable direction[27] would be for the theorist to attempt to argue that the additional features that lead to unattestability might fail for certain kinds of conceivable but non-actual thinkers. This thought might be developed in either of two directions. If a hypothetical theorist could consider our discourse of future contingencies from a standpoint outside our time, for example—that is, from an *unimmersed* vantage point—then perhaps he might be free to affirm instances of each of the conjuncts of a witness to (*Rel*) for future contingents as uttered by us. Conversely, we might cast ourselves in the role of theorists concerning the discourse involving future contingents of hypothetical speakers who again occupied an incommensurable time, and seek to argue that, in view of other similarities between their hypothetical discourse and our actual one, the possibility of affirmable witnesses, from our perspective, to a relativistic account of their discourse would allow whatever independent reasons there might be to offer an assessment-relativist account of it to transfer to such a view of ours, even though the view would be unattestable by us actual speakers.

We mention these ideas only to show we are aware of them. For the aristotelian case, they depend on the difficult idea that an assessment of the truth-values of future contingents from a situation incommensurable to ours in time—a temporally unimmersed situation—is intelligible; more specifically that a form of assessment-context is conceivable which, while, ratifying a conjunction of the form, '$\sim T(U, CA_2)$ & $T(U, CA_1)$' for CA_2 and CA_1 constituted by stations in a particular time, itself involved no station in that time and delivered no assessment of U. And for the case of epistemic possibility, they clearly go nowhere since the idea of an assessor, even a counterfactual assessor, who has no particular state of knowledge, is incoherent.

---

[27] Pressed in seminar discussion by Herman Cappelen and Elia Zardini.

10. Concluding Remarks

Attestability problems are just one potential hazard for unwary relativists. What we have offered is merely a specimen investigation of one within a conspectus of questions that have tended to be displaced by the modern debate which, largely content with the notion that contemporary truth-relativism is an interesting but, from the point of view of semantic theory, essentially modest twist to the supposedly straightforward Lewisian precedent, has been mostly focused on marshalling and evaluating linguistic 'data', for and against, in different regions of discourse. This is unfortunate. For one thing, there are very deep-reaching issues in the philosophy of language about just how straightforward the Lewisian precedent really is, and about how modest the "twist."[28] But in any case we should also still aspire to engage the underlying issues about philosophical status, coherence, and possible generalization with which critics have badgered relativism ever since its Protagorean gestation and which still bear on its modern incarnations. We still need to know, for example, which are the coherent multi-order combinations of relativisms and absolutisms, what is the proper statement of the traditional benefit of even-handedness, and what are the conditions for its deliverability, what is the impact on the stability and benefits of relativist approaches in particular localities of variable phenomena like immersion, blindness, and perhaps others yet undisclosed; and what impact on all of this is carried by the issue whether philosophy itself should be seen as an assessment-sensitive domain.[29] The present climate is indeed one in which it may be easier than before to get this range of questions into focus and debate them effectively. But the debate is, for the most part, barely engaged.[30]

Appendix

Interdependencies of orders of absolutism (and relativism)

Where U ranges over the utterances of a discourse, D, for which truth-relativism has been proposed, a *first-order assessment* is any statement of either of the forms, $T(U, CA_k)$, or $\sim T(U, CA_k)$; a *second-order assessment* is any statement of either of those forms in which the occurrence of 'U' is replaced by the name of a first-order assessment; and an n*th-order*

---

[28] For exploration, see Cappelen and Hawthorne (2009).

[29] See Hales (2006).

[30] We are grateful to the members of the Arché *Contextualism and Relativism* project seminar for very helpful discussion of an earlier draft. Thanks also to Giorgio Volpe and Giuliano Torrengo. Especial thanks to Elia Zardini and Roberto Loss.

assessment is any statement of either of those forms in which the occurrence of '*U*' is replaced by the name of an $(n - 1)$th-order assessment.

First-order absolutism about D is the view that the only contextually variable features contributing towards determination of the truth-conditions of its utterances are features of their contexts of *use*. Utterances with this property will be termed, correspondingly, *first-order absolute*. Thus for such utterances U, this principle will hold:

$$(\text{First-order absolutism}) \quad (\forall ca_1, ca_2)(T(U, ca_1) \equiv T(U, ca_2))$$

First-order absolutism about D holds that no variation in parameters of assessment makes a difference to the truth-conditions of its utterances. Assessment-contexts are idle wheels in the determination of the truth-value of utterances in the range of U.

There is, obviously, an analogous second-order doctrine about the absoluteness of the truth-values of first-order assessments of utterances of D. *Second-order absolutism* amounts to the idea that once a value for a parameter of assessment of an utterance U of D is fixed, the result—the truth-value which U takes for that value—is *itself* absolute: there is no further assessment-relativity attending its determination. If that is granted, this principle will hold:

$$(\text{Second-order absolutism}) \quad (\forall ca_1, ca_2, ca_3) T(T(U, ca_1), ca_2)$$
$$\equiv T(T(U, ca_1), ca_3)$$

By contrast *second-order relativism* for a class of utterances is the thesis that there are first-order assessments of members of that class that are themselves assessment-sensitive: two second-order assessments can correctly evaluate the same first-order assessment in different ways. We now prove four theses.

Thesis (I)

(On a natural assumption) First-order absolutism entails second-order absolutism.

Here is a proof by classical *reductio*. Assume first-order absolutism:

(1) $(\forall ca_1, ca_2)(T(U, ca_1) \equiv T(U, ca_2))$

Assume for *reductio* that second-order absolutism fails for U:

(2) $(\exists ca_1, ca_2, ca_3)(T(T(U, ca_1), ca_2) \& \sim T(T(U, ca_1), ca_3))$

Let CA_1, CA_2, and CA_3 witness of the truth of (2):

(3) $(T(T(U, CA_1), CA_2) \& \sim T(T(U, CA_1), CA_3))$

The "natural assumption" referred to is that, if first-order absolutism holds for U, it holds as an absolute, theoretical truth. Hence it should hold irrespective of any context of assessment in which it is considered:

(4) $(\forall ca_k, ca_m, ca_n)\,(T(T(U, ca_m) \equiv T(U, ca_n)), ca_k)$

From this, taking CA_1 for 'ca_m' and CA_2 for 'ca_n' and 'ca_k', we get

(5) $T(T(T(U, CA_1) \equiv T(U, CA_2)), CA_2)$

whence, distributing the context of assessment across the enclosed biconditional,[31] we obtain

(6) $T(T(U, CA_1), CA_2) \equiv T(T(U, CA_2), CA_2)$

From (6) applying the first conjunct of (3), a *modus ponens* across the biconditional yields

(7) $T(T(U, CA_2), CA_2)$

By analogous steps, taking CA_1 for 'ca_m' and CA_3 for 'ca_n' and 'ca_k' in (4), we obtain

(8) $T(T(U, CA_1), CA_3) \equiv T(T(U, CA_3), CA_3)$

From (8) applying the second conjunct of (3), a *modus tollens* across the biconditional yields

(9) $\sim T(T(U, CA_3), CA_3)$

By the quasi-disquotational principle, (8) and (9) entail

(10) $T(U, CA_2)\ \&\sim T(U, CA_3),$

contradicting assumption (1) of first-order absolutism.

Evidently this reasoning manifests a template that is (classically) good when U is a statement of any kind. In particular, it is good if U is itself an nth-order assessment of some other utterance. So we have the generalized result that nth-order absolutism entails $n + 1$th order absolutism.

We do not, of course, expect the converse entailment, from second- to first-order absolutism, or more generally from nth to $n - 1$th-order absolutism, without qualification.

---

[31] If a biconditional holds in a context of assessment, and so does one of its limbs, then so too does the other.

It is, for instance, quite consistent with first-order relativism about matters of taste to hold that truths about which opinions are sanctioned by which standards of taste are themselves absolute. That the proposition that Sassicaia is better than Barolo is true as assessed by Paul's standards, but not as assessed by Barry's, may be an absolute truth, invariant under change not just in standards of taste but in any assessment-contextual parameters.

However, although second-order absolutism does not itself enjoin first-order absolutism, it does so if *inward* trumping also holds. In fact, inward trumping precludes the combination of regular (first-order) relativism and second-order absolutism.

Thesis (II)

Second-order Absolutism and trumping entail First-Order Absolutism

This is very straightforward to see. Suppose that second-order absolutism and inward trumping hold for an utterance U:

(1) $(\forall ca_1, ca_2, ca_3)T(T(U, ca_1), ca_2) \equiv T(T(U, ca_1), ca_3)$ (Second-order Absolutism)

(2) $(\forall ca_1, ca_2)(T(U, ca_1) \supset T(T(U, ca_2), ca_1))$ (Inward trumping)

and assume for *reductio* that first-order relativism holds for U:

(3) $(\exists ca_1, ca_2)(T(U, ca_1) \& \sim T(U, ca_2))$ (First-order relativism)

Let CA_1 and CA_2 be two contexts of assessment which witness the truth of (3), specifically, suppose that the utterance U is true relative to the context of assessment CA_1 and untrue relative to the context of assessment CA_2:

(4) $(T(U, CA_1) \& \sim T(U, CA_2))$

By the quasi-disquotational principle, the second conjunct of (4) yields

(5) $\sim T(T(U, CA_2), CA_2)$

As an instance of (1), taking CA_1 for 'ca_3' and CA_2 for 'ca_1' and 'ca_2' we obtain:

(6) $T(T(U, CA_2), CA_2) \equiv T(T(U, CA_2), CA_1)$

And from (5) and (6) by contraposition we get

(7) $\sim T(T(U, CA_2), CA_1)$

But now from (2), taking CA_1 and CA_2 for 'ca_1' and 'ca_2' respectively, together with the first conjunct of (4), we obtain

(8) $T(T(U, CA_2), CA_1)$,

which contradicts (7).

Since first-order absolutism entails second-order absolutism, first- and second-order absolutism must hold together if inward trumping holds. So—as noted in the main text—if there is a case for first-order relativism about a certain area of discourse and if in that area of discourse inward trumping holds, second-order relativism is enforced for that area too.

Second-order absolutism also entails first-order absolutism if *outward* trumping holds. Again, the proof is very immediate. Suppose that second-order absolutism and outward trumping hold for an utterance U:

(1) $(\forall ca_1, ca_2, ca_3) T(T(U, ca_1), ca_2) \equiv T(T(U, ca_1), ca_3)$ (Second-order Absolutism)

(2) $(\forall ca_1, ca_2)(T(T(U, ca_2), ca_1) \supset T(U, ca_1))$ (Outward trumping)

and assume for *reductio* that first-order relativism holds for U:

(3) $(\exists ca_1, ca_2)(T(U, ca_1) \,\&\, \sim T(U, ca_2))$ (First-order relativism)

Let CA_1 and CA_2 be two contexts of assessment which witness the truth of (3); specifically, suppose that the utterance U is true relative to the context of assessment CA_1 and untrue relative to the context of assessment CA_2:

(4) $(T(U, CA_1) \,\&\, \sim T(U, CA_2))$

As an instance of (1), taking CA_2 for 'ca_3' and CA_1 for 'ca_1' and 'ca_2', we obtain:

(5) $T(T(U, CA_1), CA_1) \equiv T(T(U, CA_1), CA_2)$

Taking 'CA_2' for 'ca_1' and 'CA_1' for 'ca_2' in (2), we have

(6) $T(T(U, CA_1), CA_2) \supset T(U, CA_2))$

The second conjunct of (4) together with (6) then yield by contraposition

(7) $\sim T(T(U, CA_1), CA_2)$

which by (5) and a further contraposition yields

(8) $\sim T(T(U, CA_1), CA_1)$

By the quasi-disquotational principle, (8) yields

(9) $\sim T(U, CA_1)$

which contradicts with the first conjunct of (4). It follows that in the presence of outward trumping, first-order relativism for a certain area of discourse is a commitment to second-order relativism as well.

In general: if either form of trumping holds, nth- and $n + 1$th-order absolutism collapse into each other, and so do nth- and $n + 1$th-order relativism.

Let Absolute Absolutism for a discourse D be the view that all its basic statements and every nth-order assessment of them are absolute. Let the extended discourse of D, D^*, include D and all nth-order assessments of statements of D. Then:

Thesis (III)

Absolute Absolutism for a discourse D entails that both inward and outward trumping hold unrestrictedly within D^*.

Both cases are very immediate. First, inward trumping. Let U be any statement of D^*. Assume the antecedent of inward trumping holds for U and an arbitrary context of assessment CA_1:

(1) $T(U, CA_1)$

By the quasi-disquotational principle, we have that

(2) $T(T(U, CA_1), CA_1)$

Since by absolute absolutism, any arbitrary assessment-context, CA_2, agrees with CA_1 in the assessment of $T(U, CA_1)$, we have that

(3) $T(T(U, CA_1), CA_2)$

Steps of Conditional Proof and Universal Generalization then yield inward trumping.

Now, assume the antecedent of outward trumping:

(4) $T(T(U, CA_1), CA_2)$

Since absolute absolutism holds, we have that since all contexts of assessment agree in the evaluation of $T(U, CA_1)$, CA_1 will agree with CA_2:

(5) $T(T(U, CA_1), CA_1)$

The quasi-disquotational principle then yields the consequent of outward trumping,

(6) $T(U, CA_1)$

with steps of conditional proof and generalization to follow.

References

Cappelen, H. and J. Hawthorne (2009), *Relativism and Monadic Truth*, Oxford: Oxford University Press.

Greenough, Patrick (n.d.), "The Open Future" (unpublished manuscript).

Hales, S. (2006), *Relativism and the Foundations of Philosophy*, Boston, MA: MIT Press.

Kölbel, M. (2004), "Faultless Disagreement," *Proceedings of the Aristotelian Society* 104, 53–73.

Lewis, D. (1980), "Index, Context, and Content," in S. Kanger and S. Ohman (eds.), *Philosophy and Grammar*, 79–100. Reprinted in his (1998), *Papers in Philosophical Logic*, Cambridge: Cambridge University Press, 21–44.

Lukasiewicz, J. (1970), "On Determinism," in L. Borkowski (ed.), *Selected Works*, Amsterdam: North Holland.

MacFarlane, J. (2003a), "Epistemic Modalities and Relative Truth," MS available at http://sophos.berkeley.edu/macfarlane/epistmod.pdf (unpublished).

MacFarlane, J. (2003b), "Future Contingents and Relative Truth," *The Philosophical Quarterly* 53, 321–36.

MacFarlane, J. (2005a), "The Assessment Sensitivity of Knowledge Attributions," in T. Szabó Gendler and J. Hawthorne (eds.), *Oxford Studies in Epistemology*, Vol. 1, Oxford: Oxford University Press, 197–223.

MacFarlane, J. (2005b), "Making Sense of Relative Truth," *Proceedings of the Aristotelian Society* 105, 321–39.

MacFarlane, J. (2007), "Relativism and Disagreement," *Philosophical Studies* 132, 17–31.

MacFarlane, J. (2008), "Truth in the Garden of Forking Paths," in M. García-Carpintero and M. Kölbel (eds.), *Relative Truth*, Oxford: Oxford University Press.

Macfarlane, J. (2011), "Epistemic Modals Are Assessment-Sensitive" in B. Weatherson and A. Egan (eds.), *Epistemic Modality*, Oxford University Press.

Thomason, R. H. (1970), "Indeterministic Time and Truth-Value Gaps," *Theoria* 36, 264–81.

Wright, C. (2006), "Intuitionism, Realism, Relativism and Rhubarb," in P. Greenough and M. P. Lynch (eds.), *Truth and Realism*, Oxford: Oxford University Press, 77–99. This volume, chapter 2.

Wright, C. (2007), "New Age Relativism and Epistemic Possibility," in E. Sosa and E. Villanueva (eds.), *Philosophical Issues* 17 (special number on *The Metaphysics of Epistemology*), 262–83. This volume, chapter 3.

Wright, C. (2008), "Relativism about Truth Itself: Haphazard Thoughts about the Very Idea," in M. García-Carpintero and M. Kölbel (eds.), *Relativizing Truth*, Oxford: Oxford University Press. This volume, chapter 4.

Zimmerman, A. (2007), "Against Relativism," *Philosophical Studies* 133, 313–48.

7

Assessment-Sensitivity

The Manifestation Challenge

1

MacFarlane's core project in his deep-reaching, superbly crafted book is the defence of the claim that there is a theoretically respectable, interesting, useful species of relativism about truth—to wit, the species he captions by the term, *assessment-sensitivity*. Assessment-sensitivity contrasts, however, with classic truth-relativism—if indeed there is such a thing—in three important respects. First, it is potentially a *local* feature of discourses. MacFarlane, unlike Protagoras, is making no general claim about the metaphysics of truth. So he finesses a broad sweep of traditional concerns about the coherence of truth-relativism, from the *Theaetetus* onwards, which take it to be a global thesis (so hence, e.g., self-applicable). Second, whereas traditional relative truth is a property of the contents of attitudes, assessment-sensitivity is a characteristic in the first instance of token assertoric utterances—though MacFarlane allows it to apply derivatively to the propositions expressed thereby (which he understands in the usual intuitive way as what are asserted, what are believed, what sustain relations of incompatibility and entailment, and so on).[1] Finally, MacFarlane's project is harnessed to the task of giving *descriptively* adequate semantic theories for certain regions of discourse as actually practiced, rather than, at least in the first instance, to any specifically metaphysical controversies. Traditionally, truth-relativism is a player in the *normative* debates about realism and objectivity, one kind of paradigm of anti-realism, alongside and contrasting with non-cognitivism, error-theory, expressivism, and the rest—and indeed a paradigm that in the modern (twentieth-century) debates was largely discarded. MacFarlane, as it appears, intends no direct contribution to those debates.

The interest of MacFarlane's thesis is nevertheless unquestionable. The remarks to follow will bear on the theoretical respectability, broadly conceived, of truth-relativism as he develops it, and—indirectly—on its utility.

---

[1] See MacFarlane (2014, p. 49 and following). Unless otherwise stated, all references below are to MacFarlane (2014).

Essays on Relativism: 2001–2021. Crispin Wright, Oxford University Press. © Crispin Wright 2023.
DOI: 10.1093/oso/9780192845993.003.0008

2

A class of utterances is assessment-sensitive if and only if, for each member U of that class, the question whether an assertor of U speaks truly turns not merely on the circumstances obtaining on the occasion of the assertion but depends additionally on aspects of a "context of assessment": perhaps the information state, or interests, of an assessor, or her moral standards, or tastes, or just the time of assessment. A single such utterance may thus receive *variable but nevertheless correct* assessments of truth-value, depending on the variable characteristics, broadly conceived—"parameters"—of assessors of it. There is no once-and-for-all answer to the question whether the assertor of U spoke truly, even after the content and circumstances of the assertion are fully determined. Thus the truth-conditions for assessment-sensitive utterances involve a double relativity: U is true (or not) as uttered in C_1—the *context of use*, serving to fix the content expressed by U (as well, perhaps, as other relevant features of the circumstances of evaluation)—and assessed in C_2—the *context of assessment*, serving to fix the values of the relevant parameters of assessment.[2]

Now, if a semantic theory that centralizes such an assessment-sensitive notion of truth is to prove descriptively superior, we need a clear account of how the assessment-sensitivity of a class of utterances might be distinctively manifest in the discourse concerned. What is wanted, at first blush, is clear evidence that a pair of assessors who diverge in their assessments of an utterance U, one regarding it as true and the other as false, can both be not merely justified but *correct*—and this purely in virtue of their satisfaction of different relevant parameters of assessment. How might that highly theoretical-sounding circumstance show in linguistic practice?

I think this matter has always been problematic, and my principal point here will be that it remains so. Of course there would be no problem if we could just assume that each speaker X has the resource in the object language of a *correctness* predicate, contrasted with all three of (absolute) truth, truth as assessed by X, and epistemic justifiability in the object language. In that case X can simply *say* that Y's assessment is correct, even though false (as assessed by X), and even though X does not mean to say (merely) that Y's assessment is fully (epistemically) justified in Y's situation. But the theorist of assessment-sensitivity cannot simply assume that such resources are in play. We are asking after the *pre-theoretic* manifestation of the fact that the discourse is assessment-sensitive: we want to be told about patterns of use that will display that fact even if the only alethic predicate in currency in the discourse itself is the unreconstructed "true." The task is to give sense to the idea that a semantic theory featuring an assessment-sensitive notion of truth has genuine, distinctive operational content.

---

[2] The extension of this idea to propositions is outlined in ch. 4. MacFarlane's.

3

MacFarlane himself is very respectful of the manifestation challenge. His response to it is fashioned in reaction to another type of proposal that comes into focus in his framework—one, indeed, which may seem to chime better with certain folk ideas about relativism than MacFarlane's own. Suppose Tim affirms, correctly by his taste, that stewed rhubarb is delicious, and Paul affirms, correctly by his taste, the contrary. And suppose I want to say, even-handedly, as an expression of an intuitive relativism, that neither is making any kind of mistake. (Their disagreement is "faultless.") That is something it seems I cannot say if utterances of "Stewed rhubarb is delicious" are assessment-sensitive, since then I will have to assess both claims by *my* taste, and whatever that may be, it cannot sustain both Tim's and Paul's verdicts. Suppose therefore that we retain the idea that the truth of such assertions is standards-of-taste-relative but stipulate instead that the standards by which they are to be assessed are those of their *authors*. The proposal is, in effect, that C_1 and C_2 are to coincide: the context of assessment is to be the context of use. Then now I can say that both Paul and Tim speak truly.

This proposal is what MacFarlane calls *non-indexical contextualism*.[3] Non-indexical contextualism may seem at first glance like a pretty decent approximation to Everyman's notion of relativism. (It allows that there is "your truth" and "my truth.") MacFarlane scorns the idea that such a view is properly relativist, primarily on the ground that, unlike assessment-sensitivity, it assigns once-and-for-all truth-values to Paul's and Tim's utterances. That reflection, notably, misses the point that if Paul insincerely but obsequiously defers to Tim, one and the same proposition will be false in his mouth but true in Tim's. The reader may think that is relativism enough to fulfil the Protagorean spirit.

Perhaps it is pointless to debate further which view has the better title to the term, "relativism." What is significant for MacFarlane's purposes is that non-indexical contextualism and assessment-sensitivity potentially diverge in their predictions of use. For suppose I assert U and then later have occasion to re-visit the question of the truth-value of my former utterance of it: non-indexical contextualism bids me defer to the standards of the context in which the utterance was originally made, and if it was correct by those standards—let's suppose it was—I should now regard my assertion as having been made truly, whatever the standards of the context that I now occupy. Assessment-sensitivity, by contrast, will have me assess my earlier utterance of U precisely by the standards of my

---

[3] "Non-indexical" indicates that the view does not postulate that the propositional content of "Rhubarb is delicious," e.g. varies as a function of variation in parameters—here, standards of taste— in Tim's and Paul's respective contexts of use. What Tim affirms is what Paul denies. But the view is contextualist in granting that the truth-value of the proposition concerned *is* variable with parameters set by context of use.

present context and I may thus be led to regard my assertion as having been made falsely, even if it was correct by the standards of its original context.

4

This contrast is key to MacFarlane's response to the manifestation challenge. He approaches the matter via a remark of Michael Dummett in the latter's paper, "Truth," to the effect that in order to grasp the notion of truth, it is necessary not merely to know under what circumstances sentences are true, but also to understand the connection between their truth and the proprieties of their assertion.[4] MacFarlane casts this as the claim that assertion is constitutively governed by the following:

Truth Rule.   At a context C, assert that P only if P is true at C.[5]

We presumably know well enough what it is for speakers to manage their linguistic practice in conformity to the Truth Rule. Correspondingly, it ought to suffice to allay qualms about the theoretical respectability of assessment-sensitive truth to formulate a corresponding rule for it—a rule such that it is clear what it would be to manage a relevant linguistic practice in conformity to it—and maybe thereby to show what would be for practitioners to have *implicit* grasp of assessment-sensitive truth.[6]

MacFarlane, however, fails to find any suitable such rule distinctive of assessment-sensitive truth. He discusses various options and finds all wanting,[7] with the best candidate being:

Reflexive Truth Rule.   An agent is permitted to assert that P at context C_1 only if P is true as used at C_1 and assessed from C_1

—and the evident problem with this is that since it identifies the contexts of use and assessment, it predicts nothing that is not predicted by non-indexical

---

[4] P. 98 and following.

[5] P. 101. In speaking of this rule as constitutive, MacFarlane intends, I imagine, not that an utterance is an assertion if and only if compliant with it, nor if and only if the utterer intends so to comply, but that it is of the essence of assertion to be *answerable* to it—to be subject to negative appraisal, just on that account, if in breach of it. Cf. n. 7 on p. 101.

[6] This, to be sure, will only address the question of theoretical respectability narrowly conceived: the question of giving sense to the theoretical primitive. The broader project is that of rendering fully intelligible a practice for whose description the notion of assessment-sensitivity is needed. For this, the relativist needs not merely to characterize the outlines of a practice in which the operation of assessment-sensitivity would be distinctively manifest but to show how such a practice could be *rational* and *useful*. MacFarlane encroaches on this vital task in ch. 12—but I have no space to consider his suggestions here.

[7] Pp. 103–4.

contextualism. In fact it is clear that no rules for assertion alone can do what's wanted, since rules for assertion—at least, rules which agents can effectively follow—have to relate to features of prospective contexts of use, and so can make no room for an active contrast between context of use and context of assessment.

MacFarlane's solution is to invoke the idea of *retraction*. The assessment-sensitivity of an utterance will show, MacFarlane contends, in its being constitutively subject to a norm of retraction along the following lines:

Retraction Rule. An agent in context C_2 is required to retract an (unretracted) assertion of P made at C_1 if P is not true as used at C_1 and assessed from C_2

Non-indexical contextualism need have no quarrel with the Retraction Rule as such. But, unlike assessment-sensitivity, it will require an assessor at C_2 to return the same verdict as a correct assessment from the standpoint at C_1 and so will mandate retraction only if the assertion was not correct by the lights of the latter. So the two views will thus potentially diverge in their predictions of retraction.

5

Retraction phenomena are thus a crucial component in the empirical distinguishability of MacFarlane's proposal from non-indexical contextualism. They are also key to MacFarlane's main strategy of argument against regular—indexical—contextualism. Regular contextualists about "knows," for example, make much of the apparent variation in the assertibility of knowledge ascriptions in the light of switches between so-called "low" and "high" contexts. However when, in the scepticism seminar, I decline to ascribe knowledge to a subject—say, myself—to which earlier over breakfast I laid claim, I will characteristically *deny* that I spoke truly in making that claim, saying things like "I realize now that I didn't know anything of the kind." Yet on the face of it, standards-contextualism about "knows"—whether indexical or non-indexical—can explain only my denial that I know *now*; it should predict no quarrel with what I said earlier, since the relevant form of words has undergone a shift in content with the tightening of the standards.[8] It is similar with epistemic "mights" and "coulds." High up on the Cuillin ridge during a misty scramble, a large peak briefly looms into view seemingly just a short way ahead. "That could be the summit," you encouragingly say. Later, warming your feet by the fire and poring over the map, you say, "You

---

[8] That I regard my former assertion as false is the crucial point in this instance; in view of the factivity of all (serious) uses of "knows," contextualism can of course predict that I will no longer wish to endorse the truth of my earlier utterance. What it seems it cannot predict is my denial that what I said is true.

know, I was wrong. That peak couldn't have been the summit. It's not visible from where we were standing." That seems like an acceptable piece of conversation, in which you correct—retract—an earlier claim which, we can suppose, was proper enough in the original context of use. For MacFarlane, it is the task of accounting for data of correction and retraction of this kind that provides the principal *raison d'être* for relativism. Since no form of contextualism can, apparently, account for such data, assessment-sensitivity is the superior theory.

6

Does this address the manifestation challenge? Let us grant that if the issue was only whether we should prefer a (regular) contextualist or an assessment-sensitivity-relativist account of a given region of discourse, then differences in retraction behaviour may well favour the latter. Caution is, admittedly, needed with the point, for it depends on how exactly the notion of retraction is understood and how it in turn is manifest in linguistic practice. Generally, MacFarlane characterizes retraction as an operation on speech acts: it is the *withdrawal* of an assertion, comparable to the withdrawal of a question, the cancellation of a command, or the revoking of a promise.[9] There is an issue, which I cannot adequately enter into here, about whether this notion of retraction—contrast: *denial* of the former assertion—will underwrite the problem MacFarlane thinks it makes for contextualism in all the relevant cases. Generally, one will regard a previous assertion as retractable in this milder sense whenever considerations emerge which *undermine*[10] the original grounds for it—and this is so whether or not the content of the utterance in question was sensitive to the context of use. The consequent worry is that some at least of the retraction patterns that seem characteristic of our use of, e.g., epistemic modals may accordingly be readily explicable by contextualism. This is plausibly so, for example, in the Cuillin peak example: the *evidential relevance* of the appearance of the false summit through the mist is undermined by the later information that the relevant peak was not visible from that location.[11]

However whether the intuitions that MacFarlane tries to excite concerning retractions in some of his case studies really do provide for crucial experiments between assessment-sensitivity and contextualism is not an issue I can take further here. The issue I wish to press is whether enough has been done to have assessment-sensitive truth make clear theoretical sense in the first place. MacFarlane writes that "What makes relative truth intelligible is the potential difference between the context at which an assertion is made and the contexts at

---

[9] P. 108.
[10] I have in mind the usual contrast between undermining and overriding defeaters.
[11] Contrast the Chainsaw example in Wright (2007). This volume, ch.3, p. 83).

which challenges to it will have to be met and retractions considered."[12] But he knows very well that only that much does *not* make relative truth intelligible, since that potential difference will engage any non-relativistic discourse where shifting evidential states can mandate the retraction of previously warranted claims.

If we are already persuaded of the intelligibility of relative truth, we can characterize the difference between the two kinds of case like this: when new evidence comes in that potentially mandates retraction of a non-relativistic assertion that was warranted in its original context, the justifiability of the retraction will require grounds for thinking that the original warrant was misleading. In a relativistic case, however, so one would suppose, there should be no such requirement. That is: if a practice is to distinctively manifest a relativistic character, then something about the way that retraction of an assertion is done will need to evince not merely that the assertion is acknowledged to have been fully justified in its original context, but that there need have been nothing misleading about the support it then had—that it was, as it were, *alethically faultless* back in that context. But the question we keep coming back to is: how might ordinary object-level practice manifest that element?

My sense is that MacFarlane underestimates the difficulties that his proposal encounters at this point because he envisions a theoretical landscape in which there are essentially just three players: assessment-sensitivity, one or another form of contextualism, and invariantist *realism*. The latter will expectably also predict the patterns of retraction behaviour that McFarlane believes favour assessment-sensitivity. The reason why he thinks that assessment-sensitivity is prioritized by retraction phenomena is because he has *already* discounted realism in the relevant cases. There is thus a metaphysical lemma required by his strategy of argument.

It may be rejoined that, for the relevant range of cases, that is surely a point of no great moment. There is no major metaphysical hostage involved, surely, in the rejection of realism about basic taste, comedy, or epistemic possibility (though the issue is of course much more controversial when it comes to the case of knowledge). The real concern, though, is not about the warrant for discounting a third possibility—realism—but about that for discounting a fourth: minimalism.

I can here offer only the briefest outline of this direction. For the minimalist, the object language truth-predicate that features in the discourses in which we are interested is, more or less, a deflationary—merely disquotational—truth-predicate. And with that, as he notes, MacFarlane can agree.[13] But minimalism rejects the idea that any special notion of truth is required in framing a semantic theory for these discourses. With that, again, MacFarlane can agree provided the interest of the theorist is merely in the mechanisms of semantic composition. But if the project is to recover and make sense of (diachronic) patterns of assent

---

[12] P. 116.   [13] Pp. 38–9 and 93–4.

and dissent, MacFarlane will disagree; it is here that the invocation of assessment-sensitivity is supposed to come into its own. Minimalism disputes that. For the minimalist, understanding the practice of these discourses is a matter of under-standing the conditions under which their signature statements may be asserted, and the conditions under which such assertions are defeated and should be withdrawn or denied. The former are typically subjective states: states of infor-mation, or various kinds of affective state. The defeaters are various and variously topic specific but, to illustrate for the case of taste, will include evidence of impairment of appropriate capacities (you just cleaned your teeth, or are still suffering the effects of dental anaesthesia), evidence of lack of community ("No-one but you likes that stuff"), overriders drawing on superordinate values ("Do you have any idea how they treat the geese?") and evidence of instability in one's relevant responses. It is the role of such defeaters that gives sense to the contrast between the "objectified" idiom: "This paté is delicious" and the mere report of one's personal affect: "I like this paté" which share their assertibility conditions but differ in their conditions of retraction—both withdrawal and denial. The general tenor of the defeaters in the case of taste is to register our interest in stable, shareable, (morally) acceptable gustatory responses.

The foregoing is just an illustration, and a sketchy one at that. But perhaps it is enough to give focus to the challenge I want to table. Suppose we are given a refined and elaborated description of the conditions of assertion and defeat that are characteristic of the signature claims of one of the discourses for which MacFarlane is proposing an assessment-sensitive semantics. Suppose we are also given a plausible informal theory of the social purposes characteristically served by a discourse that is so patterned. And suppose finally that we have an orthodox compositional semantic theory for the discourse. Then what further legitimate explanatory ambition is there, so far unaddressed, which a semantic theory based on assessment-sensitivity might show its superiority by accomplishing?

It may be helpful to sketch the contrast, in the most general terms, between the relativist and the minimalist approaches to disagreements in basic taste. If the intuitive idea that such disagreements can somehow be faultless is not to reduce to the banality that the respective opinions may be fully justified, then the intention of the idea has to be that they may somehow reflect no *alethic* fault. This is, naturally, a hopeless idea if the discourse is thought of as answerable to a single norm of truth with which no statement and its negation can simultaneously comply. So if faultless disagreement is to be a possibility, there must be no such single alethic norm. That leaves two options. One is, in one way or another, to—as it were—fracture the norm, multiply the ways of being true, and spread the pieces around, so that conflicting opinions can each alight on a shard. Any relativistic account of faultless disagreement offers a particular implementation of that option. The other option is to suction out the substance of the alethic norm, leaving only the deflated residue, and look elsewhere for the substantive norms that operate over the discourse—to look, as Wittgenstein urged, at the *use*. I regard it as a strength of the combination of propositional minimalism and alethic pluralism defended in *Truth and Objectivity* that it provides a natural setting for the elaboration of the second direction, which I hope to return to in further work.[14]

References

Dummett, Michael (1958), "Truth," *Proceedings of the Aristotelian Society*, Supplementary Volume LIX, 141–62.

MacFarlane, John (2014), *Assessment-Sensitivity: Relative Truth and Its Applications*, Oxford: Oxford University Press.

Wright, Crispin (1992), *Truth and Objectivity*, Cambridge, MA: Harvard University Press.

Wright, Crispin (2007), "New Age Relativism and Epistemic Possibility: The Question of Evidence," *Philosophical Issues* 17, 262–83.

[14] I would like to thank Filippo Ferrari for helpful comments on an earlier draft and John MacFarlane for valuable advice. The research for this paper was conducted under the aegis of the Relativism and Rational Tolerance project funded at the Northern Institute of Philosophy at Aberdeen University by the Leverhulme Trust.

8

Talking with Vultures

Co-authored with Filippo Ferrari

1

At the time of its first publication, relativism was proclaimed by the publisher's advertisement for Herman Cappelen and John Hawthorne's book to be 'currently the hottest topic in philosophy'. Maybe that was commercial licence but there is no denying that the debates provoked by the reinvention of relativism as a thesis not of speculative metaphysics but of descriptive semantic theory[1] have been intense and have attracted much attention. Relativism, as understood in these debates, is the claim that, for at least certain distinguished regions of discourse—in the recent literature, the relativistic case has been argued for discourses concerning each of epistemic 'mights' and 'coulds', knowledge, taste, indicative conditionals, probability statements, and future contingents[2]—we obtain the best theoretical characterization of our actual linguistic practice by allowing that the truth-value of an assertion is not determined purely by the state of the world in relevant respects[3] but depends upon and may vary with additional parameters whose values may be different across different thinkers.[4]

---

[1] See, for instance, Kölbel (2004); Lasersohn (2005, 2009); Glanzberg (2007); Recanati (2007); Stephenson (2007); Richard (2008); Egan (2010, 2014); MacFarlane (2014).

[2] Relativism about epistemic modals has been defended, among others, by Egan (2007, 2011), Gillies (2010), MacFarlane (2014); among the advocates of relativism about knowledge are Kompa (2002), Richard (2004), Stephenson (2007), Brogaard (2008) MacFarlane (2014); advocates of relativism about taste include Kölbel 2004, Lasersohn (2005), Richard 2008, Egan (2010), MacFarlane (2014); relativism about indicative conditionals is discussed by Weatherson (2009), Kolodny and MacFarlane (2010); relativism about probability statements has been proposed by Douven (2011); a relativistic treatment of future contingents has been discussed by Belnap, Perloff, and Xu (2001) and MacFarlane (2014).

[3] That is, roughly: respects of which mention is made in the assertion.

[4] This formulation deliberately ignores the distinction between the claim that a certain region of discourse is, in MacFarlane's terminology, *assessment-sensitive*, whereby the truth-value of one of its characteristic assertions is allowed to vary with aspects of the context of an assessor, and the thesis—dubbed by MacFarlane *non-indexical contextualism*—whereby tokens of the same type-assertion are allowed to vary in truth-value with aspects of the context of their assertor and without concomitant variation in content. This distinction is of great importance when it comes to predicting patterns of correction and retraction, on which MacFarlane's own strategy of argument for relativism is primarily based. Somewhat surprisingly, though, Cappelen and Hawthorne make little of it. We shall not be preoccupied with it here.

Essays on Relativism: 2001–2021. Crispin Wright, Oxford University Press. © Crispin Wright 2023.
DOI: 10.1093/oso/9780192845993.003.0009

Relativism and Monadic Truth[5] belongs to the first wave of reaction against this tendency, and at the time of writing remains the only book-length critique of it. Its heart is a systematic defence of a cluster of traditional ideas that together amount to the thesis that its authors caption as *Simplicity*, incorporating the following five ingredient claims (p. 1):

(T_1)   There are propositions[6] and they instantiate the fundamental monadic properties of truth *simpliciter* and falsity *simpliciter*.

(T_2)   The semantic values of declarative sentences relative to contexts of utterance are propositions.

(T_3)   Propositions are, unsurprisingly, the objects of propositional attitudes, such as belief, hope, wish, doubt, etc.

(T_4)   Propositions are the objects of illocutionary acts; they are, e.g., what we assert and deny.

(T_5)   Propositions are the objects of agreement and disagreement.

It is immediately striking that no relativist need want to demur at any of (T_2)–(T_5). Indeed, of these four theses, only the last is worthy of comment at this point. (T_5) is open to weaker and stronger interpretations. Weakly interpreted, it says that any proposition can be a focus of agreement and disagreement: propositions, understood as per (T_3) and (T_4), are things whose truth-values thinkers can agree or disagree about. No big deal there. But under a stronger interpretation, (T_5) says that any genuine agreement/disagreement involves conflicting attitudes to some single proposition in the sense of 'proposition' determined by the other clauses: that genuine agreement/disagreement requires convergent/conflicting attitudes to some such propositional content shared between the protagonists. Of course, we customarily invoke the notions of agreement and disagreement in ways that relax that—as when we describe people as agreeing or disagreeing about what they want or what to do.[7] Still, there is a core notion of agreement/disagreement for which (T_5) is correct. And this is a crucial point in relativistic thinking, which draws motivation from the thought that it is this notion that is in play in, e.g., many disagreements about taste or value. If the situation during dinner together in a Japanese restaurant when Ferrari opines that the sushi is delicious and Wright that it is actually rather bland and slimy is to be captured in terms of the notion of disagreement pointed at by (T_5) under its strong interpretation, then there has to be a proposition—presumably: <this sushi is delicious>—that provides the focus of the disagreement. And once that is granted, there is no ducking awkward

---

[5] All page references are to this text unless otherwise stated.
[6] Cappelen and Hawthorne espouse no particular theory of the nature of propositions.
[7] See, for instance, Gibbard 2003, Huvenes 2012, 2014, MacFarlane 2014.

metaphysical questions about the truth-conditions of that proposition, to which relativism gives the answer that Cappelen and Hawthorne are keen to avoid. Hence the general tendency of their argument in this book: to propose a semantic contextualism that enables them to deny that, in general, such 'disagreements' genuinely count as such under the aegis of (T_5).[8] Rather, there is in such cases only an illusion of disagreement; there is, in the Japanese restaurant scenario, no single proposition that is respectively affirmed by Ferrari and rejected by Wright.

Be that as it may, the point of collision between relativism and Simplicity that Cappelen and Hawthorne intend has to be found in (T_1). However, the formulation above does not seem to be the most felicitous possible for their purposes. For one thing, it is strange to read of ordinary, non-relativistic truth—the (non-deflationary) notion of truth that Cappelen and Hawthorne surely intend Simplicity to evoke in their readers—characterized as a *monadic* property. Truth, so intuitively understood, is a *relational* property: a property conferred on a proposition by the state of the world in relevant respects. Relativism parts company with truth so understood not in regarding it as relational but in raising the degree of the relation one level: from a dyadic property to a triadic one—a relation between a proposition, a circumstance of evaluation and 'context of assessment' or 'perspective'. But more importantly, as Cappelen and Hawthorne themselves point out, relativists have no trouble introducing a monadic truth-predicate, or predicate of disquotation, and an associated truth operator,[9] and can accordingly agree that propositions lie within its range, and so buy into the letter of (T_1) to that extent. The crucial point about (T_1) is thus its inclusion of the word 'fundamental': for the relativist, when in a particular context a proposition is correctly characterized simply as 'true', the characterization will mask the triadic complexity just noted. At the *fundamental* level, the level at which the triadic relationship obtains, no property of truth *simpliciter*, as Cappelen and Hawthorne like to say, is to be found—or at least, none that applies to that proposition.

So, there are issues about what exactly is the happiest formulation of (T_1) for Cappelen and Hawthorne's purposes. But maybe its spirit is clear enough. It had better be, for perhaps their most important project in *Relativism and Monadic Truth* is to illustrate how to bring within the sanctuary of (T_1) those areas of our talk that have encouraged the, in their view, misguided tendency to relativism. The discussion proceeds through four chapters. Chapter 1 provides a useful overview of the recent debates, of the key moves and terms of art they have generated, and an account of the roots of relativism as a style of systematic semantic theory in the earlier work of Lewis and, especially, Kaplan on the semantics of indexicals.[10]

---

[8] They do allow, though, that certain such apparent disagreements *are* genuine. We'll come to this below.

[9] See pp. 12–14 and 134–7. The point is emphasized by MacFarlane in his (2014) at pp. 93–4.

[10] See especially Lewis (1980) and Kaplan (1989).

Chapter 2 focuses on the crucial question of shared content, and proposes an agreement-based diagnostic for it that structures the core arguments of the book. Chapter 3 is an in depth critique of the semantic and metaphysical motivations for the kind of (anti-Simplicity) conception of propositional content that informs Lewis's and Kaplan's respective treatments of tensed discourse and their introduction of the idea of a temporally neutral proposition (the so-called Operator Argument) which Cappelen and Hawthorne identify as the root of, and core mistake in, the modern movement to relativism. Chapter 4, finally, on predicates of personal taste, attempts to show how (a sophisticated) contextualism, backed by the agreement-based conception of shared content, can provide a satisfying account, in at least this one area. This, in turn, is taken to show how relativism can be avoided and (T_1) saved consistently with recognition of the role of subjectivity in our talk of taste and avoidance of an extreme and incredible realism about the subject matter. Relativism, they contend, is thus unmotivated even in what might be considered, lay-philosophically, the most promising-looking area for it. In addition, so Cappelen and Hawthorne argue, relativism here encounters serious difficulties with, for example, 'bound' uses (e.g., 'Everyone at the party will find something fun to do') and the embedding of relativist contents in factive attitudinal verbs.

This is a large sweep of ground, covered in a brisk, adversarial but good-humoured style, in a short book full of interesting ideas and arguments. In the discussion to follow, perforce highly selective, we mainly concentrate on its treatment of discourse concerning personal taste. To come clean, our sympathies are with two principal claims: first, that Cappelen and Hawthorne do not actually succeed in making out a form of contextualism adequate to discourse of basic taste; second, that contextualism is anyway an unmotivated direction for this particular area—that a much more promising model is provided by *minimalist* conceptions of truth and truth-aptitude.[11] A plague, in short, at least for basic taste, on both the relativist and contextualist houses.

2

Why, or when, should anyone be drawn to relativism about some discourse? In John McFarlane's work on epistemic modals, it is certain putative patterns of correction and retraction in our talk involving epistemic 'mights' that provide the primary motivation.[12] With predications of taste, however, matters are different. Consider again the Japanese restaurant example:

---

[11] As first introduced and elaborated in Wright (1992; see also 2006).
[12] MacFarlane (2011, 2014); Cappelen and Hawthorne (2009, ch. 10).

Ferrari: This sushi is delicious.[13]

Wright: I don't know how you can say that. It is not in the slightest delicious—it's insipid.

Why might reflection on the kind of *contretemps* illustrated by this exchange encourage relativism? Cappelen and Hawthorne identify the core motivation as that of avoiding a kind of *chauvinism* (p. 101). Imagining us in dispute with a talking vulture who provocatively affirms, 'Rotting flesh is fabulous; there is nothing disgusting about it at all',[14] they write:

> even once it is conceded that there is a common content to 'Rotting flesh is disgusting' in the mouths of humans and talking vultures, that does not yet vindicate relativism. But, assuming that we have reason to play the game of broadly truth-conditional semantics as opposed to expressivism, there is now some motivation for relativism. After all, it seems very intuitive to think that there is symmetry between our situation and the vulture's. There would be something bizarrely chauvinistic about claiming the vulture is wrong, we're right, and leave it at that.

And it would impress as similarly bigoted or arrogant if Wright, or Ferrari, were to flat out insist, without further ado, on the correctness of his rating of the sushi. Still, this diagnosis is not quite right. The avoidance of chauvinism is at one remove from the real springs of relativist motivation here. Chauvinism/bigotry of that kind presumes a *fact of the matter*—something for one to be right about and the vulture / other guy to be wrong. And if there is such a fact of the matter, philosophy now demands some kind of account of its nature, and of its epistemology—of what it takes to be sensitive to it and of why one might reasonably take it that in the particular case one *is* so sensitive and the vulture / other guy insensitive. So the pressure, ultimately, is philosophical, not moral. To anyone who lacks any clear idea of how such a philosophical story might plausibly run, the attraction of relativism is that it allows one to respect the appearance of genuine disagreement in the examples, but without thereby incurring a commitment to regarding at least one of the antagonists as mistaken about the real fact;

---

[13] Cappelen and Hawthorne castigate a tendency they find in the literature to focus on generic examples like 'Sushi is delicious', 'Stewed rhubarb is disgusting', 'Roller coasters are fun', and so on, suspecting that the well-known vagaries of generics are apt to somehow skew our intuitions about them—see, in particular, p. 113. It seems to us open to question whether or why that is so, but in deference to their concern we will for the most part steer clear of such examples here. However, see footnote 29 below.

[14] The narrative of *Relativism and Monadic Truth* is punctuated with such phantasmagoric examples involving dialogue with a variety of talking animals such as vultures (pp. 100–1), cats (p. 113), and rats (p. 120). As the authors seem to realize (p. 116), the reader may feel some methodological unease at this, but we will not make anything of it here.

rather we can be judging correctly in the light of our gustatory sensibilities, and the other guy correctly in the light of his, and there need be nothing to choose between the two sensibilities. So the case can be one of 'faultless' disagreement: neither judgement need be out of kilter with the facts; neither judgement need be inappropriately arrived at.

Thus the impetus to relativism in the area of taste, we suggest, is a resolution of the forces exerted by three ingredient, individually attractive, assumptions: a broadly truth-conditional conception of the content of the claims put forward in the kind of *prima facie* disagreement illustrated; an acceptance that such a *prima facie* disagreement is a genuine disagreement in the sense of (T_5), strongly interpreted; and a rejection of the idea that the world bestows determinate truth-values on the contents thereby in dispute. Expressivism drops the first assumption; contextualism drops the second; (naïve, or rampant) realism the third. But relativism allows us to accept all three.

3

A stock anti-contextualist complaint is indeed the charge of *lost disagreement*: that contextualism comes at the cost of misconceivedly compatibilizing the conflicting claims in examples such as this. But how might a relativist (or anyone) argue that this *is* a disagreement in the sense of (T_5), involving shared content and genuinely conflicting claims expressed in terms of it? And how should a contextualist argue, to the contrary, that there is no such shared content, that there is context sensitivity in the predicate, 'delicious', which prevents it? This is the central issue for Cappelen and Hawthorne's chapter 2.

One simple and sensible-seeming first thought is that the context *in*sensitivity of an expression shows in its amenability to accurate homophonic speech reporting. Certainly, core indexicals—personal pronouns, tenses, demonstratives—are not generally so amenable. If someone says, 'I feel tired', or 'It is raining today', for example, another, or someone at a later date, cannot accurately report what was said by using the very same form of words. More generally: if an expression is context sensitive, there will be aspects of a context of its use, $c1$, variation in which will cause its semantic contribution to vary; so then, one might expect, a report made in a different context, $c2$, differing in relevant aspects, of what was said by the expression's use in $c1$ will have to use a different expression in order to preserve the appropriate truth-conditions.

This simple and sensible-seeming thought fails. As Cappelen and Hawthorne illustrate, there are just too many counterexamples: expressions whose semantic values are unquestionably sensitive to certain aspects of a context of use but are standardly available for homophonic speech reporting even in contexts differing in just those aspects. The reference of uses of 'nearby', for example, is sensitive to the location of the speaker. But if in a transatlantic phone conversation someone says, 'There is an excellent Japanese restaurant nearby', her conversant, quizzed about what she said, can perfectly properly reply, 'She said that there is an excellent Japanese restaurant nearby'. Similarly, for 'local', 'left' and 'right', 'overhead', 'future', and so on. The phenomenon is one of what Cappelen and Hawthorne call *parasitic* context sensitivity whereby a reporter of an utterance defers to features of the context of the reportee, rather than their own, to fix the contribution of a context-sensitive expression. It is widespread, and it blocks any fast track argument for the context insensitivity of 'delicious', e.g., from the fact that one can smoothly report that Ferrari affirmed that the sushi was delicious and that Wright affirmed that it was not in the slightest.

Cappelen and Hawthorne review a refinement of the simple thought proposed in their own earlier work.[15] The basic idea is that parasitic context sensitivity is incapable of explaining possibilities of smooth *collective* speech reports, whereby if a number of speakers, Mary and John and Fred..., all affirm a sentence S, they may—always? usually?—felicitously be reported by: 'Mary and John and Fred all said that S'. For, assuming S were context sensitive, and that relevant features of context would (be likely to) vary across Mary's, John's, Fred's, etc., respective utterances, to whose context of use would the semantic value of S as used in the collective report be answerable? As Cappelen and Hawthorne nicely express the matter, a parasite can only feed off one host at a time! But while that is true, 'nearby' and its ilk seem to submit to smooth collective reporting too. If in a three-way Skype conversation, John, in his office on the USC campus, affirms 'There is an excellent Japanese restaurant nearby' and Herman, in Oslo, affirms the very same words, Jason can perfectly felicitously report: 'They are both saying that there is an excellent Japanese restaurant nearby'.[16] The explanation of the felicity, Cappelen and Hawthorne plausibly contend, draws on essentially analogous resources to those needed to disambiguate the two salient readings of:

Herman loves his partner and so does John.

Under the reading relevant here, the property ascribed to both Herman and John is:

... is an x such that some y is uniquely the partner of x and x loves y.[17]

---

[15] See, for instance, Cappelen and Lepore (2005) and Cappelen and Hawthorne (2007).
[16] Interestingly, there are uses of 'nearby' that are not ambiguous and where the 'distributive' reading is forced. Jason says: 'Herman and John are so lucky to have good Japanese restaurants nearby' where it is known that there's no Japanese restaurant near Jason and that Herman and John are in distinct locations.
[17] Contrast: being an x such that some y is uniquely the partner of Herman and x loves y.

Following that model, the property ascribed by Jason to both John and Herman may be rendered as:

... is an x such that x said that there is an excellent Japanese restaurant near to where x is.

The felicity of the collective report is thus perfectly consistent with the context sensitivity of 'nearby'.[18]

How then, in a controversial case, should battle between a contextualist and an invariantist (of whatever stripe) be joined? In the second part of the chapter, Cappelen and Hawthorne introduce a new range of diagnostics for sameness and difference of content, based on the behaviour of 'agree' and 'disagree'. Their key thought is that while, in the above example, Jason's report that both John and Herman are saying that there is an excellent Japanese restaurant nearby is felicitous enough, it would be quite inappropriate for him to report this as an *agreement*—to affirm that John and Herman *agree* that there is an excellent Japanese restaurant nearby. The felicity of that report would require that John and Herman be speaking of the same location. In the circumstances of the example, their each having the property, merely, of saying that there is an excellent Japanese restaurant in their own locality grounds a point of similarity, not of agreement.

This proposal impresses as progress. Spurred by it, Cappelen and Hawthorne put forward (though with some hesitancy it must be said) three specific diagnostic principles whose overall gist, very roughly summarized, is as follows:

Where sincere utterances of S and 'not-S' *cannot* correctly be reported as expressive of disagreement, S is context sensitive; and where they can, that is evidence of semantic invariance.

Where a pair of sincere utterances of S can correctly be reported as expressive of agreement, that is evidence of semantic invariance; and when they cannot, that is evidence of context sensitivity.[19]

---

[18] In the interests of brevity, we here prescind from Cappelen's and Hawthorne's own sophisticated discussion of the point and its ramifications on pp. 46–50.

[19] So roughly summarized, the proposals invite, to be sure, qualifications and clarifications that Cappelen's and Hawthorne's more nuanced formulations address. These do not affect the main point in our comments to follow, so we decline to review them here. For the benefit of a reader who wishes to think further about Cappelen's and Hawthorne's proposals, the exact formulations (pp. 54–5) of the three agreement-based diagnostics are these:

Agree-1:   Let u be a sincere utterance of S by A in C and u' a sincere utterance of 'not-S' by B in C'. If from a third context C''; they cannot be correctly reported by 'A and B disagree whether S', then S is semantically context sensitive. Meanwhile, if from a third context C''; they can be correctly reported by 'A and B disagree whether S', that is evidence that S is semantically invariant across C, C', and C''.

As Cappelen and Hawthorne realize and discuss, there are still points of strain in this general direction but we shall not attempt to explore their proposals further here. What is striking for present purposes is that even a correct capture of the relationship between agreement/disagreement and context sensitivity / invariance doesn't promise any immediate leverage on the task in hand. The relativist is saying that, in the Japanese restaurant example, Ferrari and Wright are in disagreement about the merit of the sushi, that this requires a shared propositional content which they respectively endorse and reject, and that a semantics for the discourse in question should therefore be invariantist. The contextualist is saying that 'delicious' is a context-sensitive expression in a way that entails that Ferrari's and Wright's respective assertions are not expressive of a genuine disagreement but are compatible, and that a semantics for the discourse in question should therefore spell out the appropriate form of context sensitivity. The theorists are accordingly *on the same page* about the connections between disagreement and shared content. What is wanted, in order to adjudicate their dispute, is some *independent* grip on one or other of the intertwined notions: some way, for example, not going via the question of shared content, of determining whether genuine disagreement is involved, or some way, not going via the question whether a genuine disagreement is involved, of determining whether there is shared content.

We do not suggest that Cappelen and Hawthorne are unaware of this. Nevertheless, they provide, it must be said, almost nothing by way of the needed independent grip. The issue comes to the fore only in chapter 4, and there they are content for the most part to make the case for their preferred contextualism simply by appeal to the presence or absence of 'intuitions of contradiction' or our 'sense' of disagreement in particular cases. Yet these 'senses' and 'intuitions' are exactly what are disputed by their relativist opponents—the sense of 'lost disagreement' is, after all, presented as an intuitive datum that relativism urges we take very seriously.

To be sure, it is not easy to see how to do better. But here is one suggestion.[20] If 'S' contains context-sensitive expressions, then distinct tokens of 'S' in different mouths may have different truth-conditions. So distinct token *questions*, 'S?', in different mouths may have different conditions for truthful affirmative answers. Hence if 'delicious' and its ilk are context sensitive, it should be possible to design a pair of conversational contexts within which a pair of tokens of the question,

---

Agree-2: Take two sincere utterances u and u' by A and B of a sentence S in contexts C and C'. If from a third context C''; they can be reported by an utterance of 'A and B agree that S', then that is evidence that S is semantically invariant across C, C', and C''. Meanwhile, if the report in C''; is incorrect, that is evidence that S is not semantically invariant across C, C', and C''.

Agree-3: Let an A-Triple for a sentence S be a triple consisting of two sincere utterances u and u' of S by A and B respectively in distinct contexts C and C', and one utterance of 'A and B agree that S' in a third context C''. If, for *all* A-triples involving S, the last member is true, then that is evidence that S is semantically invariant.

[20] Cf. Wright (2017).

e.g., 'Is the sushi here really as delicious as people say?' presented simultaneously to a single agent—maybe a waiter—can respectively properly deserve *prima facie* conflicting yet sincere answers.[21]

This *Forked Tongue* test, as we may dub it, is pretty crude—for instance, it won't distinguish context sensitivity from simple ambiguity. Still, its credentials as at least a necessary condition for context sensitivity seem good. Consider a simple illustration. Suppose Herman and John have been waiting quite a while for a table at the Japanese restaurant, which is very busy, and are wondering whether to duck out and go and eat somewhere else. The head waiter standing nearby is on the phone, and Herman overhears him say, 'Yes, sir, actually there is. There is an excellent Italian restaurant just two minutes away where they serve superb home-made pasta and seafood sauces. You can almost always get a table without waiting'. Herman says, 'Excuse me, but did you say that there is an excellent Italian restaurant just two minutes away?' The head waiter replies, 'Ah. Actually, no. I mean: I did say that, but I was talking to one of our regulars about another location downtown'. Thus: 'just two minutes away' passes the test. It was the context of a question of the regular customer, rather than Herman's, that set the reference of 'just two minutes away' in the waiter's overheard remark. When Herman puts a token of essentially the same type-question, the reference shifts and the correct answer changes.

Can we get a similar result with 'delicious'? Let's try to construct an analogously shaped case, but where the questioners' respective contexts differ in respect of their standards of taste. We need to presuppose, of course, that the agent questioned is somehow aware of that. So: let Ferrari and Wright be seated in the Japanese restaurant, yet to order, menus in hand, head waiter in attendance. Wright mentions that he has never before tried sushi and asks the head waiter, 'Is the sushi here really as delicious as people say?' Ferrari, a regular customer at the restaurant, is most surprised when the waiter replies, apparently completely seriously, 'No, sir. It's not delicious at all'. 'I beg your pardon', Ferrari exclaims. 'Why would you say that? I eat here often, as you well know, and have always found the sushi excellent'. 'Indeed it is, sir', the waiter smilingly explains. 'But I was answering your inexperienced companion'.

Thick-skinned contextualists may find this dialogue unexceptionable. We would suggest, to the contrary, that the waiter has chosen a very strange and inept way to convey to Wright that the sushi will (very probably) not be to his

---

[21] Why simultaneously? Because restaurant standards—ownerships and chefs, for example—can change. (We needn't require strict simultaneity though. It will be enough to ensure that the material practices in the kitchen are unlikely to have altered within the interval when the two questions are put.) Why a single agent? Because we want to ensure that if different answers are appropriate to the distinct token questions, they are so because of variations in relevant factors operative in their respective conversational contexts, rather than variations in the information of those questioned.

liking. Why is that if 'delicious' and 'excellent' are sensitive to speakers' standards of taste as 'nearby' and 'just two minutes away' are sensitive to speakers' location?

4

The range of expressions, captioned by 'Predicates of Personal Taste', that are included within the scope of the discussion of chapter 4 of *Relativism and Monadic Truth* is pretty broad. It includes, for instance, 'spicy', 'funny', 'disgusting', 'fun', 'nauseating', and 'delicious'. However, Cappelen and Hawthorne lead off with a discussion of a predicate, 'filling', as it features in, e.g., 'This pasta is very filling', which they recognize might seem less than paradigmatic of the ilk. They do so because 'a number of the key relevant distinctions can be made, with minimal distraction, using that predicate' (p. 102). Their aim is that 'of producing the bare bones of a contextualist story about the truth-conditions of claims in which that predicate figures'. The general tendency of the chapter is to build on this to argue that, and illustrate how, a contextualism of the same broad stripe can, in almost all instances, both explain away the appearances of contradiction or disagreement in cases where we intuitively feel they should be explained away and sustain such appearances, in cases where they should be sustained, without recourse to relativistic manoeuvres.

The 'bare bones' contextualist semantics is glossed as follows (p. 103):

> on an occasion of use, a predication of 'filling' to some item will tacitly relate that item to a particular individual or group. In the simplest case, a claim of the form 'That is filling', as made by X, where 'that' refers to Y, will express the proposition that Y is filling for X (where the truth-conditions turn on how X is disposed with regard to Y).

Obviously, any such account will provide the resources to disarm any suggestion of contradiction in the simple kind of case illustrated, e.g., by a ballerina's saying of a serving of leek and potato soup, 'This is rather filling. I had better not have any more', and the assertion of a sumo wrestler, of a similar-sized portion, 'This isn't filling enough; I am going to need several portions at this rate'. That is a good result if it is taken as obvious that the ballerina and the wrestler are not really in disagreement, which Cappelen and Hawthorne assume is so.[22]

Included among the 'key relevant distinctions' that uses of 'filling' serve to illustrate is that between *autocentric* and *exocentric* uses: in the former, the operative perspective is that of the speaker or a group to which the speaker

---

[22] For the record, one of the present authors didn't find that obvious at all.

belongs; in the latter it is that of a third party or group to which the speaker does not belong. Thus someone may say, menu in hand, 'The leek and potato soup won't be very filling; I am going to have a main course as well', and then on another occasion in the same restaurant, advising his small daughter what to order, 'Be careful: the leek and potato soup will be filling'. Here, very plausibly, there is no serious question of inconsistency, or change of mind, expressed by the two utterances; and a similarly explicable illusion operates, Cappelen and Hawthorne are suggesting, in some of the apparent 'disagreements' of taste that provide impetus to relativism.

Well and good. But of course no relativist about taste ought to want to maintain that *all* apparent disagreements involving judgements of taste are genuine disagreements in the sense of (T_5), strongly interpreted. Relativists are free to take on board the distinction between autocentric and exocentric uses of taste predicates—indeed to write this into the account of how contexts of assessment can vary. Nor do they have any interest in denying that there are some uses of taste predicates in which speakers effectively do talk merely about their own propensities. The charge will be, though, that these considerations fall well short of the means to disarm an appearance of genuine disagreement in all cases. Indeed, one can foresee one reason why they may fail to do so in a point of disanalogy between 'filling' and other, more paradigmatic predicates of personal taste on which Cappelen and Hawthorne themselves remark at the outset of their discussion (p. 99) but make nothing of. 'Filling', for the purposes of their discussion, is treated as ascribing a disposition to induce a certain distinctive complex of sensations when ingested. It does not express any kind of evaluation. But 'funny', 'disgusting', 'fun', and 'delicious', (though probably not 'spicy', and 'nauseating' only in some uses) are predicates of *value*: in applying them in a particular case one places value, positive or negative, on the object, activity, or performance to which they are applied. If one adds to that point the thought—to be sure, it is not an immediate consequence—that in expressing a certain evaluation of something, one thereby presents it as a *fitting* evaluation and represents the object, etc., as *suitable* for it, then one can see how paradigmatic predicates of personal taste may be at the service of claims that are in a crucial respect more *adventurous* than mere ascriptions of dispositions to induce certain kinds of affect and for that reason potentially more controversial and answerable to an additional range of potentially defeating considerations.

Depending on the specific predicate concerned, 'suitability' for a certain evaluation may cover a range of possible cases: the object, etc., may be being represented as such that it *ought* to be accorded the value in question, or *deserves* to be accorded the value in question, or can at least *appropriately* be accorded the value in question, or can *defensibly* be accorded the value in question, or can *intelligibly* be accorded the value in question...and these, even the last, are all, in particular cases, debatable and potentially controversial. Clearly there is ample scope for a much more fine-grained exploration of these nuances of predications of personal taste than we have space to attempt here. The present point is only that, by lumping dispositional predicates like 'filling' along with the other usual suspects as all 'predicates of personal taste', Cappelen and Hawthorne encourage neglect of one potential reason why one might expect that some members of the group are more likely to service the expression of genuine disagreements than others.

The ballerina/wrestler and father/daughter examples illustrate two kinds of case where a contextualist semantics of the kind prefigured will—quite correctly, as many will feel—explain away any appearance of contradiction. But there are other kinds of case, Cappelen and Hawthorne emphasize, where, consistently with contextualism, the appearance of contradiction is saved and genuine disagreement occurs. What *doesn't* occur, in their view, is faultless disagreement. Rather, there is a kind of see-saw: if, when further detail is specified, the appearance of disagreement is sustained, the impression of faultlessness will be a casualty; and conversely, insofar as the impression of faultlessness persists, the appearance of genuine disagreement will weaken.[23]

In what kinds of case can genuine disagreement be identified consistently with a contextualist semantics?[24] Suppose Herman has an invitation to the warden's garden party. 'I'm going to go. It will be good fun', he says. 'Indeed it won't', rejoins John. Three possible cases are:

(1) Herman is using 'fun' autocentrically and John is using it exocentrically to point out that the party will not be fun for Herman—he imputes to Herman a mistake in thinking that the party will be fun for him, believing that when he gets there, he will rapidly feel like a fish out of water.

(2) Herman's intention is to claim that the party will be fun for a certain group of friends and colleagues who will be there. John corrects him by pointing out that the party will not be fun for him, i.e. John (who belongs to that group).

(3) Herman, in claiming that the party will be fun, merely intends the claim to apply to himself alone, but John misunderstands him, thinking he's claiming that it will be fun for both Herman and himself, and is confident that he—John—would hate it if he were to go.

These illustrate the see-saw. In cases (1) and (2), there is genuine disagreement, but no faultlessness—Herman is mistaken in case (2) and, let's suppose, in case (1)

---

[23] Cappelen and Hawthorne are quite explicit on this. They write: 'Disagreement intuitions subside as "no-fault" intuitions gain ground' (p. 120) and later on they claim 'Cases where the sense of no fault runs deep are ones where the sense of disagreement runs shallow' (p. 132).

[24] See their discussion on pp. 110–11.

as well. In case (3), there is the same appearance of disagreement (we are supposing that the dialogue proceeds in exactly the same form in all three cases) but this time there is a misunderstanding, with the result that neither Herman nor John need be wrong, but nor are they contradicting each other.

Very well. But what about:

(4) Both Herman and John are speaking autocentrically?

This is the case intendedly illustrated by Ferrari's and Wright's exchange about the sushi, and the dialogue with the talking vulture. And so far as we have been able to determine, all that Cappelen and Hawthorne have to offer about it, in the end, is that, insofar as people do have a sense of disagreement or contradiction in such cases—and they do not deny that many people may—they are confused about the content of what is being said. The correct model is supplied, rather, by the ballerina/wrestler example.

The playing of this 'semantic blindness' card is of course a familiar contextualist move in other contexts, notably in the debates concerning contextualism about 'knows'. We have no space here to enter into the methodological issues it raises, except to remind the reader that we are here dealing with proposals for a *descriptive* semantic theory, and that it is therefore prospectively a critical weakness in such a theory if it is forced to pooh-pooh the data of which it is supposed to be giving a theoretical reconstruction.[25] The case for relativism, as diagnosed earlier, rests crucially on the impression that there is genuine disagreement in such cases, focused on a shared content—that there is no 'talking past' going on. Cappelen and Hawthorne seem prepared in the end—once their repertoire of contextualism-friendly cases is exhausted—simply to insist otherwise. But the fact doesn't go away that it seems absolutely natural to report, e.g., 'Ferrari and Wright completely disagree about whether the sushi is awful'—in a way that, for example, it would be highly unnatural and misleading to report, 'Paul and Tamsin disagree about whether Ottie is ready', when Paul is talking about Ottie's upcoming grade six piano exam and Tamsin is talking about her state of dress for the party. The issue is an empirical one but we do not believe that Cappelen and Hawthorne have much support from ordinary speakers' 'intuitions' or 'senses' about the kind of cases where the relativist will complain of lost disagreement. In particular, we reject the idea that ordinary speakers' 'intuition' would dismiss the sushi case as one of genuine disagreement on the grounds that Ferrari and Wright are really just obliquely talking about their own personal tastes, though they are, of course, *expressing* their own tastes, and they may—a point we are about to come on to— *retreat* to talking about their own personal tastes.

---

[25] For an excellent discussion of the issues here, see Baker (2012).

But we are spinning our wheels. Again, how is shared content, or the lack of it, to be *argued* for? Maybe the Forked Tongue test gives us some purchase on the matter. We will suggest, though, a different way past the threatening *impasse*.

5

There is, in ordinary discourse, a distinction in use between what we shall here dub the *objectifying* idiom exemplified by 'This sushi is delicious' and 'The party is going to be fun' and the corresponding *subjective-relational* reports: 'I find this sushi delicious', or 'This sushi tastes delicious *to me*', and 'I'm going to enjoy the party' or 'The party will be fun *for me*'. Moreover, it appears that the objectifying claims are in general treated as somehow stronger; witness that, in a wide class of contexts, a subjective-relational claim provides a fall-back when an objectifying statement runs into difficulty.[26] Ferrari asserts, 'The sushi is delicious' but then finds that all his dining companions are expressing regret at ordering it and falls back to, 'Well, I am enjoying it at any rate'.

A naïve realist has no difficulty with this: for the naïve realist, the objectifying claims purport to record the 'out there' taste facts; and the relational claims describe characteristic responses by the speaker which may or may not indicate the obtaining of the relevant fact. But how is this pattern to be accounted for if not as it is by naïve realism? Relativism, too, can take the point in stride. For relativism, the objectifying claim, unlike (presumably) the corresponding subjective-relational reports, will be true, or not, as assessed in a particular context and so may match the latter in truth-value when originally asserted but cease to do so when assessed from a later standpoint when some material change in the parameters of assessment has taken place. However, contextualism has little option but to try to identify some still relational claim that is more adventurous than the original subjective-relational report and make a case that it is generally this stronger claim that is put forward by one who speaks in the objectifying mode. A move in that direction, of course, will have the resources to block the suggestion that in the autocentric-autocentric type of case, expressed in objectifying idiom, the antagonists are merely obliquely talking about their own individual affective states and thus 'talking past' each other, and should be able thereby to obviate any immediate need for manoeuvres with 'semantic blindness'.[27] Indeed, to be fair to

---

[26] For a more detailed discussion of the distinction between the objectified form of idiom and various subjective idioms in terms of their defeasibility conditions, see Ferrari (2014).

[27] One suspects, though, that in one way or another, contextualists of any sophistication will have to play the semantic blindness card sooner or later: in general, presuppositional accounts may save the appearance of conflict in the superficial dynamics of an exchange, but once it's clear that the presupposition has failed they have no choice but to say that the protagonists were talking past each other all along without realizing it.

them, Cappelen and Hawthorne do dismiss any simple-minded version of contextualism that finds no difference in truth-conditions between 'This sushi is delicious', in the mouth of a speaker, S, and an utterance at the same time of 'This Sushi tastes delicious to S'.[28] Still, it merits emphasis that, beyond the provisional reference to 'a group' featuring in the bare bones rubric cited earlier, they offer nothing by way of a more definite, less simple-minded proposal. Indeed, the constructive part of chapter 4 concludes on a very downbeat note about the prospects of saying anything much that is clear and definite (pp. 120–1):

> A confession is in order, however. Suppose one emerges from one's Pyrrhonian reflections with no powerful relativist axe to grind. Still, there is no easy recipe for the right contextualist semantics. The distinction between cases wherein one of two parties has a distorted verdict from cases where two parties speak past one another is vague and confusing. We do not pretend otherwise.

The reader may understandably feel short-changed by this anti-climactic admission. Surely if contextualism does have the resources for an intellectually more satisfying response to the original problematic than naïve realism, expressivism, or relativism can provide, we are owed a much more concrete indication of how a contextualist semantics for predicates of personal taste should run.

Let's try to see how what Cappelen and Hawthorne offer might possibly be improved. It is natural to ask: what does an objectifying judgement—an O-statement—add to an associated subjective-relational (explicitly autocentric) report—an S-R statement? But let's first ask a slightly less loaded question: what are the salient connections and contrasts in use between the two types of claim?

We have already noted two. First, S-R statements often provide a fall-back in cases where a corresponding O-statement emerges as inappropriate, or defeated. 'This ride is terrific fun!' says John to his companions on the Coney Island Cyclone but then, noticing their frozen, grey-faced expressions, retreats to 'Well, I am enjoying it, anyway'. More generally, S-R statements characteristically express an *assertibility condition* for a corresponding O-statement: the O-statement may be asserted on the basis of one's recognizing in oneself an affect or response (an S-R *response*) that would verify the S-R statement. Simple

---

[28] In discussing the problem of 'lost disagreement' (pp. 124–6) Cappelen and Hawthorne accuse the relativists of being 'guilty of an all-too naïve understanding of how the predicate "spicy" works [and thus of attacking] a simplistic version of contextualism that no contextualist worth his salt ought to be defending'. However, they offer little about how a less simplistic version should run. The only qualification they add is the following: 'When one says something of the form "X is spicy", one transcends the question of whether it is spicy to oneself, and the contextualist will recognize this.... When one uses "spicy", one realizes that there are public standards on its application and realizes that, whether a meal tastes spicy to oneself does not settle the question' (pp. 124–5). But this, of course, does not help much in clarifying how the contextualist thesis should be properly understood. We are about to press this point in the main text.

contextualism explains this by identifying the two statements' truth-conditions. But any such proposal bumps up against the fact that they generally diverge in their conditions of withdrawal or denial—their defeaters. A less simple contextualism that enlarges the relevant 'group' may perhaps accommodate the divergence. That will depend on, *inter alia*, the detail of the admissible defeaters, on which more in a minute. Note, though, that a familiar potential difficulty for group-style contextualist proposals is thereby introduced. If the truth-conditions for the O-statement involve the reactions of a group, that commits the assertion of it to a certain ambition: a speaker who bases that assertion on her own affect, or response as described in the corresponding S-R statement, is then *asserting* that her reaction, or something relevantly similar, will be shared across the relevant group. That opens up a risk of irresponsibility if the speaker has given little thought to what might constitute the relevant group or is unclear about its membership or lacks reason to think that her reaction will be shared across it. We suggest, although the issue is again an empirical one, that ordinary speakers habitually do speak in the objectifying mode purely on the basis of their own reactions, without any clear intention about a relevant group or evidence that their reactions are typical. If that is true, it is a point against 'sophisticated' contextualism. We'll come back to it in a moment.

The second point of contrast noted earlier is that O-statements often carry a normative payload (of the target's *deserving* or *being suitable for*, etc., the relevant subjective affect) which a corresponding S-R statement lacks. One can find funny things which additional information may cause one to reckon are not funny at all, and when that happens, the characteristic effect of the additional information is to call into question the fittingness of one's original response. One's natural sense of humour may also be overridden by moral considerations. Children have to learn not only that they shouldn't laugh at certain kinds of thing but also that they shouldn't find them funny in the first place.

Does, e.g., 'delicious' pattern with 'funny' in that respect? It is a nice question. Information about how *pâté de foie gras* is produced may properly disincline one ever to eat it—even perhaps to campaign against the cruelty involved in its production. But it is not clear that it should tend to defeat the claim that it is delicious, or to show that one shouldn't find it delicious *if* one eats it. Mindful that different taste predicates may differ in subtle such respects, and making no claim to comprehensiveness, we can nevertheless propose a provisional taxonomy of potential defeaters for O-statements of taste that, crucially, are not also defeaters for corresponding S-R statements. It should include at least the following:

(a) *Stability*: Lack of stability in one's subjective reactions across a relevantly similar range of cases may defeat an O-statement. More specifically, it may undermine the status of one's S-R response as warranting the assertion of the O-statement. Sometimes, let's suppose, you enjoy playing a not-too-serious game of Bridge and the 'craic' over the cards; other times—it's not clear why—you cannot get involved and quickly get bored. Mindful of this, you can truly report, on an appropriate occasion, 'I am enjoying the cards tonight', but should not assert, 'Bridge is fun'.[29]

(b) *Community*: A substantial lack of agreement often functions as a defeater for an O-statement—recall John's reaction to the dismay of his companions on the rollercoaster, and Ferrari's to his dinner companion's reaction to the sushi.

(c) *Robustness*: One's subjective response may be widely shared yet still defeated as a ground for an O-statement by relations of subordination among different kinds of values. The comic magician Tommy Cooper's slithering down the stage curtain during a trick got a laugh from most of the audience until they realized that it wasn't part of his act but signalled that he was unwell—actually, suffering a fatal heart attack. More generally, statements about what is funny, and also about what is fun, are defeasible by moral considerations about hurt and harm. Conversely, an O-statement of disgust prompted by, say, witnessing a birth may be defeated by considerations of its sheer biological normality and the value of the end product, a new human life brought into the world.

(d) *Typicality*: Certain physical or psychological conditions—for instance, intake of laughing gas or alcohol, bipolar mental illness, residues of strong toothpaste or blue cheese in one's mouth, depression, or the side-effects on one's taste buds of recent chemotherapy—are standardly treated as dependable sources of distortion, inhibition, or exaggeration of a relevant range of S-R responses and consequently as disqualifying them as grounds for a normally associated type of O-statement.

Now, it is one thing to grant that considerations in these four categories are potential defeaters of O-statements in circumstances where a suitable S-R statement is true, i.e. that they disqualify the occurrence of an otherwise appropriate subjective response as a ground for the assertion. It is another thing to assume that they do so because they tend to override, or undermine, the status of that response as *evidence* for the obtaining of a state of affairs that would make the O-statement true. However if, like Cappelen and Hawthorne, we are approaching these matters in the spirit of Simplicity, it is hard to see how to make sense of these disparities in the respective uses of O-statements and S-R statements except by associating them with appropriately contrasting non-relativistic truth-conditions and postulating an appropriate evidential relationship between them. The required kind of truth-conditions for an O-statement will have to be such that each of the admitted kinds

---

[29] We here breach our self-imposed restriction (see footnote 13 above) to avoid generic, or apparently generic, examples.

of defeater will spoil the evidence for their satisfaction that would otherwise be provided by an appropriate *S-R* response. And at this point, the move towards something not too distant from, though enlarging upon, the kind of contextualism at which Cappelen and Hawthorne casually gesture may seem inevitable. The *O*-statement will be a claim whose truth requires dependable (Stability) shared *S-R* responses of an appropriate kind across a contextually relevant group (Community) under normal circumstances (Typicality), and the evaluation it expresses must be resilient in the light of other, superordinate values of the group[30] (Robustness). There will accordingly be scope for contextual determination, in the light, presumably, of the intentions of the speaker, both of the population of the group and of the range of circumstances wherein the relevant kind of *S-R* response is germane.

So, why be uncomfortable with a contextualist proposal along these lines? Two principal, related concerns are salient. One is the resultant rarefaction of the conditions for genuine disagreements expressed using *O*-statements. Ferrari and Wright respond in their different ways to the sushi and go straight into what they take to be a disagreement, based just on their own reactions. But if the sketched contextualism is correct, the conditions for there to be a genuine incompatibility in their claims are quite demanding, involving overlap of their intentions about a number of matters to which they are very likely giving no thought. Competent speakers are not usually so casual about identifying themselves as in disagreement where context-sensitive language is involved. But the second concern, already noted earlier, is perhaps the more serious. It is that the ground for an *O*-statement provided by an appropriate *S-R* response, which ought to be canonical, now begins to look suspiciously *slight*. I laugh at a joke and say, 'That's funny'. But if the kind of contextualist account gestured at is correct, ought I not first to settle on a constituency for my remark, to get some evidence of the response to the joke among other members, to think about possibly off-colour moral ramifications of the jest, and so on?

Remember, however, that the drive to a contextualism on this broad model is driven by an assumption: that both the evidential connection and the disparities in use between *O*-statements and corresponding *S-R* statements need to be recovered from *the relations between their respective truth-conditions*, between the kinds of states of affairs that are apt to make them, respectively, true. This assumption is non-compulsory. We can, and should, drop the idea that assertoric content has to go hand in hand with truth-conditional content as implicitly interpreted by Simplicity. To be sure, assertoric content does go hand in hand with amenability to a disquotational truth-predicate but it is a further step to take this to be content fit for the representation of real-worldly states of affairs. The discrepancies in the conditions of defeat of *O*-statements and *S-R* statements do not and, we contend,

---

[30] —or maybe: values which the group *ought* to have.

should not be taken as demanding explanation of the kind that the contextualism adumbrated above implicitly attempts.

This is not the occasion to embark on a full development of the minimalist alternative. But in barest outline, the question to ask, we propose, is not: what kind of fact must O-statements be taken to describe if both their assertibility on the basis of an appropriate S-R response and their conditions of defeasibility adumbrated above are to be explained, but: what point would the institution of such assertions serve—why would it be worthwhile having a practice wherein such statements were treated as assertible on the basis of S-R responses but defeasible under the kinds of conditions reviewed? And here is where it helps to be mindful that in core cases of O-statements of personal taste, we are dealing with expressions of *value*: of things to cherish, pursue, discourage, and avoid. Not all values are things that everybody cares about. Amorality, ecological indifference, and philistinism are, in varying degrees, not unusual. But values of personal taste are important to everybody. And we care because the S-R responses on which they are grounded are absolutely integral to our humanity and our engagement with life. A world in which we found nothing funny, or fun, or delicious, or exciting, or attractive..., would be a world in which it was not worth living. And a world in which our lives were dominated by negative S-R responses—of disgust, distaste, boredom, blandness, and ugliness—would be a living hell.

Focusing now on the positive cases, a reminder is apt of a range of mundane and contingent but very important facts about these responses. First, in a wide class of cases our enjoyment of values of taste, the intensity of the associated S-R responses, is characteristically enhanced by *sharing and socialization*: the ride is more fun when others are with you and enjoying it too; we like to eat together; we—most of us, at least—prefer to go to the theatre with friends. Second, we do *naturally* share many of these responses. Third, they are also in many cases to a high degree *tractable*—one can acquire and refine patterns of response of these kinds by experience and education. Fourth, many of these responses have a *rich causal provenance* in their objects, which is receptive to study, technique, and manufacture—to the arts of cuisine, comedy, dance, and drama. Fifth, we do regard them as subject to conditions of *appropriateness* in the light of other of our social and personal values. All of these factors combine to create a situation where we have an interest in having an idiom that enables us, more than merely reporting a response we have, to *project* it as a possible point of coordination, something which may be shared and thereby enhanced, something which is dependable rather than ephemeral, something which is a reaction of our normal, healthy selves, and free of taints of spite, *schadenfreude*, cruelty, or other morally reprehensible features, and whose causal prompts it may be worthwhile understanding with a view to developing an associated art.

We are not of course suggesting that ordinary speakers characteristically have such considerations in mind in making O-statements. Rather, even in this whistle-stop overview, the beginnings can be seen of how an account might run of the *social utility* of an objectifying idiom of taste which both assigns the importance it had better assign to grounding in personal responses and explains the broad range of defeaters we have noted without any need to reconceive the content of O-statements along contextualist lines or to query appearances of disagreement where ordinary speakers take it to occur. This minimalist approach shares with expressivism a rejection of the idea that, in making such statements, we are normally in the business of trying to report the facts; but its expressivism is advanced as a thesis of pragmatics, not a claim about the semantics of the statements in question. And it agrees with relativism both in accepting that basic disagreements about taste are just that—disagreements focused on exactly the shared propositional content that they seem to concern—and in rejecting the idea that in asserting or denying such a content, one purports to represent an objective fact; but this anti-realism is accomplished without any need for relativistic manoeuvrings with the truth-predicate.[31]

It has been, in our view, a major weakness not just of *Relativism and Monadic Truth* but of almost all the recent and contemporary writing about these issues that this minimalist, use-theoretic orientation has been invisible to most of the protagonists, relativist and anti-relativist alike. But its more detailed and positive development, as well as responses to objections, must await another opportunity.[32]

References

Baker, Carl (2012), "Indexical Contextualism and the Challenges from Disagreement," *Philosophical Studies* 157 (1), 107–23.

Brogaard, Berit (2008), "In Defence of a Perspectival Semantics for 'Know'," *Australasian Journal of Philosophy* 86, 439–59.

Cappelen, Herman and John Hawthorne (2007), "Locations and Binding," *Analysis* 67, 95–105.

Cappelen, Herman and John Hawthorne (2009), *Relativism and Monadic Truth*, Oxford: Oxford University Press.

---

[31] For a minimalist-friendly account of the so-called phenomenon of faultless disagreement in the domain of basic taste, see Ferrari (2016).

[32] The research for this paper was, for the most part, conducted in the course of the *Relativism and Rational Tolerance* project which was financed by the Leverhulme Trust at the Northern Institute of Philosophy at Aberdeen from 2012 to 2015. We gratefully acknowledge the support of the Trust. Filippo Ferrari would also like to acknowledge the support of the German Research Foundation (DFG—BR 1978/3-1, 'Disagreement in Philosophy'). Thanks also to Patrick Greenough and Giacomo Melis for helpful discussion.

Cappelen, Herman and Ernie Lepore (2005), *Insensitive Semantics: A Defense of Minimalism and Speech Act Pluralism*, Malden, MA: Blackwell.

Douven, Igor (2011), "Relativism and Confirmation Theory," in S. Hales (ed.), *A Companion to Relativism*, Oxford: Wiley-Blackwell, 242–65.

Egan, Andy (2007), "Epistemic Modals, Relativism, and Assertion," *Philosophical Studies* 133, 1–22.

Egan, Andy (2010), "Disputing about Taste," in R. Feldman, and T. A. Warfield (eds.), *Disagreement*, Oxford: Oxford University Press, 247–92.

Egan, Andy (2011), "Relativism about Epistemic Modals," in S. Hales (ed.) *A Companion to Relativism*, Oxford: Wiley-Blackwell, 219–41.

Egan, Andy (2014), "There's Something Funny about Comedy: A Case Study in Faultless Disagreement," *Erkenntnis* 79 (1), 73–100.

Ferrari, Filippo (2014), *Disagreement and the Normativity of Truth beneath Cognitive Command* (PhD thesis, University of Aberdeen).

Ferrari, Filippo (2016), "Disagreement about Taste and Alethic Suberogation," *Philosophical Quarterly* 66 (264), 516–35.

Gibbard, Allan (2003), *Thinking How to Live*, Cambridge, MA: Harvard University Press.

Gillies, Anthony (2010), "Iffiness," *Semantics and Pragmatics* 3, 1–42.

Glanzberg, Michael (2007), "Context, Content, and Relativism," *Philosophical Studies* 136, 1–29.

Huvenes, Torfinn (2012), "Varieties of Disagreement and Predicates of Taste," *Australasian Journal of Philosophy* 90(1), 167–81.

Huvenes, Torfinn (2014), "Disagreement without Error," *Erkenntnis* 79(1), 143–54.

Kaplan, David (1989), "Demonstratives: An Essay on the Semantics, Logic, Metaphysics, and Epistemology of Demonstratives and Other Indexicals', in J. Almog, J. Perry, and H. Wettstein (eds.), *Themes from Kaplan*, Oxford: Oxford University Press, 481–566.

Kölbel, Max (2004), "Faultless Disagreement," *Proceedings of the Aristotelian Society* 104, 53–73.

Kolodny, Niko and John MacFarlane (2010), "Ifs and Oughts," *Journal of Philosophy* 107, 115–43.

Kompa, Nikola (2002), "The Context Sensitivity of Knowledge Ascriptions," *Grazer Philosophische Studien* 64, 79–96.

Lasersohn, Peter (2005), "Context Dependence, Disagreement, and Predicates of Personal Taste," *Linguistics and Philosophy* 28, 643–86.

Lasersohn, Peter (2009), "Relative Truth, Speaker Commitment, and Control of Implicit Arguments', *Synthese* 166, 359–74.

Lewis, D. (1980), "Index, Context, and Content," in S. Kanger and S. Ohman (eds.), *Philosophy and Grammar*, Dordrecht: Reidel, 79–100. Reprinted in D. Lewis (1998), *Papers in Philosophical Logic*. Cambridge: Cambridge University Press, 21–44.

MacFarlane, John (2011), "Epistemic Modals Are Assessment Sensitive," in A. Egan and B. Weatherson (eds.), *Epistemic Modality*, Oxford: Oxford University Press, 144–78.

MacFarlane, John (2014), *Assessment Sensitivity: Relative Truth and its Applications*, Oxford: Oxford University Press.

Recanati, François (2007), *Perspectival Thought: A Plea for (Moderate) Relativism*, Oxford: Oxford University Press.

Richard, Mark (2004), "Contextualism and Relativism," *Philosophical Studies* 119, 215–42.

Richard, Mark (2008), *When Truth Gives Out*, Oxford: Oxford University Press.

Stephenson, Tamina (2007), "Judge Dependence, Epistemic Modals, and Predicates of Personal Taste," *Linguistics and Philosophy* 30, 487–525.

Weatherson, Brian (2009), "Conditionals and Indexical Relativism," *Synthese* 166, 333–57.

Wright, Crispin (1992), *Truth and Objectivity*, Cambridge, MA: Harvard University Press.

Wright, Crispin (2006), "Intuitionism, Realism, Relativism and Rhubarb," in P. Greenough and M. Lynch (eds.), *Truth and Realism*, Oxford: Clarendon Press, 38–59 this volume ch. 2.

Wright, Crispin (2017), "The Variability of 'knows': An Opinionated Overview," in J. Jenkins Ichikawa (ed.), *Routledge Handbook of Epistemic Contextualism*, London: Routledge. This volme, ch. 9.

9

The Variability of 'Knows'

An Opinionated Overview

1. The Variabilist Reaction against Traditional Epistemology

It is fair to say that from the time of the *Theaetetus* until relatively recently, theorists of knowledge tended to conceive their central task as being to explain in what knowledge consists; more exactly, to explain what further conditions need to be satisfied by a true belief if it is to count as knowledgeable. The widely accepted failure of the post-Gettier debates to execute this task convincingly has motivated a very different tendency in mainstream contemporary epistemology. This, influentially promoted by Timothy Williamson in particular, is *epistemic primitivism*: to concede that knowledge is, as Williamson puts it, 'prime'—that it is a fundamental, irreducible cognitive relation. Knowledge, on the primitivist view, is a basic epistemological kind, and to know is to be in a basic, *sui generis* attitudinal state. There can therefore be no correct analysis of it in terms of other, supposedly constitutive or more fundamental cognitive states (true belief + X). The post-Gettier "X knows that P if and only if..." cottage industry was doomed to disappointment for this reason. To the contrary, it is in terms of knowledge that other epistemic notions—justification, evidence, warranted assertion, and rational action—are to be understood.[1]

This primitivism, however, still shares three traditional assumptions with the reductionism it is set against. They can be wrapped together as the compound idea that knowledge is a unique, objective, purely cognitive type of state—hence something at which the aspiration of reductive analysis could be sensibly (even if mis)directed. If we unpack that, however, we find the following three distinct thoughts. First, ascriptions of knowledge, that X knows that P, are *contentually invariant* as far as the semantic contribution of 'knows' is concerned. More specifically, once the referent of 'X', the identity of the proposition that P and the time reference associated with 'knows' are settled, the result is a unique proposition, the same for any competent thinker who considers it.

---

[1] This second aspect—Williamson's "Knowledge First" programme—is of course strictly independent of and additional to the primitivism.

Essays on Relativism: 2001–2021. Crispin Wright, Oxford University Press. © Crispin Wright 2023.
DOI: 10.1093/oso/9780192845993.003.0010

Second—although this would normally be taken to be entailed by the first point—this unique proposition has one and the same truth-value, no matter who asserts or assesses it. Third, this truth-value is determined purely by the cognitive achievements of the subject, irrespective of what else, other than that part of her total information relevant to the judgement that P, is true of X. In particular, such aspects as X's (or anyone else's) *interest* in whether P, is true, or *what is at stake* for her in its truth, or the range and specifics of counter-possibilities to P that occur, or are *salient*, to X—in short: such, as they are often described, 'non-traditional' or as I shall say *pragmatic* factors—have no bearing on the matter.

The striking recent tendency that provides the subject matter of this chapter is the rejection of one or more of these traditional assumptions in favour of one or another form of *variabilism*: broadly, the notion that whether an ascription of knowledge may correctly be regarded as true may depend on pragmatic factors that pertain to the circumstances of the ascriber, or to those of a third party assessing the ascription, or on pragmatic aspects of the circumstances of the ascribee. Although well short of a consensus, a considerable body of opinion has been developed that agrees that *some* form of epistemic variabilism is called for if justice is to be done to the actual employment of 'knows' and its cognates. In what follows, I will review some of the principal considerations that are taken to support that view, critically compare and assess some of the resulting variabilist proposals and recommend a conclusion both about them and about the prospects for primitivism.

2. Three Types of Consideration Suggestive of Variability

(i) Hume remarked long ago on the contrast between the potency of sceptical doubts, at least in their subtler forms, when developed in the philosophical study and their apparent fatuity when considered in the pub over beer and backgammon.[2] We may of course address the tension by proposing that one or the other—study or pub—response has to be misconceived; but then we remain in a state of cognitive dissonance until we have given a convincing account of which. No need, however, for such an account if "One normally knows that one has two hands" is false in the study but true in the pub—either because the semantic value of 'knows' is context-sensitive (and the context shifts in relevant respects as one moves from

---

[2] "The *intense* view of these manifold contradictions and imperfections in human reason has so wrought upon me, and heated my brain, that I am ready to reject all belief and reasoning, and can look upon no opinion even as more probable or likely than another. . . . Most fortunately it happens, that since reason is incapable of dispelling these clouds, nature herself suffices to that purpose, and cures me of this philosophical melancholy and delirium . . . I dine, I play a game of backgammon, I converse, and am merry with my friends; and when after three or four hours' amusement, I wou'd return to these speculations, they appear so cold, and strain'd, and ridiculous, that I cannot find in my heart to enter into them any farther" (*Treatise* I, IV, 7; Hume 1738, pp. 268–9).

the study to the pub), or because the truth-value of the single proposition expressed by tokenings of that sentence in both locations is not absolute or because *we* change in relevant pragmatic respects as we move from the study to the pub.

(ii) John Hawthorne and others have emphasized problems generated by our ordinary practices of knowledge-ascription for the principle of the closure of knowledge across known entailment.[3] A range of cases exists where one might naturally self-ascribe knowledge of a premise of what one knows is a trivially valid entailment but might then hesitate to self-ascribe knowledge of its conclusion. Some of the most striking are so-called lottery cases. Suppose you buy a ticket in next week's UK National Lottery (the first prize has built up to about £50 million). You are under no illusions about the odds and sensibly expect (truly, let's suppose) that you will not win. But, despite this true belief's being overwhelmingly strongly justified, there are powerful reasons for denying that it is, strictly, knowledgeable. For one thing, if it is knowledgeable, then your buying the ticket is irrational—but that seems a harsh verdict; indeed if the scale of the prize and the odds suitably combine, the expected utility may actually rationalize the purchase. Moreover having bought a ticket, you will have, if you *know* that it won't win, no reason not to tear it up. But actually, once having bought a ticket, tearing it up would seem irrational so long as you have every reason to think that the lottery is fair.

Suppose it's agreed that, for such reasons, you don't strictly know that you won't win the lottery. On the other hand, there are plenty of things that in ordinary contexts you would take yourself to know—for instance, that you won't be able to afford to buy a new Maserati next week or to retire at the end of the current academic year—that entail that you won't win the lottery. And in general there are plenty of things we would ordinarily be regarded as in position to know about our future circumstances in all kinds of respects (indeed, had better know if knowledge is the basis of rational practical reasoning to conclusions about what to do) that, in turn, entail that we won't be the subject of various forms of unlikely happenstance—even in cases, like lotteries, where it is sure that someone will be—which, once contemplated, we will be inclined to acknowledge that we don't strictly *know* will not occur.

There is the option of regarding such cases as actually challenging the validity of closure, of course. But that is a hard row to hoe.[4] Variability offers a different recourse. Perhaps the very act of bringing to mind the conclusion of an entailment of relevant kind 'ups the ante' in some way. Maybe the correctness of your self-ascription of knowledge that you will not be able to afford to retire at the end of the current academic year is originally relativized to a range of salient

[3] Hawthorne (2004); Dretske (2005).
[4] See Hawthorne (2005); see also Ichikawa (2017, ch. 12).

counter-possibilities which do not include lottery wins and which you *are* in a position to rule out—and maybe this range enlarges with the purchase of the ticket.

(iii) Perhaps the dominant motivation towards variabilism, however, springs from a range of putative linguistic 'intuitions' concerning proprieties of knowledge-ascription provoked, at least among many of the philosophers who think about them, by imaginary cases of a kind first put forward by Stewart Cohen and Keith DeRose.[5] We can illustrate by reference to a version of DeRose's famous Bank Case. Suppose it is Friday afternoon, and Ashley and Bobbie are considering whether to bank their salary cheques. There are long queues at all the bank counters. Ashley recalls being at the bank on a Saturday morning two weeks ago and says, "Let's come back tomorrow. **I know the bank will be open tomorrow morning.**" Suppose that the bank will indeed be open on the Saturday morning.

Case 1 (*Low stakes*):   Suppose that there is no particular reason to ensure that the cheques are banked sooner rather than later—say, by the following Monday. Then

Invited intuition: Ashley's recollection of Saturday morning opening two weeks ago suffices for her to speak truly.

Contrast that scenario with

Case 2 (*High stakes*):   The couple's mortgage lender will foreclose unless the cheques are in the account by Monday to service their monthly repayment. Ashley and Bobbie know this. Bobbie says, "But what if the bank has changed its opening hours? Or what if the Saturday morning opening was some kind of one-off promotion?" Ashley says, "You're right. **I suppose I don't really *know* that the bank will be open tomorrow** (even though I am pretty confident that it will). We had better join the queue."

Invited intuition: Again, Ashley speaks truly. Too much is at stake to take the risk of, e.g., a change in banking hours.

So the suggested conclusion is that "I know the bank will be open tomorrow" uttered by Ashley is true in Case 1 and false in Case 2 even though all that is different between the two are the costs to Ashley and Bobbie of Ashley's being wrong. Only the pragmatic factors have changed. Everything that might be mentioned in a traditional account of knowledge—as we would naturally say, all Ashley's relevant evidence or information—remains the same.

Two further cases may seem to prompt another important conclusion:

---

[5] Cohen (1986); DeRose (1992).

Case 3 (*Unknowing high stakes*):   The couple's mortgage lender will indeed foreclose unless the cheques are in the account by Monday to service their monthly repayment but Ashley and Bobbie are unaware of this (they habitually leave what looks like circular mail from the mortgage company unopened and have missed the reminder). The dialogue proceeds as first described above, with Ashley asserting, "**I know the bank will be open tomorrow morning.**"

Invited intuition: This time, Ashley speaks falsely.

Compare that with

Case 4 (*Unknowing low stakes*):   Ashley and Bobbie actually have no good reason to ensure that the cheques are banked before Monday but, misremembering the notice from the mortgage company, they *falsely* believe that Monday will be too late. The dialogue proceeds as in Case 2.

Invited intuition: This time Ashley's disclaimer, "I suppose I don't really know that the bank will be open tomorrow" is false.

The suggested conclusion from Cases 3 and 4 is this: when changes in pragmatic factors convert a true knowledge-ascription into a false one, or vice versa, it is *actual* changes that matter, rather than thinkers' impressions of what changes in such factors may have taken place.

3. The Varieties of Variabilism

We have already, in effect, noted that the space of theoretical options here must include at least three quite different kinds of proposals: one for each of the traditional assumptions distinguished in Section 1. First, there is the option of maintaining that although knowledge-ascriptions are contentually invariant (in the sense there specified), the proposition thereby expressed may take different truth-values in different circumstances, depending on variation in the pragmatic factors applying to its subject, X. This is the thesis, proposed separately by Stanley and Hawthorne,[6] that is most often termed *interest-relative invariantism* (IRI).[7] The details of a proposal of this kind will naturally depend on just what kinds of pragmatic factor are deemed relevant—saliences seemed to be the germane factor for the issue about closure; but variation in stakes is what seems germane in the various scenarios in the Bank Case. IRI allows, apparently, that a pair of subjects may both truly believe that P on the basis of the same evidence or cognitive

---

[6] Hawthorne (2004), Stanley (2005); see also Fantl and McGrath (2007). See Ichikawa (2017, ch. 19).
[7] Or sometimes: subject-sensitive invariantism.

achievements yet one knows that *P*, and the other fails to know that *P* if they suitably differ in pragmatic respects. I'll come back to this.

Second, there is the option of maintaining that the variability in truth-value of knowledge-ascriptions across the kinds of situation illustrated is actually a product of variation in *content*. The specific version of this proposal made by DeRose and Cohen is standardly termed *ascriber contextualism* (henceforward simply 'contextualism'). In its original and basic form, this view holds that the (level of) cognitive achievement that is required of *X* by the truth of an utterance of "*X* knows that *P*" varies as a function of pragmatic aspects—needs, stakes, saliences— *of the speaker*. Thus, in an example like the Bank Case, variation in pragmatic aspects of a *self*-ascriber across actual, or hypothetical, cases may result in (actual or hypothetical) tokenings of "I know that *P*" demanding different—more or less exigent—levels of cognitive achievement if they are to count as true. The truth-conditions, hence content, of tokens of such an ascription can vary, even though the only differences in their respective contexts of utterance pertain to the situation of the speaker in purely pragmatic respects.

The third option—that of *knowledge-relativism*, fashioned on the model of assessment-sensitivity as developed by John MacFarlane[8]—shifts the location of the pragmatic factors once again, this time to anyone who evaluates a knowledge-ascription, whether or not they are its original author. So a single token of "*X* knows that *P*" may properly be assigned different truth-values in differing contexts of assessment, whether or not distinct assessors are involved, depending on the situation in pragmatic respects of the assessor. Thus, Ashley may again quite correctly return different verdicts on a self-ascription of knowledge that the bank will open on the Saturday in the two contexts described. A smooth account of Hume's observation is likewise in prospect if the knowledge-relativist can make a convincing case that travel between the philosophical study and the pub is apt to change the context of assessment in some relevant respect; a relativistic treatment of lottery cases will require a similar story concerning the potential effects of explicit consideration of certain of a statement's consequences. But I shall not here consider in any detail how such an account might run.

It will not have escaped the attention of the alert reader that the three types of variabilist views distinguished exhibit disagreement in two dimensions. Agreeing that the truth-value of a knowledge-ascription may vary as an effect of variation in non-traditional pragmatic factors, they disagree about the *location*—subject, ascriber, or assessor—of the relevant factors; but they also disagree about the *semantic significance* of such variation. For both knowledge-relativism and interest-relative invariantism, variation in pragmatic factors is of no semantic significance at all; rather, one and the same proposition gets to vary in truth-value in tandem with

---

[8] MacFarlane (2005 and 2014); see MacFarlane (2017, part V).

variation in the pragmatic characteristics of the subject or assessors of that proposition. For knowledge contextualism, by contrast, at least in its classic form, it is the proposition expressed by a particular knowledge-ascription that varies in a fashion sensitive to the pragmatic factors. Ashley's tokens of "I know the bank will be open tomorrow morning" express different propositions in the low-stakes and high-stakes scenarios outlined. Thus, conceptual space exists for three further types of views that are the duals in these two dimensions of the three distinguished. There is, first, scope for a kind of contextualism—an instance of *non-indexical* contextualism[9]—that agrees with classical contextualism on the matter of location but disagrees on the matter of semantic significance. On this view, Ashley's two imaginary tokens of "I know the bank will be open tomorrow morning" express the same proposition in the low- and high-stakes scenarios, but this proposition takes a different truth-value as a function of the difference in what is at stake for the ascriber—Ashley—in those scenarios. Second, there is scope for a view which, like classical contextualism, regards ascriptions of knowledge as varying in their content (truth-conditions) as a function of variation in pragmatic characteristics but holds, like interest-relative invariantism, that the relevant characteristics are those not of the ascriber but of the subject, or subjects, to whom knowledge is ascribed. On such a view, a predicate of the form "... knows that P" will vary in its satisfaction conditions rather as, e.g., "... is sharp enough" so varies depending on whether it is being applied to a bread knife or a surgical scalpel. And finally, there is scope for an example of the view that *content itself* is, locally, assessment-sensitive: that what proposition is expressed by a token knowledge-ascription is itself a function of pragmatic characteristics of an assessor of it, with assessment-sensitivity of truth-value merely a consequence of such assessment-relativity of what is said.[10] I do not know if anyone has ever seriously proposed a view of either of these two latter kinds for the semantics of 'knows' but in any case neither will feature further in the discussion to follow. However, in view of the difficulties, to be touched on below, that classical contextualists have encountered in trying to make good the claim that 'knows' is indeed semantically context-sensitive, its non-indexical counterpart presents as worthy of serious consideration. We'll touch on it from time to time below.

4. The Location Question

So, *whose* standards (saliences, interests, etc.) count? The cases considered to this point involve *self*-ascriptions of knowledge. So they have the subject of the

---

[9] As MacFarlane terms it.
[10] For experimentation with a version of this kind of view, see Cappelen (2008). Weatherson (2009) makes an interesting application of it to address certain puzzles with indicative conditionals.

knowledge-ascription coincide with both the ascriber and an assessor. They therefore can suggest, at most, that we should be receptive to *some* sort of variabilism. They are powerless to motivate one rather than another of the variabilist views. Can we find some crucial experiments?

Here is a simple kind of case that has seemed to contextualists to favour their view over IRI:

Case 5 (*High-stakes ascriber, low-stakes subject*):   Ashley and Bobbie are situated as in Case 2. They ask Chris, another customer who is leaving the building, whether the bank will be open tomorrow. Chris says "Yes, I happen to know it will—I was in here a couple of weeks ago on a Saturday." Ashley says to Bobbie *sotto voce*, "Hmm. **That person doesn't know any better than we do**. We had better join the queue."

Invited intuition: Ashley speaks truly even though—as we may suppose—there is nothing at stake for Chris, the subject, in whether the bank will open on the Saturday or not. Here, it seems the interests that count are those of the ascriber, even when the subject is someone else whose interests are different (and less urgent).

The significance of this kind of case is *prima facie* countered, however, by the following simple case that may seem to point back towards IRI:

Case 6 (*Low-stakes ascriber, high-stakes subject*):   Ashley, Bobbie, and Chris are again situated as in Case 5. Chris is puzzled that Ashley and Bobbie have joined the queue again notwithstanding the advice they were just given about a Saturday opening and asks them about this. They explain their concern about the risk of foreclosure of their mortgage. Chris says, "OK, I understand now. I guess you guys had better not assume that the bank *will* be open tomorrow."

Invited intuition: Chris speaks truly. But since "You know that *P* but had better not assume that *P*" is some kind of conceptual solecism, Chris's remark is presumably a commitment to "**You do not know that the bank will be open tomorrow.**"[11]

So, neither contextualism nor IRI does well in all the cases—in fact they do just as well and as badly as each other: well enough in cases where subject and ascriber

---

[11] This is different from—but perhaps not quite as clean-cut as—Stanley's (2005) tactic which is to develop examples where a low-stakes ascriber does not know that the subject is high stakes. For instance, suppose Chris does not notice Ashley and Bobbie join the queue. But Denny, Chris's partner, who has overheard the exchange, does and nudges Chris with a quizzical glance in their direction. Chris says, "Oh, I guess they must have remembered some reason why they can't come back tomorrow—after all, **they now know that the bank will be open then**." This time, we are supposed to have the intuition that the knowledge-ascription is false.

are identified, but badly in various kinds of cases where they are distinct—which are of course the crucial cases. This might encourage the thought that *both* have the location issue wrong, and one might therefore wonder whether knowledge-relativism promises an overall better ride. And indeed we can very simply modify Case 5 to get one that seems to favour knowledge-relativism over contextualism *and* IRI:

Case 5*:   Ashley and Bobbie are dithering in the foyer and then merely overhear Chris (in a phone conversation) say, "Look, I don't need to wait here now. My partner, Denny, was here a couple of weeks ago on a Saturday and can vouch that this bank will be open tomorrow." Ashley remarks, *sotto voce*, "We can't rely on that; **that Denny doesn't know any better than we do.**"
Invited intuition: Ashley speaks truly.

However while knowledge-relativism may possibly best explain some intuitions in cases like this where subject, ascriber, and assessor are all distinct, it faces the basic problem that it must coincide in its predictions with contextualism in any case where ascriber and assessor are one. So any two-agent problem cases for contextualism, like Case 6, are problems for relativism, too.

These conflicting intuitions present a potential paradox if we think that they do, near enough, show that there is *some* kind of relativity to pragmatic factors in the offing. How can that be so if the intuitions also suggest that each of the possible hypotheses about location is open to counterexample?

5. Attempts to Explain away the Hard Cases

Maybe (some of) the intuitions are misleading and should be explained away rather than accommodated. What might contextualism (and knowledge-relativism) say to explain away Case 6, where the intuition is that the correctness/incorrectness of the knowledge-ascription is determined by the subject's relatively high standards, rather than the ascriber's/assessor's relatively low ones?

We should flag one tempting but futile tactic of explanation: that Ashley's and Bobbie's relatively high stakes and standards have an adverse effect on their confidence. It might be suggested that they do indeed not know that the bank will be open on that Saturday, as Chris's remark implies, but this is not because, as IRI would have it, the question is properly assessed by reference to their own high standards, but rather because they don't believe—or anyway *sufficiently confidently believe*—that the bank will then be open.

This suggestion has three problems. First, there is no general prohibition on the idea of a relatively diffident belief being knowledgeable. (Think of the school-teacher's encouraging remark to a hesitant pupil: "Come on, Jonny: you *do* know the answer to this.") Second, there is anyway no need to make it a feature of the example that Ashley be in any significant degree of doubt that the bank will be open on that Saturday (and indeed I explicitly refrained from doing so, as the reader may care to check). Finally, Case 3—involving low ascriber stakes, but *ignorant* high subject stakes—may be adapted to refurbish the objection as follows:

Case 7:   Ashley and Bobbie are situated as in Case 3—the risk of foreclosure if the cheques are not banked by Monday is real, but they are unaware of this. They ask Chris, another customer who is leaving the building, whether the bank will be open tomorrow. Chris says, "Yes, I happen to know it will—I was in here a couple of weeks ago on a Saturday." Ashley says to Bobbie, "Great. Let's get out of this and go get a coffee." Asked to explain why Ashley and Bobby have left the queue, Chris would doubtless say, "**Because they now know that the bank will be open tomorrow.**"

Invited intuition: Chris speaks falsely. Given Ashley's and Bobbie's—the subjects'—actual high stakes, they are in no position to acquire knowledge by testimony from Chris, even though Chris's low-stakes self-ascription is unexceptionable.

There is, however, another response that at least one leading contextualist has offered to this kind of case that is potentially something of a game-changer. Keith DeRose observes[12] that in taking patterns of conversation like those illustrated by Cases 6 and 7 to constitute *prima facie* counterexamples to contextualism, we are implicitly taking it for granted that the mechanism whereby the context of a token knowledge-ascription contrives to set the standards for its truth is simply by identifying them with the standards of the ascriber: that "X knows that P" as uttered by Y is true just if X's relevant epistemic situation, replicated by Y but without change in the pragmatic aspects of Y's situation, would suffice for the truth of "Y knows that P." DeRose points out that there is absolutely no reason why that has to be the only kind of case. It is very familiar that in a wide range of examples—'impure indexicals' like some personal pronouns, demonstratives, and gradable adjectives—the semantic values of context-sensitive expressions featuring in particular utterances are settled as a function, in part, of the intentions of the utterer. It is therefore open to the contextualist to allow a similar role for the intentions of the author of a knowledge-ascription in determining the standard of epistemic achievement to be applied in fixing its truth-conditions. This can of course be the standard she would (take herself to) have to meet in order to satisfy the relevant ascription. But it need not be. In certain contexts—like those of Cases

---

[12] See DeRose (2009, ch. 7).

6 and 7—an ascriber may instead set a standard that defers to the needs, interest, or saliences of the subject. In such a case, IRI and contextualism will coincide in their predictions of the truth-conditions of the knowledge-ascription.

I described this 'flexible contextualist' manoeuvre as a potential game-changer. It is, of course, merely *ad hoc* unless a principled and comprehensive account is provided of the conditions under which relevant variations in a speaker's intentions can be expected, enabling empirically testable predictions of variable truth-conditions. DeRose expends some effort in that direction, to not implausible effect. His basic suggestion is that knowledge-ascriptions may be harnessed to two quite different kinds of project: whether X knows that P may be of interest because one wishes to rate X as a potential *source of information*; but it may also be of interest in the context of assessing X's performance as a *rational agent*. In the former type of case one will naturally impose standards on X's claim to knowledge appropriate to one's own needs and interests. (Just this is what seems to be happening in the high-stakes ascriber, low-stakes subject cases reviewed.) But in the latter type of case, when the focus shifts to what it is rational for X to do, it may well be (one's conception of) X's needs and interests that determine what level of cognitive achievement it is reasonable to demand if X is to be credited with the knowledge that P. And this seems to be the driver for the (invited) intuitions operative in the low-stakes ascriber, high-stakes subject cases like Cases 6 and 7.

I have no space here to consider further whether the flexible contextualist manoeuvre can be developed so as to deliver fully satisfyingly on its initial promise. However two points are worth emphasis. The first is that an exactly analogous flexibility on the location question is, obviously, available to knowledge-relativism. Whatever potential shifts of interest are offered to explain variations in the location of standards from the point of view of a knowledge-ascriber, they will be available also to explain such variations from the perspective of a knowledge-ascription assessor. Flexibility thus offers no prospect of an advantage for contextualism over relativism. Second, there is no analogous move open to IRI, which is stuck with the idea that the standards for the truth of a knowledge-ascription are inflexibly set as a function of the needs, interests, or saliences of its subject. If IRI is to restore dialectical parity after (and presuming the success of) the flexible contextualist manoeuvre, it must therefore explain away cases, like Case 5, where the location seems to go with an ascriber (or assessor), rather than the subject, as some kind of linguistic mistake. What are the prospects?

It is important to take the full measure of the challenge. Any presumed *knowledgeable* ascription of knowledge to a third party entails—by closure and factivity—an ascription of the same knowledge to oneself. And of course if IRI is right, and one's standards are relatively high, one may not have that knowledge. In that case, one won't be in position to ascribe it to a third party either, whatever their standards. There is therefore, in general, no difficulty for IRI in explaining our *reluctance to ascribe* knowledge in such cases. That, however, is not the relevant *explanandum*. What the defender of IRI has to explain—what the high-stakes ascriber, low-stakes subject examples are meant to illustrate—is a readiness of high-stakes ascribers to (falsely) *deny* knowledge that P to a relevant low-stakes subject. (Thus Ashley: "That person doesn't know any better than we do.")

It would take us too far afield to pursue the details of all the responses that defenders of IRI have offered to this challenge.[13] Suppose, however, that it proves that IRI has no good account to offer of the patterns of knowledge-ascription and - denial that we seem to apply in certain high-stakes ascriber, low-stakes subject cases. How damaging is that? Jason Stanley[14] contends that contextualism has an exactly matching set of problems as soon as we consider the relevant *self-ascription* by the low-stakes subject. Thus in Case 5 above, the subject—Chris— affirms that "I happen to know that it [the bank] will [be open tomorrow]" and, from a contextualist point of view, this self-ascription ought to be (absent any detail in the example suggesting the contrary) in perfect order: a true knowledge-ascription made by a low-stakes ascriber on adequate evidence. Yet is that not (a truth-conditional equivalent of) the very claim that Ashley, in a high-stakes context, correctly—by contextualist lights—contradicts?

Non-indexical contextualism will accept that consequence: Ashley and Chris are, in their respective contexts, perfectly correctly endorsing incompatible claims. But historically contextualists have shown no stomach for this near-enough[15] relativistic stance. Rather here is a place where the putative context-sensitivity of 'knows' is made to do some serious theoretical work. When Chris affirms "I happen to know [that the bank will be open tomorrow]" and Ashley affirms "That person [Chris] doesn't know any better than we do [that the bank will be

---

[13] John Hawthorne (2004, ch. 4 at pp. 162–6) attempts to enlist the help of what he calls the "psychological literature on heuristics and biases." Hawthorne's idea is that one lesson of this literature is that the becoming salient of a certain risk in a high-stakes situation (e.g., that of the bank's changing its opening hours) characteristically leads us to overestimate its probability in general and hence to project our own ignorance onto subjects in low-stakes situations too. DeRose (2009, ch. 7, §3) counters that the phenomenon to be explained—high-stakes agents' denial of knowledge to low-stakes subjects—extends to cases where the former take it that they *do* nevertheless know the proposition in question (because they take themselves to meet the elevated standards demanded by their high-stakes context). That seems right, but I do not see that Hawthorne needed the "projection of ignorance" component in his proposal in any case; a tendency to overestimation of the probabilities of salient sources of error would seem sufficient to do the work he wants on its own. The objection remains, however, that if an overestimation of the risk of a certain source of error underlies a high-stakes ascriber's denial of knowledge to himself, the good standing of that denial is already compromised— whereas IRI requires precisely that the high-stakes context should validate it.

[14] Stanley (2005, ch. 7).

[15] Non-indexical contextualism allows speakers of the same proposition in distinct contexts to speak truly and falsely, respectively. That may seem relativistic enough for most people's money, but it stops short of the contention, essential to MacFarlane's understanding of relativism, that a single speaking of a proposition may take distinct truth-values as assessed in different contexts.

open tomorrow]," the contradiction is finessed by the shift in the semantic value of 'know' engineered by the differing standards operative in their two contexts.

We'll return to this shortly.

6. Ugly Conjunctions

We have so far been concerned with the challenge to the different variabilist views to capture and explain not just some but all the pragmatically variable patterns of use of 'knows' and its cognates that, according to the 'intuitions', competent speakers seem to find acceptable. And at this point, provided they are prepared to go 'flexible', and thus steal the cases that otherwise favour IRI, contextualism and relativism seem to be tied in the lead. But there is also an obverse challenge: to avoid predicting uses to be acceptable which are apt to impress as anything but. How do the different theories fare on this?

IRI imposes a condition on knowledge-ascriptions as follows:

X knows that P at t is true only if X's belief at t that P is based on cognitive accomplishments that meet standards appropriate to X's practical interests (or whatever) at t,

and consequently appears to do very badly. Suppose X fails this condition—his practical interests are such that it is vitally important at t for him to be right about whether or not P, and he does at t truly believe that P, but does so on the basis of evidence that, though probative to a degree, impresses us as too slight to confer on him knowledge that P. Then IRI seems to treat as on an equal footing either of two remedies: X can either improve his evidence, or he can work on his practical interests in such a way that much less is at stake whether he is right about P or not. He can grow his evidence to meet the standards for knowledge imposed by his practical interests at t, or he can so modify his practical interests as to shrink, as it were, the standards of knowledge that P requires. Suppose he takes the latter course. Then a situation may arise at a later time, t^*, when we can truly affirm an 'ugly conjunction' like:

X didn't (have enough evidence to) know P at t but does at t^* and has exactly the same body of P-relevant evidence at t^* as at t.

Such a remark seems drastically foreign to the concept of knowledge we actually have. It seems absurd to suppose that a thinker can acquire knowledge without further investigation simply because his practical interests happen to change so as to reduce the importance of the matter at hand. Another potential kind of ugly conjunction is the synchronic case for different subjects:

X knows that P but Y does not, and X and Y have exactly the same body of P-relevant evidence

when affirmed purely because X and Y have sufficiently different practical interests. IRI, as we noted earlier, must seemingly allow that instances of such a conjunction can be true.[16]

So far, so bad for IRI. But does contextualism escape any analogue of these problems for its competitor? Certainly, there can be no commitment to either form of ugly conjunction so long as we are concerned with cases where the relevant standards are set as those of an ascriber distinct from X and Y. In that case the same verdict must be returned about X at t and at t^*, or about X and Y, simply because some single set of standards is in play. But what if the context is one where contextualism has gone *flexible*, availing itself of the licence to defer to standards set by the (changing) pragmatic characteristics of the subject(s)? In that case, *non-indexical* contextualism, at least, can offer no evident barrier to the assertibility in suitable circumstances of either type of ugly conjunction. So much is simply the price of the flexibility it appropriates to accommodate the cases that seemed to favour IRI.

Regular (indexical) flexible contextualism, by contrast, stands to suffer a commitment only to the metalinguistic counterparts:

"X doesn't (have enough evidence to) know P" was true at t but "X does (have enough evidence to) know P" is true at t^* and X has exactly the same body of P-relevant evidence at t^* as at t;

"X knows that P" and "Y does not know that P" are both true and X and Y have exactly the same body of P-relevant evidence.

These are spared 'ugliness' by the postulated shifts in the semantic values of the occurrences of 'know' which are the trademark of the classical contextualist view and block disquotation. Nevertheless, they are unquestionably extremely strange to an English ear.

Does knowledge-relativism fare better with these potential snags? Again, the interesting question concerns a flexible relativism, one with the resources to handle cases where the pragmatic features of its subject determine the standards

---

[16] If evidence, too, were an interest-relative notion, then a possible direction of defence for IRI against these ugly conjunctive commitments would be to try to make the case that variation in the interests of a subject sufficient to make the difference between her knowing that P and failing to do so must also affect what evidence she possesses, thus undercutting the assumption that evidence may remain constant for a subject at different times or for distinct subjects when their interests differ. Stanley canvasses this suggestion (2005, p. 181). It misses the nub of the difficulty, however, because there will presumably be cases where the relevant evidence is known with certainty and hence must be reckoned to be in common no matter what the practical interests of the subjects or subject at different times.

that a correct knowledge-ascription has to meet. And of course for the relativist, as for the non-indexical contextualist, there are no complications occasioned by shifts in the semantic value of 'knows'. We know to expect that relativism will coincide in its predictions with non-indexical contextualism in all scenarios where knowledge is ascribed in the indicative mood and where there is no contrast between the ascriber and an assessor. It is therefore no more than the price paid for the flexibility to copy the verdicts of IRI in cases that reflect well on the latter that relativism, like non-indexical contextualism, will sanction certain cases, both synchronic and diachronic, of ugly conjunctions.

So, here is the scorecard.

IRI is, seemingly, encumbered by a commitment to the assertibility, in suitable circumstances, of both forms of ugly conjunction.

However, commitments of this kind are not, as is sometimes assumed, a distinctive problem for that particular form of variabilism.

Non-indexical contextualism and *relativism* both share that commitment provided they avail themselves of the option of 'flexibility'. And, of course, if they do not so avail themselves, the IRI-favourable cases stand as counterexamples to their proposals.

Classical (flexible) contextualism is committed only to metalinguistic versions of ugly conjunctions. That is not as bad only provided (i) the metalinguistic versions are not as ugly and (ii) their disquotation is indeed blocked, i.e. provided 'knows' is indeed context-sensitive.

7. Is There Any Good Reason to Think that 'Knows' Is Context-Sensitive?

When utterances of the same type-sentence in different contexts appear to be able to take differing truth-values, context-sensitivity—that is, sensitivity of the content expressed to features of the utterance-context—is plausibly the most natural explanation. So, anyway, it must have seemed to the original authors of contextualism when first reflecting on the apparent variability of 'knows', but that was before the rival invariantist kinds of explanations considered here entered the scene. Can evidence be mustered to restore the presumption that context-sensitivity is at the root of the variability phenomena, and so give classical contextualism an edge?

The literature on the matter is complex, extensive, and inconclusive; it is fair to say that there are no uncontroversial, or even generally agreed upon, criteria for (non-)context-sensitivity.[17] Jason Stanley argues persuasively[18] that the alleged

---

[17] For discussion, see Cappelen and Hawthorne (2009, ch. 2).   [18] Stanley (2005, ch. 3).

context-sensitivity of 'knows' is not felicitously assimilated to that of any of gradable adjectives ('rich', 'tall'), pronouns ('I', 'you', 'this') or quantificational determiners ('all', 'many', 'some'). Schaffer and Szabo grant this but suggest instead a comparison with so called A-quantifiers ('always', 'somewhere').[19] Still, there is no reason in any case why a bone fide context-sensitive expression should behave exactly like context-sensitive expressions of other kinds. Is there any *general* reason to think that 'knows' and its cognates are context-sensitive, whether or not their behaviour sustains close comparison with that of other, uncontroversially context-sensitive expressions?

Here is a natural litmus. If 'S' contains context-sensitives, then distinct tokens of 'S' in different mouths may have different truth-conditions. So distinct token questions, "S?" in the mouths of different questioners may have different conditions for affirmative answers. Hence, if 'knows' and its cognates are context-sensitive, it should be possible to design a pair of conversational contexts within which a pair of tokens of the question, "Does X know that P" presented simultaneously to a single agent—the *questionee*—can respectively properly deserve *prima facie* conflicting answers. Why simultaneously? Because 'knows' *is* of course context-sensitive, at least to the extent of admitting of significant tense and X, the subject, may know different things at different times. (We needn't require strict simultaneity though. It will be enough to ensure that both the questionee's and (if distinct) the subjects' information states are relevantly unaltered throughout the interval when the two questions are put.) Why a single questionee? Because, again, we want to ensure that if different answers are appropriate to the distinct token questions, they are so because of variations in pragmatic factors determined by their respective conversational contexts, rather than variations in the information of the questionee.

Call this the *forked-tongue test*. It's pretty crude—for instance, it won't distinguish context-sensitivity from simple ambiguity. Still, its credentials as at least a necessary condition for context-sensitivity seem good. Let's construct a simple illustration. Suppose Ashley and Bobbie are wondering whether to duck out of the queues at the bank and go to get coffee and cake. Chris meanwhile, standing nearby, is on the phone to Denny. Bobbie overhears Chris say, "Yes, my dear, there is. There is a Caffè Nero just two minutes away where they serve excellent coffee and *torta di cioccolata*." Bobbie says, "Excuse me, but did you say that there is a nice coffee shop just two minutes away." Chris replies, "Ah. Actually, no. I mean: I did say that, but I was talking to my partner about a location downtown."

Thus, "just two minutes away" passes the test. It was the context of Denny's question, rather than Bobbie's, that set the reference of "just two minutes way" in Chris's original remark. When Bobbie puts a token of essentially the same type-question, the reference shifts and the correct answer changes.

---

[19] Schaffer and Szabo (2013). Their proposal deserves a properly detailed discussion. I believe the comparison is flawed but I have no space to enlarge on that here.

Can we get a similar result with 'know'? Let's try to construct an analogously shaped case, but where the questioners' respective contexts differ in respect of the stakes they have in the truth of the answer.

In Case 8, Ashley and Bobbie are dithering in the foyer of the bank as before. They talk about the risk of foreclosure and Bobbie says, "Look, we had better ask someone." Chris and Denny, standing near the back of one of the queues, happen to overhear their conversation. Denny is also perturbed by the length of the queues and says to Chris, "Do you know if the bank will be open tomorrow? We could come back then if it will, but I'd rather not leave it till Monday since I have a hairdresser's appointment on Monday morning and am meeting Stacy for coffee and a chat in the afternoon." Chris, recalling the Saturday morning visit of two weeks earlier says, "It's OK. I happen to know the bank will be open tomorrow. I'll drive you over after breakfast." Ashley, overhearing, says, "Excuse me, but did you say that you know the bank will be open tomorrow?" Chris, mindful of Ashley and Bobbie's overheard priorities, replies, "Ah. Actually, no. I mean, I did use those words, but I was talking to Denny here, who has less at stake than you guys."

Case-hardened contextualists may find this dialogue unexceptionable, but I would suggest that Denny, Ashley, and Bobbie might reasonably be baffled by Chris's last reply. It is also striking that, if the dialogue *is* regarded as unexceptionable, it should remain so if all play with 'know' is dropped and the operative question is rephrased as simply, "Will the bank be open tomorrow?" But in that case the explanation of the acceptability of Chris's final remark will presumably have nothing to do with context-sensitivity in the operative question. So it looks as though the contextualist faces a choice between admitting that 'know' fails the forked-tongue test in this instance or insisting that it passes but that this fact has no significance for its putative context-sensitivity.

8. Is There Any Good Reason to Think that 'Knows' Is *Not* Context-Sensitive?

The consideration that has proved perhaps the most influential in this regard in the recent debates, and indeed has provided the prime motivation for knowledge-relativism, is provided by ostensible patterns of *correction and retraction* that our knowledge-talk seems to exhibit. Here's a toy example of the relevant kind. Chris and Denny have gone away for the weekend and have left Ashley and Bobbie the keys for the use of their car:

Ashley: Do you know where their car is parked?

Bobbie: Yes, I do—Chris texted me that they left it in the multi-storey lot as usual after badminton on Friday.

Ashley: But, as you very well know, there have been several car thefts in the neighbourhood recently. We should have gone to get it earlier. What if it's been stolen?

Bobbie: I wasn't reckoning with that. OK, I guess I don't *know* that it is in the multi-storey lot—we had better go and check.

Here, the reader is intended to understand, Ashley's second question doesn't change Bobbie's epistemic situation—it doesn't give her any more evidence. But it does persuade her that it is appropriate to impose more demanding standards of evidence on her answer than she started out doing—and she now disavows the knowledge she originally claimed.

Now, the crucial point for the opponent of contextualism is the suggestion that this disavowal is to be understood as a *retraction*. Consider this continuation of the dialogue:

Ashley: Was your first answer, about knowing where the car is, true when you originally gave it, before I raised the possibility of the car being stolen?

and two possible responses:

Bobbie: *Either* (a) Sure, but I could not truly repeat the words I used, once I was reminded of the recent incidence of car theft.

Or (b) No; as I just said, I wasn't thinking about the possibility of the car being stolen. I shouldn't have claimed to know that it is in the multi-storey lot.

The relativist's idea is that contextualism ought to predict that answer (a) can be acceptable. For if the content of a knowledge-ascription is relative to standards set by the context of ascription, then suitable changes in that context may be expected to go along with a shift in content consistent with tokens of a single type-ascription being respectively true in an original context but false in a later context. But in fact answer (a) is, on the face of it, simply bizarre, and the natural answer, in context, is answer (b), which notably not merely supplants but critiques and retracts the original. That is evidence, it is alleged, that the content of the knowledge-claim has not shifted in response to the change of standards, but has remained invariant throughout.[20]

Note that the contextualist can of course allow Bobbie to affirm not merely that she doesn't know now where the car is but that she *didn't know* when she made her first answer. That is because the referent of 'know', even as used in that past-tense claim, will—according to contextualism—have shifted to some high-standards knowledge relation in response to Ashley's invoking the possibility of

---

[20] See Ichikawa (2017, ch. 20).

theft, whereas Bobbie's original claim will have involved some different, low-standards relation. So contextualism can actually predict what *sounds like* a retraction: "I didn't know that *P*." What, the critic will charge, it cannot predict is agents' willingness to treat such remarks *as* retractions—their refusal to stand by the different thing that, according to contextualism, they originally said.

Challenged to explain that refusal, some contextualists[21] have taken recourse to the idea—usually captioned (by their critics) as 'semantic blindness'—that ordinary speakers are ignorant of the context-sensitivity of 'know' and its cognates and so are prepared in certain respects to (mis)use this family of expressions to talk misguidedly as if they were not context-sensitive. It can be said in mitigation of such a move that a kind of semantic blindness was anyway part of the epistemic contextualist package from the start: after all, the contextualist has to allow that her thesis is controversial—that it is not just straight-off evident to us that 'knows' is a context-sensitive term.[22] Still, it is one thing to maintain that we are ignorant about the gist of the correct semantic theory for an expression in common parlance, and another to hold that we systematically use that expression in ways that conflict with that theory; that is, that we systematically *mis*use it. It is, at least until more is said, rank bad methodology for proponents of a theory whose whole project is systematically to describe and explain aspects of our linguistic practice, to fall back too readily on the idea that aspects of that practice which fail to accord with the theory may be discounted as misuses.[23] At the least, contextualism needs to show how a prediction of the recalcitrant aspects of our practice may be elicited from its own theoretical resources. If no such account is forthcoming, the retraction data, *provided they are solid*, must constitute a serious strike against the view.

9. But Are the Retraction Data Solid?

It is, however, a further question whether our patterns of apparent retraction of knowledge-claims really *do* provide the powerful argument for relativism that its supporters, notably MacFarlane, have urged. I'll canvass two doubts.

To begin with, there are issues about what exactly should count as the manifestation in practice of the relevant kind of retraction. Do we, in response to changes in pragmatic factors, really retract former ascriptions of knowledge in exactly the sense that relativism needs? A moment ago we already noted an important distinction in this connection. Consider this dialogue:

Ashley (on a fast moving train): *Look, there is a cougar!*
Bobbie: Where? I don't see it.

---

[21] See, e.g., Cohen (2001).   [22] See Ichikawa (2017, ch. 24).   [23] Cf. Baker (2012).

Ashley: Just there, crouching by those rocks.

Bobbie: I still don't see it.

Ashley: Oh, I am sorry. I see now that it was just a cat-shaped shadow on the rocks. *There wasn't a cougar.*

Here Ashley's last speech is a retraction in anyone's book: she is denying, using appropriately changed context-sensitive language, exactly the thing she originally said. But to accomplish this, it suffices merely to change the tense of the original and negate it. Whereas under the aegis of contextualism about 'knows' corresponding moves do *not* suffice for retraction of a knowledge-ascription, as we observed. Contextualism allows that Bobbie may perfectly properly admit, in response to Ashley's canvassing the possibility of car theft, both that she does not know where the car is and *did not know when first asked.* The latter admission is not a retraction of the original claim, since—according to contextualism—it concerns a different, high-standards knowledge relation. Accordingly, the relativist needs to point to clear evidence in our linguistic practice that the disposition to retract knowledge-claims when the stakes are raised goes deeper than the apparent denial involved in merely changing the tense and negating the result. Speakers will have to be reliably and regularly disposed to say things that distinguish what they are doing from such merely apparent retractions that contextualism can take in stride.

What kinds of sayings would manifest that distinction? Bobbie was presented above as doing something of the needed sort by saying, "I wasn't thinking about the possibility of the car being stolen. *I shouldn't have claimed to know that it is in the multi-storey lot.*" But that is exactly *not* what she should say on the assumption of knowledge-relativism. Relativism allows that the earlier claim, in the lower standards context then current, can have been perfectly appropriate—indeed, from the standpoint of that context, true. So if that were the form that retractions of knowledge-claims were generally to assume, the fact would be at odds with rather than advantageous to relativism. What is wanted, it seems, is a form of repudiation which is neither a simple denial, modulo any needed changes in tense, etc., nor a repudiation of the propriety of one's making the earlier claim in its original context.

The salient remaining possibility is something along the lines of "What I said before is false." So, let the relativist contention be that we are characteristically prone to retractions on this model of former knowledge-ascriptions when pragmatic factors suitably change. Unfortunately, even this pattern of retraction, should it be prevalent, is too coarse to be unpredictable by contextualism. The reason it is so is because in order to give what passes as an appropriate disquotational specification of what was said by some utterance in a previous context— "What he said before by *S* was that *P*"—it is not necessary, or indeed possible, to adjust *every* kind of context-sensitive expression that *S* may have contained. To be sure, if Ashley says, "Right now, I am going crazy waiting in this queue," then in order to specify what she said we'll need to shift pronouns and tenses and temporal adverbs in routine ways: what Ashley said was that, *at that time, she was* going crazy waiting in *that* queue. But this does not apply in general to, for instance, gradable adjectives nor, so the contextualist may contend, to 'knows' and its cognates. If an inexperienced hospital theatre orderly asserts, "This scalpel is very sharp," intending roughly that you could easily cut yourself if handling it carelessly, he may quite properly be reported to an expert surgeon as having said that *that particular scalpel is very sharp*, even when the context set by conversation with the surgeon is understood as one in which the notion of an instrument's sharpness is high standards—for instance, is tied to its suitability for refined neurosurgery. And in such a context, the orderly may have to accept a reprimand and allow that "What I said—viz. that that scalpel is very sharp—was false." In short, where some kinds of context-sensitive language are involved, admissible ways of specifying what was said are not guaranteed to deliver an actual content previously asserted rather than a counterpart spawned by differences between the original context of use and the context of the specification.

Of course it's usually easy enough to disambiguate in such cases if the conversational participants find it important to do so. The hospital orderly may (perhaps unwisely) protest that all he meant was that the scalpel had enough of a fine edge to be dangerous if handled carelessly. Perhaps therefore the relativist argument should be that we don't go in for such disambiguation where knowledge-claims are concerned but, as it were, *simply* retract. But is that true? With "sharp" now annexed to high (neurosurgical) standards, the orderly has to have recourse to other language to explain what he originally meant to say. If that is allowed to constitute sticking by his former claim, then we surely will want to say something similarly exculpatory about the credentials of our erstwhile epistemic situation and an associated knowledge-claim even as we feel obliged to revoke the latter purely because of pressure of elevated standards.

It is, accordingly, open to question whether relativists have succeeded in tabling a notion of retraction with each of the needed features (a) that we do go in for retraction of knowledge-claims under changes of pragmatic parameters of context; (b) that relativism predicts this; and (c) that contextualism cannot predict as much.

The second doubt about the alleged pro-relativistic significance that our patterns of retraction of knowledge-claims supposedly carry concerns the *extent* of the phenomenon. Relativism predicts that two contexts of assessment, c_1 and c_2, differing only in the values of pragmatic parameters, may be such that one mandates an endorsement of a knowledge-ascription and another its repudiation. The examples so far considered have tended to focus on one direction: where a knowledge-ascription is made in a relatively low-standards context and then, apparently, retracted as the stakes rise, or certain error-possibilities become salient, or whatever the relevant kind of change is proposed to be. What about the converse direction? Does our practice pattern as relativism should expect?

Let's try an example:

Case 9 begins exactly as Case 2. It is Friday afternoon, and Ashley and Bobbie have arrived at the bank to deposit their salary cheques. However there are long queues at all the bank counters. Ashley recalls being at the bank on a Saturday morning two weeks ago and says, "Let's come back tomorrow. **I know the bank will be open tomorrow morning.**" Suppose that the bank will indeed be open on the Saturday morning. However the couple's mortgage lender has written to say the company will foreclose unless the cheques are in the account by Monday to service the monthly repayment, and Ashley and Bobbie are mindful of this. Bobbie says, "But what if the bank has changed its opening hours? Or what if the Saturday morning opening was some kind of one-off promotion?" Ashley says, "You're right. **I suppose I don't really *know* that the bank will be open tomorrow** (even though I am pretty confident that it will). We had better join the queue."

Invited intuition: Ashley correctly retracts her original claim. There is too much at stake to take the risk of, e.g., a change in banking hours.

But now let's run the example on. Let it so happen that Eli, who is the manager of the local branch of Ashley and Bobbie's mortgage company, is also waiting in one of the queues and overhears their conversation. Remembering "that nice young couple" and taking pity on them, Eli comes across and says, "Don't worry, guys. Just between us, there is a degree of bluff about these 'final reminder' notices. We never actually foreclose without first making every effort to conduct an interview with the borrowers. It will be absolutely fine if this month's payment is serviced by the end of next week." Ashley and Bobbie are mightily relieved and Ashley says, "Aha. **So actually I *did* know that the bank will be open tomorrow!** Let's go and get a coffee and come back then."

Relativism predicts that Ashley's last emboldened remark is perfectly in order—indeed it expresses a commitment: the context after Eli's intervention is once again low stakes, so low standards, so Ashley's knowledge-claim is now mandated by the original evidence, and the intermediate knowledge-denial should be retracted. But while relief and the decision to get a coffee are reasonable enough, Ashley's last remark is actually utterly bizarre.

This is a crucial issue for knowledge-relativism. I have no space here to pursue it in detail, but I conjecture that there are actually no clear cases where, moving from a high- to a low-standards context, and *mindful of the fact*, we are content, without acquiring any further relevant evidence, simply to retract a former knowledge-disclaimer and to affirm it's contradictory. Where *P* was the proposition of which knowledge was denied, we may well say things like, "Well, I guess it's reasonable now if we take it that P" or "We can now probably safely assume that P." But the claim to now *know* that P will simply invite the challenge to re-confront the error-possibilities made salient in the previous high-standards context. And when the changes involved in the context shift are wholly pragmatic, we will tend to regard ourselves as, strictly, no better placed, epistemically, to discount those possibilities than we were before. For example, Ashley should not now after conversation with Eli, any more than earlier, want to claim *knowledge* that the Saturday opening of two weeks ago was not a one-off promotion.

The qualification "mindful of the fact" is crucial. No doubt it may happen that, forgetting altogether about a previous high-standards situation, we may in a new, relaxed context be prepared to make knowledge-claims that contradict earlier disclaimers. But these claims will properly rank as *retractions* only if we recall the previous context and what we said then. And if we do that, recollection of the error-possibilities that drove the early disclaimers is still likely to inhibit our outright claiming the relevant bits of knowledge even if it no longer seems urgent to reckon with those possibilities. Relativism, by contrast, predicts that there is now a mandate for such claims and that any such inhibitions about them conflict with the correct semantics for 'knows'.[24]

10. Conclusion

Variabilism, in all its stripes, is motivated by an *appearance*: that the language game of knowledge-ascriptions and -denials incorporates a dependence of their truth-values on pragmatics—on interests, or saliences, or stakes. Each of the four theoretical proposals here considered, albeit offering very different accounts of the nature of the dependence involved, takes this appearance to be veridical. If, as has been the general tendency of the foregoing discussion, none of these accounts is satisfactory—if each under-predicts (fails to predict some uses) or over-predicts (predicts uses with which we are uncomfortable)—the natural conclusion is that

---

[24] This objection should be contrasted with another made by Montminy (2009). His contention is that when *in a high-standards context* we disclaim knowledge that P, we will also judge that we will be wrong to reclaim knowledge that P in a subsequent low-standards context, even though—he allows— that is what we will do once such a context is entered into, and relativism says we will be right to do so. I agree with the first part of that—namely, that we will take a dim view, while in the high-standards context, of the envisaged subsequent reclamation, and that since relativism says that there is nothing wrong with the subsequent reclamation, there is here a tension between something we are inclined to think and what relativism thinks we ought to think. But, unless I misread Montminy, I'm saying something different and stronger as well: namely, that we *won't actually make a retraction* of the previous knowledge-denial when we get into the low-standards context.

Knowledge-relativism, in other words, mispredicts not just aspects of our attitudes to our practice with 'knows' but our practice itself. (MacFarlane responds to Montminy in §8.6 of his 2014 book, see especially pp. 198 and following. His response does not engage the objection made here.)

the appearance is *not* veridical: that our discourse involving 'knows' and its cognates is subject to no genuine pragmatics-sensitive variability of truth-conditions.

If we draw that conclusion, two possibilities remain. One, of course, is invariantism. But invariantism must come to a view about where the invariant threshold for knowledge falls, and, wherever it is placed, it will have to be acknowledged that a significant body of our knowledge-claims, or knowledge-disclaimers, are false, and an explanation will therefore be owing of why so much of our linguistic practice with 'knows' and its cognates falls into error. Invariantists have not been slow to respond to this challenge.[25] I here record the opinion, for which I have no space to argue, that to date their efforts have been unpromising.

The other possibility is a view concerning 'knows' and its cognates that stands comparison with what deflationists about truth say about 'true'. For the deflationist about truth, very familiarly, it is a metaphysical mistake to ask after the character of the property that 'true' expresses. The proper use of the word is accountable, rather, not to the nature of an assumed referent in the realm of properties, but to the service of certain practical purposes—notably indirect endorsement and generalization—that it enables us to accomplish. Correspondingly, a deflationism about knowledge will discharge the idea that there is any determinate epistemic relation or—in deference to contextualism—family of relations that the proper use of 'knows' serves to record and whose character determines the truth-conditions of knowledge-ascriptions. Rather the use of the word needs to be understood by reference to the practical purposes—notably, for example, as DeRose observed, the accreditation of potential informants and the appraisal of agents' rational performance—that it enables us to accomplish. The variability phenomena surface as one or another of these purposes comes to the fore in a particular pragmatic context. But is a metaphysical mistake to project these phenomena onto the putative nature of an assumed referent, or referents, as IRI and contextualism attempt to do, and seek to explain them thereby.

Relativism doesn't make *that* mistake. Someone who holds that "*X* knows that *P*" is assessment-sensitive has already discharged the realism about the knowledge relation that deflationism would counsel us against. But if the suggestion of the preceding section about the asymmetries between our apparent retractions of knowledge-ascriptions and apparent retractions of knowledge-denials are correct, then the concept of knowledge we actually have betrays an (inflationary) invariantist tendency which relativism simply misdescribes. Of course it is open to a relativist to acknowledge this, and to present relativism as reformist. That proposal, however, stands in need of an argument that any purpose would be served by reform. The essence of the case for deflationism about 'knows' is twofold:

---

[25] See, e.g., Williamson (2005). See Ichikawa (2017, chs. 7, 16, and 17).

negatively, that the combination of our tendency to allow the standards for its application to inflate indefinitely while unwilling to accept, with the sceptic, that it never applies, betrays a concept with certain inbuilt tensions and no determinate reference; positively, that the word nevertheless supplies the valuable resources that the variability phenomena reflect. The first part of that might suggest the desirability of reform, but that is compensated for by the second.

Such a general conception of knowledge—or better, of the function of 'knows'—is nothing new,[26] although the present suggestion, that its correctness is the principal lesson which the variability phenomena have to teach us, may be so. If it is correct, the idea that knowledge should come first in analytical epistemology could not be further from the truth. Knowledge—the presumed substantive referent of 'knows'—comes nowhere. But I must defer the further exploration of this form of deflationism to another time.[27]

References

Austin, John Langshaw (1946), "Other Minds," *Proceedings of the Aristotelian Society*, Supplementary Volume 20, 148–87.

Baker, Carl (2012), "Indexical Contextualism and the Challenges from Disagreement," *Philosophical Studies* 157(1), 107–23.

Cappelen, Herman (2008), "Content Relativism and Semantic Blindness," in M. García-Carpintero and M. Kölbel (eds.), *Relative Truth*, Oxford: Oxford University Press, 265–86.

Cappelen, Herman and John Hawthorne (2009), *Relativism and Monadic Truth*, Oxford: Oxford University Press.

Cohen, Stewart (1986), "Knowledge and Context," *The Journal of Philosophy* 83, 574–83.

Cohen, Stewart (2001), "Contextualism Defended: Comments on Richard Feldman's 'Skeptical Problems, Contextualist Solutions'," *Philosophical Studies* 103, 87–98.

DeRose, K. (1992), "Contextualism and Knowledge Attributions," *Philosophy and Phenomenological Research* 52, 913–29.

---

[26] The germ is famously present in Austin (1946, pp. 97–103) where a view is outlined on which utterances of the form "I know that such and such" serve a *performative* rather than a descriptive function, and the function of "I know" is in effect to offer a *promise* of truth, on the basis of which others are entitled to act, form beliefs, or claim to know, in turn. Austin's ideas receive a thoroughgoing, sympathetic development in Lawlor (2013), though I do not know how far she would welcome the deflationism prefigured here.

[27] I am grateful to Jonathan Jenkins Ichikawa for giving me the opportunity to write up and publish this material, the principal ideas in which were generated in graduate classes at New York University in 2005 and further refined at seminars at the Arché research centre at St. Andrews that took place as part of the AHRC-funded *Contextualism and Relativism* project (2006–9). Thanks to those involved on those occasions and to Filippo Ferrari, Patrick Greenough, Jonathan Jenkins Ichikawa, Carrie Ichikawa Jenkins, and Giacomo Melis for more recent helpful discussion.

DeRose, K. (2009), *The Case for Contextualism: Knowledge, Skepticism, and Context*, Vol. 1, Oxford: Clarendon Press.

Dretske, Fred (2005), "The Case Against Closure," in M. Steup and E. Sosa (eds.), *Contemporary Debates in Epistemology*, Malden, MA: Wiley-Blackwell, 27–40.

Fantl, Jeremy and McGrath, Matthew (2007), "Knowledge and the Purely Epistemic: In Favor of Pragmatic Encroachment," *Philosophy and Phenomenological Research* 75(3), 558–89.

Hawthorne, John (2004), *Knowledge and Lotteries*, Oxford: Oxford University Press.

Hawthorne, John (2005), "The Case for Closure," in M. Steup and E. Sosa (eds.), *Contemporary Debates in Epistemology*, Malden, MA: Wiley-Blackwell.

Hume, David (1738), *A Treatise of Human Nature*, ed. L. Selby Bigge (1888), Oxford: Clarendon Press.

Lawlor, Krista (2013), *Assurance: An Austinian View of Knowledge and Knowledge Claims*, Oxford: Oxford University Press.

MacFarlane, John (2005), "The Assessment-Sensitivity of Knowledge Attributions," in Tamar Szabó Gendler and John Hawthorne (eds.), *Oxford Studies in Epistemology*, Vol. 1, Oxford: Oxford University Press, 197–233.

MacFarlane, John (2014), *Assessment Sensitivity: Relative Truth and its Applications*, Oxford: Oxford University Press.

Montminy, Martin (2009), "Contextualism, Relativism and Ordinary Speakers' Judgments," *Philosophical Studies* 143(3), 341–56.

Schaffer, Jonathan and Zoltan Szabo (2013), "Epistemic Comparativism: A Contextualist Semantics for Knowledge Ascriptions," *Philosophical Studies* 168 (2), 491–543.

Stanley, Jason (2005), *Knowledge and Practical Interests*, Oxford: Oxford University Press.

Weatherson, Brian (2009), "Conditionals and Indexical Relativism," *Synthese* 166, 333–57.

Williamson, Timothy (2005), "Contextualism, Subject-Sensitive Invariantism and Knowledge of Knowledge," *The Philosophical Quarterly* 55, 213–35.

10

Alethic Pluralism, Deflationism, and Faultless Disagreement

1. Anti-Realism and Relativism, Old and New

The issues raised by the 'New Age' Relativistic tendency are in many ways orthogonal to those concerning relativism as a broadly anti-objectivist metaphysical stance. New Age Relativism is, as we have several times observed in these chapters, a *descriptive* thesis: a thesis that our actual discourse, in certain regions of thought, displays patterns of which the best—empirically most adequate—semantic theory will make central use of a notion of relative truth. It would be possible to accept that view about a particular discourse and at the same time maintain a revisionary stance towards its relativism-suggestive aspects, on the grounds that the actual subject matter concerned was fully objective, or in other ways unsuited for articulation in terms of statements apt only for relative truth. Conversely, a traditional relativist about, say, ethics—like Harman—could perfectly properly be quite undismayed by the consideration, if true, that our actual moral discourse does not assume the patterns that would invite theoretical description by the relativistic styles of semantic theory that MacFarlane and others have developed. Traditional philosophical relativism is a *normative* thesis: a thesis about the *proper* way to think about a certain subject matter and its claims to objectivity. New Age Relativism is non-normative, and those advocating it for certain specific regions of discourse have mostly been unconcerned with issues concerning realism and objectivity.

2. Faultless Disagreement and the Simple Deduction

Still, notwithstanding their empirical semantic motivation, the ideas developed by the New Age Relativists—provided at least that they are coherent; provided that it *makes sense* to think of truth as relative and to admit contents capable only of relative truth—have, at least *prima facie*, a natural site of application within the metaphysical debates. That site is within the space occupied by what are sometimes described as *merely minimally truth-apt* discourses—discourses that fail to

Essays on Relativism: 2001–2021. Crispin Wright, Oxford University Press. © Crispin Wright 2023.
DOI: 10.1093/oso/9780192845993.003.0011

qualify for what Wright (1992) characterized as *cognitive command*[1] and (as I conjectured) thereby fail to meet any other realism-suggestive constraint. Just how wide that space is, of course, is controversial but among its less controversial members would be, precisely, discourse about the comic, about the obscene and revolting, and about the tasty. It is characteristic of such discourses that they may give rise to *disputes of inclination:*[2] disagreements where one thinker apparently takes the view that *P* and another that not *P*, and where there is little plausibility in the idea that further information, or sophistication of a relevant sensibility, could justifiably lead to an assessment of one view or the other as superior. Some—of course, not all—disagreements about the comic, or the tasty, seem to be like this. In such cases, folk philosophy—this, to stress, is not a linguistic datum, or an 'intuition', but a piece of proto-philosophical theory— says that *both opinions can be in good standing*, and that it can be perfectly rational for the protagonists to hang on to them, undismayed by the apparently equally good standing of the dissenting opinion of the other. More specifically, the folk-philosophical view is that such a case can manifest *faultless disagreement:*[3] there can (i) be a genuine contradiction between the opinions concerned; (ii) neither need be in error; and (iii) neither protagonist should feel that the credibility of his own opinion is weakened by the situation.[4] The question on which the idea of some form of relativization of truth might seem to hold some prospect of assistance is whether, and if so how, this *prima facie* adventurous piece of folk philosophizing might be developed and stabilized.

The problems about stabilizing the folk-philosophical idea are obvious enough. Suppose you and I, dining out in a North African restaurant, find ourselves in a

---

[1] "A discourse exhibits Cognitive Command if and only if it is *a priori* that differences of opinion arising within it can be satisfactorily explained only in terms of 'divergent input', that is, the disputants' working on the basis of different information (and hence guilty of ignorance or error, depending on the status of that information), or 'unsuitable conditions' (resulting in inattention or distraction and so in inferential error, or oversight of data, etc.), or 'malfunction' (e.g. prejudicial assessment of data, upwards or downwards, or dogma, or failings in other categories already listed)" (Wright 1992, pp. 92–3).

[2] The term is from Wright (2006). (This volume, ch. 2).

[3] So far as I have been able to tell, this caption, now standard in the debates, first occurs in print in Kölbel (2004), where he writes as follows:

> A faultless disagreement is a situation where there is a thinker *A*, a thinker *B*, and a proposition (content of judgement) *p*, such that:
> (a) *A* believes (judges) that *p* and *B* believes (judges) that not-*p*
> (b) Neither *A* nor *B* has made a mistake (is at fault).
> I believe that most people have a healthy pre-theoretical intuition that there can be and are faultless disagreements in this sense. (pp. 53–4)

[4] Wright (2006) this volume, ch. 2 called these features *Contradiction, Faultlessness,* and *Sustainability* respectively. We will retain those labels here. In the more recent terminology of the peer disagreement literature, sustainability corresponds to the local justifiability of *steadfastness.*

fairly vivid dispute of inclination about the merits of a dish of stewed camel fries[5] and woodland toadstools in béchamel sauce. If your opinion, that what we have been served is delicious, and mine, that it is disgusting, are genuinely incompatible, then logic decrees that they are not both true—and *classical* logic decrees that one at least is false. Either way, the opinions involved cannot both be in good standing unless 'good standing' is consistent with untruth. Moreover it is no part of ordinary thought *in general* to regard an opinion as in good standing if there is no better reason to uphold it than to uphold a contrary. And we can readily suppose in such a case that neither you nor I can adduce any consideration to break the tie; there may be vanishingly little room for discussion in such a case, and the mere fact that an opinion is mine (or yours) is not, for me (or you), or anyone else, a *reason* to regard it as true.

So there are two problems. One is to make sense of the idea that, in this particular kind of case, logically conflicting opinions can each remain in good standing and tenable, once the grounds for them are fully explicit and it is found that neither has a case to be superior. That's a problem for Sustainability. But there is the more glaring underlying problem that Faultlessness and Contradiction just seem to be incoherent in combination—that elementary logic seems to enforce the idea that one of us has to be mistaken.

It will be useful to articulate the tension in the following natural deduction:[6]

1	(1) You accept P	—	Assumption
2	(2) I accept Not-P	—	Assumption
3	(3) Our disagreement involves no mistake	—	Assumption
4	(4) P	—	Assumption
2, 4	(5) I am guilty of a mistake	—	2, 4
2, 3	(6) Not-P	—	4, 5, 3 Reductio
1, 2, 3	(7) You are guilty of a mistake	—	1, 6
1,2,	(8) Not-(3)	—	3, 3, 7 Reductio

Laying the objection out in this way immediately makes it clear how some form of alethic relativism might be expected to help. It might be expected to help because it might be supposed that it will allow us to demur at the transitions from (4) to (5) and from (6) to (7). For the relativist, presumably, a mistaken opinion will be one that is false relative to some relevant set of standards. By whose standards is P being supposed to hold at line (4)? If yours, the transition to (5) is invalid. If mine, that transition is good, and the deduction up to and including line (6) is sound, provided (6) is affirmed relative to my standards. But then the transition to (7) is invalid.

---

[5] That is, camel testicles.
[6] Dubbed the Simple Deduction by Wright (2001). Compare Kölbel (2004 at p. 56). This reasoning was originally offered by Shapiro and Taschek (1996) as a problem for the coherence of the idea of failure of Cognitive Command.

3. The Intuitionistic Proposal and the Parity Constraint

Before turning to whether relativism really does help, let's ask: what else might help? Well, not an invocation of *dialetheism*: that is, the idea that the disputed opinion might be both true *and* false. That would certainly allow us to say that your opinion and mine are on a par. But what about good standing? Even among those hospitable to the possibility of "gluts" of truth-values, there is little support for the idea that glutty statements—statements simultaneously both true and false—can be *acceptable*. The problem, rather, is to explain the sense—contrasting with denial—in which such a statement should be *rejected*. There seems no prospect that a dialetheic account can save Sustainability.

In a variety of places in earlier work,[7] however, I have canvassed the suggestion that a broadly *intuitionist* framework can conserve what might be regarded as the most important element in the folk-philosophical view, namely that in such a dispute there need be no presumption that either disputant *in particular* need be at fault, either by the manner in which they arrive at their view or by its misrepresentation of the facts. Such an intuitionistic account acknowledges that your and my respective views about the dish of stewed camel fries cannot both be true: that much is just a consequence of the law of non-contradiction. But when the principle of bivalence, and associatedly the law of excluded middle, fail for broadly intuitionistic reasons, that consideration does not force us to say that one in particular of the disputants has to be incorrect.

What this comes to is, in effect, the suggestion that the Simple Deduction is perfectly acceptable, but that we misunderstand its conclusion. It seems unacceptable only because, with our usual 'knee-jerk' classical instincts, we implicitly pass from its actual conclusion, which is the negation of a conjunction of negated propositions, to the affirmation of the disjunction of those propositions. The appearance of aporia tacitly involves this extra step. Let A = I am mistaken, and B = you are mistaken. Then the extra step is an application of the De Morgan inference:

$$\frac{\text{Not } (\text{Not-}A \,\&\, \text{Not-}B)}{A \vee B}$$

whose conclusion will indeed commit us to the, as it were, distributive thought that either you are wrong about the dish or I am, and its unwelcome implication that the metaphysics of taste sustains a 'fact of the matter'. However, save for instances of A and of B for which bivalence is acceptable, the extra step is intuitionistically invalid. So if we can motivate intuitionistic distinctions for a

---

[7] Wright (2001, 2002, and 2006).

logic appropriate to judgements of taste, we will have the resources to accept that you and I disagree about the Tunisian dish—that our opinions about it are genuinely contradictory—without being forced to think that one of us in particular has been mistaken.

That is to satisfy Contradiction and (an interpretation of) Faultlessness. The intuitionistic proposal also promises an attractive treatment of Sustainability. When cognitive command[8] is missing for a certain range of statements, so is any *a priori* guarantee that a dispute about one of them involves anything worth regarding as a cognitive shortcoming. And once there is no presumption that one or the other disputant in particular has to be guilty of such a shortcoming—no presumption that distributively, as it were, either you are at fault or I am—then there is no rational pressure on us individually to think, "... and *the guilty party* could as well be me," so no pressure to qualify or abandon our respective views. So there is a *prima facie* case that my earlier intuitionistic proposal, if it can be otherwise well motivated, can capture (something of) each of the three noted desiderata gestured at by the folk idea of faultless disagreement: the opinions in the dispute can be allowed to be genuinely contradictory, yet there is no justified presumption that either in particular has to involve any fault, and no extant reason for either protagonist not to persist, even in the face of an opposing, no less well-supported view.[9]

However there is a serious objection to the proposal. If my opinion is genuinely incompatible with yours, am *I* at least not committed to regarding you as mistaken (and you, me)? Maybe there is no pressure, flowing from a misguided acceptance *a priori* of the principle of bivalence for the kind of statement concerned, to suppose that one of us in particular *has* to be mistaken. But still, do we not both, just in taking a view, commit ourselves to regarding the other as *de facto* mistaken? In short, it seems that *the disputants themselves* in a disagreement of this kind cannot regard the dispute as faultless, even if there is no general philosophical pressure, bearing upon a neutral witness, to suppose that there has to be fault in such a dispute. So something important in the folk-philosophical idea may seem to have been lost. The scope for considered tolerance—part, plausibly, of what was meant to be implicated by "faultlessness" and conveyed in the acknowledgement we are wont to make in such cases that *your opinion is just as good as mine*—has not yet been made available to those actually involved in the disagreement.

Call this fourth requirement *Parity*. In effect, it is the requirement that faultlessness be appreciable, and endorseable, from the point of view not just of neutrals but also of the committed parties in a dispute of inclination. The folk-philosophical

---

[8] Cf. n. 4 above.
[9] My own hitherto most complete development of this proposal, and some responses to objections, are offered in Wright (2006 This volume, ch. 2 at pp. 42–52).

thought, when pressed, is, I expect the reader to agree on reflection, that disputes of inclination should manifest each of Contradiction, Faultlessness, Sustainability, *and* Parity. The intuitionistic proposal, it seems, cannot accommodate Parity.

4. Two Recent Relativisms

I myself later seemed to realize this and moved to propose a form of relativism.[10] But can relativism really do better?

Well, what should we take relativism to be? At least two importantly different relativistic proposals have been distinguished in the recent discussions. MacFarlane's own preference, *assessment-sensitivity*, is the proposal that, for statements in the discourse in question, truth-value is a function of parameters fixed by the context of an *assessor*. Applied to discourse of taste, this has the effect that my statement (or opinion), that camel fries and woodland toadstools in béchamel sauce are disgusting, may be correctly assessed as false by you, but true by me, as a function of variation in the relevant parameter (standards of taste[11]) in our respective contexts of assessment. According to assessment-sensitivity, then, a given historical token of an assessment-sensitive statement, or opinion, has no settled once-and-for-all truth-value—it takes a truth-value whenever it is assessed, and what truth-value it takes depends on the value of relevant parameters determined by the operative context of assessment, which may vary.

The second relativistic proposal is what MacFarlane has chosen to call (rather unhappily, in my view) *non-indexical contextualism*.[12] MacFarlane's own ter-minological preferences notwithstanding, this is properly a version of relativism, rather than contextualism as normally understood, since it is integral to it that the content that you endorse when you affirm that camel fries and woodland toad-stools in béchamel sauce are delicious is indeed the very content that I implicitly deny when I affirm that camel fries and woodland toadstools in béchamel sauce are disgusting. And the truth-value of the content so affirmed or denied, respect-ively, is indeed, as before, a function of variation in the value of the relevant parameter (standards of taste). What distinguishes the view from assessment-sensitivity is that the truth-value of your affirmation is now to be determined relative to *your* standards of taste, and the truth-value of my denial is to be assessed relative to mine. So we can both be right! And now a given historical token statement, or opinion, *does* have a settled once-and-for-all truth-value, as

---

[10] The intuitionistic proposal was first made in Wright (2001 This volume, ch. 1) as part of a simultaneous treatment of vagueness. In (Wright 2006) go over some of the same ground in more detail, but eventually raises the objection from Parity (not there so termed, however) before proposing a relativistic alternative.

[11] I do not think it is at all clear in what sense basic taste is subject to *standards*, but I leave the issue aside for present purposes.

[12] The damage is probably done, but if it is not too late, let me put in a plea for "author-sensitivity."

fixed by the values taken by the relevant parameters in the context of its actual authorship, though there may be variation in truth-value among other tokens, authored in other contexts, of the same propositional content.

Well, it is pretty immediate that assessment-sensitivity is useless for the purpose of securing Parity. By its rules, I am constrained to assess your opinion in the light of my standards, rather than yours. So of course I will assess it as false. Since I assess my own as true, I can then, surely, hardly regard your opinion as just as good as mine, and Parity is surrendered from my point of view, the point of view of a participant in the dispute.[13] It is also lost from the point of view of any third party who happens to have their own standards of taste. If their standards determine a view, they will be bound to disagree with at least one of us. If their standards mandate neutrality on the matter of dispute, they will regard us both as overstepping the mark. And if they have no relevant standards by which to form a view, they will be in no position to judge ours as on a par.

Relatedly, assessment-sensitivity gives us no leverage with the Simple Deduction, since the supposition of *P* at line (4), and the subsequent moves, will all take place under the aegis of the relevant standards of the agent of (the particular instance of) the argument schema. So interpreted, the conclusion, that the disagreement cannot be mistake-free, is validly drawn.

These limitations of assessment-sensitivity when it comes to sustaining Faultlessness and Parity should come as no surprise. For they are a consequence of the very feature that MacFarlane designed into his relativism in order to enable it to accommodate the, as it seemed to him, compelling data about retractions,

---

[13] There has not always been clarity about this point but Mark Richard, for one, is commendably clear about it. He writes,

> Suppose I think that Beaufort is a better cheese than Tome, and you think the reverse. Suppose (for *reductio*) that each of our thoughts is valid—mine is true from my perspective, yours is from yours. Then not only can I (validly) say that Beaufort is better than Tome, I can (validly) say that it's true that Beaufort is better than Tome. And of course if you think Tome is better than Beaufort and not vice versa I can also (validly) say that you think that it's not the case that Beaufort is better than Tome. So I can (validly) say that it's true that Beaufort is better than Tome though you think Beaufort isn't better than Tome. From which it surely follows that you're mistaken—after all, if you have a false belief, you are mistaken about something. This line of reasoning is sound no matter what the object of dispute.
> (Richard 2008 at p. 132)

Another who is clear-headed on the matter is Paul Boghossian who, citing the above passage from Richard with approval, glosses the central thought as:

> just because p is at best relatively true, and just because it is true from my perspective and false from yours, it is not *therefore* right to say that our disagreement is faultless. For even if all of this is true, it will still be true that if I validly (that is, truly, relative to my perspective) judge that *p*, then it will also be valid for me to judge that 'It is true that p' and also 'It is false that Not p.' And if I can validly judge that 'It is false that p' then I must regard anyone who believes that p to have made a mistake. (Boghossian 2011 at p. 62)

primarily for the cases of knowledge-ascriptions and epistemic modals, that argue against contextualism. The (alleged) phenomenon of the retraction of hitherto correctly asserted epistemic modal claims purely on the ground of increased information, precisely amounts to a disavowal of Parity in a *prima facie* disagreement with one's former self ("I was wrong") about the claim in question.

At first blush, however—as noted—non-indexical contextualism (author-sensitivity) does better. Indeed it may seem to turn the trick. For now your opinion and mine are both properly assessed relative to the standards of their authors. So my opinion may be assessed as true—and your contrary opinion can *also* be assessed as true, assuming that they are indeed sanctioned by the respectively different standards involved. This upshot seems to chime exactly with the promise of relativism as intuitively intended: my opinion is 'true for me' and yours is 'true for you'. And the Simple Deduction can be faulted on exactly the grounds prefigured earlier: the supposition of *P* at line (4) has to be taken as the supposition of its truth in the context of an author of that thought; but once that is fixed, there is no valid inference, under the aegis of non-indexical contextualism, that someone else who holds not-*P* does so mistakenly.

The trouble, though, is that this very result is bought at the cost of interference with aspects of the interaction between contexts of propositional attitude and ascriptions of truth-value which seem so integral to a proper understanding of both that their compromise wears a face of incoherence. In considering whether *your opinion* that the serving of camel fries and woodland toadstools in béchamel sauce is delicious is true, I must answer affirmatively, since you are the author of that opinion, so the relevant standards of assessment to use are yours, and you are right (or so we are supposing) by those standards. But in considering whether to agree with you—whether *the proposition* is true that the dish of camel fries and woodland toadstools in béchamel sauce is delicious—I must answer negatively, since now the question is of my authorship and the appropriate standards of assessment are mine. So I wind up affirming that you believe something truly although what you believe isn't true. That sounds like pretty excellent nonsense. It is certainly no intended aspect of the folk-philosophical thought we are trying to articulate and stabilize. But something of that form would be affirmable by each participant in a dispute of inclination if non-indexical contextualism were correct.

5. Multi-Mundialism (I) and Genuine Disagreement

There is a well-known joke that the celebrated Cambridge mathematician, G. H. Hardy, once found something obvious after several minutes' hard thinking about it. It may be that it is beginning to seem obvious to the reader in that kind of way that there is no squaring this particular circle: that once Contradiction is accepted, Parity is simply a desideratum too many. No doubt it is that thought that has prompted many philosophers to dispute the reality of the disagreement in 'disputes of inclination' by proposing various kinds of contextualist accounts of the content of the targeted claims that allow them to be compatible with each other. If you and I are not really disagreeing, then of course we are not committed, by our respective opinions, to regarding the other's opinion as inferior, and there need be no difficulty with any of Faultlessness, Sustainability, and Parity. But this move gives up on Contradiction; we are no more in contradiction about our Tunisian supper, on this interpretation of the situation, than we would be if, looking out of the train window, I were to correctly observe, "Look! There is a Bald eagle perched on that post," and you, looking out one minute later and seeing none, were to counter, "There is not even a post to be seen!" That we contradict each other in disputes of inclination is as intuitively robust as any other datum of the problem.[14] Is there any other Contradiction-preserving option?

A positive answer is returned in recent work of Carol Rovane.[15] Relativism has little attraction for her, but she is interested in the question of what is the most robust and potentially useful form of the view. Rovane argues that there is another alethic-relativistic option, *multi-mundialism*, which in effect—though she does not express herself in exactly these terms—promises to save Contradiction along with the other three constraints.

It is more than slightly deflating, however, when one learns that this salvage is to be bought at the cost of surrender of the connection, so far taken for granted, between Contradiction and disagreement! Rovane is explicit that, in her view, there is no saving faultless *disagreement*. Granting that we are affirming contradictory opinions in our dispute about camel fries, it does not follow—she in effect suggests—that we contradict *each other*. Let it be that our opinions are mutually contradictory in the sense that neither of us could consistently add an endorsement of the other to an endorsement of our own. Still there can be daylight between that admission and the claim that we disagree: that is, the claim that we are committed to regarding each other's opinions as false, and hence rejecting Parity. Parity can be saved if, although I could not add an endorsement of your opinion to an endorsement of my own and remain consistent, still I am not, in endorsing my opinion, repudiating your endorsement of yours. What is needed is that, where our standards vary, our taking the views that we respectively do is simply to *have no bearing on* the propriety of the other's view.

How might this work? According to multi-mundialism—as according to anything worth calling relativism—the very content, *stewed camel fries and woodland toadstools in béchamel sauce is delicious*, that you affirm does indeed recur,

---

[14] Of course it may be queried. The datum, it may be suggested, is merely that we *presume* a contradiction, and there are contextualism-friendly ways of making that a defeasible presumption. See, e.g., López De Sa (2008). I myself do not believe that Contextualism can offer a satisfactory alternative development of the folk view but it would take me too far afield to review the issues here.

[15] Rovane (2011, 2012, and 2013).

contradicted, in my very different opinion. Our dispute does not have us talking past each other in any sense that would be gratifying to contextualism. What is true, though, is that we are talking about *different worlds*. The multi-mundialist takes seriously—and must in due course explain—the idea that relativistic parameters, for example, standards of taste, literally contribute to the *constitution of a world*: a domain of facts, to which statements informed by those standards are then answerable, but which is merely one among a range of *alternative worlds*, constituted by differing standards, to which judgements informed by *those* standards will answer in their turn. So we are talking past each other in a different sense, viz. that our claims, though semantically contradictory, are answerable to different worlds. That is why your opinion can be just as good as mine.

Rovane's proposal highlights something interesting that has, in effect, been noted by other recent commentators,[16] viz. that, contrary to its standard presentations, alethic relativism need actually involve no adjustment in traditional conception of the *degree* of the truth-predicate—there need be no raising of the 'adicity' of truth. Someone who is attracted to the idea of truth as consisting everywhere in correspondence, for instance, can still be a relativist about certain kinds of truth if they are prepared to make the metaphysical multi-mundialist move of abandoning the conception of a single Tractarian all-encompassing totality of facts in favour of a many-worlds view of the relevant subject matter.

Now, there is a wave of obvious concerns about the interpretation, and legitimacy, of this metaphysical move. How can there not be a single totality of all the facts that there are—if the various denizens of the many worlds are indeed all *facts*? How are they, as it were, to be segregated, except notionally, by some form of subdivision of a more comprehensive world? If that is how it goes, will not that more comprehensive world then lurk in the background and offer absolute truth-makers after all? But if, more exotically, we try to think of our respective worlds of taste, e.g., as more than notional segregations of the facts—as genuinely alternative complete determinations of reality—what can that mean and how can we accomplish it?

To help fix the issues, consider a somewhat Pickwickian application of relativism. In my home in Scotland on the 20th of January 2015, I speak to Rovane in New York on the phone and tell her it is snowing hard with visibility down to less than 50 yards. She replies that it is sunny, very cold, and clear. Suppose we set aside any semantics of these remarks that interprets them as containing some form of inexplicit indexicality of place, and take it instead, relativistically, that the content of Rovane's statement is the very same content that I would affirm if I were to use her words in my location, and that it is a complete, truth-evaluable content—something that can contribute, for instance, to a complete specification

---

[16] Thus Fine (2005) and Beall (2006).

of the content of a wish or a belief. And let us assume the same, *mutatis mutandis*, for my statement. So then we are affirming contradictory contents. But, the relativist proposal is going to be, these are contents that take a truth-value only relative to a parameter of place.[17]

A version of multi-mundialism is one option for the interpretation of this weather report relativism. The idea of the many worlds required by the view may here be interpreted perfectly straightforwardly. Rovane's and my respective remarks are answerable to different *locations*. Our remarks are mutually incompatible insofar as they cannot both be true when directed at any single location. But that element of contradiction is quite consistent with there being no good sense in which we disagree. And surely in this case, we do not disagree. The relativist—multi-mundialist—interpretation of the semantics has no tendency to introduce a genuine disagreement here that a contextualist semantics would not recognize.

Maybe it is obvious to the reader why there is no disagreement in the case. But let me spell it out a little, since we are going to ask in a minute what reason there may be *not* to assimilate the weather report case to the Tunisian restaurant case. A genuine disagreement should involve the existence of rational pressure, perhaps likely to be stubbornly resisted, to *change one's mind* if one comes to see merit in the opposing view. But no pressure is exerted on my weather report by my coming to know that Rovane is speaking truly. Indeed, I can add an *informational equivalent* of what she is saying to my present state of information without any tension at all: I can merely add it to my stock of beliefs as a belief about the weather in New York. And if there were any risk of confusion, I could ask Rovane to be specific about what location she intends her claim to be answerable to. The explicitly relational claim, "It is sunny, very cold, and clear in New York," thus stands to her original claim as a *clarification*. And it is because the clarification is consistent with my own weather report, and something that I can cheerfully take on board alongside it, that there is no genuine disagreement, not withstanding the fact that, on the multi-mundialist semantics, I cannot add the proposition that Rovane expressed to my belief set without inconsistency. So, on that view we do indeed have Contradiction without disagreement.

This version of the multi-mundialist proposal is coherent enough—provided of course we grant the coherence of its play with trans-locally invariant weather report contents. (And, it hardly needs emphasis, to vouchsafe such semantic invariance is a cardinal point of any interesting alethic relativism.) But the surrender of disagreement really is a major drawback if the ambition is to do justice to the intuitive character of disputes of inclination. To be sure, Rovane announces in advance that we are going to have to give up on the idea that

---

[17] The proposal is meant to bear analogy to the temporalist view of tensed propositions.

relativism can save genuine disagreement in such cases. And about that, at any rate if the relativism involved is to be multi-mundialism on the weather report model, she is surely right. But the tendency of that point should not be to raise a doubt about whether genuine disagreement can be involved in disputes of inclination, as folk philosophically conceived. If, sitting in the Tunisian restaurant, plates of the steaming casserole before us, we take ourselves to be discussing, and disputing, a mutually understood topic, the merit of choosing stewed camel fries and woodland toadstools, we are as confused—on this account of the matter—as Rovane and I would have been if our remarks had been part of an argument on the telephone about the weather on the day in question. But we do not consider—and surely *rightly* do not consider—our restaurant conversation to involve anything like that kind of confusion. I may indeed say, to cut the discussion short, "Well, it's a disgusting dish by my taste." But if I do say that, I will not be *clarifying* my original claim—indeed we can assume that you are in no doubt that I find the dish revolting—but *retreating from* it. The remark about my standards of taste is a *conversational mitigation* of my original unqualified claim, not an expansion of it.

The failure of this first, simple multi-mundialist account of disputes of inclination teaches us that we need to raise the stakes again. The folk-philosophical thought is yet more demanding than we allowed: it demands each of Contradiction, Faultlessness, Sustainability, Parity, and *Genuine Disagreement*.[18] The Contradiction constraint requires that neither of the disputants can consistently add the proposition affirmed by their antagonist to their own stock of acceptances. But in order to do justice to the folk-philosophical thought about disputes of inclination, we need to impose the further condition that neither can the disputants add anything that would reasonably pass as an informational equivalent, or explanation, of what their antagonist accepts without inconsistency. Rovane's and my contradictory weather reports do not meet this condition. But your and my *contretemps* about the Tunisian dish does, at least as folk-philosophically conceived.

6. Multi-Mundialism (II)—Lewisian Worlds of Taste

In the weather report model, the *mundi*—the worlds—are *partial*: they co-exist alongside each other as part of a greater, single world, and there really is no conceptual difficulty involved in, as it were, amalgamating the bodies of meteorological information respectively associated with them. True, we cannot accomplish that amalgamated body of information when the mode of expression is restricted to

---

[18] I have simply added Genuine Disagreement to the list, rather than also delete Contradiction, because I do not wish to consider in this paper the question whether non-contradictory acceptances might nevertheless compose a genuine disagreement—as they might in a case where addition of a clarification or elaboration of the information involved in an acceptance on one side could introduce inconsistency into the other.

the simple (putatively) relativistic propositions instanced above. But, as we stressed, when I accept that it is clear, very cold, and sunny *in New York*, I am *agreeing* with what Rovane says when she simply affirms it is clear, very cold, and sunny. By contrast, I do not, in granting that camel fries and woodland toadstools in béchamel sauce is delicious by your standards effectively agree with what you are saying when you affirm the statement, unqualified, that the dish is delicious.

It is the *locality* of the *mundi*, their proper parthood in a larger reality, that underwrites the compatibilities that frustrate genuine disagreement. This is the point on which the weather report multi-mundialist model breaks down most fundamentally. If there are to be permissible alternative sets of standards of taste, determining different worlds of taste, they will each have respectively to determine potentially *all* the facts about what is tasty or not, and in that sense compete over the determination of those facts. Nothing analogous to that is involved in the restriction of claims of a certain kind to one location or another. New York City and Fife, Scotland are different actual locations, and truths about the weather conditions respectively obtaining at them hold of a single actual world. The same point, granted, holds for truths about, respectively, what is sanctioned by your standards of taste and what is sanctioned by mine, even if there is contradiction between the propositions that our standards of taste respectively sanction. That your standards validate the proposition that camel fries and woodland toadstools in béchamel sauce are delicious and that mine validate it's contradictory are both truths about the actual world. But the, so to say, corresponding relativistic truths, that camel fries and woodland toadstools in béchamel sauce is a delicious dish, and that it is not, will have to be, for an improved multi-mundialism, truths about *different* worlds—albeit worlds that must in some sense be conceived of as simultaneously competitive and potentially complete.

The reader may feel we are teetering on the verge of nonsense here, but I think a degree of sense can be made of the needed idea. A partial precedent for what the multi-mundialist seems to need is provided by the way that a modal realist of the stripe of David Lewis thinks of possible worlds. For such a modal realist, there is a sense—a transcendental sense—in which all possible worlds are on a par: each is actual *for its denizens*, and the truths in each are as robust as the truths in any other. For *us*, though, situated in *the* actual world, as we like to think, real truth is truth at our world, the only truth-making world that there is, and truths at other worlds are merely *possibilities*. On this conception, the opinion, of my Lewisian counterpart in a world in which there are talking donkeys, *that there are talking donkeys* is as robust a truth as my own opinion that there are none. Faultlessness, Sustainability, and Parity hold from the transcendental perspective. But from the perspective of a station at a particular world, only that world is actual and the truths that distinguish other worlds from it are merely possible, actually false propositions. Contradiction, and Genuine Disagreement, belong with a committed, intra-world perspective.

You may feel that this is at best an explanation of the obscure *per obscurius*. Moreover the analogy limps in the crucial respect that, on the Lewisian model of modal truth, there is, for compelling theoretical reasons, no possibility of *trans-world dialogue*, let alone apparent dispute, between the denizens of different worlds. Still, there is the possibility of contradictory opinions, and maybe that's enough to give the analogy a degree of grip. It remains, however, that there is no obvious prospect of saving all the five facets of the folk-philosophical notion of faultless disagreement at one pass, as it were. If we are to adapt the analogy to the consolidation of that idea, we will have to say that the *collective* appeal of the five facets results from an aspect switch—a switching between committed and transcendental perspectives. From my—committed—perspective as we sit, looking at the steaming casserole in front of us, there is only the world of taste that I inhabit: and, regarding our conversation from that perspective, the fact is that we disagree, and you are wrong, about stewed camel fries and woodland toadstools in béchamel sauce. But then I, as it were, sit back, and slipping into a transcendental perspective, recognize a plurality of worlds of taste in which none is privileged for a truth-making role, and each makes only for its local truths; and I recognize that, from this perspective, neither of us is at fault, that both our views are, or can be, correct respecting our own worlds of taste, and just as good as each other.

Very well, but there is still no real progress. At best we are being offered an account of our exchange of opinions about the Tunisian dish that involves Genuine Disagreement from one perspective, and Parity from another. This is to short-change the folk-philosophical idea. Parity was supposed to hold from the perspective of the disputants, not a transcendental perspective whose adoption involves disengaging from the dispute. I want to say, *even while recognizing that we are disagreeing*, that your opinion is as good as mine, and not that because our views concern different worlds, we are not really disagreeing at all.

7. A Fifth Type of Relativism

Thus, in the project of making coherent sense of the folk-philosophical view, each of the four relativisms so far distinguished—assessment-sensitivity, non-indexical contextualism (author-relativism), and the two forms of multi-mundialism— variously comes short. And so indeed does the fifth relativistic proposal mooted in the last section of Wright (2006 this volume ch. 2). That was the proposal to construe truth, in discourses apt to give rise to disputes of inclination, as a form of *superassertibility*[19] but then to allow (ordinary) assertibility to fragment into a range of properties determined by the relevant non-cognitive propensities of different participants in the discourse. Thus, very crudely: let amusement be a non-cognitive

[19] First introduced in Wright (1992, see ch. 2 at p. 44 and following).

response, and let claims of the form, 'X is funny', be, absent reason otherwise, default assertible just when one finds oneself amused by X. Since senses of humour may vary, and vary, by hypothesis, without cognitive defect, 'X is funny' may be properly assertible by you but not by me. Assertibility thus becomes a context-sensitive—indexical—property for reasons other than variation in one's information. Superassertibility idealizes away that latter kind of indexicality, by requiring that in order to be superassertible, a statement must remain assertible under arbitrary additions to, and improvements of, one's information. But no matching idealizing effect is thereby exerted on a non-cognitive assertibility base. So superassertibility potentially fragments too.

This fragmentation will allow us to give a quite literal construal of "true for me" and "true for you," and will make straightforward theoretical sense of the notion that your verdict about stewed camel fries and mine, though contradictory, are each true for their respective authors. In that respect it matches the achievement of non-indexical contextualism, but it avoids the latter's crucial drawback of sanctioning solecisms like "X judges truly that p but it my opinion it is not true that P." It avoids this because there is no selection of a superassertibility-predicate for "true" that sustains both conjuncts. Again, however, even this proposal limps when it comes to accounting for Parity and Genuine Disagreement. Suppose I bring an explicit clarity about my superassertibilist-relativist proposal to the dinner table. When you affirm that stewed camel fries and woodland toadstools in béchamel sauce are delicious, you present your opinion as true. How, when I take it that we are disagreeing, do I understand that claim? If I take it that it is answerable to superassertibility on the basis of *your* relevant affective propensities, well, that is certainly an opinion which I can regard as no worse than my own, but why should I feel that that is anything with which I should want to disagree? So understood, you are claiming that *stewed camel fries and woodland toadstools in béchamel sauce is disgusting* has a property which, in denying that claim, I am not denying that it has. But if I take it that your claim is answerable to superassertibility on the basis of *my* relevant affective propensities, then I egregiously misunderstand you, and *erroneously* take us to disagree. So, no progress.

That completes the first part of the brief of the chapter: to argue that no foreseeable—anyway, no foreseen—form of relativism can provide a fully satisfactory explanation of what a relevantly faultless disagreement might consist in, in accordance with our preconceptions about that notion.

8. The Intuitionistic Solution Provisionally Repaired...

How should we react to this situation? It very much depends, I acknowledge, on what, on this question, we believe that philosophy should try to accomplish, and what should constitute satisfaction with its products. If our priority generally is to articulate, in the sharpest possible theoretical form, what we conceive as the *wisdom* incorporated in our ordinary take on the various issues that engage our philosophical interest, then we will probably want to go on trying to understand and stabilize what I have called the folk-philosophical idea, and will merely dismiss the claim of relativism to be of any value in that project. But we may instead be more doubtful now about the claim to intuitive wisdom. If we think it likely that folk-philosophical ideas—slowly and haphazardly evolved under the successive influence of the more or less primitive, often superstitious, variously theological and scientific images that have enjoyed temporary hegemony over the centuries—are as likely to spawn paradox and incoherence as wisdom, then we may be inclined to suspect that the various relativistic offerings fall short of capture of the folk thought only because it is confused, so that the remaining question is only which of the relativisms is the best of an acceptably sub-optimal bunch.

I hope it is not too pig-headed to incline to the former stance. I think we should persevere, and that the correct conclusion from the foregoing is only that the relativistic turn was a *faux pas*. We need a fresh approach.

Let's begin by re-visiting the intuitionistic proposal. The problem which seemed to require that we look past it was Parity: in opining that stewed camel fries and woodland toadstools in béchamel sauce is delicious, you opine that it is false that it is disagreeable, and hence that my opinion is false. So how can you regard that opinion as no worse than your own?

Well, regarding my opinion as false compromises its parity with yours only if 'false' carries its *customary normative punch*.[20] Wright this volume, ch. 2 missed a trick here. A central contention of my (1992) was that—at least over merely minimally truth-apt discourses, where cognitive command fails—truth need carry no payload of accurate substantial representation. When merely minimally truth-apt claims are at stake, to regard a statement as false need not be to attribute any *representational* fault to someone's acceptance of it. So if there need be no *other* kind of fault, the way is open for the idea that, in such a case, to describe an opponent's view as 'false' is, in effect, to go no further than to record one's disagreement with it, with no implication of any further deficiency. There would be an imputation of fault, and hence a compromise of Parity, only when 'true' demands a richer interpretation or when the fact of disagreement itself has to indicate some kind of fault of process. But that, where merely minimally truth-apt discourses are concerned, is just what there need be no reason to suppose.

Nor, on this account, is there any evident difficulty with finding room for genuine Disagreement. The relativistic tendency is to try to accommodate Parity

---

[20] The suggestion that a rescue of the idea of faultless disagreement might be accomplished by disarming the truth-predicate of its usual "normative punch" is also canvassed by Boghossian in §II of his (2011). However it is there developed under the aegis of explicitly relativistic norms of belief and assertion and, as he in effect argues, thereby runs into the same difficulties in conserving the disagreement component that multi-mundialism meets with.

by, in effect, one way or another, compatibilizing the disputants' claims: by construing the kind of truth they enjoy, or the kind of truth-makers that bear on them, as capable of peaceful co-existence, even though the claims themselves are contradictory. It then followed that in taking you to be making a claim that genuinely disagrees with mine, I have to misunderstand the constraints to which, if you are clear-headed, you intend it to answer. The minimalist direction avoids this bind. No relativized notions of truth now feature. When you affirm the truth of your view, you are not, for instance, to be interpreted as committed merely to its satisfaction of a truth-concept that simply has no role in my assessment and whose application I do not dispute. Rather just as, on the surface, it appears, you are committed to an appraisal of stewed camel fries that I do indeed reject. But, again, your commitment to its truth need be no imputation of fault to me. You are indeed committed to the falsity of my opinion. But, since this is merely minimal falsity, and tagging my opinion as 'false' is simply another way of expressing your disagreement with it, with no implication of shortcoming on my part, my view can be none the worse for that.

The suggestion, in summary, is that locally minimal—fully deflated—notions of truth and falsity are available to allow one to describe a contested opinion as *false* without thereby doing more than recording one's disagreement with it, and in particular without imputing any kind of cognitive, or other, shortcoming to its author. "Locally" is of course important. A global deflationist who takes this line will need to explain what makes the difference when, in imputing falsity to a view, one precisely *does* intend to impute fault. That does not mean that global deflationism cannot avail itself of the present suggestion. But it does mean that an account of the distinction between disputes of inclination and disputes of more substantial matters, where shortcoming of some kind is essentially involved, will have to proceed in other terms. That someone thinks something false, merely, will underdetermine the issue. By contrast, within an *alethic pluralist* framework, fully deflationary conceptions of truth and falsity can be reserved for the problematic subject matters with which we are currently concerned, without any commitment to so conceiving of truth across the board.

9. . . . and Then Re-Punctured

I alleged above that I "missed a trick," implying that my own pluralist views about truth provide the resources for a better response to the Parity objection than the move to relativism that I went on to suggest. In mitigation, though, it needs to be said that there is a fairly immediate snag with the foregoing line, at least for the author of *Truth and Objectivity*. It is that invoking the notion of a non-normative truth-predicate seems in blatant conflict with the central argument—the much discussed so-called 'inflationary' argument—of chapter 1 of Wright (1992). There it is argued that deflationism is inherently unstable because even the disquotational scheme, or equivalence schema, implicitly commits us to truth's having some kind of distinctive normative role that contrasts with that of assertibility. That is something that cannot be acknowledged by any deflationary theorist for whom the role of the truth-predicate is purely that of a device of indirect endorsement and generalization.

Either that argument is mistaken, it seems, or the suggested reconciliation of the intuitionistic proposal with Parity cannot get off the ground. Which is it?

Let's look carefully at the inflationary argument. We start with the disquotational scheme:

DS   'P' is true iff P

Substituting 'Not-P' for 'P' in DS provides

'Not-P' is true iff Not-P

And negating each side of DS provides

Not-'P' is true iff Not-P

So by transitivity of the biconditional, we have the so-called negation equivalence:

NE   'Not-P' is true iff Not-'P' is true.

However, in any case where neutral states of information may be envisaged—total states of information justifying the assertion neither of 'P' nor of 'Not-P'—the corresponding schema for assertibility:

'Not-P' is assertible iff Not-'P' is assertible

will fail from right to left. So the DS itself—given only the seemingly uncontroversial principle of the equivalence of the negations of equivalents—enforces a potential divergence in extension between 'true' and 'assertible'.[21] Moreover, since deflationists regard the DS as an *a priori* principle, providing a complete explanation of the concept of truth, this potential divergence is of the very essence of that concept.

I argued that this conclusion becomes problematic for deflationism as soon as one reflects that the DS also imposes a certain normativity on "true." Specifically, it enjoins that reason to assert, or to accept, that 'P' is true is *eo ipso* reason to assert, or to accept P. Hence "true" is in that sense minimally normative over

---

[21] It is assumed here that the biconditional that features in the argument generates an extensional context.

assertion of the members of the substitution class for P in the DS. So, of course, is "assertible." Indeed, as I observed, a stronger conclusion follows from the status assigned to the DS, viz. that "true" and "assertible" *coincide* in positive normative force over belief and assertion: reason to regard P as true is *eo ipso* reason to regard it as assertible, and conversely. The potential divergence in extension ensures, nevertheless, that although to pursue the one norm is in this sense to pursue the other, successful capture of the one need not be successful capture of the other. And this result, it was suggested, is too big for deflationism, as normally formulated, to chew.

It's important to stress that the significance of this finding is not in its content but its provenance. Richer—for instance representationalist—conceptions of truth will likely regard it as the merest banality that being true is one thing and being assertible (acceptable) something else. What is, perhaps, surprising is that the distinction is apparently enforced merely by the DS and the possibility of neutral states of information.

How should a proponent of the intuitionist rescue respond to this train of thought? Before trying to answer that directly, it will be useful to approach its conclusion from another angle. Consider not negation but tense. It is constitutive of our understanding of the tenses that certain principles (the so-called truth-value links) operate to connect *a priori* the truth-values of differently tensed sentences uttered at different times. Thus, for example, "It is raining today" if uttered today is true if and only if "It will be raining tomorrow" was true if uttered yesterday. And "It was raining" is true if uttered today if and only if "It is raining" was true if uttered at some time in the past. Let's regiment the tenses as operators, 'Past', 'Pres', 'Fut', etc., on tenseless propositional radicals—(making no assumption about whether that is ultimately a philosophically felicitous treatment)—and write {'Past P'\t}, {'Fut P'\t}, etc., to denote utterances of the enquoted sentences at a variable time t. Then when t_1 antedates t_2, we get a battery of principles among the simplest of which are, for example, these:

Fut/Pres	$(\forall t_1)[\text{True}\{\text{'Will}\,P'\backslash t_1\} \text{ iff.} (\exists t_2)(\text{True}\{\text{'Pres}\,P'\backslash t_2\})]$
Past/Pres	$(\forall t_2)[\text{True}\{\text{'Past}\,P'\backslash t_2\} \text{ iff.} (\exists t_1)(\text{True}\{\text{'Pres}\,P'\backslash t_1\})]$[22]

For deflationism, the Disquotational Scheme is to serve to underwrite all essential aspects of the notion of truth. So the deflationist is obliged, I would suggest, to provide a suitable derivation of these or equivalent truth-value links from the DS and suitable collateral principles concerning the tenses. If no means present

---

[22] The form displayed won't serve, of course, for compound tenses.

themselves for accomplishing that, then that is bad news for deflationism's signature thesis concerning the DS. Suppose, accordingly, that deflationism can indeed establish the above principles. Then once again it is striking that the corresponding principles with all occurrences of "true" replaced by "assertible":

Fut/Pres^{Ass}	$(\forall t_1)[\text{Assertible}\{\text{'Will}\,P\,'t_1\}\text{ iff.}(\exists t_2)(\text{Assertible}\{\text{'Pres}\,P\,'t_2\})]$
Past/Pres^{Ass}	$(\forall t_2)[\text{Assertible}\{\text{'Past}\,P\,'t_2\}\text{ iff.}(\exists t_1)(\text{Assertible}\{\text{'Pres}\,P\,'t_1\})],$

fail of validity in both directions. Fut/Pres^{Ass} fails left to right because of the possibility of *disappointments*—because it may happen that a fully assertible prediction is never fulfilled, with all later states of information warranting its denial. It fails right to left because of the possibility of *surprises*—because it may happen that a present tensed claim is warrantedly assertible although its future tensed counterpart was never assertible in any previous state of information. Past/Pres^{Ass} fails left to right because of the possibility of *retrospective discoveries*—because it may happen that we acquire a warrant for thinking that something was earlier so for which there was no evidence at the time. It fails right to left because of the possibility of *defeaters*—because new information overrides or undermines an earlier warranted assertion about a then contemporaneous situation.

So, the inflationary argument is reinforced. The ways in which "true" and "assertible" respectively interact with tenses and negation conspire to enforce the idea that "true," as characterized by the DS and by the truth-value links, marks a dimension in which an assertion can be in good/bad standing that potentially contrasts with warrant. And that won't marry with the conception of it as a device whose presence in the language is needed only for the purposes of generalization and indirect endorsement recognized by deflationism.

But there is, I think, some room for manoeuvre. These considerations certainly do allow of interpretation as enforcing a conception of an assertion's truth as a circumstance of good standing, contrasting with its being warranted in a particular state of information. And, for my part, I think the wholesale repudiation of any such conception of truth, which I take to be part of the stock in trade of deflationism, is both unattractive and unmotivated. To accept such a 'substantial' conception of truth is not immediately to segue into an acceptance of truth as consisting in successful representation, or correspondence, in some metaphysically substantial sense—that proposals working with coherence, or one form or another of idealized assertibility, for example, can identify suitable alternative 'circumstances of good standing' to service the contrasts imposed. *However:* what the inflationary argument enforces *at a minimum* is only that, in any discourse dealing in truth-apt contents subject to the DS and standard behaviour by negation and tense, there will be norms operative over assertion additional to simple assertibility—norms of *restraint*, as required by the possibility of neutral states of information, and norms of *retraction*, and *denial*, as required by the possibility of shifting states of information serving to undermine, or override, existing warrants. Any discourse controlled by such a complex pattern of norms will, once "true" is introduced via the DS, throw up the contrasts between "true" and "assertible" that drive the inflationary argument. The deflationist counter should thus be that while this behaviour by the truth-predicate does indeed mark the operation of norms over the discourse contrasting with simple assertibility, it is a further step to associate it with a 'circumstance of good standing' so contrasted. There is an alternative: the enforced contrasts between "true" and "assertible" may be taken to reflect, still under the aegis of a fully deflated understanding of the former, the operation of norms—of abstention, denial, and retraction—that supplement norms of assertibility and articulate the shifting patterns of evidential significance and dominance relationships sustained by the variable states of information that we enjoy at different times.

10. The Puncture Patched

My suggestion is going to be, now, that this refined deflationism is available to help us sustain after all the idea that while, in suitable cases, to deny an assertion— that stewed camel fries in béchamel sauce is delicious, e.g., or that former president George W. Bush's many public gaffes were comical—is of course to be committed to regarding it as false, there need be no imputation of fault, of some relevant norm violated. The relevant train of thought proceeds in two stages.

First, we reflect that the judgements/assertions in which we are interested— about basic taste, about comedy, about what is revolting, or attractive, etc.—are indeed disciplined by norms of restraint, denial, and retraction as well as by norms of acceptance. In each case, competence requires a firm grasp not merely of circumstances in which one is in no position to have an opinion but also of circumstances in which an opinion should be controverted or withdrawn. The latter consideration is particularly important since it is here that we can begin to get an insight into the functional differences between the 'objectified' propositional surface characteristic of the discourses in question—"That's funny," "This is delicious"—and the purely subjective reports—"I found that funny," "I'm really enjoying this dish,"—which there is some temptation to (wrongly) think we might as well, or perhaps better, be affirming. Judgements of basic taste, for example, may be undermined by evidence of a (temporarily) distorted palate—you just cleaned your teeth with a strong toothpaste, or are suffering from a bad sinus infection, or sipped the wine with the taste of Danish blue cheese still lingering on your tongue. And they may be overridden, or at least challenged, by evidence of idiosyncrasy—"Well, you should be aware that nobody but you likes it,"—or by the adduction of certain relevant background facts—"Really? Do you have any idea what it's made of?"—or by the invocation of superior (usually moral) values—"Really? Do you have any idea what they do to the geese?" Judgements about what is and isn't funny run much in parallel. They may be undermined by evidence of temporary distortion of mood, up (laughing gas) or down (depression), or oversights or mistakes about details (you mishear what is said, so overlook a rather clever pun). And they too may be overridden by weight of contrary reaction—"Well, no-one else (everyone else) is laughing"—by the adduction of relevant background facts—you realize that what seemed to be a rather amusing gaffe by an unpopular colleague was actually in context a rather clever piece of manipulation, and the smile is wiped off your face—or by invocation of superior values—you learn that the clown's Monty-Python-esque silly walk is not part of his act but is rather an extreme case of Trendelenburg gait, caused by a painfully arthritic hip. The impression that the subjective mode of judgement would serve just as well as the 'objectified' idiom is an illusion, fostered by the match in their conditions of assertion and restraint, but shattered as soon as we review the differences in their conditions of retraction and denial.

A much more refined account of this than I can attempt here would be illuminating since the idea, to which I like everyone else am strongly attracted, that the discourses in question have, *au fond*, no other subject matter than our subjective reactions, perennially tempts us to suspicion or at least puzzlement about the 'objectified' pattern on which the whole impression of possibly faultless *disagreements* rests. But the foregoing is detail enough both to suggest why we should resist that temptation and to set things up for the second stage in the advertised train of thought. Assume that negation operates over these contents as normally: i.e., that the negation of P is identified as the weakest proposition incompatible with P, and thus is entailed by any proposition incompatible with P. And assume that the canonical assertibility-conditions for P and its ilk are constituted by the occurrence in the agent of an appropriate affective state—say, pleasure or revulsion, to consider two extremes—either intentionally directed upon a relevant object or merely presumed caused by it. Then your pleasurable satisfaction as you savour the tender stewed camel fries chunks will, absent other relevant information, entitle you to assert, "Hmm, this concoction is pretty good," while I, wincing at the slimy, lip-sticking texture, underwhelmed by the bland, woodland mushroomy flavour, and perhaps repelled by thoughts of the anatomical origin of the dish, will be entitled to rejoin, "I am sorry. I cannot eat this. It is awful," and hence to affirm the negation of what you said. However, the grounds for your perfectly proper assertion need not support any expectation that any information is accessible which ought to motivate me to withdraw, let alone deny, my verdict. There will be conceivable circumstances under which competence will require that I do so. That much is a consequence of the operation over the discourse in question of the norms of denial and retraction which underwrite the contrasts, stressed by the inflationary argument, between "true" and "assertible" and give point to its objectified propositional surface. But the discourse is so set up that there is a disconnection between the satisfaction, for you, of conditions mandating your contradiction of my verdict, and the satisfaction, for anybody, of conditions mandating my retraction or denial of it. Thus, your being in position to deny what I say neither defeats my warrant for saying it nor need indicate that any defeater of any of the kinds scouted above need obtain. You may be in a position where you are mandated in that denial without any reason to think that your reaction will be shared by a very significant majority, or that my taste is impaired by alcohol, or that my judgements on these matters have proved historically quite unstable, or that my response is inhibited by mistaken beliefs about inhumane treatment of the camels, or . . . and so on.

In sum, the suggested account is this. Differences of opinion, meeting simultaneously all of the five conditions we have imposed—Contradiction, Faultlessness, Sustainability, Parity, and Genuine Disagreement—can arise within a discourse D when four conditions come into alignment:

(i) The norms of assertion operative over D mandate X in asserting P and Y in asserting Not P.

(ii) The norms of retraction for D are such that, as it happens, there is no accessible further information which will mandate X in retracting P or Y in retracting her denial of it.

(iii) Neither X nor Y has any reason to expect anything other than that condition (ii) is met; and

(iv) Assertions of D are subject to no ulterior norm of correctness—such as truth, *non*-deflationarily conceived, would supply.

11. Beyond Relativism and Intuitionism: The Simple Deduction Again

We need, finally, to re-visit the problem posed by the Simple Deduction. Have we secured the materials to corroborate the intuitionistic response to it? I have space only for an impressionistic discussion of the issues, but the upshot is, I think, interesting.

What sort of shape should be assumed by a semantics for a discourse of the character we have been concerned with? The work of characterizing the meanings of the elements of its signature vocabulary, and thereby of its atomic sentences, will naturally have to be discursive and informal, and the kind of pattern that work will assume is, to an extent, prefigured in the preceding. But what about the connectives? Bearing in mind that the notion of truth that operates over the discourse is now being conceived as wholly deflated, there are strong, widely accepted reasons for dismissing any truth-conditions-based approach.[23] In any case, the salient approach is assertibility-conditional, with clauses in the spirit of the following adaptations of the Heyting semantics for intuitionist logic in its mathematical applications recommending themselves for conjunction, disjunction, and the conditional (note that the biconditionality of the formulations has the effect that we thereby also characterize conditions of restraint and withdrawal):

Conjunction.	One is in position to assert 'A and B' just if one is in position to assert 'A' and in position to assert 'B'
Disjunction.	One is in position to assert 'A or B' just if one is a position to assert that one can get into position either to assert 'A' or to assert 'B'
Conditional.	One is in position to assert 'If A, then B' just if one is a position to assert that if one gets into position to assert 'A', one will thereby be in position to assert 'B'

With negation, though, the Heyting precedent does not recommend itself. A clause that followed the Heyting precedent would run:

One is in position to assert 'Not-A' just if one is a position to assert that there is no getting in a position to assert 'A',

whose drawbacks include the apparent issuance of a licence to deny, "Ancient Etruscan cuisine was on the whole delicious" purely on the ground that no records survive of the details of the ancient Etruscan diet, or the style of cooking. A more natural approach would be to appeal to a primitive notion of incompatibility among atomic predications in the discourse in question to underwrite a clause along these lines:

Negation.	One is in position to assert 'Not-A' just if one is a position to assert some 'B' that is incompatible with 'A'.

which in turn would motivate inference rules for negation whereby (simplifying to the single premise case) being in position to assert that 'A' and 'B' are incompatible would license the inference from 'B' to 'Not-A', and possession of licences for the inferences from 'C' to 'A' and from 'B' to 'Not-A' would put one position to assert that 'C' and 'B' are incompatible.

Now, the more general question of what specific propositional logic should be motivated by semantic clauses in the style illustrated will depend upon how one proposes to think of validity for inferences among contents drawn from

---

[23] I have in mind the line of thought, going back to Dummett (1958), that there is an actual inconsistency in trying to marry deflationism about truth with truth-conditional semantics.

the discourse in question—specifically, it will depend upon what property valid inferences will be required to preserve. There are two salient options. The first is simply that valid inference should preserve assertibility: a valid inference will be one which ensures that an agent who is in position to assert each of its premises will also be in position to assert its conclusion. However, as the reader can speedily verify, that proposal would have the effect that the stated clause for disjunction would not underwrite the standard rule for disjunction elimination. We could avoid the difficulty by reverting to the stricter clause for disjunction:

One is in position to assert 'A or B' just if one is a position to assert 'A' or to assert 'B'

But the effect of that would be that any (warranted) disjunctive assertion would violate (Gricean) constraints of cooperation, since one would always be in a position to do better by asserting one of the disjuncts in particular. Since the more relaxed clause for disjunction seems thus forced, a second option for the property preserved across valid inference recommends itself: a valid (single conclusion) inference should be such as to ensure that if one *can get into a position* where each of its premises is assertible, then (from there) one *can get into a position* where the conclusion is assertible. In a familiar terminology, valid inference should preserve *propositional* justification.

Now there is, of course, scope for considerable philosophical discussion about the good standing of that notion. In particular, what is the modality that it embeds? So the emergence of a specific propositional logic, based on the kind of semantic proposals envisaged, is going to be hostage to that discussion. But suppose we win through to a broadly Heyting-style, assertibility-conditional validation of the standard rules (shared by classical and intuitionist propositional logic) for conjunction, disjunction, and the conditional, together with suitable generalizations of the negation rules prefigured above. So much, if nothing is added, will foreseeably yield *at least* intuitionist propositional logic. But the response originally proposed to the Simple Deduction requires that we have *nothing stronger than* intuitionist propositional logic. For we need to invalidate the De Morgan step that transitions from denial of the conjunction of conflicting opinions in a dispute of inclination to affirmation of the disjunction that one or the other is mistaken.

The question is, simply: does the style of assertibility-conditional semantics we have prefigured promise to validate Not-(A and Not-A) without validating (A or Not-A)? A positive answer to the first part of the question, if it is to draw directly on the clause for negation suggested above, will require that, no matter what one's state information, one will always be in position to assert some statement incompatible with (A and Not-A). That will be true if we can establish that there is a valid inference—for an appropriately assertibilist construal of validity—from a contradiction to any proposition, and can assume that any state of information will justify the assertion of some proposition. There are some subtleties around the question which I will not pursue here. Let us merely assume that that much is done, and we have an assertibilist vindication of the law of non-contradiction. Can we now avoid validation of the law of excluded middle?

The answer is, "Probably," but also—the crucial point—that under the kind of semantics proposed, it *will be no disaster if we cannot*, for the capacity of the intuitionistic response to fend off the problem posed by the Simple Deduction depends less on blocking the De Morgan inference than on sustaining something close to the interpretation now on offer of its conclusion. Let 'A' be any atomic statement of taste. Then (A or Not-A) will be assertible just in case one is in a position to assert that one can get into position either to assert 'A' or to assert some statement incompatible with A. And you might think that that is not so implausible for a suitable interpretation of what it takes to relevantly "get into position." You might think, for instance, that you only have to try the dish in question to wind up in a position to assert either that it is tasty, say, or to return a verdict incompatible with that. True, the vagueness of "tasty" might give pause. But if there is an obstacle to excluded middle from that source, that has nothing to do—or at least, nothing immediately to do—with the fact that the disjuncts concern taste. The important point is rather that, under the aegis of the prefigured semantics, excluded middle is now potentially entirely harmless. What made it harmful was an interpretation under which it enforced a distribution of fault to one antagonist or the other in any dispute of inclination involving acceptance and denial of a single content. It does indeed enforce such a distribution when interpreted classically. Now, though, under the proposed use-theoretic style of semantics, that implication is cancelled. All that will be implied is that any agent, in any state of information, can get into a position justifiably to insert one disjunct or something incompatible with it. There is accordingly no foreseeable need—or anyway, none driven by the specific subject matter of the disagreement—for the modifications to classical logic canvassed in the intuitionistic proposal.

12. Conclusion

Let me close with something of a bird's eye view of the track followed by our dialectic. The inflationary argument reminds us that it takes very little to so set up a discourse that its assertions are subject to both evidential and alethic normativity. If the intuitive idea of faultless disagreement is not to reduce to the banality that differences of opinion may be fully evidentially justified, then the intention of the idea has to be that they may, in the kind of case on which we have focused, reflect no *alethic* fault. But this is, naturally, a hopeless idea if the discourse is thought of as answerable to a single norm of truth with which no statement and its negation can simultaneously comply. So if faultless disagreement is to be a possibility, there must be no such single alethic norm. That leaves two options. One is, in one way or another, to—as it were—fracture the norm, multiply the ways of being true and spread the pieces around, so that contradictory opinions can each alight on a shard. Each of our five considered relativisms attempts a particular implementation of that option. The other option is to suction out the substance of the alethic norm, leaving only the formal shell to subserve the contrasts whose contours are exploited by the inflationary argument. I have argued that the first option will not deliver what is wanted, and that the second is the way to go. This does involve rejecting the conclusion about "true" that I drew from the inflationary argument. But with that qualification, I would regard it as a strength of the combination of propositional minimalism and alethic pluralism defended in *Truth and Objectivity* that it provides a natural setting for the elaboration of the second option.[24]

References

Beall, J. C. (2006), "Modelling the 'Ordinary View'," in P. Greenough and M. Lynch (eds.), *Truth and Realism*, Oxford: Oxford University Press, 61–74.

Belnap, Nuel, Michael Perloff, and Ming Xu (2001), *Facing the Future: Agents and Choices in Our Indeterminist World*, Oxford: Oxford University Press.

Boghossian, Paul (2011), "Three Kinds of Relativism," in S. Hales (ed.), *A Companion to Relativism*, Oxford: Wiley-Blackwell, 53–69.

Brogaard, Berit (2008), "In Defence of a Perspectival Semantics for 'Know'," *Australasian Journal of Philosophy* 86, 439–59.

Douven, Igor (2011), "Relativism and Confirmation Theory," in S. Hales (ed.), *A Companion to Relativism*, Oxford: Wiley-Blackwell, 242–65.

Dummett, Michael (1958), "Truth," *Proceedings of the Aristotelian Society*, Supplementary Volume LIX, 141–62.

[24] I am grateful to the participants at the Budapest *Metatheories of Disagreement* conference in October 2019 for helpful comments and criticisms, and to audiences at workshops and colloquia at Bologna, the Johns Hopkins University, St. Andrews, the Oxford Jowett Society, Leeds, Stirling, Durham and the Institute of Philosophy in London where I have given talks on these ideas in recent times. Special thanks are due to Paul Boghossian for many discussions of the issues over the years, and to my co-members of the *Relativism and Rational Tolerance* project funded by the Leverhulme Trust at the Northern Institute of Philosophy in Aberdeen between 2012 and 2015: Carl Baker, Alex Plakias, Filippo Ferrari, Giacomo Melis and Patrick Greenough. I gratefully acknowledge the support of the Leverhulme Trust.

Egan, Andy (2007), "Epistemic Modals, Relativism, and Assertion," *Philosophical Studies* 133, 1–22.

Egan, Andy (2010), "Disputing about Taste," in R. Feldman, and T. A. Warfield (eds.), *Disagreement*, Oxford: Oxford University Press, 247–92.

Egan, Andy (2011), "Relativism about Epistemic Modals," in S. Hales (ed.) *A Companion to Relativism*, Oxford: Wiley-Blackwell, 219–41.

Egan, Andy, John Hawthorne, and Brian Weatherson (2005), "Epistemic Modals in Context," in G. Preyer and P. Peters (eds.), *Contextualism in Philosophy*, Oxford: Oxford University Press, 131–69.

Fine, Kit (ed.) (2005), "Tense and Reality," *Modality and Tense*, New York: Oxford University Press, 261–320.

Gillies, Anthony (2010), "Iffiness," *Semantics and Pragmatics* 3, 1–42.

Harman, Gilbert (1975), "Moral Relativism Defended," *The Philosophical Review* 84 (1), 3–22.

Kölbel, Max (2004), "Faultless Disagreement," *Proceedings of the Aristotelian Society* 104, 53–73.

Kolodny, Niko and John MacFarlane (2010), "Ifs and Oughts," *Journal of Philosophy* 107, 115–43.

Kompa, Nikola (2002), "The Context Sensitivity of Knowledge Ascriptions," *Grazer Philosophische Studien* 64, 79–96.

Lasersohn, Peter (2005), "Context Dependence, Disagreement, and Predicates of Personal Taste," *Linguistics and Philosophy* 28, 643–86.

López De Sa, Dan (2008), "Presuppositions of Commonality," in M. García-Carpintero and M. Kölbel (eds.), *Relative Truth*, Oxford: Oxford University Press, 297–310.

MacFarlane, John (2005), "Making Sense of Relative Truth," *Proceedings of the Aristotelian Society* 105, 321–39.

MacFarlane, John (2014), *Assessment Sensitivity: Relative Truth and its Applications*, Oxford: Oxford University Press.

Richard, Mark (2004), "Contextualism and Relativism," *Philosophical Studies* 119, 215–42.

Richard, Mark (2008), *When Truth Gives Out*, Oxford: Oxford University Press.

Rovane, Carol (2011), "Relativism Requires Alternatives, Not Disagreement or Relative Truth," in S. Hales (ed.), *A Companion to Relativism*, Oxford: Wiley-Blackwell, 31–52.

Rovane, Carol (2012), "Can We Frame a Coherent Relativism?," in A. Coliva (ed.), *Mind, Meaning and Knowledge: Essays in Honor of Crispin Wright*, Vol. 1, Oxford: Oxford University Press, 238–66.

Rovane, Carol (2013), *The Metaphysics and Ethics of Relativism*, Cambridge, MA: Harvard University Press.

Shapiro, Stewart and William W. Taschek (1996), "Intuitionism, Pluralism, and Cognitive Command," *Journal of Philosophy* 20(2), 74–88.

Stephenson, Tamina (2007), "Judge Dependence, Epistemic Modals, and Predicates of Personal Taste," *Linguistics and Philosophy* 30, 487–525.

Weatherson, Brian (2009), "Conditionals and Indexical Relativism," *Synthese* 166, 333–57.

Williams, Bernard (1975), "The Truth in Relativism," *Proceedings of the Aristotelian Society*, New Series 75, 215–28.

Wright, Crispin (1992), *Truth and Objectivity*, Cambridge, MA: Harvard University Press.

Wright, Crispin (2001), "On Being in a Quandary: Relativism Vagueness Logical Revisionism," *Mind* 110(437), 45–98.

Wright, Crispin (2002), "Relativism and Classical Logic," *Royal Institute of Philosophy Supplement* 51, 95–118.

Wright, Crispin (2006), "Intuitionism, Realism, Relativism and Rhubarb," in P. Greenough and M. Lynch (eds.), *Truth and Realism*, Oxford: Oxford University Press.

Wright, Crispin (2007), "New Age Relativism and Epistemic Possibility: The Question of Evidence," *Philosophical Issues: The Metaphysics of Epistemology* 17, 262–83.

Yu, Andy (2016), "Epistemic Modals and Sensitivity to Contextually-Salient Partitions," *Thought: A Journal of Philosophy* 5(2), 134–46.

General Bibliography

Austin, John Langshaw (1946), "Other Minds," *Proceedings of the Aristotelian Society*, Supplementary Volume 20, 148–87.

Ayer, Alfred Jules (1936), *Language, Truth and Logic*, London: Victor Gollancz.

Baker, Carl (2012), "Indexical Contextualism and the Challenges from Disagreement," *Philosophical Studies* 157(1), 107–23.

Bealer, George (1989), "On the Identification of Properties and Propositional Functions," *Linguistics and Philosophy* 12, 1–14.

Beall, J. C. (2006), "Modelling the 'Ordinary View'," in P. Greenough and M. Lynch (eds.), *Truth and Realism*, Oxford: Oxford University Press, 61–74.

Belnap, Nuel, Michael Perloff, and Ming Xu (2001), *Facing the Future: Agents and Choices in Our Indeterminist World*, Oxford: Oxford University Press.

Björnsson, Gunnar and Alexander Almér (2011), "The Pragmatics of Insensitive Assessments. Understanding the Relativity of Assessments of Personal Taste, Epistemic Modals, and More," *The Baltic International Yearbook of Cognition, Logic and Communication* 6, 1–45.

Blackburn, Simon (1984), *Spreading the Word: Groundings in the Philosophy of Language*, Oxford: Clarendon Press.

Blackburn, Simon (1998), *Ruling Passions: A Theory of Practical Reasoning*, Oxford: Oxford University Press.

Boghossian, Paul (2006a), *Fear of Knowledge*. Oxford: Clarendon Press.

Boghossian, Paul (2006b), "What is Relativism?," in P. Greenough and M. Lynch (eds.), *Truth and Realism*, Oxford: Clarendon Press.

Boghossian, Paul (2007), "The Case against Epistemic Relativism: Replies to Rosen and Neta," *Episteme* 4, 49–65.

Boghossian, Paul (2011), "Three Kinds of Relativism," in S. Hales (ed.), *A Companion to Relativism*, Oxford: Wiley-Blackwell, 53–69.

Boghossian, Paul (2017), "Relativism about Morality," in C. Kanzian, S. Kletzl, J. Mitterer, and K. Neges (eds.), *Realism—Relativism—Constructivism: Proceedings of the 38th International Wittgenstein Symposium in Kirchberg* 24, Berlin: De Gruyter, 301–12.

Brogaard, Berit (2008a), "In Defence of a Perspectival Semantics for 'Know'," *Australasian Journal of Philosophy* 86, 439–59.

Brogaard, Berit (2008b), "Moral Contextualism and Moral Relativism," *Philosophical Quarterly* 58, 385–409.

Campbell, Richmon (1974), "The Sorites Paradox," *Philosophical Studies* 26, 175–91.

Campbell, Richmon (1979), *Paradoxes*, Cambridge: Cambridge University Press.

Cappelen, Herman (2008), "Content Relativism and Semantic Blindness," in M. García-Carpintero and M. Kölbel (eds.), *Relative Truth*, Oxford: Oxford University Press, 265–86.

Cappelen, Herman and Ernie Lepore (2005), *Insensitive Semantics: A Defense of Minimalism and Speech Act Pluralism*, Malden, MA: Blackwell.

Cappelen, Herman and John Hawthorne (2007), "Locations and Binding," *Analysis* 67, 95–105.

Cappelen, Herman and John Hawthorne (2009), *Relativism and Monadic Truth*, Oxford: Oxford University Press.

Cappelen, Herman and E. Lepore (2007), "The Myth of Unarticulated Constituents," in M. O'Rourke and C. Washington (eds.), *Essays in Honor of John Perry*, Cambridge, MA: MIT Press, 199–214.

Cargile, James (1969), "The Sorites Paradox," *British Journal for the Philosophy of Science* 20, 193–202.

Cargile, James (1979), *Paradoxes*. Cambridge: Cambridge University Press.

Chambers, Timothy (1998), "On Vagueness, *Sorites*, and Putnam's 'Intuitionistic Strategy'," *The Monist* 81, 343–8.

Cohen, Stewart (1986), "Knowledge and Context," *The Journal of Philosophy* 83, 574–83.

Cohen, Stewart (1999), "Contextualism, Skepticism and the Structure of Reasons," *Philosophical Perspectives* 13, 57–89.

Cohen, Stewart (2001), "Contextualism Defended: Comments on Richard Feldman's 'Skeptical Problems, Contextualist Solutions'," *Philosophical Studies* 103, 87–98.

Davis, Wayne, A. (2017), "Loose Use and Belief Variation," in J. Jenkins Ichikawa (ed.), *Routledge Handbook of Epistemic Contextualism*, London: Routledge.

DeRose, K. (1991), "Epistemic Possibilities," *Philosophical Review* 100(4), 581–605.

DeRose, K. (1992), "Contextualism and Knowledge Attributions," *Philosophy and Phenomenological Research* 52, 913–29.

DeRose, K. (2002), "Assertion, Knowledge, and Context," *Philosophical Review* 111, 167–203.

DeRose, K. (2009), *The Case for Contextualism: Knowledge, Skepticism, and Context*, Vol. 1, Oxford: Clarendon Press.

Dietz, Richard (2008), "Epistemic Modals and Correct Disagreement," in in M. García-Carpintero and M. Kölbel (eds.), *Relative Truth*, Oxford: Oxford University Press, 239–64.

Douven, Igor (2011), "Relativism and Confirmation Theory," in S. Hales (ed.), *A Companion to Relativism*, Oxford: Wiley-Blackwell, 242–65.

Dretske, Fred (2005), "The Case Against Closure," in M. Steup and E. Sosa (eds.), *Contemporary Debates in Epistemology*, Malden, MA: Wiley-Blackwell, 27–40.

Dummett, Michael (1958), "Truth," *Proceedings of the Aristotelian Society*, Supplementary Volume LIX, 141–62.

Dummett, Michael (1978), "The Reality of the Past," in *Truth and Other Enigmas*, London: Duckworth, 358–74.

Egan, Andy (2005), "Epistemic Modals, Relativism and Assertion," in J. Gajewski, V. Hacquard, B. Nickel, and S. Yalcin (eds.), *New Work on Modality*, MIT Working Papers in Linguistics, vol. 51, 35–61.

Egan, Andy (2007), "Epistemic Modals, Relativism, and Assertion," *Philosophical Studies* 133, 1–22.

Egan, Andy (2010), "Disputing about Taste," in R. Feldman, and T. A. Warfield (eds.), *Disagreement*, Oxford: Oxford University Press, 247–92.

Egan, Andy (2011), "Relativism about Epistemic Modals," in S. Hales (ed.) *A Companion to Relativism*, Oxford: Wiley-Blackwell, 219–41.

Egan, Andy (2014), "There's Something Funny about Comedy: A Case Study in Faultless Disagreement," *Erkenntnis* 79(1), 73–100.

Egan, Andy, John Hawthorne, and Brian Weatherson (2005), "Epistemic Modals in Context," in G. Preyer and P. Peters (eds.), *Contextualism in Philosophy*, Oxford: Oxford University Press, 131–69, 170.

Eriksson, John (2016), "Expressivism, Attitudinal Complexity and Two Senses of Disagreement in Attitude," *Erkenntnis* 81, 775–94.

Fantl, Jeremy and McGrath, Matthew (2007), "Knowledge and the Purely Epistemic: In Favor of Pragmatic Encroachment," *Philosophy and Phenomenological Research* 75(3), 558–89.

Ferrari, Filippo (2014), *Disagreement and the Normativity of Truth beneath Cognitive Command* (PhD thesis, University of Aberdeen).

Ferrari, Filippo (2016), "Disagreement about Taste and Alethic Suberogation," *Philosophical Quarterly* 66 (264), 516–35.

Ferrari, Filippo and Sebastiano Moruzzi (2019), "Ecumenical Alethic Pluralism," *Canadian Journal of Philosophy* 49, 368–93.

Ferrari, Filippo and Wright, Crispin (2017), "Talking with Vultures," *Mind* 126, 911–36.

Field, Hartry (1980), *Science without Numbers*, Oxford: Basil Blackwell.

Fine, Kit (1975), "Vagueness, Truth and Logic," *Synthese* 30, 265–300.

Finlay, Stephen (2014), *Confusion of Tongues: A Theory of Normative Language*, Oxford: Oxford University Press.

Fitch, Frederic B. (1963), "A Logical Analysis of Some Value Concepts," *The Journal of Symbolic Logic* 28, 135–42.

Francén, Ragnar (2010), "No Deep Disagreement for New Relativists," *Philosophical Studies* 151, 19–37.

Gajewski, Jon, Valentine Hacquard, Bernhard Nickel, and Seth Yalcin (2005), *New Work on Modality*, MIT Working Papers in Linguistics, v. 51.

García-Carpintero, Manuel and Max Kölbel (eds.) (2008), *Relative Truth*, Oxford: Oxford University Press.

Gibbard, Allan (1990), *Wise Choices, Apt Feelings*, Oxford: Clarendon Press.

Gibbard, Allan (2003), *Thinking How to Live*, Cambridge, MA: Harvard University Press.

Gillies, Anthony (2010), "Iffiness," *Semantics and Pragmatics* 3, 1–42.

Glanzberg, Michael (2007), "Context, Content, and Relativism," *Philosophical Studies* 136, 1–29.

Greenough, Patrick (n.d.), "The Open Future" (unpublished manuscript).

Greenough, Patrick and Dirk Kindermann (2017), "The Semantic Error Problem for Epistemic Contextualism," in J. Jenkins Ichikawa (ed.), *Routledge Handbook of Epistemic Contextualism*, London: Routledge.

Hacking, Ian (1967), "Possibility," *Philosophical Review* 76, 143–68.

Hale, Bob (1986), "The Compleat Projectivist," *Philosophical Quarterly* 36, 65–84.

Hale, Bob (1992), "Can There Be a Logic of Attitudes? ," in J. Haldane and C. Wright (eds.), *Reality, Representation and Projection*, Oxford: Oxford University Press, 337–63.

Hale, Bob (2002), "Can Arboreal Knotwork help Blackburn out of Frege's Abyss?," *Philosophy and Phenomenological Research* 65, 144–9.

Hales, Steven (2006), *Relativism and the Foundations of Philosophy*, Boston, MA: MIT.

Hare, Richard (1959), *The Language of Morals*, Oxford: Clarendon Press.

Harman, Gilbert and Judith J. Thomson (1996), *Moral Relativism and Moral Objectivity*, Oxford: Blackwell.

Harman, Gilbert and Judith J. Thomson (1998), "Book Symposium on Gilbert Harman and Judith J. Thomson (1996)," *Moral Relativism and Moral Objectivity*", *Philosophy and Phenomenological Research* 58, 161–222.

Hawthorne, John (2004), *Knowledge and Lotteries*, Oxford: Oxford University Press.

Hawthorne, John (2005), "The Case for Closure," in M. Steup and E. Sosa (eds.), *Contemporary Debates in Epistemology*, Malden, MA: Wiley-Blackwell.

Hawthorne, John (2007), "Eavesdroppers and Epistemic Modals," *Philosophical Issues* 17, 92–101.

Horwich, Paul (1998), *Truth*, Oxford: Oxford University Press (second edition).

Hume, David (1738), *A Treatise of Human Nature*, ed. L. Selby Bigge (1888), Oxford: Clarendon Press.

Huvenes, Torfinn (2012), "Varieties of Disagreement and Predicates of Taste," *Australasian Journal of Philosophy* 90(1), 167–81.

Huvenes, Torfinn (2014), "Disagreement without Error," *Erkenntnis* 79(1), 143–54.

Ichikawa, Jonathan Jenkins (2017), *Routledge Handbook of Epistemic Contextualism*, London: Routledge.

Jordan, James (1971), "Protagoras and Relativism: Criticisms Bad and Good," *Southwestern Journal of Philosophy* 2, 7–29.

Kaplan, David (1989), "Demonstratives: An Essay on the Semantics, Logic, Metaphysics, and Epistemology of Demonstratives and Other Indexicals', in J. Almog, J. Perry, and H. Wettstein (eds.), *Themes from Kaplan*, Oxford: Oxford University Press, 481–566.

Khoo, Justin (2017), "The Disagreement Challenge to Contextualism," in J. Jenkins Ichikawa (ed.), *Routledge Handbook of Epistemic Contextualism*, London: Routledge.

Kölbel, Max (2002), *Truth without Objectivity*, London: Routledge.

Kölbel, Max (2004), "Faultless Disagreement," *Proceedings of the Aristotelian Society* 104, 53–73.

Kölbel, Max (unpublished), "Wright on Disputes of Inclination," available as a PDF file at: https://members.phl.univie.ac.at/koelbel/wp-content/uploads/sites/2/2017/12/Wright-on-Disputes-of-Inclination_2002.pdf

Kolodny, Niko and John MacFarlane (2010), "Ifs and Oughts," *Journal of Philosophy* 107, 115–43.

Kompa, Nikola (2002), "The Context Sensitivity of Knowledge Ascriptions," *Grazer Philosophische Studien* 64, 79–96.

Lasersohn, Peter (2005), "Context Dependence, Disagreement, and Predicates of Personal Taste," *Linguistics and Philosophy* 28, 643–86.

Lasersohn, Peter (2009), "Relative Truth, Speaker Commitment, and Control of Implicit Arguments', *Synthese* 166, 359–74.

Lasonen-Aarnio, Maria (2017), "Contextualism and Closure," in J. Jenkins Ichikawa (ed.), *Routledge Handbook of Epistemic Contextualism*, London: Routledge.

Lawlor, Krista (2013), *Assurance: An Austinian View of Knowledge and Knowledge Claims*, Oxford: Oxford University Press.

Lewis, D. (1980), "Index, Context, and Content," in S. Kanger and S. Ohman (eds.), *Philosophy and Grammar*, Dordrecht: Reidel, 79–100. Reprinted in D. Lewis (1998), *Papers in Philosophical Logic*. Cambridge: Cambridge University Press, 21–44.

Lewis, David (1998), "Index, Context, and Content," in *Papers in Philosophical Logic*, Cambridge: Cambridge University Press, 21–44.

López De Sa, Dan (2008), "Presuppositions of Commonality," in M. García-Carpintero and M. Kölbel (eds.), *Relative Truth*, Oxford: Oxford University Press, 297–310.

Lukasiewicz, Jan (1970), "On Determinism," in L. Borkowski (ed.), *Selected Works*, Amsterdam: North Holland.

Lynch, Michael (2001), "A Functionalist Theory of Truth," in M. Lynch (ed.), *The Nature of Truth*, Cambridge, MA: Bradford/MIT, 723–49.

Lynch, Michael (2004), "Truth and Multiple Realisability," *Australasian Journal of Philosophy* 82, 384–408.

MacFarlane, John (2003a), "Epistemic Modalities and Relative Truth," available at https://johnmacfarlane.net/epistmod-2003.pdf

MacFarlane, John (2003b), "Future Contingents and Relative Truth," *Philosophical Quarterly* 53, 321–36.

MacFarlane, John (2005a), "Making Sense of Relative Truth," *Proceedings of the Aristotelian Society* 105, 321–39.

MacFarlane, John (2005b), "The Assessment-Sensitivity of Knowledge Attributions," in Tamar Szabó Gendler and John Hawthorne (eds.), *Oxford Studies in Epistemology*, Vol. 1, Oxford: Oxford University Press, 197–233.

MacFarlane, John (2005c), "Semantic Minimalism and Nonindexical Contextualism," in G. Preyer and G. Peter (eds.), *Content and Context: Essays on Semantics and Pragmatics*, Oxford: Oxford University Press.

MacFarlane, John (2007a), "Relativism and Disagreement," *Philosophical Studies* 132, 17–31.

MacFarlane, John (2007b), "Semantic Minimalism and Nonindexical Contextualism," in G. Preyer and Peter G. (eds.), *Content and Context: Essays on Semantics and Pragmatics*, Oxford: Clarendon Press.

MacFarlane, John (2008), "Truth in the Garden of Forking Paths," in M. García-Carpintero and M. Kölbel (eds.), *Relative Truth*, Oxford: Oxford University Press, 81–102.

MacFarlane, John (2011), "Epistemic Modals Are Assessment Sensitive," in A. Egan and B. Weatherson (eds.), *Epistemic Modality*, Oxford: Oxford University Press, 144–78.

MacFarlane, John (2014), *Assessment Sensitivity: Relative Truth and its Applications*, Oxford: Oxford University Press.

Meiland, Jack W. (1977), "Concepts of Relative Truth," *The Monist* 60, 568–82.

Meiland, Jack W. (1979), "Is Protagorean Relativism Self-Refuting?," *Grazer Philosophische Studien* 9, 51–68.

Montminy, Martin (2009), "Contextualism, Relativism and Ordinary Speakers' Judgments," *Philosophical Studies* 143(3), 341–56.

Nagel, Jennifer and Julia Jael Smith (2017), "The Psychological Context of Contextualism," in J. Jenkins Ichikawa (ed.), *Routledge Handbook of Epistemic Contextualism*, London: Routledge.

Olson, Jonas (2014), *Moral Error Theory: History, Critique, Defence*, Oxford: Oxford University Press.

Perry, John (1998), "Indexicals, Contexts and Unarticulated Constituents," *Proceedings of the 1995 CSLI-Amsterdam Logic, Language and Computation Conference*, Stanford, CA: CSLI Publications.

Plato (1973), "Theaetetus," in John McDowell (ed.), *Clarendon Plato Series: Theaetetus*, Oxford: Oxford University Press.

Preyer, Gerhard and Georg Peter (2004), *Contextualism in Philosophy*, Oxford: Oxford University Press.

Putnam, Hilary (1983), "Vagueness and Alternative Logic" in *Realism and Reason*, Cambridge: Cambridge University Press, 271–86.

Read, Stephen and Crispin Wright (1985), "Hairier than Putnam Thought," *Analysis* 45, 56–58.

Recanati, François (2002), "Unarticulated Constituents," *Linguistics and Philosophy* 25, 299–345.

Recanati, François (2007), *Perspectival Thought: A Plea for (Moderate) Relativism*, Oxford: Oxford University Press.

Richard, Mark (2004), "Contextualism and Relativism," *Philosophical Studies* 119, 215–42.

Richard, Mark (2008), *When Truth Gives Out*, Oxford: Oxford University Press.

Rosen, Gideon (2007), "The Case against Epistemic Relativism: Reflections on Ch. 6 of *Fear of Knowledge*," *Episteme* 4, 10–29.

Rysiew, Patrick (2017), "'Knowledge' and Pragmatics," in J. Jenkins Ichikawa (ed.), *Routledge Handbook of Epistemic Contextualism*, London: Routledge.

Salerno, Joseph (2000), "Revising the Logic of Logical Revision," *Philosophical Studies* 99, 211–27.

Schaffer, Jonathan and Zoltan Szabo (2013), "Epistemic Comparativism: A Contextualist Semantics for Knowledge Ascriptions," *Philosophical Studies* 168(2), 491–543.

Shapiro, Stewart and William W. Taschek (1996), "Intuitionism, Pluralism, and Cognitive Command," *Journal of Philosophy* 20(2), 74–88.

Siegel, Harvey (1986), "Relativism, Truth, and Incoherence," *Synthese* 68, 295–312.

Sorensen, Roy (1988), *Blindspots*, Oxford: Oxford University Press.

Sorensen, Roy (2001), *Vagueness and Contradiction*, Oxford: Oxford University Press.

Stanley, Jason (2000), "Context and Logical Form," *Linguistics and Philosophy* 23, 391–434.

Stanley, Jason (2005), *Knowledge and Practical Interests*, Oxford: Oxford University Press.

Stephenson, Tamina (2005), "Assessor Sensitivity: Epistemic Modals and Predicates of Personal Taste," in J. Gajewski, V. Hacquard, B. Nickel, and S. Yalcin (eds.), *New Work on Modality*, MIT Working Papers in Linguistics, Vol. 51, 179–206.

Stephenson, Tamina (2007), "Judge Dependence, Epistemic Modals, and Predicates of Personal Taste," *Linguistics and Philosophy* 30, 487–525.

Swoyer, Chris (1982), "True For," in M. Krausz and J. W. Meiland (eds.), *Relativism: Cognitive and Moral*, Notre Dame: University of Notre Dame Press, 84–108.

Thomason, Richmond H. (1970), "Indeterministic Time and Truth-Value Gaps," *Theoria* 36, 264–81.

Weatherson, Brian (2009), "Conditionals and Indexical Relativism," *Synthese* 166, 333–57.

Weatherson, Brian (2017), "Interest-Relative Invariantism," in J. Jenkins Ichikawa (ed.), *Routledge Handbook of Epistemic Contextualism*, London: Routledge.

Williamson, Timothy (1992), "Vagueness and Ignorance," *Proceedings of the Aristotelian Society*, Supplementary Volume 66, 145–77.

Williamson, Timothy (1994), *Vagueness*, London and New York: Routledge.

Williamson, Timothy (1996a), "Putnam on the Sorites Paradox," *Philosophical Papers* 25, 47–56.

Williamson, Timothy (1996b), "Wright on the Epistemic Conception of Vagueness," *Analysis* 56, 39–45.

Williamson, Timothy (2005a), "Knowledge, Context and the Agent's Point of View," in G. Preyer and G. Peter (eds.), *Content and Context: Essays on Semantics and Pragmatics*, Oxford: Oxford University Press.

Williamson, Timothy (2005b), "Contextualism, Subject-Sensitive Invariantism and Knowledge of Knowledge," *The Philosophical Quarterly* 55, 213–35.

Wong, David (1984), *Moral Relativity*, Berkeley, CA: University of California Press.

Wright, Crispin (1992), *Truth and Objectivity*, Cambridge, MA: Harvard University Press.

Wright, Crispin (1993), "Anti-Realism and Revisionism," in *Realism, Meaning and Truth*, Oxford: Basil Blackwell (second edition), 433–57.

Wright, Crispin (1995), "The Epistemic Conception of Vagueness," *The Southern Journal of Philosophy* Supplementary Volume XXXIII, 133–60 (on "Vagueness," edited by Terence Horgan.

Wright, Crispin (1998), "Truth: A Traditional Debate Reviewed," *Canadian Journal of Philosophy* Supplementary Volume 24, 31–74 (on "Pragmatism," edited by Cheryl

Misak). Reprinted in Simon Blackburn and Keith Simmons (eds.) (1999), *Truth*, Oxford: Clarendon Press, 203–38.

Wright, Crispin (2001), "Minimalism, Deflationism, Pragmatism, Pluralism," in Michael P. Lynch (ed.), *The Nature of Truth: From the Classic to the Contemporary*. Cambridge, MA: MIT Press.

Wright, Crispin (2002), "Relativism and Classical Logic," in A. O' Hear (ed.), *Logic, Language and Thought*, Cambridge, Cambridge University Press, 95–118.

Wyatt, Jeremy (2018). "Absolutely Tasty: An Examination of Predicates of Personal Taste and Faultless Disagreement," *Inquiry* 61, 252–80.

Yu, Andy (2016), "Epistemic Modals and Sensitivity to Contextually-Salient Partitions," *Thought: A Journal of Philosophy* 5, 134–46.

Zimmerman, Aaron (2007), "Against Relativism," *Philosophical Studies* 133, 313–48.

Index

For the benefit of digital users, indexed terms that span two pages (e.g., 52–53) may, on occasion, appear on only one of those pages.